MARCEL PROUST: THE CRITICAL HERITAGE

THE CRITICAL HERITAGE SERIES

GENERAL EDITOR: B.C. SOUTHAM, M.A., B.LITT. (OXON.)
Formerly Department of English, Westfield College, University of London

For a list of books in the series see the back end paper

MARCEL PROUST

THE CRITICAL HERITAGE

Edited by
LEIGHTON HODSON
Senior Lecturer in French Language and Literature University of Glasgow

Routledge

London and New York

First published in 1989 by
Routledge
11 New Fetter Lane, London EC4P 4EE
29 West 35th Street, New York, NY 10001

Compilation, introduction, notes, and index © 1989 Leighton Hodson
Set in 10/11pt. Bembo by Columns of Reading
Printed in Great Britain
by TJ Press (Padstow) Ltd
Padstow, Cornwall.

British Library Cataloguing in Publication Data

Marcel Proust : the critical heritage.
(The Critical heritage series).
1. Fiction in French. Proust. Marcel.
Critical studies
I. Hodson, Leighton, 1931–   II. Series 843'.912

ISBN 0-415-02821-3

Library of Congress Cataloging in Publication Data

Marcel Proust, the critical heritage.
(The Critical heritage series)
Bibliography: p.
Includes index.
1. Proust, Marcel, 1871–1922–Criticism and
interpretation. I. Hodson, Leighton. II. Series.
PQ2631.R63Z7255 1989   843'.912   88–15783
ISBN O–415–02821–3

Dedicated to

JACK BILES

1920–86

in remembrance of
his friendship and advice

and to
my dear wife

RUTH HODSON

1933–87

in deepest gratitude for
her encouragement and devotion

Je trouve très raisonnable la croyance celtique que les âmes de ceux que nous avons perdus sont captives dans quelque être inférieur, dans une bête, un végétal, une chose inanimée, perdues en effet pour nous jusqu'au jour, qui pour beaucoup ne vient jamais, où nous nous trouvons passer près de l'arbre, entrer en possession de l'objet qui est leur prison. Alors elles tressaillent, nous appellent, et sitôt que nous les avons reconnues, l'enchantement est brisé. Délivrées par nous, elles ont vaincu la mort et reviennent vivre avec nous.

(Marcel Proust: *Du côté de chez Swann*)

General Editor's Preface

The reception given to a writer by his contemporaries and near-contemporaries is evidence of considerable value to the student of literature. On one side we learn a great deal about the state of criticism at large and in particular about the development of critical attitudes towards a single writer; at the same time, through private comments in letters, journals or marginalia, we gain an insight upon the tastes and literary thought of individual readers of the period. Evidence of this kind helps us to understand the writer's historical situation, the nature of his immediate reading-public, and his response to these pressures.

The separate volumes in the *Critical Heritage Series* present a record of this early criticism. Clearly, for many of the highly productive and lengthily reviewed nineteenth- and twentieth-century writers, there exists an enormous body of material; and in these cases the volume editors have made a selection of the most important views, significant for their intrinsic critical worth or for their representative quality – perhaps even registering incomprehension!

For earlier writers, notably pre-eighteenth century, the materials are much scarcer and the historical period has been extended, sometimes far beyond the writer's lifetime, in order to show the inception and growth of critical views which were initially slow to appear.

In each volume the documents are headed by an introduction, discussing the material assembled and relating the early stages of the author's reception to what we have come to identify as the critical tradition. The volumes will make available much material which would otherwise be difficult of access and it is hoped that the modern reader will be thereby helped towards an informed understanding of the ways in which literature has been read and judged.

B.C.S.

Contents

CONTENTS

1912: The manuscript of *Du côté de chez Swann*

CONTENTS

B – On Proust's reputation up to his death

1923 Tributes and assessments

1924–31 Posthumous works and critical essays

CONTENTS

Preface

Proust lived only for his work. The substance of his life, after important sea-changes, became the substance of his writing. It is essential to remember, however, that *A la recherche du temps perdu* cannot be viewed fairly as being just memoirs or confessions in some sort of disguise. Elements of these there may well be, but they are transformed by imagination.

With this in mind, I have, nevertheless, tried to provide the facts behind Proust's emergence as a writer, his preparations and ploys for getting his work published and the critical reactions to him at the time up to the point, in the early 1930s, when his world reputation was at last firmly established. I have put alongside his development as a writer and public figure only what it is necessary to say of his personal biographical circumstances to make the chronological pattern clear.

For a detailed handling of the stages in Proust's career reference should be made, in the first instance, to Philip Kolb's invaluable introductions and notes to the *Correspondance*, to Henri Bonnet's *Marcel Proust de 1907 à 1914*, to Jean-Yves Tadié's *Proust* and to the standard biography by George D. Painter.

Acknowledgements

I wish to express my particular thanks to the French Institute, London; Bernard Brun, École Normale Supérieure, Paris, and Judith Moore, for their kind assistance.

For permission to reprint copyright material acknowledgement is due to the following: Arnold for No. 124; Henri Bergson estate for No. 9; M. Louis Billotey for No. 58; Bloud & Gay for No. 92; John Calder for No. 136; Cape for No. 121; Chatto for No. 132 and Nos 81–90; Richard Cobden-Sanderson for No. 104; Collins for Nos 81–90; Richard Cobden-Sanderson for No. 104; Collins for No. 16; *Le Crapouillot* for Nos 31 and 98; M. Francis A. Crémieux for No. 112 Dent for No. 137; *L'Écho de Paris* for No. 27; *Europe* for Dominique Fernandez for Nos 119, 131; Figuière for No. 134; Flammarion for Nos 41, 57, 97, 113; Francke AG Verlag for No. 109; Gallimard for Nos 1(?), 14, 103, 119; Ghéon estate for No. 22; *Journal des débats* for Nos. 8, 25, 36, 40; Kra for No. 101; Librairie Arthème Fayard for No. 52; *Les Marges* for Nos 58, 80, 116; *Le Miroir* for No. 19; *Mercure de France* for Nos 11, 54, 117, 118, 127, 130; *New Statesman* for Nos 63, 64; *The Nineteenth Century* for No. 123; *Les Nouvelles littéraires* for Nos 62, 111; *Nouvelle Revue française* for Nos 48, 67, 70–9, 96, 112, 115, 126; *L'Oeuvre de Léon Blum*, Albin Michel for No. 3; *Omni* for No. 65; *La Petite République* for No. 24; Plon-Nourrit for Nos 53, 91; Mme Rose de Pourtalès for No. 106; *La Revue de Paris* for No. 56; *La Revue hebdomadaire* for No. 47; *La Revue mondiale* for No. 46; *La Revue politique et littéraire/Revue bleue* for No. 21; Rieder for No. 135; *Saturday Review* for No. 65; Scribner, an imprint of Macmillan Publishing Company for No. 140; *Slavonic Review* for No. 122; Society of Authors for Nos 66 and 86; *Spectator* for No. 59; *The Times* for Nos 60, 95, 100, 108, 133; *Le Temps* for Nos 13, 49.

It has not been possible in some cases to locate the proprietors of copyright material. All possible care has been taken to trace the ownership of the selections included and to make full acknowledgement for their use.

Abbreviations

AD	*Albertine disparue*
Corr.	*Correspondance,* ed. Philip Kolb
Corr. gén.	*Correspondance générale*
Guer.	*Le côté de Guermantes*
Jeunes Filles	*A l'ombre des jeunes filles en fleurs*
La Recherche	*A la recherche du temps perdu*
Pl.	Pléiade edition of *A la recherche du temps perdu,* 3 volumes, 1954
SG	*Sodome et Gomorrhe*
Swann	*Du côté de chez Swann*
TR	*Le Temps retrouvé*

Summary Bibliography of Proust's Work

1896 *Les Plaisirs et les jours* (Calmann-Lévy)
1904 *La Bible d'Amiens* (Mercure de France)
1906 *Sésame et les lys* (Mercure de France)
1913 *Du côté de chez Swann* (Grasset)
1919 *Du côté de chez Swann* (Gallimard)
     A l'ombre des jeunes filles en fleurs (Gallimard)
1920 *Le côté de Guermantes I*
1921 *Le côté de Guermantes II*
     Sodome et Gomorrhe I
1922 *Sodome et Gomorrhe II*

Published posthumously

1923 *La Prisonnière*
1924 *Les Plaisirs et les jours* (reprint)
1925 *Albertine disparue*
1927 *Le Temps retrouvé*
1928 *Chroniques*
1952 *Jean Santeuil*
1954 *Contre Sainte-Beuve*

All texts after 1919 published by Gallimard

Introduction

THE RECEPTION OF PROUST'S WORK IN GENERAL

It must seem, both to the general reader and the specialist in French literature, that Proust's literary fortunes have always loomed large in the first half of the twentieth century. They have been taken for granted as a permanent presence in French and world literature alike. Of all modern French prose writers he is the one nearly everyone knows about, that some have read complete either in the original or in translation and that some have read in part, either in an anthology or dipped into, in the way Pepys is mostly read. To most readers he is a talisman of some kind that concentrates the essence of the modern aesthetic experience; to some, perhaps, he is only a badge worn to indicate they are at least aware of one of the masters of the modern sensibility. Either way, this presence, of course, was not always pervasive. It came from very small, compressed beginnings that took time to open up and expand. The origins of this unique force, as this collection of criticism will show, are very modest but endowed for all that with the deceptive fragility of young leaves whose tender shoots can seek out tiny gaps and with the vigour of their growth dislodge paving stones.

Proust's literary career is no more than about twenty-five years. He was born in 1871 and was in his mid-twenties when he made his literary début. In his remaining years – he was to die in 1922 at the age of only fifty-one – there were three joyous peaks of achievement: 1896, when he published his first work, *Les Plaisirs et les jours*; 1913, when *Du côté de chez Swann* appeared, and 1919, when *A l'ombre des jeunes filles en fleurs* secured him the prestigious Goncourt prize. His whole story, from the age of twenty, is one of unremitting devotion to combining a personal aesthetic adventure with the commercial demands of disseminating his work. Every moment of his existence as a writer is sacrificed – up to his dying breath – first, to the translating of his sensibility and his observation of reality into words, and secondly, to a strategy of presenting his creation to the world at large.

Critical reaction to Proust can, for clarity, be put into three categories:

1 The reaction during his lifetime, up to the appearance of *Sodome et Gomorrhe II* in 1922; this influenced his writing to some extent and is reflected in press notices and reviews.
2 The reaction between the time of his death and 1931, which includes the posthumous completion of the publication of *A la recherche du temps perdu* in 1927 and occasional pieces collected in *Chroniques* in 1928; this is the period of the consolidation of his European reputation and is reflected not only in reviews but also in considered essays and books devoted solely to him.[1]
3 The reaction from 1931 to the present, which saw his fortunes, seemingly becalmed, revive with the discovery of extremely important texts pre-dating *La Recherche* (*Jean Santeuil* in 1952 and *Contre Sainte-Beuve* in 1954), the establishment of an official journal of Proust studies, the *Bulletin de la Société des Amis de Marcel Proust et des Amis de Combray*, in 1950 and, most recently, the discovery by exponents of La Nouvelle Critique that Proust's art and especially his aesthetic of 'reading a text' is nothing less than the cornerstone of a renewal in theories of literature.

The present volume will naturally concern itself with the first two categories, which reveal a progression, though not always a smooth one, from a querulous havering over a talent that is seen from the start as having at least some originality, through sweet adulation on the one hand and bitter condemnation on the other, to a recognition that here is something worthy of more than passing comment, something to stimulate both bellettrist and scholar, something to be compared, indeed, with the biggest names of European literature. Since the novel was not completely before the public before 1927 I intend to go beyond the strict contemporary limit so as to show the establishing of a bridgehead by 1931 that secures Proust the position of a writer who has to be placed with reference to literary history and critically appreciated for the innumerable facets of his genius.

A unique tone of voice and an intensity of vision ensured that, from the beginning, Proust presented some kind of challenge to his readers, and one strong enough to guarantee that he always had keen admirers and keen detractors. He was never totally ignored and his progress was never really obstructed by disheartening sloughs and trials of strength. Generally speaking, he always elicited some positive response in some area or other – if not to his style, then to his psychological analyses; if not to his analyses, then to his imagery and his descriptions of nature; if not to his descriptions, then to his social caricatures; if not to his characters and their comic or tragic situations, then to his meditations on time, memory, art, etc. In answer to the challenge he threw down, French, and notably outside France, English and American, critics generated commentary of rare interest and sometimes exceptional quality. Up to the publication of *Swann* in 1913 his readers were family, friends, fashionable acquaintances, and influential connections; in 1919, however, with the accolade of the Goncourt prize the challenge was taken more seriously and a broader, more professional interest established. This continued in a widening stream from the time of his death (honoured by an unprecedented homage from a wide range of fellow writers) and drew into its ever-strengthening current the detailed attention of some of the best critics of the day. A new quality begins to appear in Proust criticism. The tone is no longer simply one of observing and judging, or just reviewing, what Proust had written but of admitting to its power over the critic. The insights of Proust's work begin to take over the commentators, who become in part readers of themselves, which, as Proust says in *Le Temps retrouvé*, is what he wanted. A reader of this collection will see the widening stream develop from the patronizing trickle at the time of Proust's first publication in 1896 into a broad river by 1931. Since that date, which could be thought of as establishing the Proust industry in European journalistic and academic criticism, Proust's reputation has gone on to become not so much a broad river as an ever-widening estuary in whose waters the most important critical exponents of modern literature, especially in French and English, but also in most other languages, have had their stamina put to the test. This collection shows a progression through flattering or acidic journalistic notices to distinguished essay writing. The period after 1931 – not dealt with here – has become in its turn an obligatory testing ground for all serious students and critics of French literature and has produced critical writing of the best quality in a number of fields that testifies further to the continuing challenge that Proust presents to the reader: comparative literature, textual analysis, literature and its connections with psychology, sociology, sexuality, time, memory, aesthetic theory, reception theory, structuralism, and intertextuality.

II
FROM 1896 TO 1913

The first phase of Proust criticism consists almost entirely of press notices, from full-scale reviews to the simpler brief paragraphs (or *échos*) and pre-publication extracts. A particular custom of the time, and one deliberately exploited by Proust, was the use of paid *échos* to maximize publicity by their judicious timing and placing.

Les Plaisirs et les jours

Following puffs in the press, which published poems and sketches, and also Anatole France's preface, as a foretaste of what was to come, the book eventually appeared in June 1896, published, after some difficulty on Proust's part in finding someone to take it on, by Calmann-Lévy.[2] It was a luxury in-quarto edition, ornamented with flower paintings by Madeleine Lemaire (who, according to Dumas *fils* had created the most roses after God), enriched with settings of Proust's poems by Reynaldo Hahn, and priced exorbitantly at 13 francs 50 at a time when the average price for books was less than 3 francs. It drew together short stories, poems, and reveries that Proust had composed from the time of his late teens. Some had appeared in short-lived reviews perfumed with the aestheticism of the period: *Le Banquet* and *La Revue blanche*. The general effect on a reader today is of a lucidly composed and delicately painted series of character sketches and evocations of mood that contrast enormously with the richly evocative and complex style for which Proust is famous. The stories, in particular, would be interesting by any account, though fitting very conventionally into the aestheticism of the time. The originality that shows through owes everything to hindsight. No one can now read *Les Plaisirs et les jours* except as a distant prelude to *La Recherche*, and consequently its themes of time, memory, melancholy, oblivion, and evanescence take on a resonance for us that no contemporary of Proust's could have conceived. Where we savour the experience of intertextuality in reading immature Proust through reading the mature Proust and respond to pre-echoes of a great imaginative work, Proust's contemporaries saw only the tentativeness, the suggestions of greater possibilities and the generally accepted image of a dilettante with some, as yet not fully realized, talent to amuse. The impression was emphasized by the preface Proust had acquired from Anatole France, after pressurizing France's mistress, Mme de Caillavet, to secure it (No. 1). There is some doubt whether Anatole France composed it himself, or merely signed it. According to France's secretary, Jean-Jacques Brousson, he was reported at the time as saying he could not be bothered with a writer whose 'interminable sentences were enough to give you a pain in the chest'.[3] This in turn has been disputed and there seems to be no real proof either way. What is certain is that the attention of a successful and popular author of the day added a cachet of elegant approval that was bound to impress the fashionable middle-class readers and flatter the image that Proust undoubtedly had of himself at this time. He very much played up to the notion of a dreamy 'poetic' young author making literature. There is no suggestion yet

4

of the obsessive and neurotic devotee of art who gladly gives up living for living in the past and justifying existence by the transformative power of words. What is evident is a desire to go his own way, regardless of any accusation of vanity. For him, *Les Plaisirs et les jours* had to be written whatever people thought of it, let it be praise or blame. Anatole France's preface, described as 'the first important text on Proust',[4] allows us to perceive among its flowery phrases an appreciation of 'a marvellously observant mind', 'a truly subtle intelligence'. On the other hand, Proust's friends from his schooldays at the Lycée Condorcet lampooned it wittily and sharply in a revue sketch called 'Les Lauriers sont coupés' (No. 6). Further negative comment came from friends who had been associated with him as far back as the schoolboy review, *La Revue lilas*, and also the more ambitious *Le Banquet*. They thought of him as debasing his talent for the snobbish approval of the denizens of the Faubourg Saint-Germain. See the reservations of Léon Blum (No. 3) and the sarcastic remarks of Fernand Gregh (No. 4) about the 'help' Proust had been able to organize from among his elegant connections.

More sympathetic observers saw much to praise. Paul Perret (No. 2) saw modernity behind the whimsicality and, in spite of reservations, admitted that 'the astonishing variety of the book' promised a bright future – comments that coming from an unknown source pleased Proust immensely.[5]

He was even more pleased with an article by Maurras (No. 5) that lavished compliments on a writer his *confrères* are recommended to heed and imitate.[6] The real sting for Proust came a year after publication in Jean Lorrain's bitchy gossip column (No. 7). He uses Proust's shortcomings as a way of lashing his mannered style and mocking the contributions of his sponsors: Madeleine Lemaire with her roses and Anatole France with his preface. On this last point he suggests that Proust might go one better next time and get something out of Alphonse Daudet through his son Lucien. It was a not very veiled personal attack on Proust's fervent friendship at the time with Lucien Daudet and led to his duel with Lorrain in which honour was satisfied with an exchange of shots.

Proust's first work, then, provided him with publicity and even notoriety within a narrow circle and for a brief moment only. The book hardly sold and was forgotten until Proust's name began to be hot property after the Goncourt prize and the accolade given him in the garland of essays from French and English writers just after his death. It was re-issued only in 1924 and was re-launched into a new life. Appreciative support for its hidden promise as stylistic and thematic connections with *La Recherche* began to become apparent can be seen in Gide's enthusiastic remarks in an article dated 1923 (No. 67).

The translations from Ruskin

Proust's first encounter with Ruskin was in reading Robert de La Sizeranne's *Ruskin et la religion de la beauté* in 1897, followed in 1899 by Ruskin's *Seven Lamps of Architecture*. In the meantime, Proust had engaged in the Dreyfus affair and continued some of the episodes of *Jean Santeuil*, begun already in 1896. His enthusiasm for Ruskin overlaps onto his first attempts at an extended piece of fiction. It was great enough gradually to dislodge *Jean Santeuil* from his mind and make him think of translating part of *The Bible of Amiens* and visiting Amiens cathedral with Ruskin's works as his guide. By the time of Ruskin's death in 1900 he was so involved that he began writing articles on him. These later became the preface to his translation which was finally submitted to his publishers in 1902. His overwhelming feeling for Ruskin comes through at the time of Ruskin's death. He wrote to Marie Nordlinger, who had to collaborate with him on the translation because his knowledge of English was so slight: 'I feel how small a thing death is when I see how this dead man vigorously lives on, how I admire him, listen to him, try to understand him and obey him more than I do many of the living.'[7] Following the publication of *La Bible d'Amiens* in 1904, Proust was still enthusiastic enough about Ruskin to want to continue and planned, therefore, to proceed to the translation of *Sesame and Lilies*. In 1905 he devised a preface for this translation in the form of a separately published essay called *Sur la lecture*, which proved to be the turning point in his aesthetic development. By writing about reading, by describing the memories associated with reading and the self-communion that resulted, he was able to put Ruskin in the context of his subjective reactions and distinguish what Ruskin had to say from the way in which his own point of view differed from it. Their contrasting individual theories about reading become the germ from which Proust's artistic maturity can be said to begin. What Ruskin saw as a conversation with another mind, Proust saw as the creative involvement of the reader with himself, and especially with that continuity of the self, the past. This stance became clear at the time to those who read Proust's commentary on Ruskin and is reflected particularly in the notice by Davray (No. 11). Through his own critique of Ruskin Proust begins to find the aesthetic that was to mature as the basis of *La Recherche*.

The publication of *Sésame et les lys* in 1906 closes off Proust's interest in Ruskin. After taking what he wanted and moving on in his own direction, Proust abandoned him, becoming impatient with him and hardly concerning himself with him again. Yet at the time Proust had every reason to be pleased with himself as the reception of his translations and prefaces was favourable. Though they were hardly widely read, he received attention from some of the distinguished names of the day. Bergson (No. 9) presented his translation of *The Bible of Amiens* to the Institut de France formally, but warmly. Albert Sorel, the historian, provided a rather long-winded review of it in *Le Temps*. When he spoke directly about Proust, however, he clearly established the value of Proust's enthusiasm in the growing French interest in Ruskin, particularly in putting over Ruskin's message of the religion of beauty. Sorel lushly described Proust's devotion as 'the hymn, or if you prefer, the marching song of this Tannhäuser of aesthetics' and goes on:

This serious aesthete does not translate his thoughts into decadent prose. In his meditations and reveries he writes a flexible French, free in movement and all-enveloping, with countless bursts of hues and colours, yet it remains translucent and, at times, puts you in mind of the glass work in which Gallé encloses his leafy traceries.[8]

Proust was so delighted that he wrote a letter of thanks to Sorel in which he appears almost servile in his gratitude. He had been to lectures by Sorel on political history in 1892 and makes great play with the idea of distinguished master praising unworthy pupil.[9] Further support came from Georges Goyau in *La Revue des deux mondes* and in *Le Gaulois* and Proust wrote to him too to express his rather fulsome gratitude.[10] Goyau had referred to *La Bible d'Amiens* as allowing the reader to 'delve deep into the understanding of the author, who is at times disconcerting, but always interesting' and described Proust as being 'past master in the study of Ruskin'.[11] Specifically on the translation, he went so far as to say it was 'a truly artistic exercise, in which we can see this interpreter of Ruskin lovingly caress his text before clothing it in refinements of respectfulness, as if attending to a work of piety'.[12] Proust's attitude to his work on Ruskin is almost touchingly protective. It seems he was always ready to beg a puff or two. Answering a letter from Edouard Rod, who had written to him about *La Bible d'Amiens*, he cannot resist asking: 'If you ever have the chance while you are doing an article to mention them [i.e. Ruskin and the translation] I would be very proud and very happy.'[13]

The important features that emerge from the reaction to his Ruskin translations are the gradual realization by the reviewers that here was an independent spirit, once grafted onto old stock but now growing free of it. André Beaunier (No. 10) is typical in sensing the strong affinity between Proust and Ruskin. He realizes how Proust uses him as a way of trying out his own thoughts, as Montaigne did in reading Plutarch, and above all he sees how the divergence between Proust and Ruskin on the attitude to reading has the enormous potential of self-discovery, not least for the recovering of the past and the communion with one's essential self. Guy de Pourtalès in 1924 takes up again the affinity between them (No. 106). His comments indicate how the comparison is destined to reappear intermittently. Two late articles further exploit these affinities, Jessie Murray in 1927 (No. 123) analyses the points of contact and divergence between Ruskin and Proust and captures exactly the obsession with morality in the one and the obsession with an aesthetic in the other. She points to the role and importance of involuntary memory in both men as does Maurois in 1931 (No. 138). In drawing his parallels, Maurois frankly links some of the inspiration for Proust's quest for lost time to Ruskin's *Praeterita*. It is only a step from these two sensitive commentaries to seeing the re-reading of Ruskin and Proust, one in the light of the other, as an important example of the current interest in intertextuality.

Du côté de chez Swann

The years 1907 to 1912 seem to form a kind of dark ages in our knowledge of Proust's creative life. While certain events can clearly be deduced, open knowledge of what he was producing is very sparse. Only after the discovery of *Jean Santeuil* and *Contre Sainte-Beuve* in the early 1950s can light begin to be shed on what transpired darkly and broodily in the years leading up to the appearance of *Swann* in 1913.

The studies on Ruskin had begun by overlapping with *Jean Santeuil* and finally took over from it. By 1907 Proust had certainly abandoned his first extended and undisclosed piece of fiction, a secret venture that was never divulged even to the closest friends except in cryptic remarks. Its importance to him was in part the discovery of the role of memory as preserver of a continuity in our apparently discontinuous existence. His hero, Jean, expresses a sense of fulfilment as memories bring the past and present together in a new experience of joy transcending the banality of the actual circumstances, in this case, memories of the sea occasioned by looking at the Lake of Geneva. This is described mainly, as is the whole novel, in the third person. However, at the crucial moment of assessing the importance of the experience Proust changes gear and moves unusually to the first person.[14] This piece of crucial experimenting with transcribing reality in the first person was, naturally, to remain unknown until 1952. The first public expression of such self-communion appears as a result of his opposition to Ruskin's view of reading in *Sur la lecture*, and that, of course, is in the first person. Proust's discovery, deriving from both *Jean Santeuil* and Ruskin, is his ability convincingly to investigate the past in the first person and especially to speak publicly in that voice. It was this discovery that led him in 1907 to start again to create a fiction. While a great deal of *La Recherche* is in *Jean Santeuil* in embryo, the transition to writing in the first person provides the missing ingredient that will bring Proust's art to full term. It is to this period that the sketches now forming *Contre Sainte-Beuve* belong and it was out of them that the confirmation of Proust's most important technical breakthrough emerged. The first person narrator is characterized by his involvement with everyone and everything around him while recognizing his own changing position as observer. *Jean Santeuil*, in the third person, had shown everything from the outside. The sketches in *Contre Sainte-Beuve* take on the form of the insights of a privileged observer close to the real author while not being co-extensive with him. Proust was finding his way towards that character 'who says I (and who is not me)'[15] thus providing *La Recherche*, in the Narrator's progress and meditation on art and life, with its essential infrastructure.

All that Proust wrote flows directly or indirectly towards *La Recherche* and it is not surprising that what Proust published in these years was largely exploited in some form in the final version. This is particularly true of *Journées de lecture* and *Impressions de route en automobile*[16] which were used to provide episodes in *La Recherche*. They too are in the first person and confirm Proust's discovery of how he might parallel events in his life with an imaginary dimension. By the end of 1908 Proust had come to the point of seeing in his interest in Sainte-Beuve the possibility of some major work, the most important features of which were to be the integrating of a critical essay on Sainte-Beuve with a first-person narration in which he would discuss the essay with his mother. The year 1908 seems to have been a meeting-point for all manner of ill-defined projects:

I have under way: a study on the nobility – a novel about Paris – an essay on Sainte-Beuve and Flaubert – an essay on Women – an essay on Pederasty (not easy to get published) – a study on stained-glass windows – a study on tomb stones – a study on the novel.[17]

These projects, combined with his decision to embark on his Sainte-Beuve in December, show Proust as assembling, without fully appreciating what he was about, some of the material for *La Recherche*. Above all a new attitude had crystallized.

By June 1909 a proto-version of *La Recherche* begins to form with an important shift of emphasis from critical essay to novel proper. In August he wrote a long, detailed, and confidential letter on the contents of his novel to Alfred Vallette, editor of the review, *Le Mercure de France*, in the hope of getting it published in instalments:

I am putting the finishing touches to a book that, in spite of its provisional title: *Contre Sainte-Beuve, souvenir d'une matinée* is actually a novel and an extremely indecent one in certain parts. One of the main characters is a homosexual . . . Furthermore, I imagine that there are new things in that respect (forgive me!) and I would not like to be deprived of them by anybody. The name of Sainte-Beuve is not accidental. The book comes to a conclusion with a long conversation on Sainte-Beuve and on aesthetics . . . and on finishing the book, the reader will, I hope, see that the whole novel is nothing less than the application of the artistic principles set out in this last section, a kind of preface if you like, but put at the end. [18]

An early version of *Combray* had already come into existence and Proust read it in November to Reynaldo Hahn. The following month he lent it to Georges de Lauris for his opinion. [19] It was Proust's hope to get this serialized in *Le Figaro*. The plan was to fail, but with the happy result that it led him through 1910–11 to revise and remodel his whole conception. [20]

From 1910 to 1912 Proust continued to fill numerous notebooks with episodes and descriptions that eventually fell into place as part of a work now envisaged, after the failure to get *Contre Sainte-Beuve* into the *Mercure de France*, as being essentially a quite different composition, and in two parts: *Le Temps perdu* and *Le Temps retrouvé*. He gave Reynaldo Hahn a long list of possible titles, some extremely fanciful, but all revolving around the idea of time. [21] It was not until October that he crystallized the notions of time lost and time regained:

I shall give the first volume the title of *Le Temps perdu*. If all the rest can be contained in one single volume I shall call that *Le Temps retrouvé*. And above these individual titles, I shall write the general title . . . *Les Intermittences du coeur*. [22]

He had not yet devised the notion of a quest which was ultimately to materialize as *A la recherche du temps perdu*. The Sainte-Beuve work, since little is wasted in Proust, was in effect absorbed. What remains of the idea of a critical conversation on Sainte-Beuve's method becomes in *La Recherche* a series of discussions on various authors and aesthetic theories. [23]

Overtaken by a kind of elemental force that would brook no failure in putting his work before the public, Proust, the frail invalid, spent 1912 and 1913 directing all his organizational energies towards a somewhat devious, always anxious campaign among friends and connections of self-promotion with an aim to publication. A feeling of urgency and malaise lay behind all his strategy and had appeared already in 1909 when he had submitted *Combray* to Georges de Lauris. He begged his friend to see to its publication 'if I were to pass on at this time without completing the book further'.[24] The urgency that is evident in all his transactions and in all the writing still waiting to be done can be attributed to his health and life-style during these years. The Proust who prepares for the appearance of *Swann* is the Proust of popular legend: the invalid and recluse in the cork-lined bedroom at 102 Boulevard Haussmann, crippled by bronchial troubles.

Proust had a strategy for publication that was two-pronged; advance printing of extracts and the seeking out of suitable publishing houses. On the first count, Proust succeeded with the help of connections in publishing selected texts in *Le Figaro* throughout 1912: in March, June, and September.[25] In answer to remarks on this practice by Robert de Montesquiou, he began to have misgivings since it could easily give readers the wrong impression about the book, making it appear to be disjointed reminiscences and childhood memories when, in fact, it was, as he strongly insisted, 'composed and concentric in form'.[26] As it turned out, this was often to be a criticism of the book when it appeared; see Nos 17, 18, and 22. On the second count, Proust began in October 1912 to seek out a publisher and requested Antoine Bibesco to try and get the prestigious firm of Gallimard to take him on under the imprint of the *Nouvelle Revue française*, especially as the avant-garde association of the name would seem best to accord with the content of the work. At the same time he had approached a friend to approach an acquaintance who might suggest his book to the house of Fasquelle. He dispatched his two typescripts only to receive a double rejection: on 23 December from Gallimard and on the 24th from Fasquelle. The refusal by Fasquelle was based on a report made on the manuscript by Jacques Madeleine that ridiculed the work (No. 12). The NRF claimed that they could not proceed for business reasons, the book being too great an undertaking. However, the real reason for their rejection was Gide's condemnation after a cursory glance over the manuscript. His eye had fallen on the reference to 'vertèbres' which had puzzled and annoyed him. Fate decreed that he could not bear to look further; see below and No. 21.

Proust began the New Year 1913 in despondent mood but tried

once more to get *Le Temps perdu* (as the book was called at this time) into print. He sent the typescript to Alfred Humblot, head of Ollendorf's, who also rejected it, claiming, allegedly, 'I may be as thick as two planks but I cannot understand that a gentleman can take thirty pages to describe how he tosses and turns in his bed before going off to sleep.'[27] There seemed no means of moving forward except to publish at his own expense – a plan he had always had in mind but had been dissuaded from exercising on the advice of friends who could see in that only further branding as a vanity author and a dilettante, thus reinforcing the impression left by *Les Plaisirs et les jours*. Seeking an intermediary as always in a series of behind-the-scenes ploys that now appears rather comic, Proust persuaded René Blum to approach the quite new publishing house of Grasset as a special favour. Proust, who was anxious to be published regardless of cost or arrangements, wrote to Blum at this time in fervent and touching tones about his creation: 'I have been working for a long time on this work, I have put into it the best there is of my thoughts; it calls out now for a tomb to be ready for it, before my own is filled', and referring directly to Grasset remarks prophetically: 'I think the work, which is very superior to anything I have done, will one day do him honour.'[28] However, he makes clear to his go-between that he has enough objectivity regarding his work to clarify and defend what he suspects will be severe critical obstacles to *Swann*:

I don't know if I mentioned to you that this book is a novel. At least, it is from the novel that it actually departs the least. There is a gentleman who narrates and says 'I'; there are a lot of characters; they are 'prepared' from the start of this first volume, that is to say, they will in the second volume do the exact opposite of what was expected of them according to the first. Unfortunately, from the publisher's point of view, this first volume is much less of a narrative than the second. And looking at it as composition, this is so complicated that it only becomes clear late on when all the 'themes' have begun to interlock. As you see, this is just not very engaging. But on the conditions we have agreed, it seems to me that in any case M. Grasset can only gain and, on the literary level, I think that he 'will not lose face' by it.[29]

Yet for all Proust's complicated preparations for pagination and format, it seems that Grasset was indifferent to the whole business. Proust's detailed bargaining over typeface and number of words to the page is so overwrought, even silly, that the goings-on seem comic and worthy of the antics of one of his own characters. His letters to Grasset are tiresome.[30] After his innumerable additions and changes to the galley proofs (sometimes with pages glued on), it is perhaps no wonder that Grasset's only directly recorded reference to *Swann* – 'ce beau livre' – is ironic and that a reported reference he made on it to a friend as 'illisible' is flatly dismissive.[31]

The work was eventually ready to appear early in November as *Du côté de chez Swann*, a title only arrived at in May after rejection of *Les Intermittences du coeur*, the working title for the whole book until then. As the time for publication drew near Proust's intention was that there would be three volumes: the first *Du côté de chez Swann*, the second to be called *Le côté de Guermantes* or *A l'ombre des jeunes filles en fleurs* or once again *Les Intermittences du coeur*, and the third *Le Temps retrouvé* or *L'Adoration perpétuelle*, all under the general title of *A la recherche du temps perdu*.[32] There was nothing simple about the birth of *La Recherche*. It was in these confusing conditions that the eventually much expanded and complex novel we know was launched with all the disadvantages that the work was not completely prepared, that the author was not absolutely certain he had had his say and that there was still hesitation over titles. The novel's first readers in 1913 were presented with what was really, in Proust's mind, a prelude though it appeared to the public to be a unit in itself. A great deal of adverse criticism and misunderstanding stems from the necessarily introductory character of *Swann*. Proust himself, though he had a second part of the grand design prepared in general terms, was not fully to appreciate just how elaborate and circular a symphony was to develop from his opening strains. To launch the work, Grasset, aware of the difficulty of promoting a 'forgotten' name, proposed what would now be seen as a hype in that he put the book forward for literary prizes (the Vie Heureuse and the Goncourt, though too late for either) and organized a pre-publication interview, an 'article d'atmosphère' by Élie-Joseph Bois who visited Proust in his cork-lined room on 8 November.[33] Bois secured some publicity in presenting the strange invalid, gaunt of feature and confined to bed. Since then the image of the recluse behind closed shutters has become so emblematic as to be the overriding popular impression of Proust. The interview (No. 13) appeared on the eve of publication and allowed Proust to defend in advance his intentions and his ideas on time and the presentation of characters. There was also a second interview with André Arnyvelde in *Le Miroir* (No. 19) and publication of extracts.[34]

Until now Proust has appeared as a private figure with a strategy for publication in which he was dependent on good will from friends. After 14 November 1913 he becomes public property and the attention he receives falls clearly into supportive comments from friends and sharper, less openly laudatory comments from professional reviewers and critics. Even where there was an acknowledgement of talent and originality, the professional critics countered with reservations ranging from carelessness to total lack of composition and obscurity. In general, it is evident, as Alden says, that, 'No professional critic praised Proust as his friends had done.'[35]

Immediately after its appearance *Swann* was given the expected warm welcome from friends. Within the month Cocteau, at Proust's suggestion, provided a brief item in his 'Galeries des Bustes' in *Excelsior*, full of praise for the man in the cork-lined room who 'has just painted a *giant miniature* full of mirages, silhouettes and gardens, with playful games of space and time and big fresh touches of colour à la Manet superimposed on them.'[36] On a more ambitious level, his close friend Lucien Daudet provided an important article in *Le Figaro* for which Proust was particularly grateful. Daudet had had access to the work before publication and was overwhelmed by Proust's inventiveness (No. 14). His essay is the first text to appreciate the full potential of the transformed post-Ruskinian Proust and Proust's remarks on it in a letter to Louis de Robert, recommending it, reveal the strength of his approval:

What I particularly want you to read is the article by Lucien Daudet. I did not consent to acknowledge it because the letters he has written to me are enough to make me embarrassed. But also by virtue of these same letters I come to realize the extent to which I have been understood by him. I can't tell you what he has been to me. It is truly *beyond words*.[37]

As for people totally unconnected with him, the review by Mary Duclaux, in the *Times Literary Supplement*, the first to appear in English (No. 16), shows her enthusiasm in the sympathetic response she makes to his style. Both Daudet and Duclaux have another feature in common: they readily compare Proust with other writers, Daudet with Meredith and Duclaux with Henry James and Bergson, establishing in their intuitive reactions a trend in comparative criticism that after *Swann* goes on to more and more frequent drawing of parallels.

Swann was not only being noticed by critics, it was actually being read. Grasset wrote only three weeks after publication to propose translation rights and to discuss a reprint as the first run of 1750 would shortly be sold out. Soon, however, with the appearance of more independent views, Proust began to feel exposed to less sympathetic handling. Chevassu in his article in *Le Figaro* (No. 17) took him to task on the form and especially on the detail of the composition of the work, and Souday (No. 18) even more severely on questions of style and even of French. Proust was hurt to the quick by the charge of writing bad French when it was really a question of proof-reading and misprints, of which there were not a few. He was on the point of writing a public article, as would have been his legal right of reply, but, more wisely he dealt with the matter privately and salved his honour in a letter mingling thanks for the compliments with sarcasm for what he saw as unfairness. Charged with misprints himself, he was able to trounce Souday for passing 'une sens' and even more for misattributing his Latin quotation and misunderstanding it to boot.[38] On balance, the acceptance of the attention, even if sharply qualified, of an influential critic, one of the literary big guns on the Paris scene at the time, was more beneficial than the expression of injured vanity. A similar experience came with the New Year. The *NRF* published on 1 January 1914 a long article by Henri Ghéon (No. 22) which Proust felt was unfair. He began his New Year by sending off a sixteen-page letter to Ghéon by way of defence. Again he was open to the charge of not composing his work, merely drifting along aimlessly, at leisure.

He justifies himself against Ghéon's strictures more or less point by point, implying that Ghéon has not been appreciative enough of his originality. To boost his position he quotes in his defence a letter from Jammes who makes some extravagant comparisons which he uses to show Ghéon 'that one *can* think differently from you on this book'.[39]

This prodigious fresco swarming with life, steadily increasing in definition, this element of the unexpected in the nature of the characters, so *logical* in its seeming illogicality, the Tacitus-like sentences, informed, subtle and balanced – that's where you see this genius revealing itself in masterly colours. The sheer depths of the heart. Therein you mix with the greatest, with Shakespeare, Cervantes, La Bruyère, Molière, Balzac, Paul de Kocq . . . . When you allow us to penetrate with incredible truth into Swann's devouring jealousy etc. etc. etc. I recognize in that the touch of a master. Who, I ask you, has taken analysis as far? in France nobody. That is why it is infinitely to be regretted that this book cannot be displayed everywhere as a model of *form, the most sophisticated I know of*, as a model of analysis without equal.[40]

With this last point, and underlining his words, Proust hoped to scotch Ghéon's repeated criticism of the organization of *Swann*.

In general, there was more that was encouraging in the reaction to *Swann* than discouraging. Souday and Ghéon saw positive worth in spite of misgivings, some of which were inevitable given the perspective from which they were obliged to view it. Apart from the positive English reaction of Mary Duclaux, a German view by Rilke and an Italian one by Lucio d'Ambra were full of insight and enthusiasm. Rilke thought *Swann* was a very important and remarkable work and Lucio d'Ambra recommended Proust as a name to be remembered and put alongside Stendhal.[41] At home, *La Vie heureuse* confirmed the general feeling of acceptance and referred to *Swann* as one of the most original books published for a long time.[42] Support was as much by word of mouth as it was in print. Edith Wharton remembers first reading *Swann* with emotion and recommending it forthwith to Henry James who was equally enthusiastic.[43]

The most important effect of the publicity in the French press – especially from Souday and Ghéon – was to alert the *NRF* to a work of quality. Jacques Rivière, the director, wrote to express his interest and revealed perceptive views that he was to go on to develop in a number of critical pieces later. Proust reacted with pleasure: 'At last I find a reader who has some *inkling* that my book is a dogmatic work and a composition.' He went on in his letter to elaborate the complexities of his views on presenting his characters so as to emphasize the considered planning behind his work in spite of the apparent arbitrariness of behaviour and psychological motivation.[44] Proust's greatest pleasure, however – and also surprise – was to receive Gide's abject apologies for the blunder over the NRF's rejection of *Swann*:

For the last few days, I have not been able to put your book down; I soak myself in it with delight over and over again; I wallow in it. . . . The rejection of this book will remain the most serious mistake of the NRF – and (for I am truly ashamed of being largely responsible for it) one of the most searing regrets, one of the greatest pangs of remorse of my life . . . it really is not enough to explain my mistake simply by saying that I had formed a picture of you based on a few encounters 'in society' going back nearly twenty years. For me, you had always been the man who went to Mme X's or Z's, the fellow that wrote for *Le Figaro* – I thought of you – shall I admit it? – as being from 'the Verdurins' way'. A snob, a dilettante and an amateur, something absolutely noxious for our review. . . . And now, it is not enough for me to *love* this book, I feel that I am overwhelmed by a kind of strange affection, admiration and predilection both for it and for you.[45]

The feeling was evidently growing stronger that Proust had become an important and exploitable property. Fasquelle, having second thoughts about his cavalier handling of Proust, made an offer to publish subsequent volumes and Grasset also tried to hang on to terms in their contract with a touching reluctance to let a work he had once thought unreadable slip from his grasp. However, Proust found himself called from all sides, not least the NRF, and the attraction of being an NRF author, which he had always hankered after, began to materialize when he received requests from the review for advance publication of work in progress on the second volume. Drawn between the lure of the NRF imprint and being polite to Grasset, Proust eventually made it plain where his heart's desire lay. All fell into place in March 1914 when Gide, realizing that Proust was not fully bound to Grasset, was able to offer to take over the whole work: 'The NRF is ready to take on all expenses for publication, and to do the impossible to get the first volume to form with subsequent ones part of its collection as soon as the present edition is sold out.'[46] It was a unanimous decision and closes the saga of the publication of *Swann* and the mixed, interesting, but above all influential critical reactions that it occasioned.

Though Proust seems not to have been entirely happy with the reception of *Swann*, yet on balance the positive points outweigh the negative. All the critics who spoke against it saw it as remarkable. For Paul Abram (No. 24) there was too much detail, but it was 'a book apart'. Ghéon and Souday were thoroughgoing in finding fault, but Souday found good things to say about Proust's talent and about his affinities with English writers and Ghéon, in spite of his remarks on composition, appreciated Proust's meditative side and compared him with Montaigne. Chevassu, while imposing the stricture that the work was autobiography, nevertheless appreciated Proust's powers of analysis and especially the uses of involuntary memory which he thought better than Wells' time-machine. Where the work was criticized for its form it was still admired for its descriptions. For Maury (No. 21) it was a 'beautiful but disorganized book'. For Jean-Monique (No. 28), who greatly disliked its lack of composition, it was a book rich in the analysis of behaviour, and similarly Potez (No. 29), though hating its structure, was keen on its perceptiveness: 'no one has gone so far in psychological analysis'. To him the book was 'a contradictory monster'. Indeed, all these criticisms play on a series of contradictions.

Among the most appreciative, where the mixture is reversed – more positive than negative – Blanche's article (No. 27) was the one Proust most liked and even directly helped to promote. Blanche saw *Swann* as 'difficult to classify' but uniquely French and to be rated highly for its imaginative insight. The quality of *Swann* as potential Prix Goncourt material had even been touched on by Rachilde. She thought that he 'deserved not one prize, but ten', even though she had reservations, finding the book soporific.[47] Great enthusiasm for Proust's gift of total recall came from Paul Reboux who thought the book revealed 'one of those beings who seem to be born loners, who since childhood have suffered from being misunderstood, and who seem later to have as magnificent compensation, the gift of expressing all at once what they have silently and intensely felt'.[48] The article Proust least liked was Rostand's (No. 20), unctuous and embarrassing. Latourette (No. 26) found it 'a first rate book'. Chaumeix (No. 25) appreciated this 'epic of memory' and made perceptive comparisons with English writers. Duclaux, too, responded to the atmosphere of the childhood scenes (No. 16). Drouet (No. 15) was very appreciative of stylistic effects: 'adjectives of stunning precision' and Pawlowski (No. 23) of analytical scenes, though critical of what he construed as Bergsonism. Finally, the whole series of reactions had Lucien Daudet's enthusiasm to start them off, and certainly Proust was pleased with that.

III
FROM 1914 TO 1922

Gide's offer to have the publication of *La Recherche* taken over by the NRF, though agreed in 1914, came to fruition only after the war. In the meantime, Proust withdrew officially from Grasset in 1916. The delay in publication became a vital opportunity to expand the existing novel. The original two parts were to be extended with a middle section called *Le côté de Guermantes*; in fact, the process led to the crystallizing of *Jeunes Filles* as we now have it. The new material grew in turn to become eventually the present *Le côté de Guermantes*. Along with it came the beginnings of *Sodome et Gomorrhe* and the Albertine story, later published as *La Prisonnière* and *Albertine disparue*. Finally, Proust elaborated, especially for the war scenes, what was intended as the second part of the original two-part plan: *Le Temps retrouvé*. All this came into existence only because of the delays in publication caused by the war. The original design of two parts had become three and then expanded into seven. Proust had always maintained the plan of a work with an aesthetic conclusion ever since the days of *Contre Sainte-Beuve*. What the new possibilities afforded him was the full treatment of the theme of sexual inversion only hinted at in *Swann*. *Jeunes Filles* provided a picture of adolescence following on the picture of childhood but also further hints of homosexuality. This theme, which Proust had always had in mind, comes into its own, along with his tendency to develop his work by a process of constant addition, during the fallow years of the war, and represents a large part of what he had always wanted to say. Its force was such that it dominates most of the characters' lives right up to the finale in *Le Temps retrouvé* and indeed marks a turning-point, to be described presently, in Proust criticism.

Jeunes Filles eventually appeared in June 1919, simultaneously with the re-publication of *Swann* under its new imprint and also with a collection of assorted pieces entitled *Pastiches et mélanges*. The general reaction to Proust's come-back was favourable, even though he was moving more purposefully into an area he knew would be challenging to average public taste. The main image of Proust associated with *Jeunes Filles* either revives some of the objections to length and composition previously mentioned in connection with *Swann* or questions the text's relevance as a book worthy of consideration for the Goncourt prize.

While the difficulties over Proust's morality as a writer were still a little way off, he had, in the meantime, to weather the reactions to the award of the Prix Goncourt for *Jeunes Filles*, which was made on 10 December. Proust received, after a certain amount of lobbying and rigging, six votes against four for Roland Dorgelès and his war novel, *Les Croix de bois*.[49] This was the moment when Proust was at last officially recognized, though a great deal of hostile criticism surfaced at the same time. An important amount of the feeling against him turned on his age (he was forty-eight), on the need to give the prize to a young writer in order to stimulate talent, and on the untopical nature of his text, especially as Dorgelès in his novel was more patriotic. In financial terms the award turned out to be more favourable to Dorgelès, though Proust gained in prestige.

Although the war period meant that Proust criticism was in abeyance, his reputation as creator of *Swann* continued to grow. The publicity that came with the Goncourt prize fell, therefore, like seed on prepared ground. It was at first more a question of name than first-hand knowledge as Gallimard had already sold the summer printing and had little left at the time of the award in December. [50] After the war, Giraudoux was among the first to comment. This he did in an inimitable flowery style (that said, in effect, more about Giraudoux than Proust) pointing out Proust's individual way with memories. He revived the pre-war legend of the recluse in his cork-lined room and presented Proust as providing a poetic escapist literature for readers weary of the war years. Proust was disillusioned: 'It was delightful, crammed with wit, and disappointing to a degree'.[51] Favourable remarks alerting the reading public before the Goncourt award was made continued in notices by Abel Hermant (No. 30) who was enthusiastic about the analysis of adolescent love and Binet-Valmer (No. 32) who rhapsodized on the poetry of *Jeunes Filles*. Praise, engineered by Proust himself, also came in an article by his friend Robert Dreyfus who spoke of 'this work of poetry and meticulous analysis, that must gradually continue to rise like a monument of psychology, both subtle and mysterious'.[52] André Billy (No. 37) found difficulty in deciding whether *Swann* and *Jeunes Filles* were really novels at all or merely memoirs but recommended them while Jacques-Emile Blanche reasserted that Billy's view was mistaken and that Proust was providing 'a book which had a new form, new cut and new meaning' for French literature.[53] Dominique Braga was typical of the enthusiastic and insisted in an article bubbling with praise that 'everyone should be acquainted with one of the most original talents of our time'.[54]

As soon as the Goncourt award was announced on 10 December numerous articles appeared throughout the press particularly in the next four days often criticizing the committee's choice more on personal than literary grounds. Jean Pellerin's outburst (No. 34) represents the voice of the incredulous while Léon Daudet (No. 35) and Jacques Rivière (No. 33) see the choice as reflecting the work of a master. Pierrefeu (No. 36) is typical of an ambiguous attitude. He tries to do justice to Proust's quirkiness while seeing him as unsuitable material for the Goncourt prize because his work is the product of a recluse out of touch with the new victorious post-war generation. Rivière began the New Year with a further defence of Proust over the prize, rejecting personal non-literary objections (No. 38). Pertinent literary comment, however, was made at the same time, especially about the length of the work and its old-fashioned content. Rachilde's annoyance in her brief notice proves that tact over demands made on the reader was not Proust's strong point (No. 39). Levaillant (No. 43) accepts there are literary problems but sees these as something to be overcome in order to get to grips with a worthwhile text. He sees Proust as emerging from the affair with honour. Vandérem at greater length (No. 41) brings the literary and non-literary objections to *Jeunes Filles* into focus and emphasizes the value of the work by referring to it as one of the most important and enthralling.

The art of Proust to date is assessed in two contrasting studies. For Rivière (No. 42) Proust's essential quality lies in the role of traditional analyst and moralist. Lasserre, on the other hand, finds the effort Proust demands of his readers to follow his complex analyses to be a weakness which he mocks with some relish (No. 45). A more deliberately amusing piece of mockery shows how Proust had indeed arrived. The image of the recluse, sensitive to the nth degree and unable to take anything like a snap decision, is parodied in Louis Léon-Martin's 'A l'ombre d'un jeune homme en boutons' (No. 31). This is evidence that Proust was thought important enough for his increasing reputation to be satirized and the growing bubble pricked. As Proust himself has often shown, criticism can be expressed not only in essay form but in parody too.

The period from *Jeunes Filles* to Proust's death takes us into the post-Goncourt phase where it is evident that, whether they speak favourably or unfavourably, critics know they are dealing with an author who has become established and from whom everything that is promised is going to be either curiouser and curiouser or rich in unexpected developments. We have only to contrast Lasserre's hostile view of Proust's style (No. 45) with Gide's hymn of praise (No. 48) to become aware of these two extremes. What is annoying preciosity to Lasserre is 'a whole treasury of analogies' for Gide, who defends Proust on all counts – for his analyses, his imagery, his inventiveness, and even the complexity of his sentences. In turn, Gide's exaggeration was put in its place by Souday (No. 49). Thibaudet firmly links Proust with the French tradition of analytical writers (No. 44), and Marx (No. 46) and Mauriac (No. 47) are full of praise for his contribution to the renewal of the genre of the novel. Marx, in particular, emphasizes the value to fiction of his 'generalized "I"' and Mauriac is taken with his frankness and determination in analysing our secret thoughts while being also 'the "Summa" of contemporary sensibility'.

Proust, in his post-Goncourt phase, then, had become some kind of public figure, with snobbery, perhaps, also helping to spread his readership. More important for Proust's reputation is the feeling that his introverted vision was providing, for a younger audience, as Alden claims a 'revelation and an escape; this was the principal factor in raising him overnight from the rank of a secondary author to that of the most discussed author of his times'.[55] The established critical view, however, persisted in emphasizing Proust the moralist in the French classical tradition, though Mauriac (No. 47) was already hinting at a kind of amoralism in his defence of Proust's art. While insisting that Proust's works will last 'because they possess to an eminent degree a classical character' he has to go on to defend the point that, although Proust's analyses are ruthless, there is 'no question of immorality'. He sees Proust in the tradition, generally accepted as revived by Stendhal, of the moralist 'as disinterested as the sun' and prepared to examine in full light what others thought unmentionable. Rivière (No. 42) praises Proust's rejection of emotionalism in favour of close analytical attention to detail, thus linking up with the classical tradition of psychological enquiry such as we find in Racine. The change in approach to Proust over his psychological analyses is already hinted at in Mauriac's awareness of an underside to life that Proust is becoming obsessed with. It is reflected in his reservations about Proust's obsession with jealousy in his review of *La Prisonnière* (No. 96) and even more in his memorial article not long after Proust's death: 'Sur la tombe de Marcel Proust'.[56] This is where, moralist or not, Proust is condemned for his lack of faith: 'God is terribly absent from the work of Marcel Proust.' Proust is not condemned for his entry into the world of Sodom and Gomorrah but for doing so in an amoral frame of mind: 'Simply from the literary point of view, this is the weakness of this work and its limitation: human conscience is absent from it.' His characters are not morally alert and the good ones are so without knowing it: 'the lack of moral perspective impoverishes the human world Proust creates and narrows down his universe.' His greatest fault is 'the absence of grace. . . . Behold, then, the man of letters at his highest: a man who has turned his work into an idol and is devoured by it.' There were those who tried to temper Mauriac's view by asking for charity from the Catholic moralist and quoted the death of Bergotte.[57] The change in atmosphere that can be detected here emerges more and more with the publication of *Guermantes* and *Sodome et Gomorrhe*. In general *Guermantes* was well received; Henri de Régnier, for example, emphasizes Proust's gifts as a satirist and a creator of a comedy of manners (No. 51). However, *Sodome et Gomorrhe I*, tacked on to *Guermantes*, and later *Sodome et Gomorrhe II* become the turning-point in attitudes to Proust. André Germain scathingly drew attention to the underside of sexuality in *Sodome et Gomorrhe I* by calling it the mustard in the sandwich, since it appeared to be an addition to the *Guermantes* volume to whet the public's appetite. In referring to these 'thirty pages with a mouth-watering title', Germain points to the change in Proust's readership and to a change in assessing exactly the world of sensations he is concerned to examine: 'The effect is prodigious and Paris greedily scoffs up the latest fashionable dish.' Proust, he says, is about to land us with further sensationalism: 'this brood of sodomites would be completely unbearable.'[58] The debate is now more frankly open between the Proust as classical analytical moralist and Proust as sensationalist, irrationalist, and primitive. Arguments can be made to suit both sides. Proust relentlessly pursues his investigations (like a moralist) but he also obsessively pursues views on sexuality and love that deal more with the underside of human emotions, flaunts them and comes to a totally pessimistic conclusion about our emotional lives as a consequence of them. Though the shift in attitudes and the resulting shift in criticism has more recently been examined by Eva Ahlstedt, [59] Alden already clearly indicates this change in direction:

Hermant, back in 1919 [see No. 30], had claimed to find a 'frisson' in Proust; in truth, there was many a 'frisson' in Proust, for in spite of all that the 'classic-seekers' claimed to find, sensations were undeniably the raw material from which the *Temps perdu* was manufactured. This fact probably contributed in no small way to its success even before *Sodome*. And, even before *Sodome*, Proust had been in the habit of dismantling his characters to discover their hidden, subconscious motives. The resurgence of scientific psychology in modern times is to be explained by this desire to discover the primitive part of human nature. In this respect also, Proust was a primitive and appealed to primitives. With *Sodome*, he went even further with this grovelling into the slime of human nature, and, this time, there could be no doubt about the primitive character of his work.[60]

The defence of Proust as moralist facing up to, and compassionately understanding the scabrous subject of homosexuality that became even more evident with *Sodome et Gomorrhe II*, is made notably by Roger Allard. In No. 50 he appreciates that in *Sodome et Gomorrhe I* Proust is breaking new ground and showing a disinterested vision in doing so: 'a landmark in literary history'. In No. 55 he senses an indulgent understanding of sexual deviation and a relating of these observations to multiple viewpoints in time that raises questions of the relativity of the moral values of the scenes described. The tendency to see the scabrous side of homosexuality solely as part of a disinterested, objective analysis of behaviour is further clearly evident in Vandérem (No. 57) who compares Proust with Balzac precisely on this point. Proust, he finds, has a compassion, a grace, and a comic understanding that makes his approach unique and tolerable to the public. Vandérem even stresses that the vogue for Proust advances every month with an ever-growing acquaintance with his characters as if they were 'old friends'. Bidou (No. 56), in his reminder of Proust's incredible subtlety in analysis, reinforces the trend that sees him, even in *Sodome et Gomorrhe II*, as master analyst of behaviour.

While Billotey's Rabelaisian skit (No. 58) restores the popular image of Proust the obsessional scribbler, the recurrent theme is, as it had always been, to do with questions of style and vision and particularly with the interaction of intuition and intelligence. By the time of *Sodome et Gomorrhe* the old duality of sensation and analysis moves clearly into a new area. Alden sees an important critical shift at this time: 'The year 1922 witnesses serious beginnings of a new approach, the study of Proust as the expression of a new age.'[61] The recurring impressions readers had had since *Swann* of a Proust who not only describes outward appearances but hankers after the deeply buried emotions of memory or the elusive sensation of the moment are formalized in two important studies. Charles Du Bos (No. 52) finds in the Martinville towers episode, eight years after *Swann*, material that repays a close analysis which he puts over in a brilliant commentary, and Lalou in his *Histoire de la littérature française contemporaine* tackles the question of intuition and intelligence with Proust prominent in his enquiry.[62] The sense of Proust's sheer intellectual ability to analyse sensations is appreciated by Boulenger (No. 53) with whom it is important to couple, for this interplay of intuition and intelligence, the essay on Proust's investigation of reality by Curtius (No. 109). The analysis of Proust's inspiration and his methods of expression bring out both his subjectivism and his exploitation of the unconscious. Pierrefeu is the first formally to examine Proust's inspiration. In his sharply analytical essay (No. 40), he finds behind it not only Proust's subjectivist views but necessarily also the morbidity of a sick man, a sick observer of reality: 'he has run away from the vision of common sense and taken refuge in pure subjective contemplation.' This is the very opposite of Marx (No. 46) who sees Proust's subjectivism not as something inwardly directed but as a device for spreading forth its revelations 'an "I" like a prism on which the light of the world converges and plays'.[63] The area that is being approached is, in fact, one for which Proust is still greatly admired today: the interaction of consciousness and the subconscious. This had been touched on in these specific terms by Levaillant (No. 43) where Proust's voyage of exploration is described as following 'the meandering streams of consciousness and the subconscious'. He compares Proust with Bergson in respect of the appeal to a secret, irrationalist streak in the human psyche in total contrast to 'the principles of the great classical writers'. This is a further reminder of the watershed that has developed since *Swann* and especially in the post-Goncourt period, where on one side we have, following Rivière and Thibaudet, those who see Proust as part of the French classical tradition of moralists and those who from this time on see Proust as equally enriching the more ambiguous areas of aesthetic and moral experience by evocations of the magical, the mysterious, and the supratemporal. The trend comes fully into its own in the cardinal essay by René Rousseau on Proust's aesthetic views and the unconscious (No. 54). For Rousseau, Proust is the writer who (like Proust's own Narrator) is not satisfied with appearances: 'Between what we reveal of ourselves and what we hide, it is what we hide that he prefers.' It is an analysis that as modern readers we immediately recognize as pointing Proustian criticism in the direction of Freudianism and Jungianism. Curiously enough, Rousseau finds in this invitation to self-knowledge a connection with the tradition of the moralists, but the process is one that is entirely modern, for in style and outlook Proust's art operates by following 'the sinuous meanderings of Dreams'.

24

If we look at Proust's own feelings in these final years regarding his reputation they fluctuate between gratitude for the recognition that followed the Goncourt prize and a sense of unease over the reception awaiting what he knew to be the controversial topics he was broaching with *SG I* and *II* and what was to become *La Prisonnière* and *Albertine disparue* (later retitled *La Fugitive*). These were originally thought of as *SG III* and *IV*.

Proust's feelings, as they emerge in remarks to his publishers or to the critics he approached as a public relations ploy, are the first signs of what was to turn into the debate about the morality of *La Recherche*. His intention to include in his work a difficult subject goes back as far as his covering letter on *Swann* to Fasquelle regarding the second volume in which he warns him of 'an indecent work'.[64] Fasquelle's reader, Madeleine, in fact picks up this reference in his report (No. 12) and concludes that the letter alone can clarify the author's intention and what seems to be 'a pathological case'. Proust also mentions to Louis de Robert in 1912 that his 'present work would be too indecent' to submit to Calmann-Lévy.[65] When Louis de Robert had suggested, after reading *Swann* in proof, that the effect of the Montjouvain scene, in which Mlle Vinteuil encourages her girl-friend to spit on her father's portrait, should be attenuated, Proust in his reply insisted on the scientific necessity of his subject. Even friendship, he says, will not be allowed to shift him from his purpose: 'Amicus Plato sed magis amica veritas. I cannot in favour of friendship . . . modify the result of spiritual experiments that I am obliged to communicate with the good faith of a chemist doing his research.'[66] Souday had hinted at this incident also in his review of *Swann*: 'And there is no necessity at all for certain episodes in doubtful taste' (No. 18). The only blatant reference to the Montjouvain scene is by Willy who jokingly advises that these sadistic pages should not be made available to girls to read; Proust's reaction to Willy's flippant tone in his humorous journal was to discourage further comment at this point.[67]

With *Jeunes Filles*, the image of Proust the moralist and analyst carries the day, and the only possible questionable incident – the scene where the Narrator meets Charlus – provoked no reaction though it was picked up by Gide and Madeleine. It is with *Guer.I* and *Guer. II/SG I* that Proust shows real apprehension for his future projects. He was at pains to insist in a letter to his brother, Robert, that his remarks on homosexuality in *SG* were to be considered neither as pro nor anti, but as merely objective. A little fearful lest his new books might affect his recommendation for the Légion d'Honneur, he writes:

The members of the Conseil may . . . think that it is a matter of pro-sodomite and pro-gomorrhean books, as did Barrès and the Abbé Mugnier who were a bit disappointed to learn that they were on the contrary anti-sodomite and anti-gomorrhean. In fact, I would have preferred it if they were neither pro nor anti, and just objective. But the fate of the characters, the fate of their natures has made them anti. But this is not included in the title. Moreover, even this 'anti' tone involves pictures that, however cruel and severe they may be, will appear terribly crude to people who have forgotten the tone of the Fathers of the church and are accustomed to literature of a mawkish kind.[68]

The clearest public reference to future problems comes in Souday's remarks on *Guer. I.* Proust had written to him to warn him of the new trends in his work:

It is possible that a book of mine – *Le Côté de Guermantes* – . . . will be out soon. I will send it to you, in any case, straightaway. This is still a 'respectable' book. After this one, things are going to take a turn for the worse, though it will not be my fault. My characters do not turn out well; I am obliged to follow them wherever their defects or their terrible vices lead me.[69]

Souday explained in his review of *Guer.* that this was preparation for the next two volumes 'which will be terrible and drag us so we are told, down to Sodom and Gomorrah' and far from softening the blow went on to attack Proust:

M. Marcel Proust is an extraordinarily sensitive individual and an indefatig-able analyst. His style, overdone, but vibrant and often brilliant, has sometimes caused him to be compared with Saint-Simon. Provided we do not exaggerate, there is some truth in this, although M. Marcel Proust is above all a nervous, rather morbid, almost feminine aesthete, and lacks the passionate expression and the raging storms of the author of the *Mémoires* – or at least lacks them so far, for perhaps that will come at the end of the Guermantes path, down Gomorrah and Sodom way.[70]

In spite of these open comments it is clear, as Ahlstedt claims, that 'it is above all Proust who talks about the "indecency" of his work. The first critics to talk about the daring side of *La Recherche* only repeat what the author has said to them or written about it.'[71]

The first strong whiff of scandal becomes apparent with *SG I*, particularly as a result of Germain's forthright remarks quoted earlier. They were pointed enough to incense Proust, who – had it not been for friendly advice – would have challenged Germain to a duel to clear the slur on his honour. But Germain was only saying directly what others referred to obliquely. Souday, for instance, when it came to him to review *SG I*, put things tactfully by saying it was difficult to follow Proust in the direction he was taking: 'According to Saint-Simon there were characters similar to the Baron de Charlus of M. Proust; but the author of the *Mémoires* restricted himself to rather more summary remarks.'[72] Binet-Valmer, on the other hand, who had written a novel on a homosexual theme, called *Lucien*, spoke out strongly against Proust, who, he suggested, was pursuing the subject so far that he was corrupting the image of France in a way no patriot should:

In 1910, disgusted by the behaviour I saw emerging in certain salons, I imagined what would be the suffering of a great man whose son – Lucien – could be said to bear the weight of an excessively portentous heredity. I have even indicated many times in this journal my admiration for the meticulous genius of M. Marcel Proust. *A la recherche du temps perdu* seemed to me to be a considerable work and I thought, along with many others, that no one had penetrated so deeply into the study of our social feelings, but if this monument is to be crowned by four volumes that will be given over to the study of sexual inversion,[73] I think that the timing is wrong. . . .

As long as it is in my power, I will prevent our nice lady readers from believing that these closing pages in a fine book, and those nasty books that will surely follow, give any adequate translation of the French soul.[74]

Even more forthright was the remark by 'Les Treize': 'The beginning of *Sodome et Gomorrhe* astonishes by its deliberate realism, and by pleas in its defence of a romantic and amoral vehemence.'[75] It is difficult to know whether 'amoral' is to be taken in the sense of immoral; either way, it is, according to Ahlstedt, the first time the word is used of Proust's work.[76]

There were, however, favourable reports that tended to see Proust's intention as objective and moral. Paul de Belleu saw Proust behaving scientifically, like a botanist recording details of his specimens and even giving the lead as to the moral stance to be adopted in the case of 'certain vices that could be better left unmentioned'. He goes on:

To suppress a vice, one must have the courage to denounce it by making it odious. It is obvious that a book like *Sodome et Gomorrhe* cannot be put into the hands of just anybody. I would almost say as much, by the way, for the whole series *A la recherche du temps perdu* . . . . The novelist does not always write for his own pleasure: if he seeks to be useful to his contemporaries, suppress certain abuses, check certain passions and correct certain vices, should he be criticized for undertaking such a task because it is a delicate one? . . . We can only thank him [Proust] for doing so and congratulate him for having succeeded in providing us with a work that is so vivid, so attractive and so moral.[77]

A similar positive view came from Allard (No. 50) who sees Proust as objective, and Jaloux who stresses the objective qualities: 'Several of his observations will obviously find a place among scientific studies, on the same footing as laboratory experiments.'[78]

On balance Proust had so far provoked as much opinion in favour of his objective observation of human behaviour as shock at his potential for immorality. With *SG II* Proust surprisingly had an interesting, if tentative, reception. Kemp was favourable but thought Proust overdid the references to sexual inversion and Souday seemed pleased he did not give lurid details, but employed rather a psychological approach to his characters.[79] Allard (No. 55) and Vandérem (No. 57) saw Proust as moralist and analyst of behaviour as did Chaumeix, 'Les Treize', and Jaloux.[80] Only Boulenger spoke out frankly enough to upset him. Proust had written to Boulenger to prepare him for *SG II* and to persuade him to see it in a favourable light. Proust insisted he would not be morally offended:

for you will see my hero, despising Sodom and getting married as the work comes to an end. There will scarcely be anything but the hero's passion for women in the following *Sodome* volumes, to which I intend, by the way, to give titles less obviously inspired by Vigny.[81] I had thought of *La Prisonnière* for the next but I don't know if that is not a bit ordinary. I will ask your advice before publishing, I am no good at titles. I would like a title you would approve of.[82]

Proust was, in fact, quite misleading in these remarks and was shocked to find Boulenger writing:

M. Marcel Proust, with the patience, delicacy and strength he has already shown, continues his analyses, interrupted by brusque generalizations. His characters are now the victims of shameful vices (and I am not only talking about their snobbery but about the title that this part of his work makes only too evident. . . .[83]

It was strong enough criticism to make him break off relations with Boulenger for good.

In general, however, Proust is seen as a moralist and no excessive attention is drawn this time to what was felt to be a scabrous subject; there was, according to Léon Pierre-Quint, 'a kind of passive resistance, a kind of non-cooperation', even 'a conspiracy of silence'.[84] For all that Proust uses daringly frank expressions for his day – homosexuality, inverts, sodomites – he is looked on as being an objective observer, using these terms scientifically and not in any immoral or pornographic way. The general impression, up to his death, was that Proust was observing abnormal phenomena that were as much part of the social world as any other, and any suggestion that Proust was part of that 'abnormal' way of life was scarcely hinted at, certainly never mentioned in print.

After Proust's death in November 1922 negative reactions are much franker. The pattern of opinions unequivocally divides into those whose critical views are clearly for him and those who see, especially on moral grounds, numerous arguments bristling with reservations or a case for condemnation. Reservations either follow on Mauriac's religious-cum-moral criticisms mentioned earlier or blatantly denounce him as corrupt. Germain, quoted above, follows Mauriac's line and so does Armand Praviel who sees *La Recherche* as the journal of a sick man.[85] Ghéon, in a similar vein, regretted Proust's willingness to speak openly of homosexuality. While accepting Proust's contribution to a renewal of the novel, he finds his weakness lies in the moral field:

Morally, his worst fault was to dare to depict and name, without any hypocrisy, as if they were accepted, normal things, vices that had remained secret or condemned until he came; it is not a question of lancing the abscess but spreading the pus everywhere and making way for 'blood-poisoning'.[86]

Other objectors, though sometimes mingling good points with their reservations, are often blatantly anti-Proust. These in particular show how Proust criticism has come a long way from the stylistic objections and the respectable psychologizing of *Swann* and *Jeunes Filles* to a moral debate on whether Proust is to be considered a good or bad thing for literature. Proust is more and more often described as sick, or as exaggerating the sexual proclivities he describes, or as frankly corrupting his readers. Dominique Braga echoes Souday's remark about Proust's feminine sensibility.[87] An anonymous critic in *Le Gaulois*, while being positive in some respects, makes it perfectly plain that he objects to Proust's interest in immoral subjects:

We have never been at ease in speaking in this paper about Marcel Proust, who has brought into literature the complacent analysis of vices which no French writer before him would have even allowed himself to name. We would be hard-pressed even to mention the titles of his latest works. In

Marcel Proust there was a sick side which explains, but does not excuse, all the morbid aspects of his work.[88]

Another anonymous writer, while considering Proust to be a major figure like Balzac or Stendhal who will eventually come into his own, nevertheless denounces the blemish of his sexual interests:

Yet everyone thinks, but no one dares to say, that he was the first, by exploiting the detailed riches of his unique style, to have conferred prestige on conduct that has at times been satirized, but celebrated never. So many people would have failed to realize that but for the insolent publicity of his latest titles and the long and complacent series of his *Sodome et Gomorrhe* novels, which will remain as his memoirs from beyond the grave, he was delightful. . . . But this magnificent crackpot has had numerous vulgar progeny, and it is partly because of him that we are inundated with pornographic novels.[89]

Even more cutting was the image, provided by Charles-Henry Hirsch, of Proust as a jaundiced historian of his times, totally discredited by the very corruption he describes:

Proust cannot receive praise for depicting his own time. All he has seen are the fungoid growths of an unhealthy society, a clique driven to vice, to petty obsessions with precedence, to malicious gossip, to trivia that have taken on the appearance of the whole of life for it, a sort of élite turned on its head: the élite of the idle and the inadequate – a caste weary of itself, a few hundred sick specimens that, like a sick man himself, he has observed and analysed with the meticulousness that belongs to a clinic.[90]

Finally, Lucien Dubech denounces Proust as virtually a pornographic writer and Ahlstedt sees in this an example of the total rejection Proust feared back in 1921 with *SG I*.[91]

IV
TRIBUTES

Proust, unlike any writer before him, received in a matter of weeks after his death, exceptional attention from friends, critics, and journalists. In spite of the change of climate that had become established since *SG*, Proust was to be given two generous sets of tributes from French and English authors. In these his reputation is not only praised on the principle of *nil nisi bonum* but is assessed in an up-to-date picture of his art by his contemporaries.

The French tribute, appropriately enough, was organized for the *NRF* by Jacques Rivière and therefore naturally reflects the image Proust had among his supporters there as analyst and moralist. Just three days after his death this particular image was re-asserted by Léon Daudet who linked him with the sixteenth century for his moralism. Daudet was convinced he had no equal in this respect among his contemporaries.[92] He repeated this claim in a later article, pointing out that 'Proust is not content to describe. He is also delighted to judge, and his position as a moralist, original as always, is also perfectly sound.'[93]

It is precisely this approach that will be reflected in the *NRF* 'Hommage à Marcel Proust' for 1 January 1923. The number was devised to make a big impression with a dozen plates of photographs and facsimiles of manuscripts. The range of contributors was very wide and the coverage dealt with memories, essays on Proust's works, foreign contributions, extracts from the forthcoming *La Prisonnière*, and a bibliography. The intention is on the grand scale, yet in the realization some of the contributions are decidedly slight.

In the section on memories, there is some interest in noting the following among the twenty-three in this section for their incidental critical remarks. Léon Daudet, briefly and predictably, saw Proust as the equal of Montaigne and better than Balzac: 'Proust has advanced introspection, the awareness man has of himself, to an extent that makes him the equal of the best moralists of any period.'[94] Robert de Billy recalls Proust's literary beginnings and in particular remembers Proust confessing a deep interest in Hardy, George Eliot, Stevenson, and Emerson and writing to him to say:

there is no literature that has comparable power over me than English and American literature. Germany, Italy and quite often France leave me cold. But two pages of *The Mill on the Floss* bring tears to my eyes. I know Ruskin detested that novel, but I can reconcile all the warring gods in the Pantheon of my admiration.[95]

This is reinforced by Walter Berry who recalls Proust's conversations on literature: 'He used to ask for details about English novels, and especially about the approach of Henry James, i.e. about the novel *seen*, completely seen, by one of the characters, one single character, notably as in *What Maisie Knew*.'[96] Gabriel de La Rochefoucauld was struck by Proust's obsession with and analysis of detail; in *La Recherche* we see life running like a slow-motion film: 'you notice attitudes you did not suspect; you would never have thought that movements could be broken down in this way; this is rather like the psychological effects we find in Proust.'[97] The best picture of Proust the observer comes from Fernand Gregh who recalls the period of *Le Banquet* with Proust playing the dandy with adolescent grace:

He sometimes exaggerated this grace in mincing but always witty ways, just as at times he used to exaggerate his amiability in excessive but always intelligent flattery; and we even made up among ourselves the verb 'to proustify' to express an attitude that was just a bit too conscious of its niceness with a touch of what the vulgar mob would have called 'la-de-da nonsense' that was delicious and went on non stop. (People have tried to explain why his sentences are long; the explanation is very simple: they proustify incomparably. A man's character as much as his mind is to be found in his writing).

He goes on to recall that the young Proust had not only grace and wit but a wealth of talk that suggested not so much Saint-Simon as Montaigne's *Essays*:

At twenty, Marcel cast upon life a look such as you might ascribe to a fly, a look with a thousand facets to it. He saw things polygonally. He could see the twenty sides of a question and go and add a twenty-first to it which was a wonder of inventiveness and ingenuity. . . . He was . . . one of those minds that are to be counted among the most original today, an 'artist-critic', one of those intellectual systems that flourish at times when there is a welter of culture and in which the critical faculty is the equal of the creative.[98]

The most important section covers the essays on Proust's works and here the predominant view reflects the justification of Proust as moralist and analyst. René Boylesve concludes his article by expressing his admiration for the combination of essayist and novelist. Henri Duvernois sees Proust as a recorder and judge of his age like Balzac. Thibaudet (No. 68), Boulenger (No. 69), and Martin-Chauffier (No. 71) are the ones most directly concerned with Proust as analyst of behaviour and André Maurois takes this idea further by presenting Proust as the impartial, scientific observer of the world around him whose method is that of the naturalist scrutinizing insects. Paul Desjardins, Jaloux (No. 70), Robert de Traz (No. 72), and Emma Cabire (No. 74) and Jacques Rivière take the same general line but stress the psychological features. Rivière draws a parallel between Proust and Freud as innovators, for both of whom subconscious motivation of behaviour is what we should be investigating in the analysis of our feelings. Vettard (No. 73) examines notions of time, Drieu La Rochelle the uses of the imagination, Benjamin Crémieux and Fosca (No. 76) memory and the reconstruction of the past, Allard (No. 75) Proust's interest in the visual world and Fierens (No. 77) Proust's modernism. Of the older generation of writers, Gide reassesses *Les Plaisirs et les jours* (No. 67), Valéry, who admits to having read scarcely any Proust, compares Proust's novel to the discourse of poetry, and Ghéon reasserts his earlier views on Proust's work as a 'Summa'. His is the only voice to speak of misgivings regarding Proust's moral stance, even going so far as to refer to Mauriac's influential comments in *La Revue hebdomadaire*. His great regret is the way Proust has proceeded, in his excellent psychological investigations, outwith God's grace:

The further he plunges into the soul, often giving the illusion he is brushing againt the ultimate mystery, the more persistently, it seems, he brings us back to the consideration of the flesh. You might almost say he never leaves the level of the senses. Everything he calls affection, passion, thought, is still sensation and he applies to the study of a human 'case' the very same gifts as for the evocation of a landscape: sensory gifts. This is no doubt a great novelty in the psychology practised in fiction. But when Proust seems to be digging deep into the field of introspection, he is, in my view, limiting it.[99]

The problem raised by *SG* is not a line the *NRF* cared to pursue since it promoted the image of Proust as part of the classical tradition of objective analysis. Rivière, especially, seems never to have suspected Proust's personal interest in scenes that appeared to him to be impartial investigations. This makes his remarks on Freudian hidden motivation particularly ironic. The most ambiguous position was Gide's since by this time he was totally convinced of Proust's hypocrisy and real motives.[100]

The contributions from this varied list of French writers reasserts and expands views that have previously been aired over the years. Their coming together in 1923 underlines the acceptance of a certain standard or sanctions a received opinion on Proust. Awkward questions are pushed aside while Proust the moralist is firmly ensconced in the place of honour. The most distinguished criticism, however, is not domestic. Curtius (No. 78) provides a German view of how Proust's genius extends the French tradition and Ortega (No. 79) a Spaniard's explanation of where exactly Proust's originality lies in relation to notions of time and space and to the transmission of visual reality. The *NRF* tribute also contained views by some English critics, which revealed how sympathetic an audience Proust had over the Channel. Later in 1923 these, and other English writers, brought out their remarkable English tribute to be examined presently.

Alden describes the timing of Proust's death as opportune 'since it served to crystallize opinion at the very moment when this crystallization could be most useful. . . . Proust's fame was truly at its zenith when he died, and few were the imbeciles who dared to protest.'[101] Most press reactions were full of praise (e.g. No. 62) with only occasional reservations. The *Figaro* gave its literary supplement for 26 November over to Proust and published excerpts from *Le Temps retrouvé*. The English translation of *Swann* had just come out (No. 59) and its welcome summed up the mood of the times: 'it seems that it is for us of his own generation to praise rather than appraise.' Posthumous appreciations in English (Nos 60, 63, 64, 65) were all sympathetic. The tone for the British reaction had already been set in July 1922 by Middleton Murry's praise of Proust's originality, which he ascribed to his new sensibility (No. 66). His article brought the British reader up to date by means of an analysis of Proust's art and comparisons with other European figures, past and present. Alden assesses the French contribution following Proust's death as worthy and conservative in attitude, repeating the established image of the moralist and psychologist: 'there is no article appearing immediately after Proust's death which really emphasizes his importance as a new literary manifestation in a new literary period.'[102] The discovery that Proust was part of a new modern development began only gradually, though already Fierens (No. 77) in his contribution to the *NRF* tribute would seem to contradict Alden's claim with his insight into the 'cinematic' metaphor applied to *La Recherche* that is only now being properly appreciated.

An English Tribute, edited by C. K. Scott-Moncrieff, translator of Proust, seems much more alert to Proust's placing both in the European tradition and as part of a new development. Among the numerous contributions there are some which are not much more than personal impressions; generally, however, the effect is more definite and pointed than the *NRF* tribute. Birrell (No. 81) presents the familiar picture of Proust as analyst of behaviour but without any feeling of outrage when Proust touches on areas of sexual inversion. What in the French press had been turned into a kind of *querelle*, between the moralist tradition and the corruption of a new generation, is here taken in a more balanced way. The contribution such observations make, both to the social picture and to Proust's art, are neatly underlined:

Proust is the first author to treat sexual inversion as a current and ordinary phenomenon. . . . Treating this important social phenomenon as neither more nor less important than it is, he has derived from it new material for his study of social relations, and has greatly enriched and complicated the texture of his plot.

Wright (No. 82) appreciates the complexities of the modern sensibility coming to terms with the world around us. Logan Pearsall Smith, in re-affirming in *Les Plaisirs et les jours* the germ of Proust's work, brings out his unique quality even at the outset of his career, viz. his 'creative contemplation of experience'. Proust is thought of as maturing into the man who tries 'to disengage from that flux of life and time the meanings implicit in it – to recover, to develop in the dark-room of consciousness, and recreate the ultimate realities and ideals which experience reveals, though it never really attains them.'[103] Carswell on Proust's perception of women (No. 83) underlines a particularly interesting psychological relationship between reader and fictional character which has been realized in a unique literary way: 'So his women set us wondering and supposing and coming to our own conclusions exactly as we do in life.' Mayne (No. 84) celebrates the spell Proust casts over his readers. Walkley (No. 85) sees Proust as having 'morbid' elements, without being diminished thereby; his sensibility is heightened as a result and the emphasis is not on the shortcomings of his vision but on its novelty, its detail, its 'psychometry'. For Middleton Murry (No. 86) Proust's work 'marks an epoch'. He gives a close analysis of what he sees as Proust's intention and describes the notion of the quest as the driving force that provides a peculiarly modern comment on the need for self-justification: 'This modern of the moderns, this *raffiné* of *raffinés*, had a mystical strain in his composition.' Conrad (No. 87) takes a completely practical look at Proust and sees less of the metaphysician and more of the observer: 'his is a creative art absolutely based on analysis.' Saintsbury (No. 88) in contrast goes for the importance of the dream element (cf. Rousseau, No. 54). Symons (No.89) takes *SG* into account, unlike the *NRF* tribute, and accepts Proust as a modern Petronius. The collection ends with Arnold Bennett's rather waspish, give-with-one-hand-and-take-away-with-the-other kind of criticism (No. 90). He is critical of composition but surprisingly finds the opening of *SG* wonderful: 'the high-water mark of Proust'. *An English Tribute* is, in the main, aware of Proust's contribution to new ways of seeing, observing, and recording but ends with Bennett's flat rejection of any breakthrough in modern art. That 'he made some original discoveries in the by-ways of psychological fiction' is all he will concede.

The tone of Bennett's contribution is reminiscent of the reactions to the *NRF* tribute. While Jaloux (No. 91) and Coeuroy (No. 92) can be seen as reinforcing the positive view of Proust's art, Charpentier's article (No. 80) sharply draws attention to the other side of the picture. He rightly denounces a certain lack of enthusiasm and insight in some contributions to the *NRF* volume. His remarks particularly apply to some big names, not only Barrès (whom he mentions) but Valéry also. He is also right to say that stringent critical attention has not been paid to the parallels with Saint-Simon or to Proust's all-inclusive method of composition. Interesting among his objections is the view that we have to 'rewrite the novel for ourselves' which, though a defect for him, is precisely one of the most interesting sides to Proust's art, and in its participatory invitation to the reader a feature that marks Proust truly as a modern. Though Charpentier's views are a little perverse in tone, at least they have a keenness to them that makes looking at Proust's art more worthwhile. He does not allow Proust to be mummified; rather by his objections he stimulates an intelligent critical response to the challenge of a new sensibility.

V
POSTHUMOUS WORKS

Proust's death and the immediate reactions that followed it ensured a coverage in the press that, regardless of whether feeling was pro or anti, fuelled greater and greater curiosity. There was a ready audience for each posthumous publication. An openness to re-assessment and to cumulative effect is the new development in attitudes to Proust's work. With it came the readiness to debate whether Proust is, as had generally been believed, classical and objective, or something now more easily understood, modern and subjective. Alden describes the change as a redefinition of Proust.[104] Certain elements in his art begin to be appreciated as evidence of a new way of seeing, and particularly a way of seeing that does not attempt to fill out by reason the parts of experience the observer cannot personally know. What is shown is what is experienced by the narrator, and in that picture gaps are part of the vision, characters may not be fully knowable, behaviour is not summarily set out. Above all, a character cannot be totally explained, certainly not as perceived in the present, and what is recollected from the past only reasserts in turn the discontinuity of knowledge. Fragmentation and shadows, pinpoint brillance and tormentingly vague speculation become the features of Proust's art from *La Prisonnière* to *Le Temps retrouvé*. With hindsight some of these modern features can be discovered in work going back to *Les Plaisirs et les jours* though not fully visible in their day. Changes in intellectual and artistic climate partly explain what readers are now able to perceive. The explanation is in part that Proust's genius from 1896 onwards was ahead of his readers' artistic understanding. His determination, which he had rightly exercised ever since the days when he obsessively had to get *Swann* into the form he did and published even when it could not make full sense, is the power behind a vision which we can now appreciate, from the opening pages on sleep and dreams, as modern. The first part of *Combray* is not simply an informative introduction but a prelude that conditions the mood of our response and summons up the whole time quest from the ill-defined shadowy areas of fluctuating memory and the unconscious. The new climate in which *La Prisonnière* is read was partly created by Proust himself.

In general, in 1924, *La Prisonnière*, the first of the posthumous publications, was well received. Apart from a virulent attack by Germain (No. 101), who is particularly critical of a deadly, becalming effect in Proust's manner, those who had reservations to make made them more temperately. Objections are either stylistic or critical of Proust's interest in sexual inversion. On questions of style, positive praise for Proust's sentences, usually thought of as an obstacle, came from Louis Laloy and Henri de Régnier.[105] For the latter: 'These sentences of Proust's, so characteristic, at times annoying in their prolixity, but always intensely expressive, are always marvellously alive.' The warmest response came from Braga (No. 98) and Guterman (No. 99) who both appreciate the poetic dimensions of Proust's writing. Rivière (No. 107), in a lecture on Proust, is also aware of a particular poetic quality in his descriptions. Guterman finds that Proust attempts to give 'a poetic form to the content of a consciousness' and appreciates the way the narrator becomes more and more the important character in the work. Braga is especially appreciative of Proust's imagination in *La Prisonnière* and describes it as 'a new way of thinking', and perceptively makes comparisons with other disciplines: philosophy and psychology. The Freudian parallel begins to be apparent at this time; see Robertfrance (No. 102). There is, indeed, a feeling that Proust's work is opening up a whole world of parallels, not only the frequently mentioned Saint-Simon, Montaigne, Balzac, and Stendhal, but also foreign writers and thinkers, a trend that becomes stronger still in the next few years.

Broad assessments of Proust at this time bring out new appreciations of areas of his work previously despised or neglected. Thibaudet, for instance (No. 93), is interesting for the way he not only links Proust with the moralist tradition and with Montaigne, but finds a new open-ended quality about his characters. This feeling that Proust is not interested in a 'closed cycle' but in leaving his characters open to change is a most perceptive appreciation of a feature of Proust's attitude to his characters – his treatment of them as becoming, evolving, changing with time relatively to the narrator who observes them – that we have come to think of as part of modernism. The reception of this side of Proust is at times full of perplexity. Falls (No. 104) is fascinated, but unsure of the range and impact of Proust. Guedalla (No. 105) is puzzled. At this time, only Crémieux (No. 103), in a series of reprinted essays, attempts a full-length appreciative synthesis of Proust's art that is not handicapped either by bewilderment or tremulous hesitancy. He is forthright in his view of Proust's analytical and expressive abilities; furthermore, in deriving Proust's poetics from his approach to reading and his critique of Ruskin, he brings out his basic modernism. The participation of the reader and his interaction with both the text and himself prepares for the subjectivism that is Proust's contribution to fiction. Crémieux further develops his approach to Proust as a writer who combines the subjectivity of impressionism with its analysis. Though he concludes by describing this 'superimpressionism' as part of 'impressionistic classicism', the latter expression, intended to cover Proust's analytical prowess, does nothing to disguise the fact that what Crémieux has described is a critical attitude by the observer/writer to his material which is totally modernist, since the observer does not merely record but watches himself doing so in a self-reflexive way. This theme, an important development in Proust criticism, is taken up by Curtius (No. 109) in his contrasting of impressionism and intellectualism in his analysis of Proust's subjective responses to his observations of the physical world.

There were inevitably views opposed to the modernist tendency not only to reflect but refract observed reality. The reaction to the feeling of the individual expressing his view of the world regardless of a moral stance was voiced most strongly by Fernandez (No. 119) in his article 'La Garantie des sentiments' for *La Nouvelle Revue française* (1 April 1924). He investigates in a philosophical vein the implications that lie behind Proust's artistry. He argues that Proust is to be condemned for lacking 'a hierarchy of values' and 'spiritual progress'. He no longer sees Proust in the image of a moralist, but of a self-indulgent artist preaching the disintegration of the personality, a dangerous modernist idea that leads to a kind of despair. Fernandez, in his turn, is criticized by Guterman (No. 99) for erroneously linking art and morality.

The major matter was sexual inversion, and strong objections were not lacking. Kemp (No. 94), Anon. (No. 95) and Mauriac (No. 96) mixed their appreciative remarks with feelings of alarm that the reader was yet again subjected to studies of deviancy. For Kemp it 'has impoverished his work'. Anon. admitted Proust's success in his portrayal of Charlus but felt, 'I simply cannot stomach him' and found Albertine to be 'another "case" of sexual pathology'. Mauriac goes further, calls Charlus 'an abscess', and rather resents the way Proust extrapolates from Albertine to commenting on love in general. A defence of Proust's use of sexual aberrations came from Raphael Cor[106] who accepts Proust's psychological observations as objective studies and finds that 'Albertine's tastes are only a pretext for a study – and a masterly one – of jealousy.' Less impressionistically, and with more strength of argument, Vandérem (No. 97) defended Proust against any charge of pornography, of which he is as free, in Vandérem's eyes, as Baudelaire. In Proust's defence is his use of satire or irony by which he is seen to be denouncing vice and making the scabrous a viable subject for artistic treatment.

The strongest defence of Proust along the lines of critic of society and realistic observer of morals came in the first book to be published as a comprehensive study: Léon Pierre-Quint's *Marcel Proust: sa vie, son oeuvre*, 1925. Apart from providing a biographical setting for his critical opinions, Pierre-Quint is remarkable for paying attention not only to Proust the observer and critic of his world, but Proust the explorer of the subconscious and analyst of sexual inversion in his search for the truth. In his recital of Proust's successes with regard to memory and especially involuntary memory, he draws attention also to his interest in sleep and dreams, i.e. a world of ambiguous realities. In this respect, Pierre-Quint is pointing in both directions; in his study, he shows not only the moralist, but the modernist who is both indicating phenomena in the world out there and investigating a subjective relationship to them. He puts this view of Proust succinctly when referring to a problem that is a particular feature of modernism, viz. the lucid expression of the unsayable:

our inner life is not intelligible. If Proust dismantles and reconstitutes states of consciousness by using the logical procedures of language, it is to tell us that logic does not apply to them. The most remarkable literary passages of the novel lead us to this conclusion: affective life has its own laws, quite different from those of the intelligence. Feelings have an association and a memory that are not those of ideas. Their obscure mechanism is hidden in the unconscious which forms the most essential part of our personality.

Marcel Proust arrives at the same results as the modern philosophers. Today these philosophers state that consciousness is only a point of light upon the vast plain of the unconscious. Some (like Freud) declare that the unconscious is so vast that its deeper parts *always* remain obscure, always repressed and are only occasionally visited by the fitful light of our dreams.[107]

The other eloquent part of Pierre-Quint's study is the apologia for the world of Sodom and Gommorah. The book as a whole is characteristic of the period 1924–5 in that it attempts to open up to the public (as the first work of vulgarization) those features that have made Proust 'difficult' to read, and on the question of sexual inversion 'difficult' to accept. Proust's work at this time is indeed at a watershed between more of the same analysis of impressions and comedy of manners or a move forward into a new world where the whole picture of society changes from the traditional portrait to a revelation less of outward appearances than of hidden secret behaviour. In this respect, the revelation of the secret Charlus and the secret Albertine becomes a token of an examination of the repressed side of social behaviour. In his chapter on Sodom and Gomorrah Pierre-Quint often waxes lyrical over Proust the commentator on a tragic side of life that other writers have failed to examine. Balzac was very oblique in approach and Zola fearful.[108] Proust, however, 'defies public outcry'.[109] Proust is defended not only as the objective observer of this facet of society but as a writer forcing it to see its repressed side. Proust, in evoking Sodom and Gomorrah:

parades in succession for all to see a continual alternating contrast – the apparent and the inner life of their inhabitants, society and the individual. From this bitter struggle, pursued throughout the work, the author extracts, so it seems, a twofold significance, social and individual. . . . In his picture of contemporary society, Marcel Proust is delighted to bring out the place – as important as it is unsuspected – occupied by inversion.[110]

By 1925 Proust's reputation was firmly established and not only in the narrow confines of a coterie audience. Whilst the books by Crémieux and Pierre-Quint still have a proselytizing and defensive quality about them, this approach is absent from the broadly assertive remarks of Edith Wharton (No. 110). Though aware of Proust's shortcomings, she places him in a tradition of writing the general reader can understand while emphasizing also his new quality. For her he is a 'renovator' extending the strengths of the past into contemporary writing: 'his strength is the strength of tradition.' His particular gift is to explain even the minutest details of sensations and behaviour, but always as part of 'purposive conduct'. Though this puts him, in her view, among the behaviourists, she clearly appreciates a range of receptivity in Proust that suggests areas that only a modern writer could have dealt with and that do not appear in Racine or Saint-Simon with whom she compares him. Her example of the goodnight kiss episode in *Combray* and the way it foreshadows, while being part of the narrator's story, the future events concerning Swann and Odette, suggests an appreciation of narrative technique and psychological parallels that have a peculiarly modern ring to them. Wharton's comments, in spite of herself, show that watershed in the understanding of Proust that goes on developing from this date. Proust undoubtedly has his roots in tradition but he speaks more and more to a twentieth-century awareness of the ambiguous and the subliminal in human relationships.

When *Albertine disparue* appeared in January 1926, the reaction in the following few months revealed strong movements in opinions on Proust's reputation. His fame had made him a bigger target than at any time in his career and 1926 proves to be a year when clear lines of demarcation are drawn between the pro and anti lobbies.

The contrast in style between *AD* and the earlier parts of *La Recherche* became almost a charge of foisting unworthy goods on the public. Pierre Loewel[111] found it lacked careful revision and was careless. Montfort (No. 116) typifies the indignation over the feeling that *AD* was a mere rough draft and warns that an anti-Proust reaction must follow this attempt to trade on the previous Proust vogue. Generally, the point that *AD* seems to be a draft is more sympathetically understood by those prepared to take a comprehensive view of the work. Crémieux, for instance, makes the point (No. 112) and does not recommend *AD* as an introduction to Proust. However, for the initiated there are rewards in spite of the lack of revision. The feeling is reflected in Vandérem (No. 113) who admired the work but found it uneven. Cf. the English translation (No. 133).

In general, Proust's detractors seek to underline three matters: his immorality, or his religious shortcomings, or his lack of psychological plausibility. Paul Souday found his psychological laws merely commonplace and Henri de Régnier found the work unconvincing.[112] On religious matters, Cor (No. 118), while admiring Proust as a moralist, regrets the absence of any feeling for the divine side of man. More directly, Georges Bernanos, the Catholic novelist, who had just published *Sous le soleil de Satan*, sees the lack of a religious dimension as a grave weakness in Proust's view of the world, especially at a time when the post-war generation had taken Proust as a leader in the literary field:

Proust's terrible introspection leads nowhere. It can for a while deceive our expectations, and in constantly opening up new perspectives, keep us on tenterhooks, give us the illusion of a lesson it is about to impart, and never does. This pursuit is incredible, not to say desperate. Oh, those creatures of reason and lust . . . for whom Christ died in vain. I am not only saying that God is absent from Proust's work, I am saying that it is impossible even to find a trace of him in it. I think it would be impossible to name him in it.[113]

The principal area of attack, however, was the question of sexual inversion both as literary subject and as encouragement given by Proust's work to other writers, notably Gide. Vandérem (No. 113) is by no means as tolerant this time as he was earlier (Nos 57, 97) of the scabrous elements for which he had seen a defence in SG and in La Prisonnière in either comic or satirical treatment. Now he insists that Proust 'would have gained, if not in eliminating these pages, at least in applying to them some severe pruning'. He is nevertheless impressed with the psychological analyses, even if he sees Proust as being closer to writing memoirs than fiction. In recommending the work, he has no compunction over 'the dire example' it might be thought to set; since Proust is offering no directives to the young, there is no danger, Gide's Les Faux-Monnayeurs being more to the purpose.

Proust and Gide are put together as being equally obsessed with sexual inversion and equally dangerous by Camille Mauclair.[114] The explanation he offers for this moral tone is the influence of Freud and Dostoevsky. He denounces Dostoevsky as the most lamentable influence on French writers and particularly on 'the two latest novels by Proust and Gide'. He is referring, of course, to AD and Les Faux-Monnayeurs:

these two novels seem to me comparable to two enormous poisoned gâteaux. . . . When one has finally swallowed these two works, one has, if I can be so bold as to say it, nausea in the soul. Why? Because with sickly charm, Proust and Gide have lovingly presented us with a nice collection of perfectly repugnant individuals. . . . Poor Proust has put lyricism, impressionism and art into it. Put in plain language, without any Proustian preciosity, his characters are people who, in real life, you would not shake hands with. . . . The names Sodom and Gomorrah are enough of an indication, yet Proust has never 'put so much' as in Albertine disparue. It is a veritable text book. As for Les Faux-Monnayeurs, that is also a text book of the same type. . . . But Dostoevsky is to blame. . . . You have to have monsters. Albertine disparue and Les Faux-Monnayeurs are two massive testaments to this literary conviction.[115]

The tone of Mauclair's remarks indicates the extent to which Proust's image has changed to analyst of repressed emotions and unhealthy sexuality. There was a suggestion, too, by Robert Honnert that Albertine was a transposition for an Albert that contributed further to this way of thinking.[116]

More elaborately, there was at this time a grand enquiry, instituted by Eugène Montfort, on homosexuality in literature, which invited answers from writers and critics to a questionnaire on the rise and impact of sexual inversion since the war.[117] The enquiry, as might be expected, bears frequently on Proust and Gide. Gérard Bauer[118] categorically sees Proust as the promoter of a subject that came into its own not only through Proust's talent but because social conditions had changed and homosexuality was more prevalent. In any case, Proust is considered to have opened the way for Gide. Louis Martin-Chauffier is equally definite in his view that sexual inversion has increased in the post-war period and is a vice to be condemned. Unfortunately, Proust's objective attitude has only served as a bad example and his lack of a moral stance is his greatest defect.[119] Equally firm are Mauriac's views. Proust and Gide are the originators of homosexuality as a literary theme in post-war France and their work is undoubtedly influential. However, Mauriac is more inclined to see sexual inversion as a social problem than a literary one. Indeed, while the general tone of contributions is critical of homosexuality and often of the roles of Proust and Gide, most views tend toward an acceptance of new social trends. Only Mauclair[120] is violently denunciatory, especially of the laxity that has led to works like *AD, Les Faux-Monnayeurs*, and *Corydon*. He repeats his charges against a 'sick' Dostoevsky and the pansexuality of Freud and attacks the sophistry that allows the writer total freedom of subject. He is firmly for the suppression of sexual inversion as being socially, physically, and artistically unwelcome:

It goes without saying that the homosexual tendency in literature must be combatted. To tolerate it in the name of the liberty and the right to say anything and everything is naively to play into the hands of writers to whom I prefer simple pornographers who do not claim to be other than they are – 'intellectual leaders'.[121]

Strong though the wave of reaction was, *AD* nevertheless had its admirers. Crémieux (No. 112) brings out an interesting dilemma in the critical assessment of *AD*. He finds that Proust systematizes his observations on love to the point of objectivizing them. This is evidence of that hesitancy between seeing Proust as objective/ classical analyst and subjective/modern interpreter. Crémieux, like Pierre-Quint, wants things both ways. He finds the dilemma easy to sense but difficult to resolve.

Massoulier (No. 120) is prepared to see *AD* as a point from which to review the whole of Proust's art. This he does sympathetically.

He is even ready to accept the technical device of sudden transformations of personality in Part 2 because they make us revise our notions about people and 'go back over the whole novel of which *Albertine disparue* seems to be the outcome'. In tracing Proust's development in general he perceptively brings out the influence of Wagner on Proust's style and Proust's own discovery of the importance of a critical intelligence. The insight into the interaction of the intuitive and the intellectual takes root in Proust criticism about this time (cf. Curtius, No. 109).

Pierhal (No. 115) also enthuses over the art of *AD*. In spite of feeling that some of the personality reversals are implausible, he finds that Proust triumphs in the organization, complexity and musicality of his work. He is a Wagnerian with the master's technique of leitmotivs and the master's energy for exhausting his subject. The power of music and some of the techniques of music as stimulant of, and means of access to, the unconscious had already been suggested by Coeuroy (No. 92). This is a side of Proust with new connotations because it had never been accommodated into the image of moralist. The reason, no doubt, is that music, as associated with Proust's work, is part of the Romantic 'big bang' and all that follows from that in terms of subjectivism.

The general tendency, however, still veers towards Proust as an objective observer capable, as always, of excellent notations of impressions and analyses of behaviour. Jaloux (No. 111) is able to perceive parallels between the Albertine story and the Swann–Odette affair and admire Proust for going, in one of his sentences, 'further into the human heart than any man has perhaps ever done'. His idea of Albertine is that she is a shadowy, even hallucinatory figure, which is put forward as a stricture on Proust. In fact, it is evidence again, in spite of Jaloux, of the twofold possibilities that have emerged in the interpretation of Proust's text. What Jaloux objects to can be seen as an important modern quality. The existence of Albertine is not presented as a portrait on the Balzacian model, but a creation of the narrator's consciousness, the whole point of *AD* being his realization of the importance of those images of her he had created in his mind and that her accidental death causes him to reassess. It was especially the psychological investigation that interested Thibaudet (No. 114) who describes the book as an 'incomparable monograph on memory'. He is typical of those who react positively in reaffirming Proust's link with the tradition of French moralists. A similar link with the moralist image is expressed by Charpentier (No. 117) who admires the work precisely for the combination of 'marvellous intuition, so well served by lucid reasoning'. He also defends Proust as an objective observer and psychologist who transforms his material, including sexual inversion, into art. Moral danger, in spite of those who rather hypocritically 'stand up against the perverse elements' in Gide and Proust, is averted by artistic expression, particularly so in *AD* and *Les Faux-Monnayeurs* which avoid explicit scandalous descriptions. Cor (No. 118) likewise is prepared to accept sexual inversion as a possible subject, since he sees Proust again as a moralist handling the substance of life, and the picture Proust gives of 'abnormal love-affairs shows a rare felicity in its daring', for what is called immorality is itself integrated into existence. Cor's perceptive comments are especially interesting in that he not only sees in Proust the moralist he has often been called but also a writer who leads the way into new areas. Cor, in his rejection of those writers who see life as decorative rather than as a substance to be investigated, praises Proust because his books 'have the warmth, the stickiness of life at its most fundamental'. What Cor has in mind here is not only the material the moralist may objectively observe, but that unknown, unconscious side of man that Proust is no less adept at handling. This Proust 'meditating on the dark treasure within him' or 'exhausting himself in the secret examination of his inmost self' and especially his examination of 'the poisonous growths that blanket his soul' is much nearer a modern mode of perception. His work, even if worthy of comparison with the lucidity favoured by the moralists of tradition, has the ambiguity, fluidity, and variability characteristic of modernist writers whose interest lies in dynamic changes rather than in fixed states. This is the Proust that Walkley discovers in his examination of an extract from *AD* published in 1925 (No. 108). He finds a clear distinction to be made between Proust as a modern and, say, Molière. Proust captures and expresses part of our mental evolution. He is not so much connected with past tradition; he is the voice of the new: 'The human race had grown itself during all those centuries an entirely new psychology . . . and didn't know it until an artist arose to express it in literary form.'

In 1926, for stylistic and moral reasons, Proust, whether praised or blamed, is at a peak. Leaving aside those determinedly against him, we find that Proust always provokes strongly felt interpretations from his serious readers. In the period after his death, and after the First World War, those parts of *La Recherche* that form the first wave of posthumous texts – *La Prisonnière* and *AD* – bring to the fore the most subjective obsessions of the narrator, and in turn re-emphasize by hindsight the themes of variability of personality and anguish in mutual relationships that had been there ever since the Montjouvain episode in *Combray*, Swann and Odette's affair in *Un amour de Swann*, and the upturning of the stones of polite life in *SG* to reveal the curious creatures beneath. Those attitudes to Proust that favoured solely the moralist have to be modified. They are never totally thrown out. Two books devoted to Proust in 1926 show this in different ways. René Gillouin wishes Proust to be 'given his place in the tradition of our psychologists and moralists'.[122] He considers Proust as observing sexual inversion scientifically, a moralist, therefore, both in his observation of human nature and his protection of it. Georges Gabory in his essay is impressionistic in approach and though as objective about sexual inversion as Proust seems to be concludes that he is an 'immoral moralist', meaning by his confusing formula possibly 'amoral'.[123]

The most interesting comments on Proust's work seem, in marking the extremes of subjective impression and detached observation, to underline the need for compromise. Time has operated precisely in this way, for what seemed to his contemporaries to be contradictory is to us complementary. Proust, after 1926, is no longer simply a post-Montaigne moralist or simply a modernist, but a writer with the genius to accommodate both these qualities. In that same year Proust is seen equally as part of the French classical tradition and as a poet connecting the correspondences of Baudelaire and the theories of Rimbaud with modern writing.[124] In terms of a balanced literary assessment, it is evident that the classical and modern views have, from the vantage point that we now see them, to forego exclusivity. At our distance we are able to appreciate that the method of the one is grafted on to the content of the other. The technique of the critical analyst, observed as operating in Proust's earlier texts, remains, but more and more his raw material is that of the poet open to sensation.

The articles in the French press, and also the few books, tended to emphasize the points of divergence over morality, art, and style in a manner that seems more concerned with scoring points than in seeing Proust in a broader context. An outsider, G. Turquet-Milnes, in a wide-ranging study of French literature has the advantage, by not getting waylaid by coterie polemics, that she can make a number of far-reaching comparisons. Her essay (No. 121) throws out stimulating connections for the general reader with Bergson, Marivaux, Sterne, and Dostoevsky (cf. also Lavrin's comparison with Dostoevsky, No. 122). She develops parallels with music (cf. also Forster, No. 124), with Romanticism (comparing Proust with René, Manfred, and Werther) and with aesthetics in remarks on Proust and Pater. From 1926 onwards there is a tendency, especially among critics writing in English, to relate Proust to recent trends and also to the European, and not only French, tradition.

Le Temps retrouvé, the final posthumous part of *La Recherche*, came out in November 1927 and reactions quickly crystallized around two subjects: morality and aesthetic theory. Extracts had appeared as early as January in *La Nouvelle Revue française* and there are some reactions, therefore, before the work came out in book form. These reactions tend to centre on moral questions. As early as February Mauriac spoke out against the amoral stance characteristic of Proust's work, repeating a line of argument he had already taken up in 1922.[125] More trenchantly, Gonzague Truc makes a similar attack against the immorality revealed in these extracts: 'To put it in a word, he gives no evidence of a jot of moral sense. The puppet figures he delights in depicting are very often odious and that is no hindrance to his enjoyment of their company.'[126] Louis de Bertrand sees Proust as perverse: 'This invalid has seen nothing beyond his own morbid state, and he has made sickness the norm. If his observations are true, then they are like hospital notes and are only directed at very special cases.'[127]

When the work appeared in book form, the reactions to moral questions remained in the forefront though placed in contexts that reveal some understanding of other matters besides the sado-masochism of Charlus in Part 2. For Gabriel Marcel (No. 125) this is something regrettable in a work that can be appreciated for the spiritual salvation it offers the narrator. Pierre Loewel, similarly, found the Charlus episodes revolting but was favourable to the aesthetic speculations of Part 2.[128] While finding that Proust goes too far, he suggests it might – if one were seeking to excuse it – be possible to see a moral intention in the scene where Charlus is in chains if the chains are looked on symbolically as a warning of the abyss of vice. Henri de Régnier also, though approving Proust's subtlety, is embarrassed by Charlus. J. Ernest-Charles found it all a tiresome 'lapse of taste'.[129]

A defence of Proust as a moralist who shows life and all that is in it, including the degradation of Charlus, came from Jaloux[130] and from Quesnoy (No. 129) who stresses Proust's powers of introspection, on the principle that he is a moralist who follows the dictum: 'know thyself'. A similar view is held by Henri Bonnet.[131] André Berge sees a moral stance in Proust's aesthetic analyses in Part 2, where he transforms his aesthetic into an ethic, a view to be compared with Gabriel Marcel, No. 125:

Since the latest volumes of *Le Temps retrouvé* have appeared it is evident that the Proustian oeuvre is nothing but a gigantic Aesthetic, but also that this Aesthetic is itself an Ethic, a moral system: a System that, in a certain sense, could be described as mystical (in the way that Spinoza is a mystic), in any case contemplative.[132]

47

It was Part 2 of *Le Temps retrouvé* that raised the most interesting speculations. Instead of moral expostulations we have more extended analysis and debate, which in turn bring out the cumulative impact of *La Recherche*. Crémieux (No. 126) is full of admiration for the overall effect of *Le Temps retrouvé* and especially for the way it shows that 'Proust's negative work is here converted into a positive one'. He can be compared on this point with Cor (No. 130) who relates Proust to Schopenhauer in terms of the saving grace of art, and with Gonzague Truc, who though severe on Part 1 of *Le Temps retrouvé*, appreciates the importance of art in Part 2.[133] Crémieux reserves his strongest arguments for an appreciation and a justification of what the final volumes reveal to be Proust's rigorous composition. On this point, Charpentier (No. 127) finds on the contrary that Proust has no gift for construction and also lacks psychological truth in so far as he does not allow his characters any independent life. A similar charge comes from Bertrand:

his biggest defect is the lack of life in his characters: they exist like portraits and not like real people. In the first place, the continuity of personality in them is very weak. Proust has been highly praised for his psychiatry, for his *Freudian* psychology. His alleged discoveries are minute.[134]

The firmest objections to Crémieux came from Louis de Robert (No. 134) who calls anything that might be described as method in Proust into question. More than just putting Crémieux in his place, Louis de Robert is interested in celebrating the freedom of Proust's genius – 'almost always characterized by excess'. Proust's unique quality of proliferation rather than condensation explains how 'He writes an enormous letter to posterity'. A more rigorous investigation into Proust's art and the values to be extracted from it is made by Fernandez (No. 131). He establishes that Proust is 'a rationalist down to his boots' and examines with precision the interplay of intuition and intelligence. The most rounded and comprehensive picture of Proust's art in 1928 comes from an 'outsider' who, like Turquet-Milnes, is above the fray of pugnacious polemicists. Clive Bell (No. 132) passes in review the objections and excellences of Proust's work for the general reader, with a broad apprehension of his subject that is absent from French criticism, which seems too near the picture for comfort. The phases in Bell's essay seem to reflect the general pattern of reactions Proust's work has always provoked. The reader is at first put out by a style and a vision marked by such detail and executed with such relentlessness; once converted, he gives in to enthusiasm but gradually gets the measure of Proust enough to take up a critical position in relation to what at first seemed monstrous and insurmountable.

Contrary to Alden, who sees in the reactions to *AD* and *TR* evidence of a public distancing itself from Proust, it is possible to argue that Proust's reputation becomes thoroughly established in these years. The Communist *L'Humanité*, no less, praised *TR* as a 'psychological monument'.[135] By 1930–1 Proust is more often spoken of as an author rich in what he can give the reader, than as one to be avoided. Abraham (No. 135) justifies Proust's introspection as a method the reader can learn to apply to himself, a point Proust himself makes in *TR* when he speaks about the reader reading himself. Beckett (No. 136) in his remarks on Proust's style is more encouraging than off-putting. It is hard to believe he is being other than provocative when he claims that Proust is 'no longer read'. The comprehensiveness, enthusiasm, and timing of Green's essay (No. 137) are truer indications of Proust's stock. Seillière (No. 139) appreciates in Proust both 'the born artist' and the skilful craftsman. This seems an unlikely appraisal of an author in decline. Last but not least, Wilson (No. 140) provides the most readable, persuasive, informed, and critical placing of Proust for the general reader of any critic of the time in his study of literature from 1870 to 1930. Again it is the distancing of a non-French view that appreciates the true stature of Proust, which is not that of a contentious subject of local interest but of a world figure.

Though by 1930–1 Proust's position has become a sure one with a readership that is now less naive than his audience of 1913 – a readership well up in the controversies and failings of his art as well as appreciative of his unique literary qualities – nevertheless, criticisms, especially on moral grounds, continue. It is possible that because of these continuing criticisms the bloom is taken off Proust's reputation in the next decade, up to the Second World War. His reputation was not to be refurbished until André Maurois launched his biography in 1949 complete with unpublished material and a consequent feeling of a forward-looking new judgment that was to revive Proust studies. Oddly enough, also in 1949, Gaëton Picon, looking back, left Proust out of his survey of French literature because his work, he claimed, had no effect on his generation.[136] The explanation for this lies, no doubt, in the vogue for the committed literature of Malraux, Sartre, and Camus. Yet *La Recherche* as a work of imagination is organic and, like all true masterpieces, has a life-force of its own that carries it through the denting of factions and fashions, lobbies for this and enthusiasts for that, detractors, fanatics, critics, and time. With the emergence of *Jean Santeuil* and *Contre Sainte-Beuve* in the early 1950s, the whole literary assessment begins anew and the obsessive arguments on morality fall away before a less hysterical reaction to his complex and better understood personality.

After *TR*, however, the anti-homosexual faction continued to hit hard even though it was obvious that Proust's reputation as a novelist of world stature was by now certain. Charles-Henry Hirsch repeats his denunciation of Proust as a 'sick' writer who would not have been honoured as he has been if 'pederasty had not, since the war, acquired such deplorable importance in literature'.[137] Louis Reynaud, in denouncing Proust's obsession with sexual inversion, suggests that far from being objective Proust was indulging his own self-interest. Proust has merely 'followed the inclination of his own morbid nature'.[138] Henri Massis, even more frankly, claims that it was Proust's intention to drag us all down with him to the accursed cities of Sodom and Gomorrah.[139] Alden associates Proust's image, in respect of his being thought a neurotic writer, with reactions against modernism itself. He mentions Souday mocking the Proust of *TR* as 'the representative of pernicious modernist literature'.[140] Souday thinks of Proust as reducing literature to nothing more than the association of sensations, a kind of 'exclusively sensory Platonism' that contradicts Plato by indulgence in an impressionism that betrays 'a symptom of aesthetic femininity'.[141] The image of Proust is further denigrated in Alden's view by Marie-Anne Cochet's *L'Ame Proustienne*. Alden describes this book as 'the most devastating study ever devoted to Proust'.[142] In it she not only relentlessly pursues the notion of subjectivism – seeing something of Proust in every character and sexuality in every element of *La Recherche* – but interprets it as a form of neurotic confession tainting everything in the novel.

While it is possible to see Proust's reputation as being undermined by these charges of sick neuroticism and decadent literary expression, it is difficult to accept along with them, as Alden also claims, 'that even more important in the reaction to Proust was the book by Arnaud Dandieu: *Marcel Proust, sa révélation psychologique*'.[143] Alden sees Dandieu as a negative critic of Proust's originality. In fact, this is not truly the case. Dandieu, unlike other French critics, turns aside from sexual inversion and directs his attention to the more critically illuminating matter of a psychological understanding of Proust's subjectivism. He agrees with Proust that the subject of *La Recherche* is only a pretext to bring out the all-important subjective attitude that encourages the reader to continue his own quest as reader of himself. All the elements of *La Recherche*, not least the Albertine–Marcel story, are paradigms of inner investigation:

In *Sodome et Gomorrhe* the drama of Albertine and Marcel takes shape; it fills the four volumes of *La Prisonnière* and *Albertine disparue*. But this drama is only the occasion for the essential drama, I mean the quest for the real, that had begun with the memories of childhood, with the first mysterious impressions in which life unexpectedly seemed to open up its secret. *To rediscover time*, is above all a matter of rediscovering these unforgettable sensations and clarifying their meaning. Friendship, love, grief, nothing has any value except in relation to this quest, the pursuit of which merges into the genesis of the work of art.

The interest of this quest, therefore, goes well beyond not only Albertine, the Duchesse de Guermantes or M. de Charlus, but Marcel Proust himself; it is of a general order, indeed a pragmatic one, for without knowing it we continue this quest within ourselves. But it seems that, thanks to Marcel Proust, we do so with a little more hope, a little more illumination.[144]

The dynamic behind this is precisely the attitude that Proust brings to the information he gives rather than the information in itself. This is most clearly evident from his attitude to time, for unlike the naturalist novelist Proust does not take up a position above time, as if he were in control of it, but within concrete duration:

Thus he runs the risk of being confused and contradictory, for the evocations are not made at will. Moreover, they are never perfect. But it is precisely this effort put into true recollection that gives Proust's novel its profoundly poetic character. In this, Proust is the heir of Romanticism which should be considered as a progressive realization of the feeling of time. But this realization is only perfectly clear in Proust. Furthermore, while the poets swoon, Proust maintains a critical attitude within the rich evocations of ecstasy, hence the great importance investing his 'rediscovery of lost time'.[145]

In the final part of his essay, Dandieu uses the term schizoid to describe Proust's intense involvement with the sensation he describes, an involvement that is in danger of dissociating him from the real world. Yet without his exercising this faculty we would not be able to understand the value Proust puts on sensation, and especially recollected sensations, as an insight into the nature of sensibility. Whatever shortcomings there are philosophically and psychologically, especially his pessimism and his willingness to sacrifice social contact for art in a kind of social suicide, Proust has achieved a poetic power that he transmits to his readers. For all his strictures, Dandieu admires Proust's prowess as a writer:

But there is no question here of illness, at most a morbid tendency; on the contrary, the incredible elasticity of Proust's imagination, that needs only a crumb of reality for it to evoke a whole world and not lose its footing,

51

remains as the example of a lucidity that brooks no rival and a sensibility that knows no limit.[146]

Dandieu is elucidating a particular Proustian dimension of the modernist attitude to the description of reality. Looked at purely in aesthetic-cum-psychological terms, Dandieu's assessment seems to be a positive contribution to the understanding of Proust's genius and not a condemnation that can be said, as Alden claims, to weaken his position with his readers. Dandieu seems, along with Wilson (No. 140) and Green (No. 137) to be confirming Proust's particular aesthetic achievement. Far from undermining Proust, he is clarifying for the general reader a worthwhile way of interpreting the aesthetic theory left as Proust's last word to the reader in *TR*. Dandieu's achievement is comparable to Wilson's brilliant overall assessment of Proust, in that, while allowing for Proust's idiosyncratic approach, he is nevertheless clear-headed about the value of his subjective vision.

Dandieu, Green, and Wilson, allowing for their due critical reservations, give the impression of confirming our arrival at a bridgehead in Proust criticism. By the time of *Axel's Castle* in 1931, whatever reservations remain in store for Proust's work over the years up to and including the Second World War – reservations that stem from the decadence with which it seems to be associated and the highly privileged world of economically protected self-reflection and aesthetic adventure that it amply spreads out before us – there is no doubting the full and rich appreciation of *La Recherche* as a totality from *Swann* to *TR*. Counting from Proust's death, this has taken nearly a decade to come about after weathering moral objections and objections to the modernism his work in part created. Even if there is uncertain ground ahead, in 1931 we stand on a high peak in the hilly terrain of Proust's critical fortunes.

NOTES

1 The first book totally devoted to Proust is Léon Pierre-Quint's *Marcel Proust: sa vie, son oeuvre*, Paris, Kra, 1925. Previously Charles Du Bos had included an important essay on Proust in *Approximations*, Paris, Plon-Nourrit, 1922. Others reproduce in book form previously published articles, e.g. Benjamin Crémieux, *XXe Siècle*, Paris, Gallimard, 1924 and Louis de Robert, *Comment débuta Marcel Proust*, Paris, Éditions de la Nouvelle Revue Française, 1925. The latter was the first to make use of unpublished letters and heralded a series of critical works based on impressions, correspondence, and reminiscences.

2 Advance publicity appeared:
   (a) in *Le Gaulois* a year earlier, on 28 May and 21 June 1895: samples of
       the poems, called *Portraits de peintres*, that had been recited at Mme
       Lemaire's;
   (b) in *Le Gaulois* on 9 June 1896: a preview of Anatole France's preface;
   (c) in Le Figaro; an announcement;
   (d) in *Le Gaulois*, 12 June 1896, publication day, quoting 'Tuileries';
   (e) in *Le Temps*, 13 June 1896, quoting 'Eloge de la mauvaise musique'.
3 Jean-Jacques Brousson, *Itinéraire de Paris à Buenos-Ayres*, Paris, Crès,
   1927, p. 26.
4 Jean-Yves Tadié, *Proust*, Paris, Belfond, 1983, p. 156.
5 *Corr.* II, p. 83.
6 *Corr.* II, pp. 108–9.
7 *Corr.* II, p. 384.
8 *Le Temps*, 11 July 1904.
9 *Corr.* IV, pp. 176–80.
10 *Corr.* IV, pp. 275–6; 398–400.
11 *La Revue des deux mondes*, 15 December 1904.
12 *Le Gaulois*, 18 December 1904.
13 *Corr.* IV, p. 126.
14 *Jean Santeuil*, ed. Pierre Clarac, Paris, Gallimard, 1971, pp. 397–402.
15 Interview with E.-J. Bois, *Le Temps*, 13 November 1913. See No. 13.
16 Published in *Le Figaro* on 20 March and 19 November 1907,
   respectively.
17 *Corr.* VIII, pp. 112–13.
18 *Corr.* IX, pp. 155–6.
19 *Corr.* IX, pp. 218 and 225 respectively.
20 *Corr.* X, p. vi (Introduction by Philip Kolb).
21 *Corr.* XI, p. 151.
22 *Corr.* XI, p. 257; cf. also p. 241.
23 *Corr.* IX p. xvii (Introduction by Philip Kolb).
24 *Corr.* IX, p. 226.
25 'Épines blanches, épines roses' (March); 'Rayon de soleil sur un balcon'
   (June) and 'L'Église de village' (September).
26 *Corr.* XI, p. 90.
27 See Louis de Robert, *Comment débuta Marcel Proust*, Paris, Gallimard,
   Nouvelle édition, 1969, p. 9. Proust, hurt by these remarks, defended
   himself against Humblot's stupidity in a letter to Louis de Robert; see
   Corr. XII, p. 83–7.
28 *Corr.* XII, p. 80.
29 *Corr.* XII. pp. 91–2.
30 *Corr.* XII. See especially pp. 95–102.
31 *Corr.* XII, p. 290.
32 *Corr.* XII, p. 298.

33 *Corr.* XII, p. 298; p. 304.

34 Pre-publication puff appeared in *Gil Blas*, 9 November 1913; see *Corr.* XII, pp. 300–1. An *écho* appeared just after publication in *Le Figaro*, 16 November by Robert Dreyfus briefly describing the book as a fine work and 'the result of several years of intense meditation'. After publication, extracts appeared in *Gil Blas*, 18 November and *Les Annales*, 23 November.

35 D. W. Alden, *Marcel Proust and his French Critics*, New York, Russell, 1940; reprinted 1973, p. 19.

36 In italics in the text. *Excelsior*, 23 November 1913.

37 *Corr.* XII, p. 338.

38 *Corr.* XII, pp. 380–1.

39 *Corr.* XIII, p. 26. In italics in the text.

40 *Ibid.* The reference to the prolific popular novelist, Paul de Kock among the great is an amusing touch of bathos, though Proust did not seem to see it as odd. The tone of pride in his work and the feeling of a master justifying himself can also be found elsewhere. See *Corr.* XII, pp. 230–1 for his defence of his use of detail 'to uncover some general law'. Cf. also *Corr.* XII, p. 394.

41 See respectively Rainer Maria Rilke, *Briefe* I, Wiesbaden, Insel-Verlag, 1950, p. 480 and Lucio d'Ambra, *Rassegna Contemporanea*, 10 December 1913, pp. 822–4.

42 Supplement to *La Vie heureuse*, 15 February 1914.

43 Edith Wharton, *A Backward Glance*, New York, Appleton-Century, 1934; reprinted London, Constable 1972:

> No one but a novelist knows how hard it is for one of the craft to read other people's novels; but in the presence of a masterpiece all of James's prejudices and reluctances vanished. He seized upon *Du côté de chez Swann* and devoured it in a passion of curiosity and admiration. Here, in the first volume of a long chronicle-novel – the very type of the unrolling tapestry which was so contrary to his own conception of form – he instantly recognised a new mastery, a new vision, and a new structural design as yet unintelligible to him, but as surely there as hard bone under soft flesh in a living organism. (p. 324)

44 *Corr.* XIII, p. 98. In italics in the text.

45 Letter dated January 1914, quoted in *Marcel Proust: lettres à André Gide*, Neuchâtel and Paris, Éditions des Ides et Calendes, 1949, pp. 9–10.

46 *Corr.* XIII, p. 114.

47 Review in *Mercure de France*, 16 January 1914, p. 364. That 'soporific' rankled. Proust was still thinking about it in April when he wrote to her husband, the editor of *Le Mercure de France*, to point out that she was both cruel and unfair; see *Corr.* XIII, p. 151.

48 Review in *Le Journal*, 23 December 1913, p. 6.

49 For a full account of the Goncourt affair see particularly D. W. Alden, *Marcel Proust and his French Critics*, New York, Russell, 1973, pp. 21–39; and G. Painter, *Marcel Proust*, London, Chatto & Windus, 1965, vol. 2, pp. 276–7.

50 See Proust's letter to Jacques Boulenger, 21 December 1919, *Corr. gén.*, III, p. 201.

51 *Feuillets d'art*, June 1919; Proust's comment appears in a letter to Jacques Porel, 15 October 1919 in *Bulletin de la Société des Amis de Marcel Proust*, 1970, p. 940.

52 'Une rentrée littéraire', *Le Figaro*, 7 July 1919 under the pseudonym Bartholo. Dreyfus explains in his *Souvenirs sur Marcel Proust*, Paris, Grasset, 1926, pp. 321 ff. that since Proust was in a hurry, he had to write his notice hastily. Proust tempered his letter of thanks by pointing out that *La Recherche* 'is not just meticulous and is not even meticulous at all'. He had in mind to reject any idea of being thought finicky.

53 *Le Figaro*, 22 September 1919.

54 *Le Crapouillot*, 1 September 1919, p. 6.

55 Alden, *op.cit.* p. 41.

56 *Revue hebdomadaire*, 2 December 1922.

57 See Henriette Charasson, *Revue hebdomadaire*, April 1923, pp. 682–7.

58 'Le dernier livre de Marcel Proust', 1921; now in *De Proust à Dada*, Paris, Kra, 1924, pp. 11–15.

59 Eva Ahlstedt, *La Pudeur en crise*, Paris, Touzot, 1985.

60 Alden, *op. cit*, p. 57.

61 *Ibid.*, p. 62.

62 René Lalou, *Histoire de la littérature française contemporaine*, Paris, Crès, 1922, pp. 639–45.

63 Cf. Alden, *op. cit.*, p. 52; he also claims in reference to Pierrefeu: 'This is the first time that Proust is seriously charged with morbidity.'

64 *Choix de Lettres*, Paris, Plon, 1965, p. 181.

65 Louis de Robert, *Comment débuta Marcel Proust*, Paris, Gallimard, 1969, p. 21.

66 *Ibid.*, p. 104; for Proust's reply see p. 66.

67 Willy (pseudonym of Henry de Gauthier-Villars, better known as husband of Colette), *Le Sourire*, 18 June 1914; for Proust's comment see *Correspondance: Marcel Proust et Jacques Rivière*, Paris, Plon, 1955, p. 18.

68 'Marcel Proust: quatre lettres à son frère', *La Nouvelle Revue française*, 1 May 1970, pp. 748–9.

69 *Corr. gén.*, III, p. 83.

70 *Le Temps*, 4 November 1920. Proust expressed his reaction in a confidential letter to the influential Souday, but not publicly:

At the moment when I am about to publish *Sodome et Gomorrhe*, and when, because I shall be talking of Sodom, no one will have the courage to come to my defence, you are in advance opening up the path (without malice, I'm sure) to all sorts of nasty people, by treating me as 'feminine'. From feminine to effeminate is only a step. People who have been my witnesses in a duel will tell you if I have the spinelessness of someone effeminate. (*Corr. gén.*, III, p. 86)

71 Ahlstedt, *op. cit.*, p. 51.

72 *Le Temps*, 12 May 1921.

73 Binet-Valmer is thinking, of course, of the possibility of *SG II, III* and *IV* as Proust originally intended.

74 *Comoedia*, 22 May 1921.

75 *L'Intransigeant*, 5 June 1921.

76 Ahlstedt, *op. cit.*, pp. 59–60.

77 *La Libre Parole*, 1 July 1921.

78 *Le Bulletin de la maison du livre français*, 22 April 1922.

79 R. Kemp in *La Liberté*, 8 May 1922; P. Souday in *Le Temps*, 12 May 1922.

80 A. Chaumeix in *Le Gaulois*, 1 July 1922; 'Les Treize' in *L'Intransigeant*, 13 July 1922; E. Jaloux in *Le Soir (Bruxelles)*, 4 August 1922 and *L'Éclair*, 7 September 1922.

81 As epigraph to *SG I* Proust used a line from Vigny's poem: *La Colère de Samson* – 'La femme aura Gomorrhe et l'homme aura Sodome.'

82 *Corr. gén.*, III, pp. 290–1.

83 *L'Opinion*, 27 May 1922.

84 Léon Pierre-Quint, *Marcel Proust – sa vie, son oeuvre*, Paris, Kra, 1925, p. 290.

85 *Le Correspondant*, 23 January 1923.

86 *La Revue des jeunes*, 10 March 1923.

87 *Europe nouvelle*, 25 November 1922.

88 *Le Gaulois*, 20 November 1922.

89 *Le Cri de Paris*, 10 December 1922.

90 *Le Mercure de France*, 1 March 1923.

91 *La Revue critique des idées et des livres*, 25 April 1923; Ahlstedt, *op. cit.*, p. 124.

92 *L'Intransigeant*, 21 November 1922.

93 *L'Action française*, 23 November 1922.

94 *La Nouvelle Revue française*, 1 January 1923, p. 23.

95 *Ibid.*, p. 38.

96 *Ibid.*, p. 79.

97 *Ibid.*, p. 72.

98 *Ibid.*, pp. 42–3.

99 *Ibid.*, p. 235.

100 Gide, *Journal* for 1921, p. 694, Paris, Gallimard, 1948. Proust, it seems, told him that he used his pleasant homosexual memories for the heterosexual *Jeunes Filles* and was now left only with grotesque and abject material for *SG*.

101 Alden, *op. cit.*, p. 69.

102 *Ibid.*, p. 75.

103 *An English Tribute*, London, Chatto & Windus, 1923, pp. 54–5.

104 Alden, *op. cit.*, p. 90:

> *La Prisonnière* led to a redefinition of Proust; . . . there is a very decided swing from the notion of an objective Proust to a subjective Proust. The explanation is that the term objective is entirely unsuitable for this volume and, since this is only a continuation of the previous work, it is soon apparent that the term is a misnomer for any part of the *Temps perdu*.

105 Louis Laloy in *Comoedia*, 26 February 1924, p. 4 and Henri de Régnier in *Le Figaro*, 1 April 1924.

106 *Le Mercure de France*, 15 July 1924 in an article signed with his pseudonym, Bergotte: 'Un psychologue du péché', pp. 307–24.

107 Léon Pierre-Quint: *Marcel Proust: sa vie, son oeuvre*, Paris, Kra, 1925, pp. 141–2. Italics in the text.

108 *Ibid.*, pp. 208–9.

109 *Ibid.*, p. 209.

110 *Ibid.*, pp. 227–8.

111 Pierre Loewel in *L'Avenir*, 27 January 1926, p. 2.

112 Paul Souday, *Le Temps*, 28 January 1926, p. 3; Henri de Régnier, *Le Figaro*, 23 February 1926, p. 4.

113 Georges Bernanos, Interview with Frédéric Lefèvre, *Les Nouvelles littéraires*, 17 April 1926.

114 Camille Mauclair, 'La vase littéraire', *La Dépêche* (Toulouse), 19 February 1926, p. 1.

115 Camille Mauclair, 'Le poison Dostoievsky', *La Semaine littéraire* (Genève), 27 February 1926, p. 105.

116 Robert Honnert, Notice in *La Revue européenne*, 1 March 1926, pp. 75–6.

117 Eugène Montfort, 'L'homosexualité en littérature', *Les Marges*, 15 March 1926, pp. 176–216.

118 *Ibid.*, pp. 178–82.

119 *Ibid.*, p. 199.

120 *Ibid.*, pp. 200–2.

121 *Ibid.*, p. 201.

122 René Gillouin, *Esquisses littéraires et morales*, Paris, Grasset, 1926, p. 194.

123 Georges Gabory, *Essai sur Marcel Proust*, Paris, Chamontin, 1926, p. 109.

124 See Marcel Braunschvig, *La Littérature française contemporaine étudiée dans les textes*, Paris, Colin, 1926 and M. J. Durry, 'Reflexions' in *Les Contemporains*, Paris, Les Editions de la Revue *Le Capitole*, 1926.

125 *La Revue hebdomadaire*, 19 February 1927.

126 *Comoedia*, 17 May 1927.

127 *Candide*, 30 June 1927.
128 *L'Avenir*, 7 December 1927.
129 Henri de Régnier in *Le Figaro*, 21 December 1927; J. Ernest-Charles in *Le Quotidien*, 7 December 1927.
130 *Les Nouvelles littéraires*, 3 December 1927.
131 *Le Rouge et le noir*, 15 April 1928.
132 *Le Rouge et le noir*, 15 April 1928.
133 *Comoedia*, 23 October 1928.
134 *Candide*, 30 June 1927, p. 3. Italics in the text.
135 *L'Humanité*, 6 June 1929.
136 André Maurois, *A la recherche de Marcel Proust*, Paris, Hachette, 1949; Gaeton Picon, *Panorama de la nouvelle littérature française*, Paris, Gallimard, 1949.
137 *Le Mercure de France*, 15 December 1929, p. 700.
138 Louis Reynaud, *La Crise de notre littérature*, Paris, Hachette, 1929, p. 200.
139 *La Revue universelle*, 15 April 1930, pp. 230–4.
140 Alden, *op. cit.*, p. 129.
141 *Le Temps*, 17 November 1927.
142 *L'Ame Proustienne*, Brussels, Collignon, 1930; see Alden, *op. cit.*, p. 130.
143 Arnaud Dandieu, *Marcel Proust, sa révélation psychologique*, Paris, Firmin-Didot, 1930; see Alden, *op. cit.*, p. 134.
144 Dandieu, *op. cit.*, pp. 17–18. Italics in the text.
145 *Ibid.*, p. 21.
146 *Ibid.*, p. 26.

Notes on the Text

I must express my particular indebtedness to two important books on the critical reception of Proust's work. All students of Proust will be grateful for their invaluable assistance.

These are D. W. Alden's pioneering *Marcel Proust and his French Critics*, 1940 and Eva Ahlstedt's expansion of part of Alden's thesis, *La Pudeur en crise*, 1985. They are both of special interest and value for their exhaustive bibliographies and the latter, in particular, for its clear analysis of the change in direction in Proust criticism following the publication of *Sodome et Gomorrhe*.

I am responsible for all translations.

1896–7

LES PLAISIRS ET LES JOURS

1. Anatole France on *Les Plaisirs et les jours*
1896

Preface to *Les Plaisirs et les jours*, Paris, Calmann-Lévy, 1896.

Anatole France (1844–1924), influential novelist, critic, and satirist, had promised Proust a preface but had to be forced to write it by his mistress, Mme Arman de Caillavet. Nevertheless, from amidst the excessively precious language there emerges a positive feeling in favour of Proust's potential talent.

Why has he asked me to present his book to the curious reader? And why have I promised him that I would take on this most agreeable but quite unnecessary task? His book is like a young face, full of charm and refined grace. It needs no recommendation, it speaks for itself and cannot help but be its own presenter.

It is certainly youthful. It has the youth that partakes of the author's own youthfulness. Yet it is old with the age of the world. It makes you think of springtime leaves sprouting on ancient branches in age-old forests. The new growths seem to be full of the sadness of the woodland's dim and distant past and to wear mourning for so many springs long dead.

Grave Hesiod recited his *Works and Days* to the goat-herds of Mount Helicon. How much sadder it is to recite these *Pleasures and Days* to the elegant and fashionable of our time if, as the English statesman claims, life would be bearable were it not for its pleasures. And our young friend's book is full of weary smiles and languorous poses that are not without beauty or nobility.

Even his sadness may be found to be pleasant and many-sided, borne and sustained as it is by a marvellously observant mind and a supple, penetrating and truly subtle intelligence. This calendar of *Pleasures and Days* marks both nature's hours by harmonious pictures of sky, sea and woods and human hours by faithful portraits and genre pictures that have a marvellous finish to them.

Marcel Proust takes equal delight in describing the desolate splendour of the setting sun and the agitated vanity of a snobbish soul. He excels in retailing the elegant griefs and the affected sufferings which, at least in cruelty, equal those that nature lavishes on us with motherly abundance. I must confess that these invented sufferings, these griefs discovered by dint of human genius and these pains created by artifice seem infinitely interesting and precious to me, and I am grateful to Marcel Proust for having studied and described some choice specimens.

He entices us into a hot-house atmosphere and keeps us there among orchids of a strange and sickly beauty which have evolved so as to dispense with nourishment from mere soil. Suddenly, a shining arrow flies through the deliciously heavy air, a lightning flash which, like the German doctor's rays, penetrates the bodies of men.[1] The poet, at one go, has penetrated secret thoughts and unavowed desires.

That is his style and art. He displays therein an accuracy surprising in so young an archer. He is by no means innocent. But he is so sincere and so truthful that he takes on an air of artlessness and in that way delights us. There is a touch of a depraved Bernardin de Saint-Pierre and a naive Petronius in him.

His book is blessed by fortune! It will make its way through the city all adorned and perfumed with the flowers that Madeleine Lemaire has strewn over it with that divine hand that goes scattering the roses together with the roses' dew.

NOTE

1 The reference is to Roentgen's discovery of X-rays in 1895.

2. Paul Perret on *Les Plaisirs et les jours*
1896

Extract from his review of Proust's first book, *La Liberté*, 26 June 1896, p. 2.

Paul Perret (1830–1904), novelist and critic, takes the work seriously and not as the effusion of a dilettante. His concern to define Proust as a 'modern' writer can be compared with Gide, No. 67. In his remarks on the short stories, he objects to their symbolist origins and remoteness from life.

The author is truly a 'modern' – and his modernity does not consist, as with many others, in the search for baroque and generally empty literary forms; he is neither creator of gobbledygook nor master-craftsman in emotionalism. M. Marcel Proust is modern because he expresses feelings that belong specifically to our present time. It is not amusing – it is even quite the opposite of broad Gallic jollity; it smells of the profound boredom, the *taedium vitae* of the Roman Empire and, in general, of all periods of decadence; it is subtly refined and just a little perverse. . . .
[Surveys the contents of *Les Plaisirs et les jours* and goes on to the weaknesses in the short stories.]

These stories, in which the psychological handling of the characters is always very exact, are set in vague surroundings; the very real characters are clothed in strange, tawdry costumes that in colour and in cut have no reality at all; they are like heroes and heroines of fairy-tales with names like princess of Styria, duke of Bohemia etc. I realize, of course, that this is the new fad; it has here been hitched up to grim Madame Psychology. It is a whim of the author, but the attentive reader is quick to see that the said grim Madame is none too happy to be so wildly paired off. . . .
[Sees Proust as lacking the exactness in the short story form to be found in Mérimée and goes on to object to his symbolist attitudes.]

The whole of M. Marcel Proust's poetic credo is in a phrase to be found in his pretty piece, *Rêveries, couleur du temps*: 'Desire flourishes but possession makes all things wither; better dream your life than live it, even though to live it is still but a dream.' Not at all, nothing is further from the truth, or less human or social. . . . To write is to throw oneself anew into the hurly-burly of life; a book is action, and to keep it wrapped in this twilight atmosphere of reverie is to deprive it of its import and its power. . . .

[Considers the saving grace of the stories to be the touches of satire and social criticism that take the author out of dreams and into reality.]

The astonishing variety of this book is not its least attraction. This richly talented young man, marked out for a fine career as a writer, has put everything he has seen, felt, thought and observed into his first work. In this way, *Les Plaisirs et les jours* becomes the literary mirror of a mind and soul. So many others only fill, or rather cram, their first pieces with unconscious imitations or shameless plagiarism.

3. Léon Blum on *Les Plaisirs et les jours*
1896

Extract from 'Les Livres', *La Revue blanche*, 1 July 1896, pp. 44–8.

Léon Blum (1872–1950) was acquainted with Proust from their schooldays at the Lycée Condorcet and shared his literary début with him on *Le Banquet*. He was a distinguished, among many distinguished, contributors to *La Revue blanche*, a little review of some originality published from 1891 to 1903. He began as an essayist and drama critic noted for his crisp style and mature judgment and later made another reputation as a socialist politician and prime minister.

Here we have M. Marcel Proust's book: *Les Plaisirs et les jours*, with a preface by M. France, designs by Mme Lemaire, printed by Chamerot and published by Lévy on fine quality, thick, luxurious paper. Hesiod counted the days by the hard toil of work in the fields; M. Proust honours them with the varied and novel pleasures of life in the city. Short-stories on fashionable society, tales of love, melodious verses, with music by Reynaldo Hahn; fragments in which the accuracy of the observation is diminished by the languid grace of the expression; M. Proust has brought all kinds of styles and all kinds of charm together. And elegant ladies and elegant young gentlemen will be moved and delighted to read such a fine work. However, I who know M. Proust, I who bear him the sympathy and esteem his talent and his very fine gifts deserve, would for my part prefer to have a much firmer control over him and I would take him aside for a few friendly but very firm words. He knows full well what I would say, he knows it better than I do myself, and one day he will show us that he does. When one has all the stylistic talent, all the natural flow of thought hidden away in this excessively elegant and pretty book, then one has gifts that cannot be allowed to go to waste. I take my hat off sincerely and amicably to salute the very fortunate and effortless début that M. Proust has had, but I somewhat regret that *Les Plaisirs et les jours* did not appear two years earlier. And it is with quiet eagerness that I await his next work.

4. Fernand Gregh on *Les Plaisirs et les jours*
1896

Extract from a notice in *La Revue de Paris*, 15 July 1896.

Fernand Gregh (1873–1960), poet and essayist, was a close friend of Proust's but felt put out, as were others of their circle, by what appeared to be a sycophantic book.

. . . the author of this book has ingratiated himself with the public using the most famous names as referees; he has coyly appealed to those whose friendship is most dear to give him an introduction into literary life. You could say that he has gathered all the kind fairies round this new-born book. It is the custom to leave one out, but it seems that here they have been invited one and all. Each has granted the child a favour: the first, a touch of melancholy; the second, a touch of irony; the third, a peculiar musicality. And every one of them has promised him success.[1]

NOTE

1 Later in the year, however, he seemed to be less piqued: 'This very fine book would make a good New Year's gift. It has the rather rare merit of being as pleasant in content as it is beautiful in appearance' (*La Revue de Paris*, 15 December 1896).

5. Charles Maurras on *Les Plaisirs et les jours*
1896

Extract from 'La vie littéraire', *La Revue encyclopédique*, 22 August 1896, p. 584.

Charles Maurras (1868–1952), at this time poet, essayist, and journalist, was soon to emerge as political figure and part founder of *L'Action française*. His notice is more blatantly given to compliments than Perret's review (see No. 2).

It is no simple matter to praise M. Marcel Proust: his first book, this newly published Treatise on *Pleasures and Days*, reveals such an extreme diversity of talents that it can be embarrassing to have to admit to all of them at once in such a young writer. Yet we must. We must even allow that such varied gifts as these do not cancel each other out, but rather form a felicitous, brilliant and spontaneous whole. For instance, the somewhat early fruits of his experience, far from harming M. Marcel Proust's powers of reflection, have combined with them to produce wisdom that is both gentle and mischievous, forthright and rather wistful. . . . The language is pure, transparent, with no strongly marked rhythm and is controlled by exquisite taste. In M. Marcel Proust instinct seems as sound as calculation is exact. The new generation must see its way to modelling itself on this young writer. . . . Take a maxim, a character, an exhortation to love or a letter, such as are found here, and only M. Proust could bring them off. I can see no equal, at least in such delicate and sure understanding and in such simple elegance. A famous master,[1] I may say, has in presenting the book, said these very things with the greatest clarity. They have been magically expressed. Thus must the first poets of Athens have spoken when, the muse having singled out a young one among them, they hung myrtles, roses and laurels round his door.[2]

NOTES

1 These flattering remarks, together with the flowery ending, sycophantically endorse the preface written by the influential Anatole France.
2 Proust wrote effusively to Maurras to thank him:
    You find treasures in the books you touch, though you do not go so

far as to suggest that you are the one who, by touching them, turns them into gold. Marvelling as I do at the transformation I thank you and the kind magician that you are with all my heart; sudden though your enchantments may be, they linger on in the memory of those graced by them. And some day a reader under the spell of what you have said will think that there must be some injustice if my book has not survived and that perhaps I had some talent after all. In the meantime I am very grateful and very proud that you have said such nice things about me. (*Corr.* II, p. 108.)

6. 'Pruning the laurels'
1897

Extract from a revue sketch called 'Les lauriers sont coupés' by Jacques Bizet and Robert Dreyfus, quoted in the latter's *Souvenirs sur Marcel Proust*, Paris, Grasset, 1926, p. 123.

The revue (given three performances on 18, 19, and 20 March 1897) harmlessly mocked the style and mannerisms of the young writers of the *Banquet* circle and others. Proust, however, was deeply hurt by the section dealing with the sheer cost of *Les Plaisirs et les jours*. It was set out as a dialogue between Proust, Ernest La Jeunesse, and Fernand Gregh.

PROUST, *speaking to Ernest La Jeunesse* – Have you read my book?

LA JEUNESSE – No sir, it's too expensive.

PROUST – Alas, that's what they all say. – Gregh, how about you, have you read it?

GREGH – Yes, I cut it up into pieces to review it.

PROUST – And did you find that the price was too high as well?

GREGH – No, not at all. It was good value for money.

PROUST – Well, of course! – Item, a preface by Monsieur France, 4 francs. Item, paintings by Madame Lemaire, 4 francs. Item, music by Reynaldo Hahn, 4 francs. Item, prose by me, 1 franc. Item, a few lines of verse by me, 50 centimes. Total, 13 francs 50, that wasn't asking too much, was it?

LA JEUNESSE – But my dear sir, there are more things than that in the Hachette Almanach, and that only costs 25 sous!

PROUST, *bursting with hilarity*, – Ah! it's so funny! – It makes me laugh till it hurts! – You are so witty, Monsieur La Jeunesse! What fun it must be to be as witty as you!

7. Jean Lorrain on *Les Plaisirs et les jours*
1897

Extract from 'Pall-Mall semaine', *Le Journal*, 3 February 1897; reprinted in *La Ville empoisonnée*, Paris, Crès, 1936, pp. 129–31.

Jean Lorrain, alias Paul Duval (1856–1906), Symbolist poet and acidic literary journalist, used his gossip column to attack what he saw as the elegant, would-be writers of the Faubourg Saint-Germain. The barbed comments, and especially the suggestion of sycophantic flattery, he makes here led Proust to challenge him to a duel.

There is no beating the fashionable set. And, my word, the sheer amateurism of society people! A book perpetrated by one of their kind, – a book much fussed over last spring – has come into my hands. Prefaced by M. Anatole France, who could not refuse the support of his name and his elegant prose to a dear lady friend (he had dined at her table often enough!), this delicate volume would hardly be thought a typical example of the genre were it not for the illustrations of Mme Madeleine Lemaire.

Les Plaisirs et les jours, by M. Marcel Proust: suave melancholic rêveries, elegiac languishings, elegant and refined little trifles, shallow emotions, inane flirtations in precious and pretentious tones, together with Mme Lemaire's flowers, scattered symbolically in the margins and over chapter-headings. One of these chapters is called: *La mort de Baldassare de Silvande*, the viscount of Silvande. Illustration provided: two pitchers. Another, *Violante ou la mondanité*. Illustration provided: two rose leaves (this is the absolute truth). Mme Lemaire's ingenuity has never been so aptly applied to an author's talent. M. Paul Hervieu, and his *Flirt*, certainly never inspired such wit as this in our charming paintress. Thus it is that one of M. Proust's stories entitled: *Amis: Octavian et Fabrice* is decorated with two she-cats playing the guitar, and another, called *Rêverie couleur du temps* is illustrated with three peacock feathers.

Yes, madam, three peacock feathers; that takes the biscuit, don't you think?

Also in these *Pleasures and Days*, there is a chapter entitled: *Mélancolique villégiature de Mme de Bresve*, Bresve rhymes with 'grève' and 'rêve', oh the elusive sweetness of that long Bresve! And three of the heroines are decked out with the charming names of Helmonde, Adelgise and Hercole, and they are three Parisian ladies of the oh so utterly noble faubourg.

Oh, come along, sir!

For all that, M. Marcel Proust has got his preface out of M. Anatole France, who would not have done as much for M. Marcel Schwob or M. Pierre Louÿs or M. Maurice Barrès; but that's the way the world goes; you can rest assured that for his next book M. Marcel Proust will get his preface out of M. Alphonse Daudet, the intransigent M. Alphonse Daudet himself, who will not be able to refuse that preface of his either to Mme Lemaire or to his son Lucien.

1904–6
TRANSLATIONS FROM RUSKIN

8. André Chaumeix on Proust and Ruskin
1904

Extracts from a review of Proust's translation of *The Bible of Amiens, Le Journal des débats*, 20 March 1904, p. 2.

André Chaumeix (1874–1955) appreciates in Proust's translation the delicate balance between his great enthusiasm for Ruskin and those reservations that become the germ of his independent aesthetic.

. . . It has been the aim of M. Marcel Proust to elucidate this book completely for us. To this task he was able to bring a deep acquaintance with Ruskin's work, a rare sense of the poetry in it, an extreme refinement of sensibility, a kind of Ruskinian enthusiasm and also a pleasing critical modesty. With his extensive knowledge, he was fully prepared mentally to want to write a book of his own. He has been content, however, to reconstruct with scrupulous piety the book of a beloved writer. Years of hard work having brought close acquaintance with Ruskin and a thorough understanding of him, he now restricts his own ambition to communicating this patiently accumulated knowledge to others. What he gives us is, first of all, an exact and complete translation; this is followed by explanations of all kinds to put us in a position fully to understand the English writer's text; lastly, there are notes, memories and comparisons whereby he helps us to recognize instantly in his author what constitute his permanent and fundamental characteristics, the intimate nature of his imagination and the general run of his thoughts. Set out in this way, this translation of *The Bible of Amiens* is a book full of good things, suitable for the student and written so as to seduce the reader. It also speaks volumes; the writer to whom we are indebted is both scholar and artist. . . .

During the period of his earlier enthusiasm, it was the soul of Ruskin that the translator looked for in Amiens; at that time the stones of Amiens took on for him the dignity of the stones of Venice and something of the grandeur that the Bible had when it was still a living truth in men's hearts. Since then, his admiration has lost none of its fervour. But he does begin to wonder how all that aesthetic became fused with so much morality and how the English writer was able to maintain his intellectual honesty untouched by any unconscious idolatry. . . . And as he digs ever deeper into himself, M. Marcel Proust begins to have doubts and is afraid he may discover something a trifle false in the keenest pleasures Ruskin's thought has given him; yet he declares it to be admirable and for him it has made the universe a more beautiful place. In pages of infinite delicacy he gathers together all the powerful and strange charm of the author of *The Bible of Amiens* and he is not afraid either to declare in what respect he is marvellous or to indicate in what respect he is disconcerting. After having had at one time a more ardent belief in Ruskin and a more exclusive and less perspicacious love for him, he has now moved towards a state of calm and reflective admiration. . . .

9. Henri Bergson on Proust and Ruskin

1904

Presentation on 28 May 1904 of Proust's translation of *La Bible d'Amiens* to the Académie des Sciences Morales et Politiques at the Institut de France; proceedings vol. CLXII, Paris, 1904, pp. 491–2.

Henri Bergson (1859–1941), famous for his works on memory, time, and intuition, was distantly related to Proust who was best man at his marriage in 1892 to a cousin of the family. Proust wrote to him in anticipation of his notice to the Académie: 'Allow me to thank you from the bottom of my heart for your great kindness. You may imagine the value I place upon a few words from the philosopher I most admire' (*Corr.* IV, p. 128). Bergson replied: 'I stressed what you say about the essentially religious character of Ruskin' (*Corr.* IV, p. 137, which also quotes Bergson's notice in a footnote). In general, though his tone is a little dry, he speaks with approval of Proust's contribution to the understanding of Ruskin's outlook.

I have the honour to present to the Academy, in the name of M. Marcel Proust, the translation with notes and preface that he has recently made of *La Bible d'Amiens* by Ruskin. The preface is an important contribution to the psychology of Ruskin. M. Marcel Proust reminds us of the contradictory assessments that have been made of Ruskin, the theorist of aesthetics. It has been said that Ruskin was a realist and an intellectualist, that he diminished the role of the imagination in art by granting too great a place in it to scientific knowledge and that he ruined science by granting too great a place in that to the imagination, that he was purely a theorist of aesthetics since his sole love was beauty and that he was not an artist since he mixed considerations alien to aesthetics with his appreciation of beauty. M. Marcel Proust goes to the root of all these differences. Ruskin's was above all a *religious* nature.[1] His aesthetic stance is that of a man who believes that the poet and the artist are limited to transcribing a divine message. He is, therefore, an idealist in the highest degree, but he is a realist too because matter is no more to him than an expression of the mind. His work will only be understood if we start from the idea that religious feeling was always, in his case, the inspirer and guide of aesthetic feelings. His judgment was that art could not flourish except through faith, and that it declined as faith declined. That is why he saw in Christian art art par excellence. That is also why he deeply loved, understood and showed others how to understand the architecture, painting and sculpture of the Middle Ages. In this sense, Ruskin's book on Amiens cathedral is one of those books that allow us to enter most intimately into his thinking. M. Marcel Proust has translated it into such vibrant and original language that you would not think, to read it, that you were dealing with a translation. He has added notes in which we find numerous comparisons between *La Bible d'Amiens* and other works by the same author.

NOTE

1 In italics in the text.

10. André Beaunier on Proust and Ruskin
1906

Extract from a review of Proust's translation of *Sesame and Lilies*, *Le Figaro*, 14 June 1906, p. 1.

André Beaunier (1869–1925), drama critic of *L'Écho de Paris* and also contributor to *La Revue des deux mondes*, gives an astute account of Proust's self-discovery while pursuing his role of translator of Ruskin.

On 6 December 1864, at Rusholme Town Hall, near Manchester, John Ruskin delivered a public lecture on reading: a good choice of subject given his obligation to contribute to setting up a library. And the orator's message was: we had better read. Or else! . . .

M. Marcel Proust has just translated *Sesame and Lilies* with exquisite care, admirable ingenuity and infinite circumspection. Attentive to the smallest detail of a sentence, as if to its tone of voice, and, so to speak, to the basic impulse behind it as well as to its twists and turns, he is a faithful translator and succeeds in writing Ruskinian prose in excellent French. His translation is a model of what a well-executed translation should be, a masterpiece of intelligent acquiescence and an astounding success.

M. Proust is very fond of Ruskin. . . . But perhaps, at bottom, he is less fond of him than he imagines. In any case, he yields to his inclination to go his own sweet way. After pursuing this difficult man a little while he begins to wonder where he will be taken to next. Yet he goes on translating with admirable docility, though pointing out his reservations at the foot of the page; and these numerous, full and varied notes are set down with both wit and knowledge. His purpose is to make clear that he is not quite of the same opinion as his author but that his author, on the other hand, is not entirely wrong and that, though he has not the arrogance to contradict him outright, nevertheless . . . ! This gives M. Marcel Proust the opportunity to make thousands of ingenious comparisons, tell us anecdotes, tease us and show what a charming essayist he is.

He reads Ruskin rather in the way Montaigne read Plutarch: he 'tries out' his own thinking by putting it in contact with a different kind of thinking; he questions himself on the greater or lesser degree of credibility inspired in him by another person's perfectly respectable opinion; he has doubts, he perceives multiple differences

71

between the other person's assertion and the one he would be happy to formulate: thus, by imperceptible degrees, he moves towards an understanding of himself. . . .

In his notes M. Marcel Proust tries to resolve the contradictions of his author; to this end he modifies the two extremes and brings them together, and all this with as much adroit good grace as the text allows. . . .

The effort he puts into setting Ruskin to rights with himself, he also puts, even more circumspectly, into avoiding any quarrel between the author and his commentator. Generally, his tactfulness is successful. However, on the issue of 'reading' they are in disagreement; to put it another way, they are only half in agreement. . . .

Ruskin . . . explains how he wants us to read: in such a way, in fact, that if we read like that we would be spending our whole life at it! . . . M. Proust replies, without arrogance or impetuosity, that this is not the way, that reading is not simply a conversation: when we read, we are alone; we retain that 'intellectual power that comes with solitude and that is immediately dispelled by conversation', and inspired though we may surely be by another, yet we remain 'deeply involved in the mind's fertile working upon itself'. Ruskin would like us to read with the sincere desire to be instructed by books, to enter into their thinking and let ourselves be persuaded by them. Ruskin demands this denial, this forgetting of ourselves. . . . Certainly not, retorts M. Proust; when I read, my independence and my mental activity are intact, I take from books what suits me: what we retain from our reading is 'the image of the places and the days when we engaged in it'.

To give foundation to this pleasing and melancholy thesis, M. Proust recalls his childhood reading, the lovely books read under the hazel and hawthorn trees, the air scented with medick and clover, sitting next to a beloved and rather talkative great-aunt; or else, by the fireside, with the maid coming in and out of the dining room, laying the table and apologizing for disturbing you; or else, at the window, a ray of sunshine or a bee breaking your concentration. . . .

Of these lovely books – for instance, *Le Capitaine Fracasse* – memory has perhaps retained only a sentence, arranging it, taking it apart and re-arranging it at will. But above all, the most precious thing that memory retains of these pleasant hours is not an idea, a moral lesson, an individual word, but a moment of your former long-lost life, the very features of your life at that moment. The book that engaged your intelligence has allowed you, without your knowing it, to be more closely attentive to the special particularity of that period in your evolution; you say to yourself – I was there, such and such a thing happened to me. Wisps of the dead past have attached themselves to that unforgettable minute. . . .

When all is said and done, reading is no more than that. M. Proust has no desire to grant it the dominating role, in our spiritual destiny, that Ruskin seems to assign to it. There are books and there is living: living is more important.

These pages in which M. Marcel Proust refutes his author are admirable, moving in their expression, in their detailed truth, in their longing for the past and in that charming melancholy and unfulfilled emotion that the regret for days gone by brings back to us. . . .

11. Henry–D. Davray on Proust and Ruskin
1906

Extract from his article: 'Lettres anglaises', *Le Mercure de France*, 15 July 1906, pp. 295–301.

Henry–D. Davray (1873–1944), foreign editor of *Le Mercure de France* and translator, brings out Proust's special pleading in his translation of *Sesame and Lilies*.

I would like to be a translator like M. Proust. But if I translated Wells as he translates Ruskin, the reader would be annoyed. . . . M. Proust is not in agreement with his author except in so far as it is a matter of faithfully transposing his thought into French. Where ideas are concerned, he quibbles with him, disputes with him and contradicts him. These are opinions, and Ruskin's and M. Proust's contradict each other but do not destroy each other. Both of them are right and both wrong. The result is that the pleasure of controversy is added to the charm of the work, as M. Proust decorates the text with an endless supply of notes that have been written with as much ingenious wit as meticulous knowledge. . . . In these two lectures there are ideas in plenty which the author develops in a rather confused and disorganized way. Nevertheless, when they were published together . . . they were a great success; they taught thousands of people, who were otherwise indifferent to it, respect for both word and thought. . . . M. Marcel Proust has written a fifty-page preface to his translation, and it turns out that his commentary is approximately the opposite of Ruskin's message.

Ruskin says, read to be informed, with the intention of being converted, persuaded, won over by the author you are conversing with. M. Proust politely refutes this doctrine. Read, he also says, but as you read keep your independence intact; remain the master of your faculties and your mental activity. Let reading be a stimulant but do not allow yourself to forget that there is life too. Reading is good, but living is much better. Reading must not play a dominant and exclusive role in our lives; to develop our thoughts, our mental faculties and our personalities, let us turn to books by all means, but life is a better educator. M. Proust's thesis is very seductive, though, if we listen to what he has to say, we need to resist the temptation to let ourselves be converted.

1912

THE MANUSCRIPT OF *DU CÔTÉ DE CHEZ SWANN*

12. *Swann*'s first critic: a confidential report

1912

Report by Jacques Madeleine (pseudonym of the poet Jacques Normand, 1848–1931), reader for the publisher Eugène Fasquelle. This long forgotten and illuminating document, in the possession of Fasquelle's heirs, was communicated to the eminent Proust scholar, Henri Bonnet, who published it in *Le Figaro littéraire*, 8 December 1966, p. 15.

The first version of Proust's novel was to be called *Les Intermittences du coeur* set out in two volumes as *Le Temps perdu* and *Le Temps retrouvé* which he described in 1912 in a letter to Fasquelle (*Corr.* XI, p. 257). The part examined by Madeleine was *Le Temps perdu* corresponding basically, in spite of the difference of names given to some characters, to the present *Du côté de chez Swann* and part of *A l'ombre des jeunes filles en fleurs*. Madeleine's bewilderment, especially at the impressionism and analysis that characterize the text, reflects certain reactions that are still evident in some readers today. However, he does make occasional slight concession to originality which comes through in spite of comments that clearly show him looking for the wrong things and missing the impact of what now are among the most widely known and admired pages.

At the end of the seven hundred and twelve pages of this manuscript (seven hundred and twelve at least, because lots of pages have numbers graced with a, b, c, d,) – after the utter depression of seeming to drown in fathomless complications and after irritating feelings of impatience at never being able to surface – the reader has simply no idea of what it's all about. What is all this for? What does all this mean? Where is it leading to? – It's impossible to make head or tail of it! It's impossible to comment on it!

75

The letter attached to the manuscript provides some clarification. But the reader of the volume would not have the letter to consult.

The letter concedes that nothing happens in these seven hundred pages, that no action is entered upon, or at least only in the last sixty pages, and in a manner that could not be perceived by anyone who has not been forewarned. For the intended character does nothing more than show his face, hidden furthermore by the mask of an outward appearance which is the opposite of what he is revealed to be later. And how could you know it was him? . . . No one will ever guess it!

The whole of the first part, says the letter, is only a 'preparation', a 'poetic overture'. A volume that is longer than one of the longest novels of Zola is surely excessive as preparation. And even more unfortunate, this preparation does not prepare anything, indeed, does not even bring to our attention what the letter, the letter alone, tells us will follow. Even with the information given by the letter we are constantly asking: Why all this? What's the connection? Just what is it all about?

What we have here is in fact a clearly defined pathological case.

The only way to get the measure of it (which is easy) and the only way to give some idea of the work (which is not so easy) is to follow the author step by step, groping along like the blind man one is obliged to be.

The first part falls naturally into three sections: *Twenty Stories!*
Pages 1–17. A gentleman is suffering from insomnia. He turns over in his bed, he goes over and over impressions and hallucinations in a half-wakeful state including some that bring back to him the difficulties he had in falling asleep, as a little boy, in his room in the family's country house at Combray. Seventeen pages! where one sentence (bottom of page 4 and page 5) is forty-four lines long and where you lose your foothold. . . .
Pages 17–74. A little boy is unable to go to sleep as long as his mother has not come to kiss him in his bed. She does not come when they have people to dinner. One of these 'people' is M. Vington. Several pages on M. Vington whom we shall never see again. Another of these 'people' is M. Swann. M. Swann is a close friend of the Comte de Chambord and the Prince of Wales; but he keeps these connections in high places secret, and is treated patronizingly by the very bourgeois family of the little boy. There is talk of a Mme de Villeparisis, a close relative of Maréchal de MacMahon, at whose house Swann frequently dines. There are lots of pages given over to these two persons, then to the old servant, Françoise. . . . And all the while we get the analysis of the case of the little boy who cannot go to sleep as long as his mother. . . .

Eventually we come to the end of the memories of childhood which lead back to the gentleman's bouts of insomnia.

P. 75–82. But this same character dips a cake into a cup of tea, and behold a quite new spurt of memories surges up.

P. 82–221. This time it's Combray. It's aunt Léonie who for years has not left her bedroom, then her bed and is now dead. She keeps abreast of the village gossip through old Françoise and a religious girl called Eulalie; she impatiently puts up with the nattering of Monsieur le Curé. There is a digression on an uncle, Charles. Another interminable one on old pictures. Another on a school-friend, Bloch, who admires a great contemporary writer called Bergotte who could pass for Barrès in certain parts of the description given. – Then a Monsieur Legrandin whom we meet coming out of mass and will not meet again in the whole book for all that he is discussed over and over in a very large number of pages. Then a noble family and a noble lady called Guermantes on whose account we hear the author go into endless finicky detail. Then Swann comes back, rather frowned on because no one can receive the woman of tarnished reputation he has married. Then it's a question again of M. Vington, whose death we hear about. And we are present (p. 187–190) at a sadistic scene where Mlle Vington, before yielding to the embraces of a 'woman friend', becomes excited as she gives her a portrait of this dead father for her to spit on. Then, once again, the Duchesse de Guermantes.

At last the first part comes to an end here. It alone would make a volume of average size. We have here the memories and the whole childhood of the character who narrates, interrupted by thousands of subtle disquisitions and encumbered with twenty stories full of people who for the most part will not recur. . . .

As for any idea where all this is leading to, that's quite another question.

NEW ELEMENTS

This story, covering two hundred pages, retails facts already dating back fifteen years, which were previously told to the little boy and which now the grown man remembers in improbable detail.

Monsieur and Madame Verdurin have a salon the main adornments of which are Doctor Cottard and his wife, a little pianist and his aunt, a painter and a few other puppet figures. They entertain a lady of ill repute, Odette de Crécy, who brings Swann, already getting on in years, to see them. Swann is in love with Odette, who is quite prepared to be kept by him and achieves this without Swann (who in the meantime is giving her from three to ten thousand francs a year) coming to terms with the idea that he is in fact maintaining her. Meanwhile he reads the situation differently, viz. that he is being outrageously deceived. He is even completely dropped and still goes on paying out.

Eventually, when all the facts have been made plain to him and he has, what is more, realized that he did not like Odette de Crécy and she 'was not his type', he leaves her.

At least the reader thinks he leaves her. But it appears it was not the case. For in the childhood memories of the first part we have seen Swann married many a long year to Odette de Crécy, having fathered a little girl called Gilberte.

Put like this the story seems relatively simple. But in the manuscript it is interrupted by as many further unrelated incidents and cluttered with as many further unbelievable complications as we have seen in the first part. Here's a sentence from it (p. 302):

'In the army . . . I had a friend that the gentleman reminded me of a bit. Take any old subject, I don't know, say, this glass, he could rattle on about it for hours, no, not about the glass, which of course is silly, but about the battle of Waterloo, anything you like and as he went along he could come out with things you would never have thought of.'

Isn't the author afraid we might apply it to him?

One would be sorely tempted! 'For hours . . . about this glass, or about the battle of Waterloo . . . as he goes along he brings out things you would never have thought of' . . . i.e. things which, to be fair, are not any sort of thoughts, but new ones, sharp, full of observation and insight, aimed at you, however, 'for hours as he goes along his road', in other words without your ever seeing where his road is leading you.

Furthermore, this sentence happens to be typical of all the other sentences. It is full of all the confusion, all the complexity that is already evident just in the letter attached to the manuscript and this makes reading unbearable beyond five or six pages.

And the 'rattling on' gets into everything. Swann happens, on one occasion, to go 'into society'. And this goes on for thirty pages (369 to 401). And there are three pages on the flunkeys lined up on the staircase and suggesting 'the predellas of San Zeno and the frescoes of the Eremitani . . . Albrecht Dürer . . . the Staircase of the Gaints in the Ducal Palace . . . Benvenuto Cellini . . . the watch-towers of a castle keep or cathedral . . . etc. etc.' As much again about each guest. . . . And there's no end to it, it's sheer madness.

There are some tiresome preparatory sections of this kind at the beginning of Balzac's novels. But once the characters are planted, that's it. The characters act. And they are characters.

Here it's nothing of the sort. Swann now goes somewhat into the background. If there is something useful in all this hotchpotch one would really like to know what purpose he, Swann, does serve or what he represents. Certainly, we shall not be spared his presence in the third part. And we cannot entertain the hope that he will not crop up again in the second manuscript. Meanwhile, we know from the letter that he will not be the main character and that he will only be able to play an episodic role. – What is more serious is that we have no means of knowing what part this fellow who has been sending us to sleep for so long with his memories and speculative musings will have in it.

EVERYONE GOES AWAY

P. 422–436. Fourteen pages on Bricquebec, where there is a church in Persian style, on Venice, on Florence. . . .

P. 436–471. On the Champs-Elysées and the public conveniences. In the Champs-Elysées the little boy plays with some little girls, including Gilberte, daughter of Swann and Odette de Crécy; she fills the little boy's heart with a great passion.

P. 472–520. Concerns M. de Norpois, or de Montfort, diplomat. And the little boy goes to see a Sarah Bernhardt-type actress called La Borma. There is talk of Swann's marriage. Then a piece on the great writer, Bergotte.

P. 521–528. Concerns La Borma.

P. 529–569. Continuation of the story of the little boy and Gilberte in the Champs-Elysées. Then the little boy is invited to the Swanns', first to the children's tea-parties given by the young lady for the little girls who are her friends, then to the private apartments of Mme Swann, who arouses a very special feeling in the little boy. The parents in the meantime keep out of each other's sight. The little boy joins in all the outings. He meets up with the famous Bergotte.

After this, we will not, for the time being at least, hear any more about a single one of all these previous characters – not one, no more about Swann, Gilberte or Bergotte than any of the others – except for the appearance, incidentally for no special reason, of a Mme de Villeparisis about whom there has been vague, though long-winded, talk five hundred pages earlier.

P. 569–655. The little boy goes to Bricquebec with his grandmother. Interminable psychologizing on the journey, the hotel room, the church in Persian style, the guests at dinner, the excursions in Mme de Villeparisis' carriage etc.etc.etc.

P. 656–672. A nephew of Mme de Villeparisis, called sometimes M. de Beauvais and sometimes M. de Montargis, comes to Bricquebec and develops a close friendship with the little boy (incidentally, how old is this little boy? We're never told).

P. 672–675 The arrival of a brother or brother-in-law of Mme de Villeparisis is announced. His Christian name is Palamède; he has possibly a princely title; he goes by the name of Baron de Fleurus or de Charlus. We are given his portrait. We hear that he has given a thrashing to a 'homosexual' who had propositioned him.

P. 675–690. The Baron de Fleurus arrives. He is strange and disconcerts the little boy by his manner. He disappears.

P. 691–706. The intimate friendship of the little boy and Montargis continues. Then Montargis goes away.

P. 706–712. A few more pages on the stay at Bricquebec. Then everyone goes away. And page 712 is the last; why this page rather than any other one?

CURIOUS AND OUT OF ALL PROPORTION

The author concedes that his first volume could end at page 633. There's nothing lost and nothing gained, after all, give or take eighty pages out of the whole number . . . !

And again all this could be reduced by half, by three quarters or by nine tenths. Besides, there's no reason why the author should not have extended his manuscript to twice or ten times its length. Given the procedure he favours of 'rattling on for hours, as you go on your way', writing twenty volumes is as normal as stopping at one or two.

Taking all in all, what have we got here?

For someone with no outside knowledge it's the study of a sickly, abnormally nervous little boy whose sensitivity, impressionable nature and reflective subtlety are in a state of irritation.

It's often of curious interest. But too long, out of all proportion. In fact one could say that you will not find a reader strong enough to stay with it more than a quarter of an hour, especially since the author does not help with the nature of his sentences – which leak all over the place.

And then what indeed do the endless stories of aunt Léonie, uncle Charles, M. Legrandin and many more matter to the study of the sickly little boy? or the quite separate story of M. Swann? This has no influence on the little boy's abnormal condition.

Yet that's all that anyone who perseveres to the end of the present manuscript can see in it.

But are we alerted in the letter as to the subject the author claims to deal with in the second volume or even in the two volumes?

It's hardly worth taking into account the very brief and misleading appearance of the future 'homosexual', Baron de Fleurus.

There remains one question that has to be put: is the little boy eventually destined to be just what the Baron de Fleurus is looking for? There seems to be nothing in the study to indicate it. The letter only mentions a concierge and a pianist.

If the little boy does not become a homosexual what is the point of the whole book? If he does – and we ought to hope so for logic's sake – the study is justified, but there is for all that an unbelievable lack of proportion.

Certainly – provided you persevere for a while with the reading – there are in the detail of the text many things of curious, even outstanding interest, and the work cannot be accused of insignificance or lack of solid worth.

In the work as a whole, indeed, and even in each unit taken on its own it is impossible not to see here an extraordinary intellectual phenomenon.

1913–14
DU CÔTÉ DE CHEZ SWANN

---

13. Élie-Joseph Bois and Proust's defence of *Swann*
1913

Extracts from an article on *Swann, Le Temps,* 13 November 1913.

Élie-Joseph Bois (1878–1941), journalist and literary reviewer of the newspaper *Le Temps*, introduces *Swann* with high praise the day before its publication and goes on to quote an interview with Proust in which he is presented for the first time as the inaccessible invalid of popular mythology. Proust attempts to forestall misunderstanding by a vindication of his style, method of work, and aesthetic.

A la recherche du temps perdu – This enigmatic title belongs to a novel, the first volume of which is about to appear and concerning which considerable curiosity has been aroused. A fair number of pages have been privately circulated and those privileged to read them speak about them with nothing but enthusiasm. This anticipatory success is often an advantage, but sometimes an obstacle. I cannot say what tomorrow's public opinion will be, whether it will, as I have heard it said, hail this first volume of *A la recherche du temps perdu* as a masterpiece . . . however, I barely take any risk at all in predicting that it will leave none of its readers indifferent. It will perhaps disconcert some. *Du côté de chez Swann* is not to be described as light reading for a train journey, to be merely glanced at while the reader skips pages; it is an original work, rather strange, profound, requiring the reader's whole attention, even demanding it utterly. It is surprising, gripping, disorientating and overwhelming. As for action – the kind usually found in most novels, that carries you along, with some degree of excitement, through a string of adventures till you reach the tragic dénouement – there is none. And yet action there is, but its strings are, as it were, discreetly hidden with an almost exaggerated concern and it is up to us, as we breathlessly follow it, to realize that we are emotionally overwhelmed by the development of the characters who, in situation after situation, have been etched with a pitiless pen. It is a psychological novel, but I do not know many psychological novels where the psychological analysis has been more profoundly pursued. . . .

M. Marcel Proust is lying in his bedroom where the shutters are nearly always closed. The electric light accentuates the matt effect of the face, though two eyes, feverish but shining with life, flash out from beneath the hair falling over his forehead. M. Marcel Proust is still a martyr to ill health but he does not appear so once the writer in him, asked to explain his work, comes to life and speaks.

– 'I am only publishing one volume, *Du côté de chez Swann*, of a novel which will have as its general title *A la recherche du temps perdu*. I would have liked to publish the whole thing at once; but no one publishes works in several volumes any more. I am like someone who has a tapestry which is too big for today's rooms and has to cut it up.

'Younger writers, and I can understand them, specify unlike me condensed action with few characters. It is not my conception of the novel. How can I explain it to you? There is, as you know, plane geometry and geometry in space. Well, for me, the novel is not only plane psychology but psychology in time. I have attempted to isolate this invisible time-substance, but to do it it had to be possible for the experiment to go on a long while. I hope that at the end of my book some little social event of no importance at all, some marriage between two people who in the first volume belong to quite different worlds, will show that time has passed and will take on the beautiful effect of the patina on some of those lead figures at Versailles which time has ensheathed in a scabbard of emerald green.

'Then, just as a town that appears to us, while the train follows its winding track, now on our right, now on our left, so the different appearances that one particular character has taken on in the eyes of another – even to the extent of seeming like a succession of different characters – will give, in this way and no other, the sensation of time that has elapsed. Such characters will later reveal themselves to be different from what they are in the present volume, different from what they will be thought to be, as so often happens, of course, in life.'

It is not only the same characters who will reappear in different guises in the course of this work, as in certain sequences of novels by Balzac, but, M. Proust tells us, certain deep, almost unconscious impressions within one and the same character.

– 'From this point of view,' M. Proust goes on, 'my book would

83

perhaps resemble an attempt at a series of "Novels of the Unconscious"; I would not at all be ashamed to say "Bergsonian novels" if I really thought so, for in all periods it transpires that literature has tried – after the event, of course – to attach itself to the reigning philosophy of the day. But it would not be correct, for my work is dominated by the distinction between involuntary and voluntary memory, a distinction which not only does not appear in M. Bergson's philosophy, but is even contradicted by it.'

– How do you establish this distinction?

– 'For me, voluntary memory, which is primarily a memory of the intelligence and of the visual sense, only gives us unconvincing pictures of the past; but should a smell or a taste, rediscovered in quite different circumstances, cause the past, whether we like it or not, to reawaken within us, we feel how different that past was from what we thought we remembered and which our voluntary memory, like a bad painter, depicted in unconvincing colours. Already in this first volume you will see the character who narrates and says "I" (and who is not me!) suddenly rediscovering forgotten years, gardens and people in the taste of a mouthful of tea in which he has dipped a piece of cake; he could, of course, recall them, but without their colour or their charm. . . .

'You see, I think that the artist ought to seek the raw material of his work pretty well only in involuntary memories. First, precisely because they are involuntary and come automatically into existence, attracted by the resemblance to an identical moment; they alone have the mark of authenticity. Next, they bring things back in an exact mixture of remembering and forgetting. And lastly, as they cause us to enjoy the same sensation in quite different circumstances, they liberate it from all contingency and they present us with its extratemporal essence, an essence which actually makes the content of a beautiful style, that general and necessary truth that the beauty of style alone translates.

'I may well reason about my book in this way,' continues M. Marcel Proust, 'but it is not in any degree a work of reasoning; its slightest elements have been given to me by my sensibility. I perceived them first deep within me without understanding them and I had as much difficulty in converting them into something intelligible as if they had been as alien to the world of the intelligence as, how shall I put it?, a musical motif. I get the impression that you think it is all a matter of subtleties. Not at all, I assure you; it is, on the contrary, a matter of realities. What we have never needed to clarify ourselves, what was clear enough before we came, for example, logical ideas, none of this is truly our own, we do not even know if it is real. It is some "possibility" that we choose arbitrarily.

In any case, as you know, such a thing shows at once in the style.

'Style is no mere embellishment as some people believe, it is not even a question of technique, it is, like colour for a painter, a quality of vision, the revelation of the particular universe each one of us sees and that can be seen by no one else. The pleasure an artist gives us is to acquaint us with yet another universe.'

– How is it, that, given these conditions, certain writers confess they try hard not to have a style? This is something that M. Marcel Proust does not understand; he insists:

– 'They can only do it by refusing to dig deep into their impressions! . . .'

And the hand of the invalid indicates the dark bedroom with its closed shutters, where the sun never enters. But the look on his face is without sadness. If the invalid has reason to pity himself, the writer has every reason to be proud. The latter has been a consolation for the former. . . .

14. Lucien Daudet on *Swann*

1913

Extract from his article in *Le Figaro*, 27 November, 1913, reprinted in *Autour de soixante lettres de Marcel Proust*, Paris Gallimard, 1929, pp. 81–6.

Lucien Daudet (1883–?), son of Alphonse Daudet and close friend of Proust's, had read *Swann* in proof form and offered to present it in a publicity article. His enthusiasm and insights are evidence enough of his being among the first to recognize and proclaim Proust's genius.

My role here is not to give a summary of this work; in any case, it could not be done briefly. . . . Simply imagine, placed between two apparently autobiographical accounts that make up the finest and richest memories of childhood, a sad love story, with the unfortunate and charming M. Swann as the victim; and . . . the first and third parts explaining and clarifying many of the facts of the middle section.

What excites us, as much as the novel itself, in these three parts, and in the now objective, now subjective domain where M. Proust takes us, is the analysis of every feeling, every sensation, every process of reasoning even, every hour of the day and every aspect of nature, and all this virtually simultaneously, for we become aware that, for the author, the invisible and the visible are constantly joined together. Never, I believe, has the analysis of all that makes up our existence been pursued so far. To find the equivalent of such an investigation, we could perhaps mention George Meredith, certain pages of *The Egoist* or of *Amazing Marriage*; Meredith's frequent obscurity is at times disconcerting, whereas the analytical procedures of M. Proust, who knows the unknowable and explains the inexplicable, are so lucid that they evoke the pure blue air of summer days . . . which is to say that vast space so inaccessible to us all: the sky.

Furthermore, analysis, even analysis less thorough than this, normally brings with it an involuntary and definite dryness, an implacable and systematic logic, which put the reader on guard against both himself and the author. M. Proust's analysis, on the other hand, is so perfectly blended with a phenomenal sensibility that the two merge together inseparably in sad emotion as in irony and we end up thinking, contrary to the normal rules, that his analysis releases our feelings and that his sensibility provokes our laughter. We soon realize that for some natures analysis and sensibility are one and the same thing, and that if the author of *Du côté de chez Swann* has not himself wept or laughed much (which is something we do not know) he has at least often enough shed tears over the sadness of an unrequited passion or over the heart-searching and irrational emotions of a cruel fit of jealousy, that chance or trust had just revealed to him, and has often enough joined in the sadness and gaiety of others with even more intensity than those sad or happy people, because he understood and divined the secret origins and the slightest consequences of their grief and joy better perhaps than they did themselves. . . .

M. Proust's knowledge of high society corresponds to the time when he was beginning to acquire knowledge of life; he did not, at the age of thirty or so, have to discover a social group that, till then, was alien to his existence. . . . Nor does he waste time in vainly and superficially describing external details; on the contrary, it is by examining them 'from the inside' that we have evidence of their reality, by dismantling and reconstituting the machinery and the motives of people who make use of these details, build their lives on them and construct the basic daily setting of their existence or their mode of living out of them.

But on top of all this: *Du côté de chez Swann* shows that its author possesses the rarest of senses, namely *a social sense*.[1] This is the sense that gives an exceptional clearsightedness to the judgment of the man who has it, as it does to the novels he writes – if he writes any at all. Knowing how to represent oneself or represent each one of us on the more or less inclined plane – often difficult to discern clearly – where we have been placed by birth, talent or chance, knowing how to look at the more or less oblique way in which it is lit, at the greater or less degree of light that emanates from it or that it receives from others, knowing how to classify different social groups and the people included in them like a botanist classifying plants or a naturalist classifying animals by families and individual members, methodically, without distraction or confusion – it is that sense, often a cause of suffering because of its precision and lucidity, that is least considered and never mentioned; yet it is the sense that ought to be our best guide through civilization.

M. Marcel Proust's style parallels his thought completely; with scrupulous precision, to a point beyond what would be thought credible, he does not fail to satisfy our expectations of the relationship of expression used to impression received. And when at first sight some of his sentences seem long, we quickly realize that they logically relate to one another, like those Japanese boxes whose diminishing size allows you to fit them all into one; that each sentence forms a unit completed by the next and that it has to be like this so that the twists and turns of the periodic sentence can fit every sinuous curve of the thought, follow its course and come to an exact stop. Each word, in fact, is the only one that could be used and even if, to express his meaning, the author is only able to find a technical term, he forces it to emerge from the abstract, specialist domain where it lay hidden, so as to send the life-blood of his work circulating through it.

So much so that a musician or a gardener, a painter or a doctor may well believe, as they read *Du côté de chez Swann*, that M. Proust has devoted years of study to music or horticulture, painting or medicine. This exactness of erudition is no mere list of words or something improvised for a book but, so to speak, innate, neatly putting M. Proust into the complete mental state needed for the art he speaks of, and even granting him such an abundance of images that here reality finds itself endlessly reflected in a mirror, a truthful but unexpected one, that completes it, comments on it and intensifies it. . . .

I have never understood the docile and ever present intellectual optical error which consists in making some show of enthusiasm, but only retrospectively, only to those who are no longer here and refuses this privilege outright to our contemporaries, especially if they are young, from a fear of being wrong, out of habit or various other reasons. Yet it is such a simple thing to say that, in the years to come, when M. Marcel Proust's book is mentioned, it will appear as an extraordinary manifestation of human intelligence in the twentieth century.

By then, *Du côté de chez Swann* will have taken its place, quite naturally, next to its peers, and will have joined its famous companions which, in a form unwillingly adapted to their respective periods, and waiting for it to join them, will all have preceded it down the ages; for every masterpiece is a great rallying cry forging ahead, and mustering beyond time in the dark cold of eternity, the other masterpieces yet to come.

NOTE

1 In italics in the text.

15. Marcel Drouet on *Swann*

1913

Extract from 'Chronique littéraire', *La Dépêche de l'est*, 2 December 1913, p. 6.

Marcel Drouet (1888–1915) reviewed *Swann* along with Alain-Fournier's *Le Grand Meaulnes*; his remarks on Proust (the 'strangest' of recent books) are less enthusiastic than for Alain-Fournier but his response to Proust's descriptive style is exceptionally positive.

. . . *Du côte de chez Swann* is not a work of imagination any more than it is a narrative; it is autobiography pushed to its extreme limits where personal analysis is characterized by extraordinary subtlety.

[Refers to *Un amour de Swann* as filling out the slight content.]

. . . But do not be put off by the banal nature of the subject matter. M. Marcel Proust, with a genius unknown to psychological analysis, not content to unveil his inmost soul, carries the elucidation of his feelings and passions to the point of implausibility. The whole of our unconscious, the thousand and one associations of ideas that, in a single second, take shape and die in our brains, the whole machinery of sense impressions set in motion by the engine of our sensibility – these have been remarkably dissected by M. Marcel Proust in pages that at first glance look heavy going but are perfectly logical and admirable.

It is not that such reading, for all its interest, cannot, in the end, weary the reader. Rather, *Du côté de chez Swann* is not a novel to skim through, but a study to get one's teeth into, the study of the experiences of life in relation to a marvellous sensibility and an ever watchful intelligence. . . .

What is even more remarkable in such a detailed, sincere, enthusiastic, almost dense work is the appropriateness of a logically organized style, in which the, admittedly, long periodic sentences overlap with an order and discipline that are quite French and in which the adjectives have a stunning precision, succeeding as they do, in defining states of mind, sensations and smells which are so elusive as to defy until now any description of them in literature.

16. Mary Duclaux on *Swann*

1913

Review of *Du côté de chez Swann* in the *Times Literary Supplement*, 4 December 1913. Reprinted in *Twentieth Century French Writers*, London, Collins, 1919, pp. 253–6.

Mary Duclaux (1857–1944), was an essayist with a strong interest in contemporary French literature. She provides a rare example of a notice in English on *Swann*. Perhaps because of her special interest in novels of childhood she is generally positive.

Of all these books – save, perhaps, Alain-Fournier's, for which I have, I own, a peculiar weakness; of all these novels of childhood – unless I except M. Boylesve's, and *Marie-Claire*, and *Jean-Christophe* (for so many of them, when, you come to think of it, are really quite first-rate) – the most delicate, the most pregnant with a sensibility extraordinarily rich, and ample, and yet sensitive as the impressions of convalescence or the first images of childhood is an immense novel published in the winter of 1913–14 by M. Marcel Proust, under the enigmatic title, *A la Recherche du Temps Perdu: Du Côté de chez Swann*. The book with which it is easiest to compare it, is Henry James's *A Small Boy*, though that, indeed, is concise and simple compared with M. Marcel Proust's attempt at reconstituting the vague shimmering impressions of a young mind, the wonderment with which – inexplicably to us – it regards places and people which in our eyes possess no magic. M. Proust's hero is a small boy living in the bosom of the most regular of families – one of those vast French families, closely knit, whose tissue unites grandparents, great-aunts, uncles, cousins in such quantity as to limit the possible supply of outside acquaintance. One most familiar friend, however, there is, the friend of the family, a 'hereditary friend', as Homer would say, M. Swann. He is a man of the world, a member of the Jockey Club, a friend of the Prince of Wales, a comrade of the Comte de Paris, a great collector; but for the small boy and his family he is especially 'le fils Swann', the son of their old friend the member of the Stock Exchange ('qui a bien dû lui laisser quatre ou cinq millions') who has made a ridiculous marriage with a demi-mondaine – a case of all for love and the world well lost.

And the world is lost the more completely that the impossible lady continues her adventures unabashed and unabated after matrimony. She therefore is not 'received', or indeed hardly mentioned, in the ample respectable home of the small boy; so that Swann and this unlikely love of Swann's, this beautiful wife of Swann's, and Swann's remote, intangible, but not invisible little girl, are the constant object of his romantic curiosity.

There are two walks at Combray: you may set out in the direction of Guermantes or else go round by Swann's: 'du côté de chez Swann', and to the childish hero of the book these two walks gradually accumulate round them the material for two views of life – Swann standing for all that is brilliant, irregular, attractive, Guermantes representing an orderly and glorious tradition. This long novel, *A la Recherche du Temps Perdu*, sets out to recover, in three volumes, a child's first impressions in both sorts; but this instalment records (in 500 closely printed pages) the earliest images '*du côté de chez Swann*': images forgotten by the intellect, mysteriously resuscitated by the senses – by a tune sung in the street, or a whiff of thyme or mignonette, or (as in the case of our author) by the flavour of a fragment of sponge-cake dipped in tea; images in which matter and memory are subtly combined in a sudden warm flood of life, revived, without the intervention of the understanding.

In all this the influence of Bergson is evident. But can we imagine the Twentieth Century in France without Bergson? As well conceive the Eighteenth Century without Rousseau. Such a delicate excess of sensibility does not exist without disorder; such a need to fuse and unite the very depth of the soul with the ambient world – such a sense of the fluid, pregnant, moving flood of life – exceeds the strict limits of a perfect art. Evidently M. Proust's novel, by its faults as well as by its qualities, is admirably adequate to the spirit of our age. Again, I repeat that while I read with delight the delicate, long-winded masters of our times, I think sometimes with regret of a Turgeneff, no less subtle, who, even as they, wrote at tremendous length and recorded the minutest shades of feeling, but having finished, went through his manuscript again, pen in hand, and reduced it to about one-third of its original length.

In the case of M. Proust's novel, the result is the more bewildering in that the book is conceived, as it were, on two planes; no sooner have we accustomed ourselves to the sun-pierced mist of early reminiscence than the light changes; we find ourselves in glaring noon; the recollection becomes a recital; the magic glory fades from M. Swann and the fair, frail Odette de Crécy; we see them in their habit as they lived and moved among their acquaintance; we smile at the evocation of an artistic coterie under President Grévy, and suffer a sort of gnawing under our ribs as we realise the poignant jealousy of the unhappy Swann. And then the light shifts again, we are back in childhood; and Swann is again the mysterious idol of a dreamy, chivalrous little boy:

He seemed to me to be such an extraordinary being that I thought it miraculous that people I visited should also know him and that in the chance encounters of any old day of the week one might be introduced to him. On one occasion my mother, merely by saying, in the course of telling us as she did every evening at dinner about her shopping during the afternoon: 'By the way, guess whom I met in the Trois-Quartiers at the umbrella counter: Swann', brought about, in the middle of the, to me, arid desert of her story, the full blossoming of a mysterious flower. What melancholy joy to learn that that afternoon, parading his magic person among the common herd, Swann had been out to buy an umbrella.[1]

Can I end better than with this brief and casual quotation, which, better than my criticism, will show the fresh and fine reality which these pages mysteriously recover from the back of our consciousness (where it exists in a warm penumbra of its own) and exhale, as naturally as vapour from a new-ploughed autumn furrow? Something older and deeper than knowledge pervades the book.[2]

NOTES

1 Pléiade I, p. 414.
2 Proust was aware of this notice and was glad of publicity in the British press; see *Corr.* XIII, p. 73.

17. Francis Chevassu on *Swann*
1913

Review of *Swann, Le Figaro*, 8 December 1913, p. 4.

Francis Chevassu (1862–1918), literary critic of *Le Figaro, Le Figaro littéraire* and *Gil Blas*, sees *Swann* as a scarcely transposed poeticized autobiography rather than fiction.

M. Marcel Proust's book is most original, though initially there is a chance that it might disconcert the reader for, at first glance, it does not fit into any genre. The liberties that freely derive from the author's imagination would seem to suggest a novel; but these liberties are not the liberties of fiction. The absence of a plot and the capricious nature of the composition show, in addition, that M. Marcel Proust's last wish was to be restricted to what is commonly called the observation of life. One would be more likely to conclude that what he wanted to write was a pleasant and picturesque autobiography, but in an unexpected format. However, the first concern of an author of Memoirs is, so to speak, to get his recollections washed, dressed and made presentable; of these, there are some to be excluded, others to be adorned with special care; in any case, he tries to conceal from us his preliminary efforts, his hesitations, his rough sketches and all the work needed to give his book its pleasing or severe layout; once the building is up, he pulls down all the scaffolding. What M. Marcel Proust presents us with, on the other hand, is the actual construction of an autobiography; he shows us the whims of memory bringing now one stone, now another; he drags us behind him, as he moves like a stubborn explorer through the undergrowth of the past.

Wells's marvellous imagination was not afraid to play with the centuries, just like a child with sliding tubes in a telescope; it invented a fantastic machine to bring the past nearer, gathering from space the vibrations that made up the lives of people from olden times, projecting them anew on our earth and reconstituting before our eyes the appearance, the gestures and the voices of contemporaries of Louis XIV or Napoleon. To M. Marcel Proust's way of thinking the past of a given individual is no less complex or forbidding than that of humanity at large; its vibrations extend into the present of each of us. Usually we let them go to waste; what priceless thoughts, what joys do we lose like this every day! For not only does the past survive, it is truly alive and well but only yielding its true worth and coming into full flower in the present. . . . M. Marcel Proust . . . has gone 'in search of lost time'. Not having a time-machine like Wells, he has invented a method of his own for rediscovering the past.

Philosophers, who are positively minded people, distinguish between two sorts of memory; the one, involuntary, whose whims are unpredictable, they despise; the other, which would seem to be controlled by our will, they value. The predilection of poets is the very opposite of that of philosophers; they take pleasure in entrusting themselves to the charming revelations of spontaneous memory; they know that this memory is linked to a thousand fleeting sensations that provide more of a base for our personality than the cold and questionable efforts made by the intelligence. Whereas most people pay scent attention to the disconnected images that go through their minds, poets attempt to keep them under the control of their inward-looking eye; M. Marcel Proust proceeds in the manner of the poets. Like them, his alertness is eager and anxious; he seizes on the slightest image, fondles it, questions it, analyses all his responses and classifies them; more often than not, he is magnificently rewarded, for this apparently insignificant image was connected by a multitude of tenuous threads to a whole section of the past that he thought had disappeared for ever. The surest way to recover lost time is to question in detail every present sensation as it arises; because it is the past that gives it its charm, though not everyone knows how to go back and discover it. . . .

[Quotes the 'madeleine' episode and goes on to refer in detail to Combray and Swann's affair.]

There is no more delicate task for a writer than to define a child's impressions; the least literary artifice can easily weigh them down and distort them. In his book, M. Marcel Proust's memories remain in their pristine state, clearly defined; and yet, the impression of the mature man who evokes them is unfailingly superimposed on them; it does not bring about any transfiguration in them; it simply prolongs them in a mood of reverie or illuminates them with tender and delicious humour; contrary to normal practice, it is the present that provides a kind of halo for the past. M. Marcel Proust's book is to be read without haste – for it is dense, which is a criticism to be levelled against it – on winter afternoons so dreary, or on summer afternoons so splendid that reality begins to give the impression that it is retreating or dissolving away; he gently leads us into the land of memory, which is also the land of poetry, and sometimes of humour too.

18. Paul Souday on *Swann*
1913

Review of *Du côté de chez Swann, Le Temps*, 10 December 1913.

Paul Souday (1868–1929), literary critic of the newspaper, *Le Temps*, was a traditionalist in his views and very influential. His review established a tendency in Proust criticism to condemn severely what appeared, at the time, as faults of presentation and yet admit some originality without analysing it precisely. His remarks on characterization should be compared with No. 54 (René Rousseau) who by 1922 was praising what for Souday were weaknesses as part of Proust's particular richness. In spite of the sharp tone of the article Proust was glad of the publicity and at being compared with English writers. He was deeply hurt, nevertheless, by the accusations of writing bad French and justified himself in a letter to Souday the following day, 11 December (*Corr.* XII, pp. 380–3) by dismissing the mistakes as printer's errors. (See Introduction p. 14–15.)

M. Marcel Proust, well-known to admirers of Ruskin for his remarkable translations of *The Bible of Amiens* and *Sesame and Lilies*, offers us the first volume of a large-scale original work: *A la recherche du temps perdu* which will encompass three volumes at least, since two others are announced and are due to appear next year. The first already comprises five hundred and twenty closely printed pages. Now what is this vast, serious subject that brings such developments in its train? Does M. Marcel Proust embrace in his grand work the history of human-kind or at the very least the history of one century? Absolutely not. He tells us about his memories of childhood. Has his childhood, therefore, been filled with a host of extraordinary events? Not at all: nothing special has ever happened to him. Holiday walks and games in the Champs-Elysées constitute the heart of the story. You may say that the content is of little import and that the whole interest of a book resides in the writer's art. Of course. Yet Horace has spoken harshly of certain cases where *materiam superabat opus*[1]; and there is every reason to fear that the remark may apply to the first five hundred and twenty pages of M. Marcel Proust, concerning whom one wonders how many folios he would accumulate and how many libraries he would fill were he to tell us his whole life-story. . . .

[Souday objects to what he calls the density and obscurity of Proust's cluttered descriptions and quotes with distaste errors in agreements of past participles and in the form of the subjunctive.]

However, M. Marcel Proust has, without a shadow of a doubt, a great deal of talent. This is precisely why spoiling such fine gifts with so many errors of taste and grammatical form is to be deplored. He has a rich imagination, a very sharp sensibility, the love of landscape and the arts and a keen sense of observation that is realistic and quick to exaggerate the comic. In his copious narratives there are traces of Ruskin and Dickens. He is often embarrassed by an excess of riches. This superabundance of tiny detail and this insistence on offering explanations of it is frequently to be encountered in English novels where the sensation of existence is produced by a sort of close cohabitation with the characters. As French and Latins we prefer a more closely integrated method. M. Marcel Proust's big volume seems to lack composition and to be as excessive as it is chaotic, yet it contains precious elements that the author could well have used to put together a quite exquisite little book. . . .

[Souday goes on to examine the childhood scenes and quotes the passage on the 'petite madeleine'; '. . . un de ces gâteaux courts et dodus' to 'de ma tasse de thé'.][2]

This is not an instance of association of ideas or even of images, but of purely sense impressions. And M. Marcel Proust, like so many contemporary writers, is above all else an impressionist. But he is to be distinguished from many others in that he is not uniquely or even mainly a man for whom the visual matters, but an emotionalist, a sensualist and a dreamer. His tendency to the

95

meditative sometimes plays nasty tricks on him. He lingers in endless reverie on the nature and destiny of quite insignificant people, a mad old aunt inseparable from her pepsin and Vichy water, a scheming and devoted old nanny and an old curé who hates the stained-glass of days gone by and has no artistic sense whatsoever. A few lines would have been enough to sketch in these fleeting characters. And there is no necessity at all for certain episodes in doubtful taste. What swingeing cuts might M. Proust have made with advantage in these five hundred pages! There are, however, some very pretty descriptions that are hardly ever restricted to rendering the mere surface texture and that are raised to a high level more often than not by the inspiration of an aesthete or poet.

[Quotes section on the hawthorns: 'La haie formait' to 'fleur de fraisier'[3] which is described as 'eminently Ruskinian'. Souday proceeds to the memories of the two ways – Swann's way and Méséglise way – then to what he dismisses as the misplaced and unconvincing episode of Swann and Odette.]

. . . But after two hundred pages given over to these memories and to anecdotes on the grandfather, the grandmother, the great-aunts and the servants we veer rather too much towards 'Swann's way': an enormous episode, taking up a good half of the volume and no longer filled with childhood impressions, but with facts that the child was to a large extent ignorant of and that had to be reconstituted later, lays before us in minute detail the love of this M. Swann, son of a stockbroker, rich, fashionable and friend of the Comte de Paris and the Prince of Wales for a flirtatious lady whose past he knows nothing of and whom for a long time he believes to be virtuous, with a naïvety that is quite unconvincing in a Parisian of this standing. She deceives him, torments him and finally gets him to marry her. It is not exactly boring, but it is rather banal in spite of a certain excessive inclination to coarse expressions and Swann's idea of comparing this mistress of his to Botticelli's Zephora in the Sistine Chapel. And what a lot of episodes within this one episode! What a mass of incidental characters, society people of all kinds and ridiculous bohemians, whose silly behaviour is spread out before us in exceedingly minute and prolix detail! Finally, the last part shows us our young hero madly in love with his little friend from the Champ-Elysées, Gilberte, daughter of M. Swann (whom the little boy's parents no longer see after his absurd marriage). This, I suppose, is intended to link up with the next volume which we await with sympathy and also with the hope of finding in it a little more order and concision, and a more highly polished style. Here is the melancholy conclusion of the present volume: a walk by the now grown up author, twenty years after, in the Bois de Boulogne where he can find nothing of what had once delighted him. He longs for horse-drawn carriages and the elegance of yesteryear; cars and hobble skirts horrify him. 'The reality I once knew was no more . . . the memory of a particular image is but the regret of a particular moment; and the houses, the roads and the avenues go flying past, alas!, like the years.'[4]

NOTES

1 The reference is not to Horace but Ovid (*Metamorphoses*, vol. I, Bk 2, 1. 5). When Proust wrote to Souday the following day he scored handsomely against Souday's sarcasm by pointing out the error. In Ovid the phrase means the very opposite of what Souday implies; when he came to reprint his essay in 1927 he tactfully omitted it.
2 Pléiade I, pp. 45–8.
3 *Idem.*, p. 138.
4 *Idem.*, p. 427.

19. André Arnyvelde: an interview with Proust
1913

Part of 'A propos d'un livre récente', *Le Miroir*, 21 December 1913.

André Arnyvelde records an interview given by Proust to continue the campaign of publicity for *Du côté de chez Swann*. He adds as subtitle: 'L'oeuvre écrite dans la chambre close – Chez M. Marcel Proust', thus playing on the image of Proust as invalid and recluse. He introduces Proust as being not as well known as he might be, partly because of this reclusive life-style and partly because of the degree of culture needed to appreciate his writing. The book is described, nevertheless, as being important; he speaks of 'the stunning arrival of this new novel'.

[He begins his interview by referring to the fact that 'a cruel malady keeps the writer away from society'; Proust opens by defending himself].

'As for this reclusiveness – I think of it as profoundly helpful to my work. Darkness, silence and solitude, by throwing their heavy cloaks over my shoulders, have forced me to recreate all the light, all the music and the joys of nature and society in myself. My spiritual being no longer comes up against the barriers of the visible world and nothing hampers its freedom. . . .'

[Proust is described as lying in bed in his darkened room with all his papers and medicines beside him.]

'When by chance a thin ray of sunlight manages to slip in here . . . my whole being, like the ancient statue of Memnon, that gave out harmonious sounds when the rays of the rising sun struck it, bursts with joy, and I feel myself transported into realms of radiant light. . . .

'But, in my imprisonment, I experience moments of profound sensuousness – For instance, I assure you, and don't laugh for you will soon see my meaning, – I don't know if there is for me any piece of reading that is the equal of – railway timetables. Ah the sweet sound and the loving caress of all those names of towns and villages on the PLM,[1] the charming evocation of the places of light and life where I will never go.'

[The subject of *Swann* is introduced.]

'This book is only the first in a trilogy that I call *A la recherche du temps perdu*. The second book will be: *Le Côté de Guermantes*, and the third: '*Le Temps retrouvé*.

'It goes without saying that each volume can be, or will be capable of being, considered as complete in itself. However, only when he has read the three books will the reader fully know my characters.

'I have tried to follow life itself, in which unsuspected aspects of a person suddenly reveal themselves to our eyes. – We live alongside people, thinking we know them. All that's missing is the incident that will make them suddenly appear other than we knew them to be. Thus, in my book, readers will see, among many others, a certain Vinteuil who, in *Du côté de chez Swann*, is a fine man, a somewhat complacent bourgeois, rather commonplace; and only in the following volume will they learn that he is a musician of genius, creator of a sublime cantata –

'In my mind, my work resembled, you might say, some vast tapestry in an apartment where it could not be contained all in one piece but had to be cut up.

'My characters will appear in their multiple aspects throughout the volumes, just as the different personalities of a given individual reveal themselves to us in the course of time.'

[Asked about his literary career, Proust is unable to ascribe dates to any of his developments.]

'Throughout our lives we have alongside us like a fellow-prisoner shackled by the same chain, a man who is different from our physical self – You see, when you think of yourself, you create a certain idea of yourself – And when one looks in a glass, the mirror reflects our real image. – The other was a stranger – It was the spiritual self. – Well, it is this one alone that matters to me. – Furthermore, the only interest I take in myself is in the manifestations of this "self" and not in events or dates.

'I only consider my objective self (take this word in the sense meant by philosophers) as an experimental instrument which has no inherent interest but that links me to my spiritual side so that I can penetrate certain realities and especially the shadowy areas of consciousness on which I try to throw light –

So I simply cannot tell you when I began to write – I took an article along to a big daily paper. They liked it. It was published. Then others got published. As for the talents I might have had, the director behaved in the way bee-keepers do with their bees. He helped me by his advice and his friendship, as people who keep bees prepare the apiaries and the combs where the honey will be made.'

[The article ends with an evocation of the bustle outside in the Boulevard Haussmann and the quiet by the fireside. 'And one gets the impression one is outside time', in a strange atmosphere, which Arnyvelde describes as lit only by the shining stars of a sick man's feverish eyes, the only concrete reality.]

NOTE

1 The Paris–Lyon–Marseille railway line.

20. Maurice Rostand on *Swann*

1913

Extract from his review of *Swann, Comoedia*, 26 December 1913, p. 1.

Maurice Rostand (1891–1968) dramatist and critic, son of Edmond Rostand, gives a near ecstatic welcome to *Swann*, particularly for its style, in an article entitled 'Quelques lignes à propos d'un livre unique'.

What is this miracle that Marcel Proust presents us with? He comes to us speaking the language that he alone speaks and that he has himself created to express his soul. . . . Unique himself, he expresses himself by unique means and the lucid and mysterious masterpiece, in which he has found the secret of expressing what seemed inexpressible and saying what seemed ineffable, is a soul masquerading as a book. In the same way, awesome Pascal by tormenting us torments himself before our very eyes. Likewise divine Shelley discovers the crystal flute through which his siren soul can reach us.

Like them, Marcel Proust seems to me to deserve to shine among the greatest, those who feel that a sacred fraternity is being established between their different souls, peerless in their uniqueness. . . . A strange fraternity that unites Leonardo da Vinci and Goethe, Plato and Nietzsche, Dostoevsky and Shakespeare. Like them Marcel Proust is a universe apart. He has his own trees and hills, his truths and silences, and his own music too. You would look in vain in Verona for the pomegranate tree in which Romeo hears the nightingale singing, because it is only in Shakespeare; in the same way you would look in vain in every garden for that pink hawthorn in the bushes that sends its perfume through several pages of this book . . . for it is contained entirely in Proust. But already its virginal and delightful perfume has become legendary and gives us its scent for ever like that of the pomegranate tree whose nightingale Romeo heard singing in the dark.[1]

NOTE

1 Proust was embarrassed by the effusiveness of this article. He described it, in a letter to Jacques Rivière, as 'perhaps the one . . . whose ridiculous

exaggeration shocks me most' (*Corr.* XIII, p. 258; see also p. 33).

The same letter gives another instance of Proust's sensitive reactions to certain comments on *Swann*. He asks Rivière to give no more inducement to further views on *Swann* by Willy (pseudonym of Henry Gauthier-Villars, husband and collaborator of Colette on the mildly scandalous sensual *Claudine* novels). Willy had already picked up the references to sexual deviation involving Mlle Vinteuil and suggested that *Swann* was hardly a book to be given to girls to read; see *Le Sourire*, 18 June 1914. Ahlstedt thinks Proust was playing safe and discouraging further outspoken views on certain features of his work; see Eva Ahlstedt, *La Pudeur en crise*, Paris, Touzot, 1985, p. 31. See Introduction p. 25.

21. Lucien Maury on *Swann*

1913

Part of a review of *Swann*, *La Revue politique et littéraire (La Revue bleue)*, 27 December 1913, pp. 821–3.

Lucien Maury is wary of the inflated praise given by Proust's friends. He sees the main weakness as a decadent self-indulgence in both matter and manner, especially when it leads to linguistic contortion.

M. Marcel Proust has good friends in the press, friends who are devoted to the point of imprudence, to the point of indiscretion. He has thus seen himself proclaimed *coram populo*[1] as a writer of genius. . . . M. Marcel Proust who, among many other qualities, gives here and there some evidence of artistic modesty, must indeed have suffered. He will plead mitigating circumstances in my favour before his impetuous friends if I maintain that what he has is a great deal of talent.

A supple, assimilative talent and one that, in the first instance, has the merit of brilliantly reflecting our intellectual fashions.

An expanse of clear water, reflecting all the grandeur of a vast and varied landscape, may turn out to be not very deep; we are attracted by the miracle of its limpidity, the magic of this smooth and deceptive surface. . . .

The mind of Marcel Proust is attractive for a similar quality; the ways of feeling, the habits of thought and the taste for aesthetic and spiritual refinement that found approval with us are obligingly reflected in it: philosophy, and science too, depict in it, in fine or insubstantial outline, a few of the peaks of generally held beliefs; the discoveries of experimental psychology in it seem to be close to us and not laboriously dragged in as was the case with those novels of twenty-five years ago, but simplified and cleverly popularized; Marcel Proust is not one to go quoting Fechner. From literature Marcel Proust has extracted a precious quintessence, though it is evident too that he is hardly less interested in painting and music.

The result is that what is immediately striking about this book is the 'culture' of the author, that prestigious, harmful culture, delicate and diverse, attraction and danger of decadent literatures. It totally dissolves the personality, and the high dignity of art falls victim to it and is brought down to the level of the false grace that accompanies mere pretence and sham.

Marcel Proust is on a beguiling – and dangerous – slope, if one is ambitious for the renown of a creator and not the mere egotistical enjoyment of the pleasures of aestheticism. . . .

The contemporary aesthete, the aesthete with his understanding of abstract connections, with his knowledge of art exceeding his knowledge of life, the aesthete with his refinements, his expressions of naivety, real and unreal, the aesthete with his memories, with his pedantry, the aesthete who can charm and deceive us, the exquisite and pathetic aesthete, the aesthete in all his horror – that is the model I cannot help perceiving on the far side of the shadowy image of Marcel Proust. Has he the will to lay this ghost?

The aesthete glories in simultaneously practising several cults. It would be possible to extract from Marcel Proust's book a collection of sayings and moral maxims, an anthology of dissertations on art and life, a gallery of portraits and genre pictures, another gallery of lyrical landscapes, even a languid little novel that would be reminiscent in more ways than one of L'Enfant à la balustrade by René Boylesve.

There are four or five little books in this novel, which taken separately might have appeared distinguished and charming, but perhaps with no special claim to fame. Are they worth more all collected together, amalgamated in one compact volume? Or did this confusion serve as a magnifying glass through which devoted friends thought they could perceive genius? . . .

I am deliberately exaggerating so as to be better understood and because it would give me no pleasure to praise defects that are blindly worshipped. If we are not the dupes of this beautiful but disorganized book, of these longueurs, of this eternal cross-referencing, of these transpositions, of everything about it that is pointlessly heterogeneous, that is artificial, that is impersonally aloof, we are all the more likely to enjoy the pages that are lively and harmonious.

Marcel Proust is capable of combining great intensity with delicacy; what sphygmograph or microphone could record with a more accurate degree of subtlety blood throbbing through an artery or barely perceptible waves of silence? For example, he writes:

[Quotes 'Dehors les choses' to 'comme ces motifs en sourdine'. Pléiade I. pp. 32–3.]

. . . Marcel Proust brings humorous and lyrical elements into realism; his ironic and sensitive evocation of a provincial family, of the everyday details of domestic life, as well as the waves of feeling that darken and illuminate by turns the heart of a child and adolescent, the picture he gives us of a quiet sleepy village, his depiction of the ceaseless round of the petty dramas going on at the bedside of an invalid aunt and in the world of a nervous youth with a lively imagination and a keen eye for detail, all that minute recording of things, people and emotions – the whole thing has a rich truth in it that would gain from being presented to us within a less hazy framework.

And what exquisite subtleties! But that is precisely where the danger lies, for Marcel Proust has the temperament of a moralist or an essayist, quick to take up and develop his themes and unable to resist the temptation to examine opposing ideological viewpoints. . . .

[Goes on to condemn first the loose connection between Parts I, II, and III and then the relentless ironic tone used in describing both Swann and the Verdurin circle because it degenerates into monotony.]

. . . After all we weary of this insistent charm long before the author. And I admit that sometimes it reminds me of *Les Liaisons dangereuses* and at other times of the psychologizing of Stendhal; meanwhile, has Marcel Proust not been afraid that these unending analyses, this assiduous attention to detail and this zeal that fails to make a real distinction between the important and the insignificant might remind us of other examples, for instance, the worst excesses of Paul Bourget?

This monotony can tolerate a style that is more lively than the wide-ranging presentation and inspiration evident in the first part of the work; Marcel Proust is to be congratulated on having rejected the frightful syntax that might well have stopped many a reader dead in his tracks at the very outset of his book; there is nothing more untidy and intolerable than those shapeless sentences in which parentheses and subordinate clauses wander about aimlessly in an unbridled free-for-all.

Here among many others is an example of this cacophanous writing:

[Quotes 'Un des dimanches' to 'un autre gros propriétaire terrien des environs', Pléiade I, p. 124.]

Marcel Proust would do well also to avoid sentences like this one:

'She held out for me to kiss her sad, pale, nondescript brow on which she had not yet, at that early hour of the morning, arranged her false hair, and where *vertebrae showed through*[2] like the points of a crown of thorns or the beads of a rosary'.

That sort of thing is unworthy of the singular, disconcerting but resourceful writer promised by *Du côté de chez Swann*.

NOTES

1 Before the people; for all to see.
2 In italics in the text. This sentence (Pléiade I, p. 52) also greatly upset Gide. See Introduction p. 11. The sentence was published incorrectly and the error is still in the text. The 'and' after 'her false hair' should be suppressed. It is not in the original MS. The sentence should read: '. . . her false hair where etc. . .', i.e. the vertebrae refer to the row of projections on the framework underlying the wig and not to the brow. See Henri Bonnet, *Marcel Proust de 1907 à 1914*, Paris, Nizet, 1971, pp. 154–5. He explains the error and provides a facsimile of the MS.

22. Henri Ghéon on *Swann*

1914

Review of *Swann, La Nouvelle Revue française*, 1 January 1914, pp. 139–43.

Henri Ghéon (1875–1944), dramatist, essayist and critic, was given Proust's novel to review by Jean Schlumberger or Jacques Rivière, directors of the NRF, possibly to make amends for its rejection by Gide. Proust was not a little put out by Ghéon's mixture of praise and censure and what appeared to be perfunctory mollifying remarks at the end. He immediately wrote Ghéon a sixteen-page letter in self-defence (3 January). The essay, nevertheless, brought Proust's work fully to the notice of the NRF and prepared the way for eventual publication under its imprint. (See Introduction p. 15).

What we have here is a work of leisure, in the fullest meaning of the word. I am not arguing against it on those grounds. Surely leisure is an essential condition for a work of art? It may also render it futile. – The whole question is whether the excess of leisure has not led the author in this case to overdo it and whether, no matter what the pleasure we take in following him, we can go on following him for ever. We sense that M. Marcel Proust has stretching out before him all the time one could need to bring to fruition, to elaborate and successfully create a considerable work. He has all the time in the world and in his own way he exploits it. He considers it from the outset as time lost. He could not, therefore, put it to better use than to reassemble the memories, which are still alive in him, of a time which is already also lost! (he admits as much) and to register a bankruptcy which he is careful not to boast about yet is determined loyally to inform us of. His past life is not a drama and he does not want to make a drama out of it. He has seen many things, read many books and associated with many people. Leisure itself has kept his senses and his mind in a state of total receptivity. Because he was not obliged to judge, he was not obliged to reject; he has rejected nothing. . . . Thus the slightest passing impression, the slightest breath of spring, as much as the merest passer-by in the street, have taken in his memory a place that is as big as, and no less privileged than, the rarest adventures, the most heart-rending passions or the people he has most intimately known. Any intention of choosing and of 'selecting' from among all that is far from his thoughts! All things are equal. All things, for the man who knows how to look at them, conceal a treasure-house of nuances that one is nowhere near exhausting and can bring into play the subtlest analytical faculties that heaven has granted us. After the leisure of living has allowed M. Proust to take interest and pleasure in every moment of life, the leisure of writing now encourages him to consider not one of them to be negligible and to produce what is, properly speaking, the opposite of a work of art, i.e. the stocklist of his sensations and the inventory of his knowledge and to draw up the successive pictures, which are never 'comprehensive', never complete, of the fleeting states of landscapes and the human heart. – Instead of condensing and restricting what he has to say, M. Marcel Proust is self-indulgent. He does not seek out the line of development in a character but rather the character's contradictions and many-sidedness. He does not even bother to be logical and even less to 'compose'. As for that organic satisfaction we get from a work where we take in all its parts, its form at a glance, he stubbornly declines to provide it. The time that anyone else would have used to let a little light into this dense forest, to open up spaces in it and provide vistas he gives to counting the trees, the various kinds of species, the leaves on the branches and the leaves on the ground. And he will describe every leaf in the way it differs from the others, vein by vein, front and back. That is what he enjoys doing and what he preens himself on. He writes 'pieces'. He puts all his pride into the 'piece'; indeed, into the sentence itself. And to say piece or sentence is not to get it quite right. There is no one further removed from writers obsessed with form – Gautier, Flaubert, Goncourt or Renard – than M. Proust. The aesthetic he cultivates is not the least bit parnassian. He does not lovingly linger over the full sonorous period or the exact and polished formulation of words; he does not hone down your brittle phrase or polish up your eloquent one. . . . For all the affectation to which he is more and more fatally drawn by his obsession with the infinitesimal details stored in his memory, he reveals an endless and extraordinary spontaneity. If he must affect a precious tone, then it is because of the subject he is writing about and the sheer mass of things turned up: and the sentence exists only to string together the greatest number of them. It stretches out a kind of net that is indefinitely extendible dragging the ocean floor of the past and bringing up all the flora and fauna in one go. It is not bitter or skimpy or wilfully tortuous or stilted; in itself it is nothing. It fits each moment completely, clinging to it; far from inflicting a chosen meaning on us, the author allows us to do the choosing, spreading out before us, steadily and confusedly what each trawling of the net

brings up. – A quotation at random: one on the stained-glass windows in Combray church:
[Quotes 'Ses vitraux' to 'douce tapisserie de verre'.]¹

There you have the fire-works display of images and observations that a stained-glass window will produce and M. Proust will not even spare us Mme Sazerat with her little box of cakes; it is enough for him to remember having seen her once in church! What, indeed, is Mme Sazerat? An incidental character that he will scarcely mention again. M. Proust, however, would feel he was being dishonest if he were to withhold from us her fortuitous appearance. Whether it is a stained-glass window, a landscape, a human figure, a matter of conscience or a trivial event it's all one and everything is deliberately spelled out. This book suffers from sincerity mania; it has the affected and mannered style of something that is trying to be too sincere. . . . So how is one to assess it?

We will look in vain for a way of linking together a child's first dreams and this affair of M. Swann and Odette de Crécy which M. Proust must surely only have learned about long after childhood, but without any clear justification is intercalated in the story between his summer walks in Combray and his games in the Champs-Elysées. The person who speaks to us is sometimes seven years old, sometimes fifteen and sometimes thirty. He mingles together events and ages. His logic is certainly not ours! And by the same token his book is not a novel, or a story or even a confession. It is a 'summa', the most complex sum of acts, observations, sensations and feelings that our age has yielded up. His book is not of the type to be judged, as a work of art, by its overall harmony, or by the beauty of a particular episode or of a sentence. . . . We have not treated it as we should have. Devoting such a short time to reading it was not the right method. His book is 'time lost': it is to be read page by page without count of time, as we read Montaigne's *Essays*. For all its defects it brings us a real treasure of documentation on modern hypersensibility. You can find poetry in it – and some of the finest, psychology – and some of the newest, irony – and some of the most original, a picture of 'society' never depicted before M. Proust, and lastly the spectacle of a nature of infinite gifts anxious to give proof of its worth before having found, and without even seeking out, its 'form'. Each thing is to be taken and tasted for what it is, as it arises. I can assure you we are far from exhausting it. – Let us get over our annoyance; even what we find annoying here is sincere. At one point M. Proust mocks his relatives for daring to claim 'that one must put before children, and that children show evidence of good taste in at first liking, those works of art that, in their full maturity, they will ultimately admire.' He humbly confesses that in his tender years he admired 'a landscape by Gleyre or some novel by Saintine'. And he adds that 'aesthetic qualities' are not 'mere physical objects that someone with an alert eye cannot fail to notice and yet feel no necessity to allow their spiritual equivalent to ripen slowly in his heart'.[2] This is evidence enough to reassure us on his aestheticism. For all that he is an aesthete, he is no ordinary aesthete and what he gives us today no one had given us before, neither the shadowy bedroom of a precocious child nor the conversations of those astonishing Verdurins, two things which are the strongly contrasting successes of the book.

NOTES

1 Pléiade I, pp. 59–60.
2 Pléiade I, p. 146. Proust's Narrator is referring to 'les soeurs de ma grand' mère'.

23. G. de Pawlowski on *Swann*
1914

Extract from a review of *Swann, Comoedia*, 11 January 1914, p. 3.

G. de Pawlowski (1874–1933) sees Proust's originality, though with reservations, as being in his psychological breakthrough.

This is certainly one of the most important books of the year by virtue of the stylistic effects involved and the way it gives startling concrete form to certain philosophical tendencies in contemporary literature. We have come a long way from the rudimentary, purely descriptive psychology of the novelists we enjoyed in adolescence! . . . This is psychology treated like the study of bacteria under the microscope; it is not psychologizing by a man-about-town with the aid of a mere monocle. . . .

Furthermore, it is not the scenario that particularly interests us in this important work, but the way that the work is handled. The author is determined to bring the details into the foreground; the slighter a detail is, the more importance it is given. . . .

This dissection of feelings . . . reminds me of the extraordinary removal of skin layer by layer from an unfortunate gentleman I once saw on a dissecting table in medical school. . . . What M. Marcel Proust dissects is not the skin, but the mind; he shows us the countless layers one on top of the other that we had not suspected. . . . What gives remarkable value to M. Marcel Proust's method is the author's aesthetic concern. . . . Involuntarily, however keen his interest in analysis, he reconstructs and selects in each scene he evokes, and in spite of himself produces an artistic synthesis. . . .

Having said that, I feel, however, that the author's psychological method is dangerously inspired by the theories of Bergson, which, though at first glance seductive philosophically because of their paradoxical nature and at the same time their profound truth, are nevertheless dangerous when one tries to draw aesthetic conclusions from them. . . .

The risk is that adhering to M. Marcel Proust's Bergsonian method provides us with *an exact photograph of the chaos of life*,[1] you might even say a microphotograph. But however interesting a work might be from the scientific point of view, it would be without artistic worth if there were no deliberate selection by the author.

Unconsciously, M. Marcel Proust has, in fact, often made this selection, for he is an artist, and also because it would be materially impossible to analyse our sensations thoroughly without coming up against the impassable barrier of infinity. . . . Excessive analysis necessarily encounters inaccessible infinity, as does science itself, which lives and breathes analysis; on the other hand, it is art alone, since it operates by synthesis, that is able to bring out the ever more simple, ever more true outline, the eternal gesture that epitomizes all others.[2]

NOTES

1 In italics in the text.
2 Proust wrote immediately to Pawlowski to deny any interest in Bergson; see *Corr*. XIII, p. 54.

24. Paul Abram on *Swann*

1914

A brief review of *Swann, La Petite République*, 19 January 1914.

Paul Abram represents those early views of Proust that warily mingle censure with admiration for something clearly perceived to be original.

The least that one can write about this book is that it stands out markedly from current literary banalities. It is special in its form and original in its content. . . . It seems that its author, M. Marcel Proust, lives isolated from the world. . . . By distancing himself from life M. Marcel Proust has succeeded in forgetting or disregarding its general rhythm to the point that he can no longer perceive anything but the details. His book is thus a collection of facts, endlessly analysed and commented on. With him everything takes on equal value. There is no variation in lay-out. Everything is on the same level. There is no perspective in it. No detail, not even the flimsiest, is left in the dark. It is psychology seen through a minute lens. In addition, M. Marcel Proust has attempted to apply the methods of exposition of various philosophical schools to the tiniest events. One chapter of his book is the virtually intact transposition of Condillac's theory of sensations. For many that will seem brilliantly original. For some there will be no more in it than a perfunctory exercise.

However, I believe that this book will remain for our time, let us say, a unique work, or rather a book apart, a kind of patient and sedulous literary marquetry, whose gravest defect is perhaps to have examined life too fully. It is perfectly true that actions, or the feelings that inspire those actions, are for the most part the outcome of a mental activity that is more often than not unconscious. It is obligatory for a treatise on experimental psychology to seek out the phases of this activity, to find the guiding thread of thought lost in the labyrinthine meanderings of intelligence in action: but a novel, that has any intention of reflecting life, must not permit itself to be drawn into analyses of this kind. For in life the unconscious, the abstract, is only revealed by its material transformation into action or volition. M. Marcel Proust's mistake can be thought of as composing a novel in the manner of a treatise on pure psychology. But, all

110

things considered, this mistake is perhaps the essential quality of his work, and far from criticizing him we should on the contrary praise him highly for it.

25. André Chaumeix on *Swann*

1914

Part of a review of *Swann, Le Journal des débats*, 25 January 1914.

André Chaumeix (1874–1955) provides an example of a sympathetic view of Proust with few reservations – mainly on presentation. He is particularly aware of the affinities between the English novel and Proust. He completely misses the distinction between voluntary and involuntary memory but ends his article with an appreciation of the rich expansiveness of Proust's evocation of Combray, his analysis of Swann's affair, and the poetic evocation of passing time in the final pages.

M. Marcel Proust has begun the publication of a work in three volumes entitled *A la recherche du temps perdu*. The first book, published recently under the rather mysterious title of *Du côté de chez Swann*, is full of rare qualities. I would like to say frankly at the outset that it is disconcerting in its form, in its composition, in its copiousness and in its complexity. M. Marcel Proust has obviously written to please himself and for those alone who will be inclined to read him in a leisurely, meditative way. From the start, he has discouraged the reader in a hurry who thinks he can follow well enough by glancing through a few pages. He has also mercilessly driven away the carefree reader who wants to be carried along and entertained without making the least effort. He has made no sacrifice to the public of his day: such independence, in the state of current literary practice, has become a precious rarity. He is a writer who talks at length and with affection on everything he holds dear, and at first a certain effort is needed to go along with him in this huge narrative.

But the reader is soon encouraged and seduced by the richness of the impressions, the diversity of the points of view and the full flowering of a delicate and inexhaustible sensibility. You wander through this strange, captivating book as if walking through a thick, truly magnificent forest where you miss the path, where there is indeed no path at all, where the branches, the scents, the simplest plants, the most sumptuous shadows and the subtle light combine to cast a spell. M. Marcel Proust unravels with marvellous fluidity the memories that make up his childhood days, the time that cannot be rediscovered, lost time. His book is a kind of epic of memory; it gathers together one by one all the author's impressions in infinite variety and thus as we turn the pages his whole former life comes back into existence.

In a book of this devising – as far as can be judged from this single volume considered separately from the ones to follow – there is no subject properly speaking. Of the three parts of unequal length that comprise *Du côté de chez Swann*, two consist of a narrative in the first person, the other, the second part, is like a huge parenthesis in which we are presented retrospectively with the life and loves of M. Swann. Yet these differences of form do not affect the general atmosphere or tone of the narrative. Even when the author is telling us the story of Swann we have the feeling that he is still speaking about himself. No work is more personal in the sense that no work gives greater space to impressions pinpointed always for their uniqueness, their subtlety, their sheer elusiveness. The tiniest details of the life of a child are recounted, all the incidents of his day, his waking up, his falling asleep, his walks, his conversations with his parents, his aunts, his neighbours, his servants, all the resonances occasioned in a fresh and morbidly sensitive soul by the daily encounter with people and things. When you read M. Marcel Proust you can understand why a philosopher one day defined man as a collection of sensations.

But this procedure would be monotonous and ineffective if the author were satisfied with this collection, however prodigious. There is nothing whose content is slighter for a psychologist than a sensation: what is general about it is adequately indicated and anatomized by a name; what is absolutely unique to a single individual is almost untranslatable. Yet between these two extremes there are a hundred shades of meaning whereby an impression general enough to be understood by all becomes colourful and original enough to appear to belong to an individual of flesh and blood. M. Marcel Proust has a sort of instinct for distinguishing them. He rounds them out by all sorts of associations. The least emotion immediately calls up many more that extend it further, explain it or surround it. The author scarcely summons up a memory than a myriad others follow as if all connected by a fine thread, and it is enough to fix the first for all the others to come and arrange themselves around it and form a web that is life itself. In the world of pure sensibility, where feelings, emotions and memories stand together or are contained one in another, M. Marcel Proust moves with surprising ease; here he is surely in his private domain with whose copious diversity and dark mystery he is wonderfully acquainted.

As he goes up and down this realm he is pulled in two different directions: he responds to the slightest vibration of memory but he also has a perspicacity that shows a very remarkable degree of self-possession. He is the proper witness of this whole sensibility: he watches over it; he could be said to spy on it with a lucid mind that observes and retains things and sometimes even clarifies and organizes them. This split in outlook, that allows the transformation of sensibility into a medium for artistic ends without either diminishing its force or hampering it, is the mark of an artist. M. Marcel Proust considers the whole jumble of memories that come flooding in on the tide of his sensibility with a combination of intellectual sharpness and presence of mind that constantly seeks to make distinctions between them; he keeps them to himself; he gently plays with them while continuing to prolong the emotion involved. He is not a man to live by imagination alone. Confronted by all the scenes of his childhood, he does not show the independence and fantasy of a Dickens who takes interest in thousands of things, recalling them and describing them with the skill of a draughtsman who is master of every line he draws; he is rather like a musician playing old melodies he knows like the back of his hand over and over again without letting you feel just yet the sadness contained in them. . . .

Nothing would be easier than to express serious critical reservations about M. Marcel Proust. It would be desirable if he took more care over his use of language and paid attention to certain slovenly expressions and even down-right errors. It would be desirable if he could see his way to cutting sentences that are over-long and cluttered up with subordinate clauses and parentheses. And since in other places – you have only to re-read the final pages to be convinced of it – he can write in a different, much more careful style, there is a suspicion that the author has a weakness for certain complicated pages that he imagines the rather puzzled reader being amazed by. Nothing would be easier to than to show just how little respect M. Marcel Proust has for composition. It is not an art greatly honoured in our day and famous examples can be cited to excuse this licence. Moreover, all these examples come from foreign literatures and it is perfectly true to say that, on the question of the structure of a book, neither Tolstoy, nor George Eliot, nor Dickens, nor Meredith shares the ideas that in our country are traditional. English novelists in particular show, as far as composition is concerned, a notorious independence. With them, as we all know, action slows down or speeds up for no reason, discussions take over the story and episodes in serial form knock it off course. All that fine structure, that balance of the different parts, that even illumination that we love in Flaubert, and whatever some people may say, in Stendhal and even in Balzac, all that seems to be ignored and replaced by an exceptional meticulousness of detail. M. Marcel Proust's book often reminds you of an English novel. In spite of the arguments to the contrary, I cannot bring myself to believe that order, clarity, the art of selection, of finding the right expression and the most telling description are negligible qualities. . . . The concern for order is a rule that may appear narrow but we should remember that it is inspired by everything that the language and literature of our country has produced over the last four hundred years. It would, of course, be unfair to deny that English literature, for instance, with its meticulousness, its accumulation of detail and its air of irregularity can create outstanding impressions, and few novelists have succeeded as much as English ones in devising with more depth and quality a picture of ordinary lives, in translating the complexity of life, the repercussion of actions on each other, the interlocking of events, the slow outcome of their consequences and the whole mysterious power of fate on human existence. It may well be that our taste for clarity has, at times, the effect of over-simplifying the representation of the adventures of the heart in our literature, and perhaps, by combining some profusion of detail with some relaxation of discipline, it is possible to bring things that are common and simple, yet rich in feeling and vitality, much more vividly to life? This is a problem to exercise the minds of novelists.

M. Marcel Proust, whichever way you look at it, has the benefit of the aesthetic approach he has chosen. His book may lack organization, but it does have that rather strange, though appetising plenitude, that profusion and richness which at times give the impression of being like the raw stuff of experience itself.

26. Louis Latourette on *Swann*

1914

Part of a review of *Swann, Les Écrits français*, 5 April 1914, pp. 60–1.

Louis Latourette sees Proust's originality not in his content but in the transmission of his sincerity.

In novelists, philosophers are saddled with compromising inter-preters. Zola's stories did a great deal of disservice to the force and gravity of Claude Bernard and Auguste Comte. And I wager that M. Bergson must consider the application of his theories in M. Marcel Proust's novel to be weak. . . . To have done, once and for all, with M. Marcel Proust's defects, I will go on to say that his scorning of action in the way incidents succeed one another is only too obvious and too many studies of personal foibles have an adverse effect on the force of his characters.

Having said that, I think it proper to note that this book – first in a trilogy – is one of the most original and one of the most composite to have been published for a long time. . . . Composite because all the feelings of recent generations and schools, all their ideas and all their turns of phrase have been assembled and arranged to set off the analyses and the descriptions. . . .

His enormous number of pages would frighten most of our present-day novelists. In such an undertaking, masterly skill is needed to avoid boredom. Not for a moment does one feel the least fatigue. Sometimes there is a kind of nervous twitching at the excessive examination of detail under the microscope. . . . However, as one comes to the end of the work one retains, looking back on the multitude of emotions one has shared, the satisfaction of having read a first-rate book. A book that will have no influence, that will not change people's behaviour or inclinations, but a book that will remain like a magnificent document, a thing of outstanding importance and rare stature.

27. Jacques-Émile Blanche on *Swann*
1914

Extract from his review of *Swann, L'Écho de Paris*, 15 April 1914, p. 1.

Jacques-Émile Blanche (1861–1942), art critic and painter, was famous for his portraits of celebrities; his well known portrait of Proust with the orchid in his buttonhole dates from 1892. The quality of his literary judgment is shown here in an article in which he uses visual metaphors to define Proust's originality. He is also the first to appreciate the nocturnal and dreamy inspiration of *Swann*. Cf. No. 54.

Du côté de chez Swann is the book of sleepless nights, of thoughts that keep watch through silence and darkness. Yet it is a book overflowing with life, diverse and one, so full of details, all equal in importance, that depending on your mood, dear reader, either you will not be able to leave it alone once you have penetrated it, or else you will give it up, should something deprive you of the sheer concentration demanded by this fearsome register of minute facts. It makes me feel as if I am in a drawing room, panelled with mirrors, that is increasing in size in all directions, the reflections expanding to infinity and at the same time getting smaller and smaller.

M. Proust has not so much been keeping a journal as amusing himself with a kind of cinema film, reconstituting the sequences and *posing*[1] in it himself for several characters, throwing, as the whim takes him, the cloak of one around the shoulders of another, or even wearing it himself.

Some have criticized him for a lack of selectivity, especially those who claim art only begins with selection; but art has no immutable rules. *Du côté de chez Swann* is a work that it is difficult to classify, even more to compare with anything else; it has no precedent in our literature. What M. Proust sees, feels and writes is completely original. Famous foreign names like Meredith and Dickens have been quoted in connection with him. Whereas what we have here comes from France, could not have come from anywhere else and dates from the end of the nineteenth century. This is the work of an impressionist with aspirations to being a line-engraver and – I hardly dare say it since the word frightens people today – of a man about town. His boldness comes out in the interlacing and the arabesques of interminable periodic sentences, clear ones, however, picturesque and, when they do not linger over weaving too many garlands, firm, sharply outlined, supple and pregnant with meaning. . . .

[Goes on to refer to the memories of Combray and to Swann's love affair.]

So here is the first volume and as such a rare treat, a breath of fresh air to blow away the soporific vapours of current writing. As soon as it appeared, it delighted some and alarmed others, for access to it, so they say, is difficult. As with all exceptional works it appears both original and beautiful.

Du côté de chez Swann . . . contains irresistible magic. It brings to mind a Paris that no longer exists; though it is not a 'roman à clef', I can recognize two or three models for each character; it has the flavour of an autobiography and an essay and overflows with sensibility and intelligence. . . .

Until now a novel of society life has seemed almost insipid, if not ridiculous. To give good descriptions of high society you must not be dazzled by it, you must like it, but laugh at it. . . . M. Proust, like a Bertillon,[2] has his record cards, his finger prints and has only to open one of his files to build up a picture of characters who are touching or absurd. He adds to his qualities of alienist and psychologist, the rare spice of a sharp irony that would be implacable if it were not tempered by sympathy. He is witty and profound. There is a touch of Granville [sic][3] in M. Proust; like this famous draughtsman he looks at people from above (foreshortened) or from below (like frescoes on a ceiling); he sees them from strange angles; I would almost go so far as to say he suggests the fourth dimension of the cubists. His triumph is in the accumulation of details; he clears the most dangerous obstacles and, as soon as our attention flags, he takes hold of us and carries us along. . . .

M. Proust's perspicacity has increased rather than been blunted in his solitude far from the madding crowd. He looks at people long and patiently with a magnifying glass and sees in them nuances that escape us, as we go scurrying through the century. This book could only have been written in the fearsome clarity of vision that comes with nights of sleeplessness. It is almost too intense for eyes that are half-blind even in the full light of day.[4]

NOTES

1 In italics in the text.

2 Alphonse Bertillon (1853–1914), detective and inventor of 'bertillonnage', the application of scientific method to the identification of criminals.

3 Jean-Ignace-Isidore Gérard, known as Grandville (1803–47) famous as caricaturist and as illustrator of La Fontaine's *Fables*.

4 Proust was very keen on this article and suggested amendments to Blanche; see *Corr.* XIII, pp. 84–6. He also arranged to pay for an *écho* quoting from it at length in *Gil Blas* a few days later; *ibid.* p. 149.

28. F. Jean-Monique on *Swann*

1914

Extracts from a review of *Swann, Effort libre*, May 1914, pp. 509–15.

F. Jean-Monique typically mingles a critical response to the analytical qualities of the work with annoyance at its composition.

Five hundred and twenty-three pages of closely printed text in search of lost/wasted[1] time! You need plenty of time on your hands to waste. . . . A set of three chapters consisting of a series of essays and confessions, in no logical order or time sequence: the protagonist is ten, twenty-eight then fifteen years old. After this, for no apparent reason, is intercalated a well drawn picture of a society salon, where Swann's love affairs occur; and I feel that at that point the author puts himself in the place of Swann.

This inorganic and powerful mass does not constitute a work. That does not seem to have worried M. Proust overmuch. However, the lack of composition is striking and presents a problem. . . . Content, topic and notion are all one. Wherever they come from they are welcome; one is of as much value as the other; there is no choice to be made; the fact that they exist is enough to justify them. . . . A book where there is no choice, will not really be a choice book: it is weakened in its human and in its aesthetic value. . . .

M. Proust's sentences are worthy of interest. They also have time to waste. The initial meanderings open up perspectives reminiscent of a certain style that belongs to memoirs of the sixteenth or seventeenth centuries; not so much as all that, perhaps; just enough to suggest some name or other; Bussy-Rabutin; then suddenly a vigorous nonchalant quality emerges such that the endless stream of images, notations and metaphors eventually confronts you with a slight little creation, original, rather forced, I daresay, but not aping the period, belonging to no school and playing the role of willing slave to the rich content embedded in it. . . .

Stendhalians will love this book in which intelligence holds sway over sensibility, accentuating and refining it, but strangling emotion; they will love the story of Swann's affairs. . . . This Swann character, the role of love in high society and the man about town, Stendhal and the bourgeoisie could together form the basis of a very interesting study. . . .

All in all then, this is an original and extremely rich book; an impressionist poet over-endowed with intelligence originated it; the man about town who took it up had too much leisure-time to complete it. The sketches and pictures remain a little off-putting, but full of things to teach a writer or any cultivated person, because they set us upon the road to that inner richness that we all carry within us without our knowing it.

NOTES

1 He plays on the two senses of 'perdre': to lose and to waste (time).

29. Henri Potez on *Swann*

1914

Extract from 'Les infiniment petits de l'âme,' *L'Écho du Nord*, 5 June 1914, p. 1.

Henri Potez, rather puzzled by the content of *Swann*, gives a review that is sometimes ambiguously complimentary.

I scarcely know of any more distinguished work that has appeared over the last ten years.

M. Proust's novel is by no means easy of access. It puts up a defence against the superficial and frivolous reader. In fact, the first thing about it is that the organization is a little disconcerting. It is enormous, dense and truncated. It contains enough material for two stout volumes. The development spreads out over an endless expanse. In already over-long paragraphs, the sentences are at times out of proportion. . . . The plan, or absence of plan, is not the least surprising thing about it. . . . But for all these reservations, we must admit that no one has gone so far in psychological analysis. . . . M. Proust scrutinizes his past. Not only does he evoke a swarm of endless impressions, like the dust-cloud surrounding the nucleus of a comet, swinging, undulating and twisting in its train, but he even loads onto the past his interpretations and commentaries in the present. . . . From this volume it would be possible to extract a little book of maxims, perhaps not so clear-cut or so highly polished, but as profound as the best of La Rochefoucauld's and Chamfort's. And even as I say that, I am afraid I can only hint at M. Proust's real quality: there is in him a poet who writes movingly of special moments, quiet evenings, reading alone, or meres, woods and heavily-scented flowers.

A master-piece? Perhaps not; possibly something better. A conscientiously contrived enchantment, a book that disturbs, stimulates and enriches, a contradictory monster, as elusive and appealing as the human soul. Of course, the man who pursues Psyche will always lose his way. But nobody, more than M. Proust, has appeared so exactly poised to take her by surprise.

1919–22

A — *A L'OMBRE DES JEUNES FILLES EN FLEURS* AND THE GONCOURT PRIZE

30. Abel Hermant on *Jeunes Filles*
1919

Part of a review of *Swann* and *Jeunes Filles* in *Le Figaro*, 24 August 1919.

Abel Hermant (1862–1950), novelist and critic, speaks very favourably before going on to discuss the problem of memory and selectivity.

. . . A memory that is so demanding in itself is not less so in the case of the artist for whom it provides the raw material of his work. Everything it has set aside seems equally valuable to him; it does not countenance his neglecting one scrap of it. In short, it deprives him of choice, of the sacrifices needing to be made, of all order, except the order imposed by chronology . . . in a word of art. . . . He [M. Marcel Proust] risks creating a confused jumble. Today when people only want short books, he has the cynicism, I would even say – to use a word he favours – the sadism, to give us volumes of 443 pages with 44 lines to the page. He seems to fall into the trap laid for him by his excessively rich memory. The funny side of it is that he drags us with him; we are caught, his charm takes over and we are the ones who are sorry that he has made cuts and choices!

– But you will object: so much writing and just about oneself, to tell us his little adventures? If you distinguish as the Germans do, the objective and the subjective, you will see that the real has no reality except in the sensibility of the subject who reflects it and that, on the other hand, there is nothing in the sensibility of each one of us which does not come from outside sources. Hence it is as clear as daylight that the most subjective of books is the most objective and vice versa. M. Marcel Proust, as he tells us his own personal adventures, tells us those of his time and provides a picture of his society. He

121

pretends to be confined to bed, but his curiosity roams free. He has bouts of ill-humour combined with refinements of etiquette reminiscent of Saint-Simon . . . whims like Mme de Sévigné, a cruel talent for portraits more extended than La Bruyère, a carefree enthusiasm, lots of wit and a touch of maliciousness as needed; and he has written the truest passages in any literature on love at the unsure and fluctuating age of adolescence.

31. Louis Léon-Martin: In the shadow of a pimply youth

1919

Pastiche of *A l'ombre des jeunes filles en fleurs* entitled 'A l'ombre d'un jeune homme en boutons' in *Le Crapouillot*, 1 October 1919, p. 7.

Louis Léon-Martin, the well-known parodist, plays here on Proust's reputation in *Swann* and *Jeunes Filles* for over-long, contorted sentences and, even more, for obscure analyses involving decisions of great personal import.

In the shadow of a pimply youth

(*Some notes outlining the appropriateness of undertaking a visit and the increasing difficulty over taking the first step.*)

I was finishing dressing when I received this note from my friend Gilbert: 'Dear friend, you, who love to savour the inner life, will learn not without chagrin that the said inner life has just, in my case, been singularly curtailed by the expulsion of a tape-worm that the School of Medicine has enjoined me to distance from my person. At the same time a profusion of pimples has broken out on my face which causes me to delay the pleasure of seeing you – '. I resolved immediately to go and see Gilbert; but, as soon as I intended to make the first step, I perceived that I had been bold indeed to take so rapid a decision, for the reason that I am, so to speak, divided and, as it were, distributed between two pans of a scale and for the reason too that, since the pros and cons are equally balanced, I cannot succeed in making the bar dip down on any side at all. I perceived it, as I said, as soon as I intended to act, for, having raised my right foot, I could not decide to let it drop for the following reason: there are no more grounds for beginning to walk with this foot rather than the other. I was in a dire quandary, my foot remained up in the air and I was trying not to commit a blunder. To bring it back to the level of my left foot would have meant making a movement to no purpose, to move it forwards was to take a far-reaching decision, for we do not know where the least movement can lead us, and besides, the unique possibilities inherent in a resolution contain within them – as does the seed the future harvest – all the ideas, emotions, incidents or catastrophes of the completed act, so that I felt myself a fool to have, if I may dare to put it like this, got ready to decamp, just as if I had completed the whole movement, because, in so doing, I had unleashed from within me, in addition to a world of already irreversible consequences, another world of painful hesitations. At that moment, the idea flashed through my mind that, since I enjoyed spending my time in the shade of budding young girls, I could well find some delight in the shadow of a pimply young man, but that thought was instantly counter-balanced by this one: namely that, if I did not hesitate, I would no longer have any reason to write, and that in addition the state of indecision is my privilege, as incidentally is splitting hairs, given that I would be incapable of wasting my time, seeing that people cannot but know the incomparable use to which, with a whole string of contradictory considerations, I can put time, even if lost. These were my reflections when, making an instinctive gesture, I shuddered with pain and dropped down on a nearby sofa uttering a cry like a hunting call. A forgotten horn-call, addressing itself to my memory, condemned me to a state of immobility to which, going by my own intelligence alone, I would not have thought I had the right to entrust myself. . .

MARCEL PROUST

32. Binet–Valmer on *Jeunes Filles*

1919

Part of 'La Semaine littéraire', a review of *Jeunes Filles, Comoedia*, 5 October 1919.

Binet-Valmer (1875–1940), novelist, journalist, and critic, welcomes *Jeunes Filles* for its readability. His rhapsodic remarks emphasize what he sees as the poet in Proust. He came to feel rather differently later over *Sodome et Gomorrhe*. See Introduction, p. 27.

. . . What a pleasure it has been! Here you have this rare civilized society, brimming with subtle distinctions, but not lacking in depth because the artists – and what a lot there were! – agonized over the slightest lapse of taste as much as any soldier hit by a bullet. So this was the state of the most cultivated men on earth! The Avenue du Bois, grand clubs, literary salons, the middle-classes within an ace of being nobility, scribblers within a whisker of being poets, innocent girls within an inch of being demi-mondaines, fastidious souls just missing passion by a hair's breadth, and this invalid, this man who is almost a genius – it would not be Parisian not to include the 'almost' – this invalid who leaves his bedroom every four months and takes precise note of the basement window through which the light reaches down into his cellar. His cellar? The darkness where lurks his subconscious, the real character of the book. As for this character, we do not know him completely. He will need another few volumes before he reveals himself to us in his magnificent complexity. When we do get to know him, we will perhaps say about Marcel Proust: before the war, there existed in Paris a civilization rich in sensibility; it was embodied in an invalid, who made foolish remarks while taking tea with friends, while walking along the avenues, while trying to fall in love with budding young girls. And he was a poet, a great poet full of sadness. . . .

33. Jacques Rivière on the Prix Goncourt
1919

Article in *Excelsior*, 11 December 1919, p. 4.

Jacques Rivière (1886–1925), essayist of distinction, had become by 1919 director of *La Nouvelle Revue française* and had been converted to an admiration for Proust on reading *Swann* which he eventually persuaded his colleagues on the NRF to acquire for their imprint. His readiness to compare Proust with other French writers, his enthusiasm for Proust's insights and his positive tone contrast with the popular reaction to *A l'ombre des jeunes filles en fleurs* to be seen in No. 34.

We have not seen the appearance of a psychological monument of such imposing dimensions since the *Mémoires* of Saint-Simon. This thick volume, by the way, is one of the least thick of books, I mean it is one of the most meticulous, most precise, most positive books I have been given to review for a long time. M. Marcel Proust's only care, where feelings are involved, is to show us the fine detail; and he pursues it with infinite patience and scrupulousness. He gets under the skin of his characters without forcing, yet he immediately gets to the bottom of them; he draws them from the inside and insists on reproducing every single fibre. He is an anatomist. There is an absence of intellectual laziness in him worthy of a scientist. And he has also the man of science's horror of exaggerated language and excessive attitudes. He is profoundly, seriously anti-romantic. Yet he is no cold fish. His object of study is the human heart and, having experienced it so long and intimately, he is only too well acquainted with its tender vulnerability ever to fall into the trap of dullness. The sensitive – not to be confused with the sentimental – reader finds a rare intoxication in his company. He recognizes his smallest agitations and transient emotional states. For a long time, since Stendhal perhaps, there was nobody in France – the only country where you might meet such a person – to take such pains in dealing with love, i.e. with the only really serious business in the world. Marcel Proust's portraits of women! Who can look at them without sweet and secret pangs of anguish, without discovering within oneself, jumbled together, that pity, desire, amazement, resistance and delighted disenchantment that combine to seize one's heart as soon as some irresistibly sweet face exerts its charm? And who can read the long analyses of *A l'ombre des jeunes filles en fleurs* without feeling oneself reimmersed in that marvellous lucid disarray into which we are plunged by all true passions?

Yes, a really fine book. The Goncourt Academy has never been better inspired.

34. Jean Pellerin on the Prix Goncourt
1919

Extract from an article in *Lanterne*, 11 December 1919, p. 1.

Jean Pellerin (1885–1920), known for his association with Le Groupe Fantaisiste and his ironic poems on modern life, expresses the general bewilderment at the choice of Proust for the Prix Goncourt when there were more readable works available and younger writers to encourage.

. . . It is possible – I confess I was not able to finish reading it – that *A l'ombre des jeunes filles en fleurs* is a very remarkable book. M. Marcel Proust's delightful *Pastiches et mélanges* reveal a great talent, solid erudition and excellent taste. But however much you pore over this prize-winner, this enormous book that beats the modern record for length . . . this meticulous autobiography that lumps together what would make four or five average novels, you are filled with dismay. Why? Because the Goncourt committee has just told the public at large: 'Read this! This is the best literary work of the year!' And the public at large, which is sure to lose heart when confronted with this impenetrable tissue of subtleties, will jeer once again at 'literature' and just turn back to Fantomas![1] Who would dare to blame them for it? . . .

NOTE

1 Character invented by the popular thriller writer, Marcel Allain.

35. Léon Daudet on the Prix Goncourt

1919

Extract from 'Un nouveau et puissant romancier', *L'Action française*, 12 December 1919.

Léon Daudet (1868–1942), journalist, critic, novelist, and part founder of *L'Action française*, was member of the committee of the Académie Goncourt. He claims with pride that they had never done better than to choose *A l'ombre des jeunes filles en fleurs* and comments here on its original features.

. . . As he tells us about other people, while giving the impression that he is telling us about himself – something achieved by a very ingenious psychological subterfuge – he examines and mulls over the most delicate problems of our inner life. . . It is a combination of easy-going manner and shrewd observation, in which astonishing viewpoints open up on you, the reader, on all of us, on the characters themselves, such as you find in our best moralists and chroniclers of the human heart: a Saint-Evremond, a La Bruyère or a La Rochefoucauld. . . .

Yesterday, one of our colleagues mentioned Meredith in connection with Marcel Proust. This is very much to the point. One could also mention Sterne in *Tristram Shandy* and Jean-Paul Richter in *Titan*. For the most spontaneous literary mentality – and this one is extremely so – does not appear among us like a bolt from the blue. It is the result of a slow maturing that draws on the manifestations of the human spirit, the works of the past and the reading that peoples our imagination with unexpected characters. Marcel Proust – and one does not have to know him to sense it – is one of the most profoundly cultured of men. . . .

A rare phenomenon to appear for many years . . . he is a writer with a sense of the comic.[1] He goes well beyond the point of sour, painful observation where this turns to bitterness, as in Vallès[2] and his successors. . . . He gives us twenty pages of the conversation of an old, solemn, pretentious diplomat who has come to dine with his parents and does so with an astounding verve that leaves you dazzled. Imagine a fresco made up of miniatures so that from a distance you can admire the general effect and from close to you are ravished by the detail. The minute descriptions Proust gives of a domestic scene, someone's attire or a face eventually correspond to

127

moral traits and intellectual characteristics which are surprisingly convincing. His tapestry looks at first as if it is back to front, with dangling threads and colourless patterns. He swiftly turns it round and then you see all its outlines, its perspectives, its bright reds, crude yellows and deep purples. It is the hand of a master.

NOTE

1 A side to Proust's genius that is not often appreciated; see also Vandérem (No. 57) and Middleton Murry (No. 66).
2 Jules Vallès (1833–85) noted for the picture of his childhood and youth in his novel *Jacques Vingtras*.

36. Jean de Pierrefeu on the Goncourt Prize
1919

Article in *Le Journal des débats*, 12 December 1919.

Jean de Pierrefeu (1881–1940), critic and novelist, reflects in his article the mixed attitudes to *Jeunes Filles* immediately following the Goncourt award.

Awaited with the same impatience as in preceding years in literary circles, the decision of the Goncourt Academy has caused a certain astonishment. Not that M. Marcel Proust was not thought worthy of this choice, but the impression is that neither his age nor the quality of his work put him in the running for possible candidates.

M. Marcel Proust is no beginner. His reputation is not still to be made, he is not in need of assistance for his début in the ungrateful career of man of letters, on the contrary, he is a writer appreciated by an élite that willingly takes rare talents not easily accessible to the common herd to its bosom. Ranged against him were precisely authors who fulfilled all the conditions demanded to date: MM. Roland Dorgelès, Alexandre Arnoux, Adès Josipovici and Francis Carco. And, by a happy coincidence, these writers presented works of unquestionable value: *Les Croix de bois, Le Cabaret, Goha le simple* and *L'Équipe*. Each of these novels was of the sort to appeal to the Goncourt Academy.

Whereas, it was possible to maintain in advance that neither *Du côté de chez Swann* nor *A l'ombre des jeunes filles en fleurs* fitted in with their tastes and theories of art.

M. Marcel Proust was known for clever, mischievous pastiches when, a few years before the war, he published a dense volume, with no beginning and no end, oddly entitled *Du côté de chez Swann*.[1] Since then, he has added a second book as extension to the first, and he is preparing others on the same subject. There is nothing to prove that he will stop now that he is off to such a good start. In my view, only sheer fatigue or death can stop him in the task he has undertaken to go in search of the time he has lost in the course of the first thirty or forty years of his existence and bring it back to life before our very eyes.

M. Proust is not one of those authors who has to cast around for a theme; he has taken himself as the subject of his books. One fine day, coming to the conclusion that he had lived long enough, he began to live his life all over again through reminiscence. Like an underwater diver working on the sea-floor of his memory, he has gone deep down into himself and has dug up bit by bit, fragment by fragment the most obscure desires, feelings and movements of his soul and the images of the external world captured by his eye and stored in his mind. Going even further, he has searched his unconscious and discovered thousands of elusive meanings, tastes, smells, joys and sorrows that scarcely impinged on the soft wax of that inmost tablet which records our life. Of all that, he has patiently made the most detailed inventory.

And it transpires that these fragments joined end to end form figures and elliptically drawn landscapes as lacking in solidity as the phantoms we create in our dreams, a pale representation of a human life engulfed in the night of time.

Certainly, this talent from beyond the grave has its charm. A very gentle melancholy mood overwhelms us as we follow the author. What life once was is always moving. Unfortunately, M. Proust, enslaved by this laborious quest in the dark places of his inmost self, gropes his way, stumbles at every step, his sentences as clumsy as a blind man's hands reaching out, lightly touching things and not properly getting hold of them.

This collection of wakeful ruminations, written by a willing recluse, will delight those sickly souls who cannot take reality and hide in dreams. It has little connection with the sympathies of the new generation who celebrate the beauty of conflict and the virtues of enlightenment; it is out of tune with the renewed classical spirit that the Party of the Intelligence declares to be the only one compatible with the greatness of our victorious nation.

NOTE

1 Pierrefeu's view is carelessly expressed and, of course, inaccurate.

37. André Billy on *Swann* and *Jeunes Filles*
1920

Part of an article on Proust reprinted in *La Muse aux besicles*,
Paris, La Renaissance du Livre, 1920, pp. 223–4.

André Billy (1882–1971), while enthusiastic over the detail of
Proust's work, revives in his notice on *Jeunes Filles* the kind of
criticism made before the war on *Swann*: Proust has written
something interesting, but are they novels?

. . . From time to time a cell forms, disintegrates then reappears,
divides and is swallowed up again in this spongy element that
constitutes M. Proust's prose. Spongy, but glistening with changing
lights. Dear me, how treacherous metaphors can be! I have risked the
word spongy and I stand by it, for I feel it is exactly right, but it may
give the impression that M. Proust has no nerves, whereas, on the
contrary, his books could actually be compared, with even greater
justification, to 'packs of nerves'.

Do you enjoy a read? Reading, not reading a novel, but just
reading, reading for reading's sake? In that case, read Marcel Proust
without worrying your head about deciding whether what you have
in your hands is a novel. *Du côté de chez Swann* and *A l'ombre des
jeunes filles en fleurs* are not novels, although, when the author is
asked if they are his memoirs, he is annoyed. Why do you want
Swann to have really existed? And Odette? Odette has no existence
either. It makes no difference, these indefinable books are not novels;
they are not memoirs; but there is a bit of both in them. By
whatever name we agree to label them, they bring back to us the
spirit and the fashions of 1880 to 1890. . . . The irritating and
ambiguous seduction of M. Proust's reminiscences partake somewhat of an anachronism, a dissonance; in tone they belong to today;
in the events described, they belong to the day before yesterday. The
divergence is already difficult to grasp, and time will make it more
tenuous. What will be left for those coming after us? I have no idea,
but M. Proust's works, even if with time they lost the mask of
make-up that, though not hiding it, creates an illusion about their
real age, would retain enough beauties of detail scattered here, there
and everywhere and, so to speak, in generous handfuls, to stimulate
the enthusiasm of commentators when Swann's victoria will have
joined, in the long perspective of history, the assault machines of the
high Middle Ages.

130

38. Jacques Rivière on the Prix Goncourt
1920

Part of 'Le Prix Goncourt', *La Nouvelle Revue française*, 1 January 1920, pp. 152–4.

Jacques Rivière follows up his article of 11 December 1919, the day after the announcement of the Goncourt Prize (No. 33), by boosting Proust's association with the NRF. He welcomes the granting of the prize for a work from which pre-publication extracts had already appeared in the review and goes on to justify the choice of the Goncourt Academy against the hostile reactions it had raised.

. . . The daily press, too often ruled by preoccupations that are alien to literature, has, to a man, risen up against the choice of the Goncourt Academy, which it has criticized for having favoured, contrary to tradition, an author who is no longer very young. Without wishing to discuss the respective merits of M. Marcel Proust's rivals, among whom several were undoubtedly talented and who will see their work duly appreciated here as favourably as possible, we may surely be allowed to say that a writer's youth must not be calculated exclusively according to his age.

Between the young man who skilfully assimilates an already exhausted formula and succeeds in giving it an ephemeral veneer of novelty, and the writer who only sets to work late in life, driven on by the sheer need to transcribe the profoundly original, and if one may dare to say, 'unusual' vision that he has of things, and especially of the inner world, – between these, which is the real 'young' man? To settle the question, should we not consider how the future is best served, how literature is least hampered and left most open to renewing itself? In other words, should we not measure the quantity of youth contained in a work, rather than the youth that its author has the good fortune to be endowed with (in itself already pleasure enough and its own reward)? If the Goncourt Academy has proceeded in this spirit to the examination of the works submitted to it, should we not congratulate it rather than condemn it? Should we not be grateful to it for having crowned, instead of the youngest, the most rejuvenating of all the novelists who aspired to claim its approbation?

Indeed, Marcel Proust, so we claim and would wish one day to be able amply to demonstrate, is a writer in the first rank of those who fill us with life. Without perhaps consciously attempting to do so, he gives a new lease of life to all the techniques of the psychological novel, he restructures in a new dimension that study of the human heart in which our natural genius always excelled but which Romanticism had, even among us, enfeebled, weakened and obscured.

The choice of the Goncourt Academy, even if it has displeased some journalists, will certainly be ratified by the coming generation. Can one wish for better proof of its just decision?

39. Rachilde on *Jeunes Filles*
1920

Part of a notice in *Le Mercure de France*, 1 January 1920, pp. 202–3.

Rachilde (1860–1953) – pseudonym of Mme Alfred Vallette – was a reviewer on *Le Mercure de France* which she founded with her husband.

A book that is too long always shows a lack of politeness, but with that said once and for all, a society author writing his journal has the perfect right not to come to a conclusion. . . .

What we have here is not a novel, but a history of a society. Thirty pages are devoted to the description of a dinner, ten to the matching of stoles to an evening dress, and also to describing mental states. All this is strongly redolent of pre-war attitudes; one senses that the author of this book has neither moved forward nor developed and he is not the only guilty party. At least he has the excuse of getting up very late, between five and six in the evening and dreaming the night away in the light of the chandeliers and opalescent lamps of boudoirs. . . .

I look on this book rather as a sumptuous, embroidered wing-chair in which all the preciosity of an invalid, accustomed to the little attentions of his servants, can take its ease, but I do not question its elegance and its lush comfort. . . .

1919–22

B – ON PROUST'S REPUTATION UP TO HIS DEATH

40. Jean de Pierrefeu on Proust's subjectivism
1920

Part of 'Le cas de M. Proust', *Le Journal des débats*, 2 January 1920.

Jean de Pierrefeu (1881–1940) sets aside the ephemeral and fashionable reaction to the Goncourt Prize to attempt an analysis of the origins of Proust's inspiration. He finds Proust's psychological observations to be a token of a sick mind, while his originality relies excessively on Kantian subjectivism at the expense of the common reader's common sense.

. . . It is common knowledge that M. Marcel Proust's work comprises two stout volumes whose unusual thickness is a source of curiosity. Though in preparation over a long period of years, they have only recently been made available to the public. One is entitled *Du côté de chez Swann* and the other *A l'ombre des jeunes filles en fleurs*.

Certainly M. Proust is no man of letters. His silence and his horror of publicity provide us with ample assurance of that. He is even less of one to go by the way he has conceived his work. Much more than entertaining the intention of being an author, it seems he has restricted himself in the first instance to embroidering on his own life. For many people, everyday tasks, their situation and their objectives in life obscure the actual fact of existence. For most people, it is at the moment of death that they perceive they have lived. M. Proust, wiser and more contemplative in temperament seems to have devoted the greatest part of his time to watching himself in the process of living. This, in my view, is not a sign of egotism but actually a faculty of inner communion that it would be worthwhile everyone mastering. . . . I imagine him turned in on himself, scrutinizing the scenes that are played out on the stage of his inner theatre, distinguishing the nuances of feeling, the fluctuatons of light and shade suggested to him by a thought or a word and that endless shower of images and impressions whose charm has been revealed to us by M. Bergson.

It is an intoxicating pleasure that enlightened moralists, casuists and catholic confessors, who are the world's first psychologists, have taken care, long before M. Bergson, to warn us against. If pushed too far, the searching of one's conscience, normally so beneficial, turns into a painful obsession. . . .

I am afraid that M. Proust may have arrived all too soon at that stage where self-examination becomes morbid, and this hyperacuity of inner vision has, perhaps, become the origin of his malaise.

How did he get the idea of turning us into the spectators of those secret pleasures that those who cherish their privacy jealously keep to themselves out of sheer refinement of sensual delight? It is beyond me. This genesis of his work that I am attempting to establish is, of course, pure speculation. Has he actually been privy to that fatal moment when we flip over the hour-glass so as to relive in memory a life we believe has become humdrum? Because of his wish to give greater duration to this resurrection of a lost past, was there a decision to fix it permanently on paper? Possibly. People who know Marcel Proust have told me strange things about him. Locked all day in his room, most often abed with all lights blazing, he passionately strives, with closed eyes, to dig out of his memory the fleeting instants that have lodged there, even unbeknown to him. During one of his visits, a friend of Marcel Proust's was shown directly into the bedroom which had briefly been vacated. Coming from outside, the visitor was struck by the musty smell and the stuffy atmosphere. 'Will you open the window?' he said to the valet, 'this bedroom is unhealthy.' 'Oh, no, Monsieur,' replied the servant in respectful tones, 'it is excellent for Monsieur's thoughts'. . . .

What M. Marcel Proust will therefore give us, having no other subject but his own life, that of his parents and the people they met, will be an account of the events he has been involved in and, in so doing, he will give us a precise picture, in both psychological and visual terms, of a family and a certain French society after 1870, in so far as each has been reflected in the consciousness of a child, then a young man and later no doubt a man of mature years.

The memoirs of Saint-Simon have been mentioned in connection with his work; others will compare it with the Journal of the Goncourt Brothers and they will be equally in the right. It is, in fact, comparable to all the memoirs in which people have undertaken to bare themselves to us while writing about others. But it also differs profoundly from that kind of work by a special tone of voice that situates it in our day.

As Schopenhauer put it: 'The world is my idea.'

This thought is nothing short of a complete and utter acceptance of the black magic old Kant devised to our cost and which has turned our whole notion of existence upside down: the external world only exists as a function of us, ourselves; what we call objective is a creation of our self: it is impossible for us to escape from this self to grasp reality. M. Marcel Proust seems profoundly influenced by the truth of Kant's words. He has accepted living in this special atmosphere with the same ease as thinking and sleeping in an airless room. So much so, that in his desire to write the story of his life, it is from inside that he will examine it in order to be sure he has not allowed himself to be influenced by a spirit of false objectivity.

In this respect he differs from the majority of people, because for all that Kant and Schopenhauer have insinuated their poison, the common run of mortals has not ceased to continue to believe firmly in the existence of the exterior world and to consider it as a reality it wanted to conquer and enjoy. We live, perhaps, by a convention, but it is universally taken over and called into question only by philosophers and intellectuals.

And of course, the world that literary people have striven to reproduce has always been the world of common sense. . . .

M. Proust's originality resides in the fact that he has run away from the vision of common sense and taken refuge in pure subjective contemplation. The whole perspective of life is changed by it, as are its lighting and atmosphere. He transports us into another world that is reminiscent of the world of phantoms. And it is obvious that this world quite resembles the one we live in, but rather in the way my reflection in the mirror resembles my true self.

[Rejects the claim that Proust's work should be seen as objectively scientific and reasserts the view that what he has created is a psychological study that should, if anything, pay more heed to the demands of literary form.]

. . . It is a kind of very detailed, very informed psychological enquiry, a summing up of the latest discoveries in modern psychiatry. . . . As he pursues his enquiry he draws a gallery of portraits, scenes from the life of the period and states of mind that, we must admit, have their interesting side. But how much we would really have liked M. Proust to have taken the trouble to marshal such valuable material according to the principles of the art of literature

135

which requires some attempt at organization, a certain over-all view and an arrangement better suited to please both our minds and the laws of beauty. . . .

41. Fernand Vandérem on the Goncourt Prize
1920

Part of a notice on *Jeunes Filles*, *La Revue de Paris*, 15 January 1920; reprinted in *Le Miroir des lettres*, Paris, Flammarion, 1921, pp. 217–25.

Fernand Vandérem (1864–1939) was literary critic of numerous well-known reviews and newspapers, including *La Revue de Paris* and, from 1921, *La Revue de France*. He presents a spirited rebuttal of Proust's treatment over the Goncourt prize in 1919.

Except for a few journals, M. Marcel Proust has had a frankly bad – and it must also be said – frankly unjust press for his Goncourt prize.

Had the Goncourt committee given their award in the case of his book to one of your run-of-the-mill, jejune works such as are selected on occasion by the academy's caprice or back-stage scheming, there could not have been a worse outcry. From every point of the literary compass, twenty to thirty slating notices have rained down on *A l'ombre des jeunes filles en fleurs*. It was declared to be boring, unreadable and written in gobbledygook. The fact that M. Proust was fifty was held against him. His reclusive life-style was held against him. His money was held against him. In short, a series of virulent caricatures, out of which emerged the picture of a superannuated bore with no style, art or talent and without even the excuse of being stony broke.

Whatever the case, allow me to point out that what we had here, in the first instance, was a nasty literary hatchet job. When a writer not only does not write simply with an eye to success, but, like M. Proust, writes almost with the opposite in mind, concerned only for the expression of his thought, piling up between his readers and himself all the obstacles of subject, psychology and style of writing, all guaranteed to repel any favourable response – such an author, even if he is mistaken, has the right to a certain respect.

Secondly, it was too easy a job. For M. Proust's defects are not like those secret failings or those subcutaneous blemishes that can be hidden either by the stratagem of smooth talk or the cosmetic effects of style. No exceptional literary acumen is needed to uncover them, no extra-strong magnifying glass, no ultra-powerful microscope. Far from it, they leap out at you from his first page. They show up with the brightness of a weft of light colours in a piece of dark cloth. They are, as it were, one of the essences of M. Proust's talent and one has the impression that should the author dispense with them he would lose half of his resources. There was not, therefore, as much distinction as all that in decrying such obvious defects with such commotion – defects so openly flaunted that their very display forestalled detractors in advance.

But even allowing that one might take delight, according to the ancient custom, in mocking the triumphant hero, it was still only right, in all justice, not to deny his qualities and particularly not to make a travesty of his defects.

When *A l'ombre des jeunes filles en fleurs* appeared last July, I intimated these defects with a sincerity that was perhaps not to everyone's taste but that I believed to be my duty. Diffuse, disorganized, virtually formless, lingering over details, getting lost in intertwining secondary episodes, written in the most contorted language and in a style overloaded with qualifying clauses – one could just go on and on in this vein. But the misunderstanding, if not the malice, begins when M. Proust is accused of boring us, when all the comedy and emotions, which playfully alternate in these difficult pages, is ignored or not mentioned, when the reader does not see, or pretends not to see, on the other side of this barbed wire, the life force and the rising sap, the strong growth of leafy branches and the colours of so many lovely roses.

With all these obligatory reservations behind me, my conclusion, in fact, was that *A l'ombre des jeunes filles en fleurs* constituted, to my way of thinking, one of the most enthralling, indeed one of the most important, works that recent fiction has produced. . . .

42. Jacques Rivière on Proust as analyst

1920

Part of 'Marcel Proust et la tradition classique', *La Nouvelle Revue française*, 1 February 1920, pp. 192–200.

Jacques Rivière, following his defence of Proust over the Goncourt Prize (No. 38), argues here for Proust's connections with tradition, as opposed to being modern and revolutionary at all costs. He claims that Proust's uniqueness is in his analytical powers, which are his special continuation of and improvement on the tradition of Stendhal and take him back to the rigorous character analysis of Racine. Among more recent writers, Flaubert and Barrès, for all their individual qualities, lack the insight of Proust and bring too subjective a lyricism to the psychological novel.

. . . The psychological novel is saturated with lyricism; it is no longer a branch of the study of human passions; it is no longer used for drawing character; with very rare exceptions, it is now only thought of as an anthology of 'impressions' on the soul, of 'introspective landscapes'.

At first glance, Proust may seem to have done nothing else but bring this genre to its peak of perfection. Is he not a prodigious 'evoker' of sensations and feelings? What else is he about, if not to bring his whole innermost past alive before the reader's very eyes?

– That may be so; but there is the question of manner. He does not rely on any magic wand to achieve it. He has no intention of making his soul 'rise up' before us 'from the depths of the sea' like a complete island, fully equipped. *A la recherche du temps perdu*: the title spells it out; it implies a certain effort, application, method, enterprise; it denotes a certain distance between the author and the object of his study, a distance that he will have endlessly to traverse by means of memory, reflection, understanding; it supposes a need for knowledge; it announces a discursive victory over the reality being pursued.

And indeed, from the outset, Proust abandons all literary devices that even slightly smack of magic. He deprives himself, even with a certain severity, of music; it is evident that he has no wish to suggest, but to rediscover.

He fastens on to feelings, to characters by close attention to detail;

he does not abdicate any claim to reveal their outlines and shapes; but he knows that that should not, cannot come except in the long term. The first thing is to nibble away at it. He is a gnawing animal: there will be a lot of debris before it becomes clear that it is not like that at all and that these are the basic materials of a vast and magnificent construction.

I cannot say enough how moving I find his renunciation of being emotional, his patience, his diligence, his love of the truth. . . .

He reveals everything from the inside; he has no intention of echoing past Time; he merely tries bit by bit to restore to it its full content. And the same goes in particular for each emotion he has experienced, for each character he recalls. He immediately searches out their nuances, their intimate diversity; it is only by dint of uncovering their individuality that he hopes to summon them back to life. . . .

Try as one may, there is no truly profound description of characters that is not based on a strict and solid understanding of oneself. Before turning one's attention outwards with any chance of success, it is essential that analysis should have bitten deeply inwards. At least, that is the law with us, in France. The shortcoming of Flaubert and all the novelists of his school was to have been able from the start to stand back from themselves. Because their wish was to be immediately and directly objective, they condemned themselves simply to posing *objects* before them, without diversifying them, without illuminating them from the inside.

Proust sees all things, even their outsides, from the angle from which he sees himself. And since he has taken to himself the habit of refraction, his eye straightaway distinguishes and specifies. In this way he manages by never separating any being from its details, always to reveal it to us in all its solidity, as rich within as it is without, amazing and familiar at one and the same time.

Thus it is that he connects with the great classical tradition. What else does Racine do but seek out others within himself? . . . Hermione, Néron, Phèdre, where do they slowly emerge from to engage us if not from the nucleus of feelings they are revealed to us as sharing? This is not, properly speaking, *creation*, but only *invention*, i.e. something *found*, perceived, unravelled, a statement, if one can put it like this, of the consciousness of other people.

Proust takes up this method, but on a grander scale, more slowly, more minutely, and not so dramatically. In everything, he rediscovers the inward path. And not following the Bergsonian method, by meditation and dreams, but on the contrary by a quiet deployment of lucidity and discrimination. . . .

In this way his work is completely opposed to the whole of

Romanticism, which has consisted without let-up of making us believe in things without demonstrating them. Because of his intervention we can expect, as far as our literature is concerned, a massive debunking. It will shortly become impossible to engage the imagination, to touch it directly: the writer will no longer be able to demand that faith in the senses to which an increasingly tyrannical appeal has been made. Explanations will have to be given, cards will have to be put on the table. . . .

In ridding us of the undifferentiated mass of ideas and feelings, Proust liberates us from what is enigmatic and unverifiable. He sets our reason to work again and makes our reflective faculties function once more. Thanks to him, we are released from all that complicity of the senses or mystical communing, which tended to be the only relationship we could be engaged in with a writer. We recover our taste for understanding; our pleasure is once more the pleasure of learning something about ourselves, of feeling ourselves totally elucidated and recognizing ourselves to be more readily explicable than we had thought.

The grand and unpretentious journey through the human heart that the classical writers had begun is once more under way. 'The study of feelings' makes progress again. Our eyes are re-opened to inner truth. Our literature, at one time suffocated by the inexpressible, becomes frankly again what it has always been in essence: a 'discourse on human passions'.

NOTE

All italics are in the text.

43. Maurice Levaillant on the Prix Goncourt
1920

Part of an article on controversies of the day: 'Les Petites
Polémiques: Du côté de chez les Goncourt', *Le Figaro*, 8
February 1920.

Maurice Levaillant (1883–?) comments on Proust's place in
the public's estimation now the dust has begun to settle
following the Prix Goncourt award the previous year.

. . . To an observer of current literary practices, the case of
M. Marcel Proust poses some rather interesting questions. It teaches
us, for instance, that a man of letters who is stubbornly attached to
his art, who refuses to be diverted from it either by politics or
literary coteries and who locks himself away for years in his tower,
even a dark tower and not a gold or ivory one, may well face a poor
reception from his contemporaries when the day comes for him to
unveil his work. . . .
    Secondly . . . the main complaint the public had against him was
his age; he was twenty around 1895. What does it matter? In any
case, is his work not young if it is new? . . .
    Now as to the prejudices and the wrongs in this dying
controversy, should they all be blamed on public opinion?
M. Marcel Proust is perhaps partly responsible. His work is only
charming and delightful for those who have penetrated it. But you
have to open up a certain amount of undergrowth and cut your way
through it before reaching Sleeping Beauty's castle. . . . Besides, his
two novels are not composed in conformity with the usual rules of
logic; though one would not claim that his only allegiance is to the
laws governing the association of ideas, the order they appear in is a
subtle, almost secret one, more in line with the flexible laws briefly
perceived by M. Bergson than with the principles of the great
classical writers. But this was what had to be paid for analyses of this
rigour and strength. M. Marcel Proust does not miss a single detail
in his voyage of exploration, as he takes us with him along the
meandering streams of consciousness and the subconscious. . . . He
calls to mind also those insects with five or ten thousand pairs of
microscopic eyes. . . ; those terrible eyes miss nothing; they do not
spare a speck of mica in a grain of sand. . . .
    M. Marcel Proust is a writer quite unlike any other and public

opinion does not take instantly to those writers who do not go out of their way to flatter it. This is the source of the misunderstanding between them. But the controversy is over. No one now questions the view that M. Marcel Proust is a great and original talent. Whether he has genius as well, only our offspring will discover.

44. Albert Thibaudet on Proust as analyst

1920

Article in the series, 'A letter from France' called 'Marcel Proust and the analytic novel' in the *London Mercury*, May 1920, pp. 111–13.

Albert Thibaudet (1874–1936) brings the French view of the immediately post-Goncourt Proust into focus. He relates him to a tradition of French analytical writers and assesses his wide-ranging style for its originality and its defects. He shrewdly isolates the mixture in Proust's style of the intellectual and the sensual and sees how in Proust style and vision go together: 'Its complexity is only the complexity of the psychology it is exposing.'

Among new French writers the one most in the foreground to-day is M. Marcel Proust. His success recalls somewhat that which greeted, from ever-widening circles of readers, Romain Rolland's *Jean-Christophe* at the time when it was appearing in Péguy's *Cahiers de la Quinzaine*. Marcel Proust has already published four volumes of a work which, like *Jean-Christophe*, will probably run to ten volumes, and will consist of five parts. The first, *Du Côté de Chez Swann*, published some months before the war, was almost unnoticed, and the second, *A l'Ombre des Jeunes Filles en Fleurs*, was recently awarded the Prix Goncourt. The work, in its entirety, is entitled *À la Recherche du Temps Perdu*.

It is one of the deepest, most elaborate, most complex novels that have ever appeared in France. The indifference which the public showed for some years (it is true that they were war years) towards *Du Côté de Chez Swann* was quite natural; it was the result of the extraordinary novelty of that analysis and of that style. Everything which is novel to such a degree must needs pass some time in

142

obscurity in order to give public and even critical taste time to become accustomed to it. But this period of time was reduced to a minimum for Marcel Proust, because behind this novel aspect three elements could be recognized with which the French reader is familiar, three reasons for this book's success – it is a picture of the world, of ordinary life and of society; it is a work of psychological analysis; and its style has remarkable originality and strength. To treat the psychology of men and women of the world in an accurate and brilliant picture of social life seems (since the time of Stendhal and Balzac) to have been one of the fondest ambitions of French novelists. Stendhal, by transposing it into an Italian Court, achieved his masterpiece, *La Chartreuse de Parme*. But Balzac fell heavily in attempting it, and critics may frequently be heard laughing at the society pictures of Bourget and de Maupassant, of Hervieu and Hermant. The novelists have given to their pictures of society either a clumsy or a jaundiced air, have confronted it either, like Bourget, with a naïve admiration which provokes a smile, or, like Hervieu and Hermant, with that rather envious hatred of the professional man of letters who from Rousseau's time onwards has contemplated a world some of whose refinements are forbidden him. It is not astonishing, then, that the title of '*romancier mondain*' has generally been taken in a derogatory sense and makes an author slightly ridiculous.

Marcel Proust, who belongs by birth to the upper middle classes (that *grande bourgeoisie* to which Abel Hermant has devoted a novel, very amusing but singularly narrow, bitter and unjust), and who acknowledges with charming frankness a keen liking for the superior world of the aristocracy, has painted the world like a man who loves the world with as much honest warmth as the Goncourts loved literature or a militarist loves the army. Unlike other novelists, he has drawn it from within with affection and pleasure. His portraits of marchionesses, of rich citizens' wives, of demi-mondaines who become fine ladies, like Madame Swann, of snobs obsessed by the fear of snobbery like the astonishing Legrandin (a Dickens character) give an impression of actuality and move with a lifelike solidity to which we have been unaccustomed since the *Chartreuse de Parme*. And, contrary to that which takes place in the ordinary novels, Marcel Proust's worldlings are never overtaken in a dramatic adventure or a passionate tragedy. Like the characters of Gyp,[1] they live their ordinary lives simply, lives most commonplace and most devoid of incident: and this equable life suffices to interest us. In reading Marcel Proust we think of that novel without a plot which the *naturalistes* dreamed of and attempted to write. 'Huysmans,' says Rémy de Gourmont, 'reflected for a long time on a book which would have been planned as follows: A gentleman leaves his house to go to his office, sees that his shoes have not been cleaned, gives them to a shoeblack, thinks about his business affairs during the performance, and then continues his way. The problem was to expand that to three hundred pages. Doubtless it is this same difficulty which hindered. M. Th— in the production of a comedy which he had projected for more than ten years. It seems it was extremely amusing. I have not had the pleasure of hearing it, but I know the plot of it, which is short. A shopkeeper goes one Sunday to his country house to bottle some wine. Incidents of the proceedings. His return to Paris. That's all.' The incidents of ordinary life from which Marcel Proust has drawn the thousand pages of his first four volumes are not more complicated. And it is a masterpiece, a masterpiece of intricacy, too, because the complication which is not in its events is in the method of the narrator and in the characterisation of his figures. Besides, the *Vin en Bouteilles* of M. Thyébaut would perhaps also have been a masterpiece if M. Thyébaut had had genius. And all humanity might have been contained within his shopkeeper's day.

But for the reader of Marcel Proust the pleasure of seeing genuine and living worldlings is only a superficial one. *À la Recherche du Temps Perdu* arrests and holds our attention chiefly by reason of the skill and depth of its psychological analysis.

The origin of the *Recherche du Temps Perdu* is curious. It is the work of a mind tempered by the moral solitude, the emptiness and the longings of a protracted illness. During this illness he employed himself in recalling, thoroughly examining, and setting in order the recollections of his past life. Like humanity in the land of its Egyptian or Greek past, he set himself to delve in his own past, in his 'lost time', which became also recovered time. He withdrew from it in order to carve anew minutely and patiently the figures of the people whom he had known. He has in fact written memoirs, but memoirs of a new kind – memoirs in which the characters and events of the past are not transferred to and called up in the past, but are, on the contrary, inspired and transformed by the present; memoirs which are a true and living memory, where the emphasis is not on the figures of bygone days, but on the very act of remembrance. It is not the past life of a man which we see in reading the book, but the man himself who is remembering it. The originality of Marcel Proust lies in the fact that he has, in spite of that entirely personal perspective which seems as if it ought entirely to shut him up in himself, discovered a means of creating so many characters as vivid as or even more vivid than those of the objective novelists, the novelists among whom, as Tourguenev said, the umbilical cord uniting them to their characters has been cut.

And, moreover, we are present at a curious and paradoxical spectacle, this psychology always concentrated upon itself and busied in rummaging in its past. Among the crowd of convincing characters whom he puts on his stage there is one more convincing and more complete, analysed at greater length and more fondly depicted than the others: Swann, in whom one recognises a man of the world, rather a celebrity, of old days. And this portrait recalls and almost equals, in its minuteness and intimacy, Stendhal's Sanseverina or Meredith's Willoughby: from the point of view of development it has something in common with both. But there is another portrait which one would have expected to see more complete even than that of Swann: it is that of the author, the narrator himself.

This psychologist who studies others only in the reflection which they shed on him ought, it seems, to have depicted his own life and his own originality with more life and pungency than those of others. Now there is nothing of that. He does not appear so far (we have not yet got half his work) except in vague touches. Nowhere does he stand out in relief like the other characters. He talks copiously about himself and with a prodigious richness of analysis. We see in him a child, nervous, sensitive, intelligent, self-centred. And the analyses of himself, which are sometimes masterpieces, relate much more often to mankind in general than to the author personally. It seems pretty clear that if he had bent his explorations in another direction he could have made himself live as Montaigne does in the *Essays*. He has preferred to observe others, to turn his lamp upon others, leaving the observer standing in shadow.

It is obvious that a work of psychological analysis like this has a long pedigree in French literature and even links with certain English figures. Men looking for a comparison to Marcel Proust have again and again brought up the three names of Montaigne, Saint-Simon, and Meredith. He reminds one of Montaigne by the originality, the independence, the discursiveness of his study of the inner world; he recalls Saint-Simon by the living force of his portraits and the tortuous abundance of his style; he resembles Meredith in the minuteness of an analysis which is not hurried and is not meant for hurried readers, and in his gift for creating, not by a vigorous spurt like Balzac, but by the slow accumulation of details, figures which, when the book has been shut, dwell in the memory with a fixed individuality. I think of that Egyptian statue in the Cairo Museum, which is made of copper plates patiently ajdusted with rivets, but which one nevertheless remembers as a fine image of a king, powerfully and simply designed.

It does not take long for lettered Frenchmen to tire of a work which is without style. Ten years ago Marcel Proust's present success was enjoyed by *Jean-Christophe*. If *Jean-Christophe*, which is still much admired abroad, has in France fallen quickly and a little unjustly into contempt, it is because Romain Rolland's greatest weakness lay in his style. Is Marcel Proust's style on the level of his feeling for life and his analytical powers? That style is widely discussed. Those who only like and understand the academic phrase find it barbarous and shapeless. Those interminable sentences, full to bursting, do not appeal to everybody. Moreover, Proust's prose lacks cadence, is difficult to read aloud, except when the author (who is marvellously supple) is seized by the whim of deliberately making a few fine classical phrases, which he can always do without effort. Effort is conspicuously absent everywhere in this style. Its complexity is only the complexity of the psychology which it is exposing, of the past which it evokes, of the lost time which it recovers. And this lack of effort is also manifested in countless pieces of carelessness, as if the author had disdained to go over his work again and even to correct his proofs for himself.

Notwithstanding all this, Marcel Proust seems to be one of the most astonishing stylistic creators of our time. Nobody has more, or more ingenious, images. To attain his ends, to seize the most delicate ramifications of sentiment and idea, images, words, turns of phrase come to him in such swarms that sentence and page give an impression of exuberant fecundity which the author might certainly have checked and regulated, but which subjugates one by its opulence like a page of Montaigne or Saint-Simon. With him certain strong qualities of sixteenth-century prose reappear in the prose of to-day. And above all the range of his keyboard is prodigious. He has an amazing repertory of ideas, sensations, colours, scents, savours. His style is at once very intellectual and very sensual. The fairies at its christening overwhelmed it with all the gifts; but perhaps the wicked fairy who came at the last moment, she who had not been invited, added the qualification that it should not be able to choose between those gifts, that it should be a style embarrassed by its riches, its overfull hands. Still, that is a pleasing defect.

NOTE

1 Gyp (1850–1932), pseudonym, as brief as her real name was long, of Marie-Antoinette de Riquetti de Mirabeau. Her light entertainments based on society life, particularly those published in the 1880s, were widely appreciated for their wit and satire.

45. Pierre Lasserre on *Jeunes Filles en fleurs*
1920

Article in *La Revue universelle*, 1 July 1920, vol. 2, pp. 19–32.

Pierre Lasserre (1867–1930) was a literary critic (for a time on *L'Action française*) and author of studies on Claudel, Jammes, and Péguy. In the wake of the Prix Goncourt, awarded to Proust in the previous year, he wrote this hostile essay on Proust's style. Reflecting a general trend, he saw it as combining the faults of introversion and preciosity.

. . . Without any shadow of doubt, this lost time we go in search of, and these trees which are young ladies in whose shade a dreamy aesthete has seated himself to indulge in his precious mental processes, might well deserve to be included in worthy histories of literature after all the examples of preciosity, mannerism, euphuism, affectation, pseudo-elegance and insipidity given classic status by the author of *Les Femmes savantes*.

For my part, I would have been very surprised that a writer so little inspired in the choice of a sign to advertise his work could have shown any inspiration in the work itself. Indeed, he has shown none. To be fair, he has, but only to a very small extent. The curious thing, however, is the considerable difference between what this work brings us and what the sign that graces it might herald. One might have expected to see the author agreeably stringing together, I won't say poetic ideas, but sweet thoughts, gallant talk, ironies, flowery cadenzas and madrigals capable of holding their own, and even to advantage against that multitude of people who, in literary matters, have more of a taste for roses on wallpaper than for the real thing. This is not at all what we find. M. Proust is the most deceptive of men. He stimulates our minds to hope for sweet pleasures. And what does he in reality provide? Hard mental exercises. Who would think that the book that resembles *A l'ombre des jeunes filles en fleurs* most is Spinoza's *Ethics*? Who would think that what has sprouted in this shade would be a veritable garden of arguments, inductive reasoning, definitions, analyses, theorems, corollaries and learned commentaries that are more dense, compact, interlocking and entangled one with another than anything to be seen in the already formidable text of Spinoza?

It is true that Spinoza and Proust deal with very different subjects.

The former tells us about the existence and attributes of God, about the general order of the universe, about the relationship of body and soul, about the nature of good and evil and man's ultimate purpose. As for M. Proust's favourite topics some insight will be gained from the following: the weather and the impressions M. Proust has had about it, especially when the weather was not out of the ordinary; the people he has met on his walks and his thoughts about them, especially when these are people he does not know; the ritual acts that make up the day of elegant young men at their sea-bathing and the ideas he receives when he executes them, notably when putting on his evening clothes . . . and the style of Baron de Charlus' trousers and the sober and calculated harmony with which it matches his socks. . . . M. Proust applies to the question of M. de Charlus' trousers a technique of dialectical analysis, of ideological argumentation and ex cathedra didacticism compared with which the geometric apparatus of Spinoza's exposition would almost give the effect of a superficial impressionism. . . . You would think that M. Proust is Spinoza in playful Marivaux mood and that M. Proust's literary creation is the scholasticism of sophisticated banter:

A line of dark green in the cloth of the trousers matched the stripes of the socks with a refinement that revealed the vicacity of a taste that was subdued everywhere else and to which this sole concession had been made on sufferance, while a red spot on the tie was barely visible, like a liberty you dare not take.[1]

If a real professor is someone who eschews superficiality in favour of argument and giving pertinent explanations of things, we can call M. Proust a professor of elegance. Nobody could speak about clothes in a more conscientiously deductive manner while keeping any trivial preoccupation about superficiality at bay. . . .

Nothing is more characteristic . . . than his comparisons. Of all stylistic effects this is the dearest to him. It is, indeed, something he never spares us. I would be really surprised if anyone could quote me even fifteen lines in his whole output which did not contain a comparison developed in all its detail and wrung out, so to speak, to the last drop. Judging by him, it is his cast of thought:

And I rather pitied all the people at dinner because I felt that for them the round tables were not planets and that they had not practised that dissection of things that rids us of their habitual appearance and allows us to perceive analogies.[2]

All good authors teach us that the first quality of a comparison is to be precise and natural. M. Proust goes looking for his on the moon; in addition, his comparisons are quite amazed to find themselves where he puts them:

These girls could not bear to see an obstacle without playing at jumping over it, at a run or feet together, because they were all exuberant and filled with that youthful energy that so calls out to be used up that, even when you are feeling low or ill, urged on more by the demands of one's age than the mood of the day, you cannot let a chance to jump or slide go by without going at it full tilt, interrupting your sauntering walk and filling it out – just like Chopin in his most plangent phrases – with elegant meanderings that mingle capriciousness with virtuosity.[3]

Now would you really have expected to meet Chopin in all that? And how overdone it all is! Here's something even better:

I rang for the lift-boy who was not silent this time when I stood beside him going up in the lift, as if in a moving rib cage sliding along an upright spine.[4]

The comparison is brilliant if we accept: (a) that there are people whose backbones are much longer than their rib cages and that their rib cages take advantage of the fact to go up and down the vertebrae and (b) that breathing movements are sometimes prepared to stop for the sole purpose of allowing the chest wall to become as rigid as a lift. . . .

[Lasserre further condemns what he considers to be a contorted style but sees Proust's strength in his observation of behaviour.]

Behaviour is M. Proust's real domain, behaviour considered not as an object of satire or as a theme for whimsical variations and amusing paradoxes, but as a subject for philosophical study and thorough observation. Lightness, facility of expression and grace are not this writer's gifts. He does not catch things on the wing. He lacks the art of understatement. Meticulous attention to detail, methodical meditation and a generalizing approach are his characteristics. He has a need to justify himself, to make a show of the detail and the method of his investigations. . . . M. Proust has an ancestor in our literature whose name may lack lustre but whose work is eminently worthwhile: I am referring to the author of *Considérations sur les moeurs*, Duclos.[5] The turmoil in present-day society and the manoeuvrings from class to class that happen with a speed that we quiet readers and students find hard to keep up with, offer a very interesting field of study for a new Duclos. And M. Proust would give us more pleasure in bringing us solid news of that world, soundly commented on, even if a little heavy-handed, than when he goes describing the cornflowers trippingly pursuing his carriage.

There is a famous surgeon in his family who could be recommended to him as an example.[6] When Professor Proust used to open his cases and put his formidable steel instruments on the theatre table, he did not do so in order to operate on heat-bumps or to trepan a patient suffering from no more than some hair condition. Unless he thought of splitting the hairs. But what a misuse of a surgeon's skills that would have been!

NOTES

1 Pléiade I, p. 753.
2 Pléiade I, p. 811.
3 Pléiade I, p. 791.
4 Pléiade I, p. 799.
5 Charles Pinot Duclos (1704–72), moralist and historian.
6 His father, Professor Adrien Proust.

46. M. C. Marx on new trends in the novel
1920

Part of 'Un rénovateur du roman', *La Revue mondiale*, 1 October 1920, pp. 220–5.

M. C. Marx gives an enthusiastic assessment of Proust and attempts to place him in relation to recent changes of approach to fiction.

To approach a book by M. Marcel Proust critically is a difficult ordeal. The dissecting knife slides over this fine, muscular, strong and supple tissue without cutting into it. Separating out its elements seems an impossible task. The work is a solid block and holds together. If the words *form* and *content* could ever have been capable of being opposed one to the other, it is impossible to do so here. Trained to follow the practices of grammar to the point of exhaustion, determined to abandon all coquetry, never was a style more subservient to ideas. Nor do the images it conveys seek an individual glory, rather they come happily and modestly into existence to render a thought with precision. It is not possible to analyse the structure of this art, born as it is directly from life itself; it mocks the usual means of analysis, which is what earned it the ill humour of some judges of literature. What does it matter! Would not its powerful unity have been sufficient refutation, if certain descriptions and episodes had not been enough to prove clearly that Proust is able to *write and compose*, when he wishes to, in the most classic sense of the word? An account of the events of *A la recherche du temps perdu*? This, too, is equally impossible! You would need to re-write it in its entirety. You have to say everything – or else nothing at all; there is no single story or rather there are thousands. . . .

[Discusses Proust's characters.]

Laden with years and honour, the Novel, so it seems, is reaching in our day the point of its obsolescence. Writers and readers today seem to want to avoid its hackneyed rules and its jejune adventures: too often disguised as what it is not, it is no more than the tiresome illustration of some philosophical or emotional argument. Narrative techniques intended to excite our curiosity or our feelings, certain expressions capable of awakening anxiety or melancholy, the story pure and simple written for our amusement – hasn't all that since France and Régnier, fallen into the hands of second-rate writers or newspaper serials? The war killed off the promise of an adorable tale, Alain Fournier's *Le Grand Meaulnes*. Perhaps – and they are exceptions – only Colette delights us with the saga of her own life and Giraudoux with his dazzling improvisations. But here comes Proust with a work of some considerable length, structured and built on new foundations. No *subject* in the traditional meaning of the word: the subject, or rather the centre, the unity of the action, is himself. Not the lyrical 'I' and even less the odious personal 'I' fashionable in a certain literary style, but a generalized 'I', an 'I' like a prism on which the light of the world converges and plays. . . .

Others drew our tears by the powerful story of man's worst sufferings. Marcel Proust does not raise his voice yet he affects us. His sensibility, at one and the same time so melancholy and so happy, finds its material in the very impressions of everyday existence. Important life-shattering events may be relegated to the second rank. Some little unimportant fact, on the other hand – an unexpected meeting, a tune, a lamp shining behind closed shutters –

re-echoes powerfully in our deepest recesses. Our inner life is well acquainted with these familiar adaptations which make up another side of reality. The inner life – some call it the subconscious or the underground galleries of the soul – that is what constitutes this writer's field, or better still, his observation post. That's where he uncovers, slumbering in the dark, thousands of things that no one else had dragged out into the light. . . .

NOTE

All italics in the text.

47. Mauriac on the renewal of the novel

1921

Part of 'L'Art de Marcel Proust', *La Revue hebdomadaire*, 26 February 1921, pp. 373–6.

François Mauriac (1885–1970) examines Proust's work from the point of view of a novelist.

M. Marcel Proust's well-known works run the obvious risk, by their mere appearance, of driving away timid or lazy readers. These dense texts were not the custom in France. From the outset we are aware that this author is out to change our ways; and, in my view, the truth is that M. Marcel Proust has hardly done less than renew a genre of literature: the novel. . . .

For this resurrection of Lost Time, M. Marcel Proust has invented the tool he needed. To say he has renewed the novel, is also to say he has renewed style. . . .

Actually, if we remain persuaded that of all contemporary works M. Marcel Proust's have the strongest chances of survival, it is because they possess to an eminent degree a classical character. The more he accumulates particular and peculiar features, the more he defies the danger of getting lost in detail, and the more his pictures take on a universal meaning. That surely is the sign of a classical work. These thousands of notes that have been accumulated, and themselves selected from among thousands, by this patient visionary, present us with the Truth, which is the ultimate quest of Art. Consequently, let there be no question of immorality where this work is concerned: an examination of conscience is the foundation of any moral life, and Proust directs an awesome light deep into our secret thoughts. His art is as disinterested as the sun: everything is dragged out from the shadows, even those things that, before he came, no one dared mention. Yet Proust avoids harshness and cruelty by some kind of warm and melancholy sympathy informing a work that is, by the way, so lucid: the 'Summa' of contemporary sensibility, in our view; but by the same token the Summa also of our absurdities and our vices. . . .

48. Gide on the riches of Proust's work
1921

Part of 'Billet à Angèle', *La Nouvelle Revue française*, 1 May 1921, pp. 586–91.

André Gide (1869–1951), totally converted to *La Recherche*, writes in praise of Proust in one of a series of critical essays in letter form.

. . . When we read Proust, we begin suddenly to perceive detail where until then all that confronted us was a solid mass. He is, you will say, what we would call: an analyst. No; your analyst distinguishes things with effort; he gives explanations and takes pains: Proust's feelings in this respect are quite natural. Proust is someone whose observation is infinitely more subtle and more attentive than our own, and who shares this observation with us the whole time we spend reading him. And as the things he observes (which he does so spontaneously that he never gives the impression of observing) are the most natural in the world, it constantly seems to us, as we read him, that it is into ourselves that he is allowing us to look; through him our essential confusion emerges from chaos into full consciousness; and since the most varied feelings exist in each one of us in embryonic state, most often unknown to us and sometimes awaiting only an example or a designation, I was about to say, a denunciation to assert themselves, we imagine, thanks to Proust, that we have ourselves experienced this detail, we recognize it, adopt it, whereas it is our own past that is being enriched by this wealth of observation. Proust's books act like some powerful developer on the somewhat misty photographic plates that make up our memories, and on which suddenly reappear the face, the forgotten smile and the very emotions that the disintegration of the latter was dragging down with them into oblivion.

I do not know what is more worthy of admiration, whether it is that superacuity of the inner eye or the prestigious art which seizes upon that detail and offers it up to us nothing less than transfigured with freshness and life. Proust's style of writing (to use a word that the Goncourt brothers had made me loathe but no longer annoys me when I think of Proust) is the most *artistic* I know.[1] He never seems to be hampered by it. If, to give form to the ineffable, the word fails him, he has recourse to an image; he has at his disposal a whole treasury of analogies, equivalences and such exact and exquisite comparisons that at times you reach the point of questioning which one provides the other with the most life, brilliance and fun, and whether the feeling is helped by the image, or whether this fleeting image was only awaiting the feeling to attach itself to it. I am trying to find the defect in this style, and I cannot. I am trying to find its dominant characteristics, and I cannot find them either; he does not have this quality or that: he possesses them all (now this may not be solely praise) not one after another, but all at once; so disconcerting is his suppleness that any other style compared with his appears stiff, colourless, imprecise, perfunctory and lifeless. Should I admit it? every time I find myself bathing in this lake of delights, I do not even dare, for a good number of days afterwards, to take up my pen, unwilling to admit – as happens during the whole period that a masterpiece exercises its hold over us – that there are other ways of producing good writing, no longer seeing, in what you call the 'purity' of my style, anything but poverty.

You have told me that the length of Proust's sentences often wears you out. But just wait for me to come back and I will read those endless sentences aloud for you: immediately everything just falls into place! the different levels simply take their places rank upon rank! the landscape of his thought just goes on deepening! I can imagine a page of *Guermantes* printed like Mallarmé's 'Coup de dés'; my voice makes the key-words stand out; in my own way, I orchestrate the parenthetical clauses, I shade them in, holding back or pushing forward the rate of my delivery; and I can prove to you that there is nothing superfluous in that sentence, that every word was necessary to keep the various levels separate and allow its complexity to blossom forth. Detailed though Proust may be, I never find him prolix; copious though he may be, I never find him diffuse.

'Minutely detailed' but 'not finicky', as Louis Martin-Chauffier judiciously put it.

Proust clarifies in exemplary fashion for me what Jacques Rivière understood by the word 'global', which he used to denounce the lazy-mindedness of those who are content to grab by the armful feelings which are so well bound together by custom that the bundle appears to us to be deceptively homogeneous. Proust, on the other hand, carefully unties each bunch and teases out the whole tangle. He is not even satisfied until he can show us, along with the flower, the stem as well, and even the delicate hairs of the root-system. What curious books! You enter them as if you were going into a magic forest; from the very first pages, you lose your way, and are delighted to do so; soon you no longer know where you came in or what distance you are from the forest edge; at times it seems you are marching ahead without moving forward, and at times that you move forward without taking a step; you look at everything as you pass; you do not know where you are, where you are going, and:

Suddenly my father would stop us and ask my mother: 'Where are we?' Tired from the walk, but proud of him, she would lovingly confess she had simply no idea. He used to shrug his shoulders and laugh. Then, as if he had pulled it out of his coat pocket along with his key, he would point out the little back-gate to our garden, there in front of us, which together with the corner of the rue du Saint-Esprit had decided to wait for us at the end of these unfamiliar paths. My mother used to say to him, full of admiration: 'You are extraordinary!'[2]

My dear Proust, you are extraordinary! The impression may be that you only speak to us about yourself, but your books are as full of people as the whole *Comédie humaine*; your narrative is not a novel, you do not set up or unravel any plot, and yet I do not know of any that is followed with more intense interest; you only present your characters incidentally and, one might say, haphazardly, but we soon know them as deeply as Cousin Pons, Eugénie Grandet or Vautrin. The impression given is that your books are not 'composed' and that you spread your profusion at random; but, though I await your future books to decide the matter, I suspect that already all the elements are deployed in them according to a hidden plan. . . . And as you go on your way, you find the means to talk about everything, mingling with the apparent diffuseness of memory reflections which are so judicious and new that I would wish to see, as an appendix to your work, a sort of index allowing easy retrieval of those remarks of yours on sleep and sleeplessness, on illness, on music, drama and the technique of actors – an index that would already be a thick one but an index where I think almost all the words of our language would have to appear, once all the volumes you still have for us have been published.

If I now try to find what I admire most in this work, I think it is its gratuitousness. I do not know of any that is more useless or that tries less to prove anything. – I know this is the aim of all works of art and that each finds its justification in its own beauty. But, and this is its essence, the elements that constitute it all make their contribution, and though the whole itself is useless, nothing appears in it, or ought to appear in it which is not useful to the whole, besides we know that all that is not relevant is detrimental to it. – In *La Recherche du temps perdu*, this subordination is so hidden that it seems that each page in turn finds its perfect end in itself. Hence that extremely slow pace, that non-desire to go faster, that continuous satisfaction. I am only aware of a similar nonchalance in Montaigne, and that is no doubt why I can only compare the pleasure I get from reading a book by Proust to what I get from the *Essays*. They are leisurely and time-demanding works. I do not only mean that the author, when he produced them, had to feel his mind was perfectly independent of the passage of time, but that they demand an exactly similar detachment from the reader. They simultaneously demand and obtain it; that is the most real benefit they confer. You will object that the peculiarity of art and philosophy is precisely to escape from the demands of time; but Proust's book is distinctive in that it takes every instant into account; it could be said to have the very passage of time as its subject matter. Though cut off from life, it does not turn away from life; brooding over it, it contemplates it, or rather it contemplates life's reflection in itself. The more anxious the image, the calmer the mirror, the more contemplative the gaze.

It is strange that such books come at a moment when events triumph everywhere over ideas, when time is short, when action mocks thought, when contemplation no longer seems possible or allowed, when, not properly recovered from the war, we have no longer any consideration except for what can be useful, for what can serve. And suddenly, Proust's work, so disinterested, so gratuitous, appears to us to be more profitable and more helpful than so many works whose usefulness alone is their justification.

NOTES

1 In italics in the text. Proust provides a parody of the Goncourts' 'écriture artiste' in *Le Temps retrouvé*, Pléiade III, pp. 709 ff.
2 Pléiade I, p. 115.

49. Paul Souday on *Guermantes* and *SG I*
1921

Part of a notice in *Le Temps*, 12 May 1921.

Souday's views are astringent. He is sarcastic about the complexities of Proust's sentences and challenges Gide's enthusiastic appraisal in his 'Billet à Angèle' (No. 48).

M. Marcel Proust tirelessly pursues his *Recherche du temps perdu*: here we have the fourth volume, perhaps not quite as long or as substantial as the preceding ones; it has only 280 pages, though they are those with very long, very wide and very dense pages without paragraphs that are peculiar to NRF publications – each one of them is the equal of two or three of a normal edition – and seem to have been invented, judging by the sheer look of the typography, to give the exact image and physical impression of M. Marcel Proust's manner before you have read a single line. 'A lake of delights' says M. André Gide in his latest 'Billet à Angèle'.

[Gide gets over the difficulty of Proust's long sentences by offering to read them aloud. Souday has no difficulty in finding a tricky example and quotes: 'Est-ce parce que nous ne revivons pas . . . colorations ambiantes.'[1]]

It is as clear as crystal. But it would be clearer still for us all thanks to the skilful enunciation of M. André Gide. . . .

I hasten to add that M. Marcel Proust's written style is not always as convoluted and that the present volume is, in fact, easier to read than the three preceding ones. . . .

NOTE

1 Pléiade II, pp. 397–8.

MARCEL PROUST

50. Roger Allard on morality and realism
1921

Part of a notice on *Le Côté de Guermantes II; Sodome et Gomorrhe I*
La Nouvelle Revue française, 1 September 1921, pp. 355–7.

Roger Allard (1885–1961), poet and reviewer, wrote particularly for *La Nouvelle Revue française*. He sees in Proust's new
volumes an author breaking new ground with an impartiality
of vision that rises above his questionable material.

. . . M. Marcel Proust has taken on a bold enterprise that could only
be fully realized at the expense of completely disorientating the
reader and acclimatizing him to an unaccustomed world. And this
implacable guide is also an observer who holds back from being a
moralist, who does not flaunt in favour of vice either the generous
hatred of a d'Aubigné or the adventurous sympathy of a Wilde, an
observer for whom the word 'vice' is after all only a convention of
discourse and who, with a passing smile for all expressions of
beauty, admires or pities without ever condemning, and has a clearsightedness that is more cruel than irony or sarcasm.

Not only has such a subject never been treated in this way, but no
writer can be said to have envisaged it with that very liberty of
outlook that is tempered in M. Proust by a singular tenderness for all
those human instincts that are so touching when they are crushed
and bruised by the constraining harness of politeness. The conjunction of M. de Charlus and the tailor Jupien is described with a
realism that could scarcely be pursued further. . . .

Without prejudice to the rest of the novel, this first chapter on
inverts is a landmark in literary history. Indeed, these pages, so
ardent in their eloquence, so bitter and so noble in their poetry,
break a spell, the aesthetic spell of sexual inversion under which the
arts and literature have remained for so long. . . .

By shining into Sodom and Gomorrah such a clear light,
M. Marcel Proust has destroyed the mystery that surrounded them,
rather like the explorer who really discovered Timbuctoo, not that
he was the first to get there, but because he was the first to come
back and describe what he had seen.

51. Henri de Régnier on *Guermantes II* and *SG I*

1921

Part of a review in *Le Figaro*, 19 September 1921.

Henri de Régnier (1864–1936), poet and novelist, places the emphasis in his notice more on the criticism of manners than on the innovation of the theme of sexual inversion.

. . . The extremely meticulous nature of M. Proust's books, their complex digressions and their substantial prolixity, make it difficult to talk about them in a mere newspaper article; they require a more fully developed review that would allow reference to earlier sections and a kind of overall assessment. Taken on its own, the volume M. Proust has just published is particularly difficult to define, as it consists, instead of a beginning and an end, of an end and a beginning. In it M. Proust concludes his investigations into the Guermantes and starts up those that take place, he tells us, in more scabrous regions whither he is guided by the magnificent and shady M. de Charlus.

M. Marcel Proust has, among other qualities, that of a great portrait painter. In the previous volumes, he prepared his M. de Charlus in minute detail before specifying his revealing feature, and in this one he completes for us his depiction of the aristocratic effigies of the Duc and Duchesse de Guermantes. M. Proust provides, as setting for these portraits, the very milieu in which he has studied them. So it is in their own home that we see Basin and Oriane de Guermantes, at a dinner they are giving and at which M. Proust invites us to be present. This account of a dinner at the Guermantes', with its intrigues and its conversations, and its most detailed detail, with its silences and its allusions, is an astonishing picture of intimate society life in its finely graded colours and nuances. In it the least gesture is noted down with relentless care, the slightest word is recorded with the sound of the voice that uttered it. This is very near the ultimate in the reproduction of life. M. Marcel Proust's realism is to ordinary realism what a chemist's precision balance is to heavy-duty scales for weighing luggage in railway stations.

If the 'Dinner at the Guermantes' 'is a picture that is destined to become famous', I will go so far as to say as much for what could be called 'The death of the grandmother'. It is because there are pages of the most delicate sensitivity and the most acute observation like these that M. Marcel Proust's books may be excused many longueurs and digressions. Besides, in M. Proust's case we have, if we are to enjoy him to the full, to set aside our usual reading habits. His books have neither the dimension nor the composition we are accustomed to find in fictional works. Nor do his sentences follow the customary model. They stretch or contract according to special laws. M. Marcel Proust is an exceptional writer. He is to be judged and admired as such. He has dedicated himself to the 'search for lost time' and if we follow in his footsteps we waste none of our own; on the contrary, exquisite pleasures are our reward. . . .[1]

NOTE

1 Henri de Régnier plays on the two senses of 'temps perdu' – lost/wasted time.

52. Charles Du Bos on the creative impulse in Proust

1921

Part of an essay, dated 1921, reprinted in *Approximations*, Paris, Fayard, 1965, pp. 89–95.

Charles Du Bos (1882–1939), essayist and literary critic, applies his keen critical insight in the first part of the essay, called 'Le courage de l'esprit', to a close reading of the Martinville towers episode in *Swann*. By 1921, as this essay shows, Proust is taken seriously enough, in reference to aesthetics, to be interpreted in closely argued detail and with great intensity. Having quoted at length the Martinville towers episode (Pléiade I, pp. 180–2), Charles Du Bos goes on to stress the importance of the need to convert the exaltation of the experience into a creative act, into words.

At the origin of all spiritual life . . . there is one single, identical source: exaltation. . . .

As long as the exaltation lasts, whoever is fired by it is transported; . . . such a state – a paradise lost and gained by turns – remains for ever our supreme aspiration, because it alone possesses the characteristic of finality: it is the state beyond which the mind can no longer move. As to that indefinable, insidious problem that the mere fact of existence always seems to present to our thoughts, we sense that it is at that moment, and only then, resolved. . . . To maintain and perpetuate that exaltation would be to live there and then in a second reality, – but it would also mean escaping from the very conditions controlling existence, and if, perhaps, exaltation is not completely denied to anyone, surging up as it does at times in brief fleeting moments without anyone being able to appreciate its causes, no one on the other hand manages to be haunted by it day and night without respite. The man of genius cannot claim, any more than the next man, to be able to capture it, or – as we only too often imagine – prolong it by some artificial means; but he does differ from others in so far as he alone knows what value to put on that exaltation: he knows that whatever he does subsequently will only have value in so far as . . . a few drops at least of the elixir will have been caught, which brings us back perfectly naturally to Marcel Proust's writing. . . . It may be that, if the exaltation has established itself in a lyric genius, it then finds its outlet, so to speak, in itself, – stimulating in the poet the outburst of song of which it is the theme. . . ; the lyric poet alone is privileged to give the lie occasionally to the adage of Heraclitus and 'bathe twice in the same stream'. But the opposite procedure is also possible and the mind, after completely opening up to the wave of exaltation, instead of trying to go, once the tide begins to turn, with the current actually examines and scrutinizes with the minutest curiosity everything thrown up on the sand: at that point the state of exaltation is no longer the theme of a song, but rather each element resulting from the examination is submitted to a relentless inquiry; each becomes the point of departure for endless meditations and ruminations, from the depths of which rises at last the clear flame of unadulterated knowledge. This is precisely the procedure with Marcel Proust. . . .

As we see from the texts quoted earlier, the truths that Proust's inward search lead him to bring to the light of day do not, at the outset, present themselves to him as arising from within. They are 'the line of the roof, the light on the stone' which without his being able to understand why seemed 'full, ready to burst open, to yield up what was hidden in them as if under a lid'; he is referring to objects which 'seem to hide behind their outward appearances something that they invite him to come and take – something they seem both to

161

contain and conceal'; and these impressions are always 'linked to an object of no intellectual value and have no relationship with any abstract truth'. For anyone seeking to understand the whole import of Proust's work, this is an essential feature to remember, – at the same time it illuminates to some extent one of the mysteries that deservedly occupy our thoughts and exercise our minds. Intellectual sensitivity, at a certain deep level, has, for all its range of reference, the peculiarity that purely intellectual notions are not of the calibre to measure up to and get the best out of its intricate structure and the richness of its resources. The unavoidable device of conceptual thought and the frequent fragility of the actual thinking are therefore overwhelmed, as it were, by intellectual sensitivity: a material object, on the other hand, which, being external, acts directly on the sense organs, undergoes in return the influence of the persistent and passionate contemplation with which a mind surrounds it: under this scrutiny the material object imperceptibly changes; without losing any of its power over the senses, indeed even intensifying it, it gradually takes upon itself the very spirituality that the mind sends in its direction, drawing it somehow into its veins. But the mind, lost in the contemplation of the object, feeling in its presence that overwhelming humility that all deep admiration is associated with, does not even suspect that it is in part the cause of this transmutation: the metamorphosis it sees before it fascinates it like a secondary state of the object itself, like the apperception of a state of immateriality within matter itself. 'Ready to burst open', will the object finally 'deliver up what is hidden in it as if under a lid'? And the mind in its fixity concentrates its attention more than ever on the point into which more and more of its fundamental substance is directed. Of course, I am not claiming that the mind does not receive as much from the object as it gives: the exchanges operating here are beyond language because they take place at the very extremes of two worlds. What, however, would seem to indicate that the mind plays a dominating role here is the fact that creative activity alone is capable of setting a limit – once and for all – to this absorption. The episode of the Martinville towers is very significant in this respect. If, after writing this page, Proust discovers he is so happy, it is because he feels that writing that page 'completely liberated him from these bell-towers and from what they had hidden behind them'; and what they hid, when all is said and done, – what every object that solicits our attention for any length of time hides – is the appeal that we make through it to our second reality and that, echoed by it, comes back to us with new amplitude, with a new sonority, to which we have no longer any reply and from which we can no longer deliver ourselves except by the very act of creation.

162

53. Jacques Boulenger on Proust's analyses
1921

Extract from *Mais l'art est difficile*, Paris, Plon-Nourrit, 1921, pp. 91–3.

Jacques Boulenger (1879–1944) defends Proust's originality in *Jeunes Filles* at the time of hostile criticism over the Goncourt prize: 'the most independent and most powerfully original writer (along with M. Jean Giraudoux) who has emerged for many a long year' (p. 86). He is among the first to appreciate the importance of intellectual analysis – though he sees it as disproportionate – in Proust's method of work. To be compared, for the balance of instinct and intellect, with Curtius, No. 109.

Pure intelligence, the 'power of understanding', is not a quality a novelist or a poet has to be endowed with to any great degree. . . . M. Marcel Proust's intelligence is remarkable; in particular, he has an extraordinary critical and analytical ability.

The psychological value of the facts he retails is immediately studied, criticized, weighed and sifted with marvellous skill and subtlety. . . .

A rare critical perspicuity and power of analysis – and not only in psychology, but in aesthetics too; I can scarcely recall having read remarks of greater insight than those he has made regarding a picture, a landscape or a musical phrase – these surely are qualities of a scientific order that few novelists have had to the same degree as M. Marcel Proust. . . . Where this 'scientific point of view' of his, which is so different from the aesthetic point of view, shows itself at its best is on examination of his complete indifference to any kind of composition. In fact, M. Proust never thinks that it is necessary to ignore a fact he remembers, provided there is sense in it, or that an explanation, however long or however slight its purpose, can be put aside; he simply cannot be bothered to adjust the length of his analyses to the importance of their subjects, and merely tries to make them as exact and complete as possible. . . . In the same way, he mentions absolutely all the significant events he calls to mind and gives us all the remarks they inspire in him without ever considering their aesthetic value and whether they make for longueurs or digressions, thinking only of their truth and scientific worth. . . .

Obviously, to say that *A la recherche du temps perdu* is not constructed like a work of art, is not to say that this wonderful book is not beautiful. For there are close connections between the beautiful and the true, although they do not exactly 'coincide'. This is why it often turns out that a purely scientific work is beautiful. M. Marcel Proust's novel, incomparable as it is in its details, is beautiful. But taken as a whole, because of its disproportion, it is a monster – but a beautiful one.

54. René Rousseau on Proust's psychology and art

1922

Extracts from 'Marcel Proust et l'esthétique de l'inconscient', *Le Mercure de France*, 15 January 1922, pp. 361–86.

René Rousseau shows in his article that Proust has arrived and is to be taken seriously for his art and ideas and no longer either to be patronized or flattered. Cf. Nos 43, 46, 66.

(a) Proust as analyst of behaviour (pp. 364–7)

. . . Marcel Proust is above all an artist who portrays our souls. He turns his attention, not to the acts that reveal our individual personality, but to the mechanism within. Professional in his approach to analysing his characters, he resembles a clock-maker whose attention moves away from the dial and the conventional representation it gives of time, to turn to the cog-wheels, the weights and the pendulum. Events as such do not interest him; he only sees in them the spring that has the potential to bring the free interaction of our motives into play. Between what we reveal of ourselves and what we hide, it is what we hide that he prefers. If he is dealing with a criminal or a man driven by ambition, he will not bother with the consequences and the episodes following and surrounding the crime and the ambition but, by uncovering the deepest corners of the soul, its fundamental blackness, its weaknesses and fluctuations, he gradually establishes the genesis of the feelings involved in their hidden development. . . .

Marcel Proust has devoted himself to bringing out, from under the labels applied to the motives of human behaviour, and given the confusing names of *avarice, ambition, vanity, jealousy*[1] etc, the preparatory and secret work that accounts for them. He has carried the problem to its ultimate conclusion; working back from the solution, he has revealed its starting point. At the heart of the boisterous and malicious action of his contemporaries, he has found the feverishly active little cinema showing the drama of their desires. . . . Delicately and scrupulously, with a rather special kind of pleasure, he has examined these images under the microscope. And straightaway, on the first examination, he has turned his lens onto the apparatus of lies standing at the threshold of our passions. . . .

Thus the novel shows us in M. Legrandin a man possessed by the demon of snobbery who, amusingly enough, does not miss an opportunity to rail against snobbery and snobs. M. Legrandin is sincere: he is yet another dupe of the seductive sirens and lends flattering colours to the crude vanity that drives him to seek out the company of duchesses.

[Quotes 'Et certes, cela ne veut pas dire' to 'sa cause primaire'. Pléiade I, p. 129.]

Marcel Proust has noted those 'secondary motives', by which we are quickly deceived, in the minutest detail. Duplicity, logic-chopping and the sly casuistry of the human heart! And what a school for modesty we have in Marcel Proust's novels! Reading books like these urges us to question our motives and to dig out unsparingly the falsely good reasons provided by our instincts. Step by step, we make our way towards the real man, the enchantment falls away; the magic disappears; wisps of smoke, filth and gall, that is what is left in our grasp! We too, without knowing it, have covered up our vices: the novelist has warned us; we know where our weaknesses lie and we will strike a sure blow. With a flick of a finger we can send the fake demigod rolling to the ground and, from beneath the cardboard scenery, we can tear out like living entrails the congealed mass of our concupiscence. Ah! this quality could only be found in the work of Marcel Proust: contributing to our self-knowledge would in itself place this writer on a level of his own, far above the literary herd and the commercial concerns of an art devoted to shoddy entertainment.

He has gone back to the tradition of the moralists and explored men's souls; he has shown faith in the things of the heart, whose passions he has described and explained. With him the tone has been raised; in the study of man he has undertaken, Marcel Proust has

joined hands with those great masters who have been acquainted
with the trials and tribulations of human existence. . . .

(b) On the subconscious in Proust's style (pp. 377–8)

Marcel Proust's 'style', more than any other, partakes of the
unconscious mechanism of dreams. In the exercising of his thought,
attention seems relaxed to such a degree that a kind of numbness is
eventually transmitted from author to reader. Do not be misled by
my opinion; this observation does not, in my view, imply any
pejorative conclusion. Even Marcel Proust's detractors recognize that
there are seductive qualities in the slow, rocking rhythm of this
prose. For my part, I believe the full understanding of the novelist
demands a bending of the rational faculties and a displacing of the
imaginative field of vision towards the vague fringes of light that
make up the halo of the soul, towards the dark zones that constitute
the infra-red and the ultra-violet of the heart. In order to become
accustomed to this chiaroscuro, we need a special supplementary
sense, like those deep ocean fish that develop in the darkness of their
normal habitat, special energy sources of light and electricity. Then
one grasps previously unnoticed shades of meaning and infinitesimal
moral points in which one discovers treasure-houses full of
psychological insights. The microcosm grows bigger, opening out
before our eyes like those Japanese playthings that, once put in
water, turn from shapeless wisps of paper into people, butterflies and
flowers. Hidden reality is revealed in movement; you would think it
was magic. Yet there is nothing to mislead us. Marcel Proust the
magician has no secrets; all he needs to do is place the prism of his
sensibility in the concentrated mass of his thought for the unstable
atoms locked in it to spurt out like a shower of diamonds and gold.

This magician does, however, have a magic wand to help him
bring about his alchemy: this talisman is, in fact, his 'style' which I
have just described as being closely modelled on the rudimentary
reasoning of dreams.

Basically, every 'style' conveys the author's method of reasoning,
or rather, it is this actual method in concrete form and put into
practice with the aid of syntax. When he writes, Marcel Proust casts
an artificial twilight over his thought and leaves the unconscious
arguments . . . proliferate at the whim of the images they attract.
The result is that the logical analysis of his sentences is no easy task;
no writer has made greater use of subordinate clauses and
parentheses. So as to liberate the nuances and particles of thought
from the dense mass, he has had recourse to a wily, tentacular
language in which each phrase is to be compared to a fan being
opened wide.

Such a 'style' does not make for easy reading. But we must, at least, in fairness to the author of *Swann*, grant that, though his sentences look as if they have been thrown blindly into the depths of the unconscious, they do land neatly on their feet. As the author proceeds through the labyrinth of his subordinate clauses, he bursts out onto some unexpected bend in his path and, from out of the shadow, the reader emerges suddenly into the light.

(c) Proust as artist of the subconscious (pp. 384–6)

We should now review our material and draw our conclusions: the art of Marcel Proust is not concerned with the intellect but with the psyche; it follows the sinuous meanderings of Dreams. It exists on the border of conscious creation and unconscious inspiration. In this respect, it is related to music, the art closest to the unconscious.

Marcel Proust, no more than a composer, could get away with choosing arbitrary and self-contained sections of the life of the psyche and removing them from the uninterrupted flow of the soul's expression. Faced with the stream of reality, which is what alone interests him, he is indeed obliged to forego all desire for cohesion and systematization. He is condemned to glide along with the current in the river of human passions. Rejecting all rules, i.e. an intellectual and hence conventional stance, he has no choice but to direct the antennae of his sensibility, once it has been aroused, to every corner where there is a living being or a throbbing heart. His field of investigation is as vast as Life – it is Life.

And if our novelist *must*[2] express everything about life, he can do so and get away with it precisely because of the atmosphere of music surrounding this symbolic impressionism . . . and the only criticism to be made of the method might be to deplore that in the narrative there is not always a touch of the driving force which was in the characters themselves and which, now broken up into successive phases, leaves us at times with the impression of a cinematograph in which the film could be said to be projected too slowly, showing us successive shots instead of giving the illusion of movement.

Whichever way you look at it, the art of Marcel Proust partakes of life, since all these vibrations and resonances are reproduced in it as on a recording machine. The art of Marcel Proust is the *exact*[3] image of Life, with its beauty and its dross – and also sometimes with the monotony of the daily round. This exactness and precision in observation are emerging – or are about to emerge – from the realm of Art to enter the realm of Science.

This is perhaps the place where we should ask ourselves whether Art does not require an element of convention and artifice, an arbitrary condensing of particular phenomena into general statements.

But the discussion of such a problem would soon be reduced to barren definitions. There is no more an absolute division between Art and Life than there is a gulf between Art and Dreams; their individual domains overlap and at times even merge together completely.

Furthermore, we will take Marcel Proust's books for what they are. As they stand, they present an extraordinary collection of facts about people; they are inexhaustible gold-mines, where a surprise awaits you every time you drive home your pick and where every excavation reveals unhoped-for levels of deposits. To read these books is truly to accomplish the most instructive and the most curious of journeys through the human heart.

NOTES

1 In italics in the text.
2 *Idem.*
3 *Idem.*

55. Roger Allard on the relativity of Proust's moralism

1922

Part of 'Sodome et Gomorrhe ou Marcel Proust moraliste', *La Nouvelle Revue française*, 1 June 1922, pp. 641–6.

Roger Allard continues his earlier line of thinking (No. 50) and finds that Proust in *Sodome et Gomorrhe*, contrary to expectations, does not take the severe attitude that deviation from sexual norms would suggest, but presents his characters with an indulgent compassion that promotes a relative view of their behaviour and avoids absolute sanctions.

The only people in respect of whom he allows the scorn of sarcasm to show through are those that are represented to us as incapable of bearing suffering themselves or of being a source of delight for others. On the other hand, M. de Charlus, the Duc de Guermantes and the violinist Morel are, even when open to ridicule because of the bizarre and grotesque adventures to which they are exposed by their sexual proclivities, no less eloquent or touching than the kings and princesses of Racine. In fact, the reader will notice that, in his latest volume, M. Proust has increased the quotations from *Esther* and *Athalie.* . . .

The indulgence one senses in M. Marcel Proust is not made up of scepticism, it is a kind of reflection of the intimate satisfaction that the moralist derives from the proven accuracy of his diagnosis. . . .

With what finesse and subtlety is the (hero's) jealousy depicted for us. . . . As long as he remains unsure of Albertine's behaviour, we see the hero ready to succumb to weariness and disgust. But it is at the very moment when doubt is no longer an option for him, when a thousand petty facts come togther and when so many paths, previously followed and abandoned, converge at the same brilliant and painful point, that he finds in the very certainty of the suspicion of her vice the determination to marry his lover.

Such analyses go beyond the limits of fictional psychology. They leave behind in us a whole residue of anxieties and remorse. . . . The word relativity comes naturally to the mind of anyone reflecting on the importance of this psychological discovery, the discovery of a truth that is subject not only to the laws of time and space, but also to the now fast, now slow rhythm of life and passion in a given observer.

It is obvious that M. Proust has added to Laclos' triangulation system new theorems and elegant solutions; should one say that he has turned psychology upside down in the way that Einstein has treated physics? . . . I cannot verify the accuracy of such a comparison. Shall I say, however, that there is something very attractive about it that appeals to the imagination? If the notion of moral relativity can be deduced from a psychological work of the imagination, surely it can from Marcel Proust's, in which points of view are multiplied ad infinitum. . . .

56. Henry Bidou on *SG II*
1922

Part of 'Parmi les livres', *La Revue de Paris*, 1 June 1922.

Henry Bidou reflects the perplexity over the way Proust divides up the sections of *La Recherche* and concentrates on presenting him as the master analyst of subtle fluctuations in social behaviour.

When we are among the characters created by M. Proust it is as if we were in a crowd of living people. I was a little bemused to see that of the three volumes he groups together for us the first had the inscription volume V marked with a II and an asterisk underneath. It is a part of *Sodome et Gomorrhe*, which is a part of *Le Côté de Guermantes*, which is a part of *A la recherche du temps perdu*. 'Never, I thought, will I find my way through all that.' The author's talent was more present to my memory than the faces of his characters, and I was afraid I might be a stranger among them. But here we are, on page one, at a reception given by the Princesse de Guermantes. And the sense of reality is so strong in our author that he transmits it to us. We experience not a reading, but a presence.

He arrives at this result without recourse to any known procedure. For thirty pages he takes us round the salons of this historic house, surrounded by people whose main business is to find out if they will acknowledge one another. No passions, or hardly any, though a few strange ones. No matter of great moment. Everything is brought down to establishing precedence, avoiding a presentation and replying with a put-down. To see or not to see, that is the question.

The danger is we might wish to leave this reception. Not so. Not only does this vanity fair hold our attention but these very characters have the appearance of living beings. Like them, or dislike them, there they are. The author has suggested an explanation for the strange interest we take in them. The life of high society – this is the gist of what he says – is an attenuated image of the history of an age. A whole period is present in a single salon, with its revolutions, its wars, its social catastrophes, its new ideas and its arts. But these great events only reveal their presence in slight and empty manifestations. Geologists with a press and a metal sheet can obtain in laboratory conditions the powerful torsions that created mountains. Others study torrents in small bowls filled with sand. It is on this scale that history gathers force around a tea-table. Moreover, this is enough for the indications and nods around this table to be the image of great things.

Though the instances are reduced to scale, they are at least described with minute precision and picturesque artistry. My impression is that this artistry consists of two things in particular: a watchmaker's talent in taking things apart and a painter's skill in taking note of signs. The author suspects that the Princesse de Guermantes has a liking for M. de Charlus: consider by what symptom he recognized it:

Once, when I had said in her presence that M. de Charlus had at that time a quite strong feeling for a certain person, I saw with astonishment taking its place in the princess's eyes that different, momentary expression that traces in the pupils a kind of hair-line crack, and that comes from a thought that our words without realizing it have stirred in the person we are addressing, a secret thought that will not be translated into words, but that will rise up to the surface, from the depths disturbed by us, distorted for a moment by the look.[1]

The whole book is in this extract which is symbolic in value. A variation in intensity in the expression of a look is an event to turn this universe upside down. This variation is a sign, and the sign may remain infinitely small while the cause of it grows indefinitely. . . .

[Considers Swann, Françoise, and Albertine as examples of this kind of close analysis.]

This relentless analysis . . . ends in the dissociation of everything. You would need the delicate processes of musical analysis to describe the results of this work; like harmonists, M. Proust discovers in human feelings strange notes, accidentals, syncopations and retard-ations; in particular, there is a study of retardation in grief, which is very strange. The human personality splits into two, into three, is divided into an infinite number of successive beings. Our yesterday's self is a stranger to us. But on occasion it returns to take up its place once more and haunt us, with the result that for a moment we become the ghost of our past. We are constantly driven out of ourselves by new images of ourselves. Our soul itself at that moment does not even belong to us. We have at our disposal only a small number of our actual feelings. The rest are buried somewhere or other, and though they do exist in us, they are of no avail. But if certain circumstances summon them back to the light, and especially

MARCEL PROUST

if the sensations that accompanied their birth are revived, they in turn drive out the feelings that annoyed them and recover all their force. These resurrections of our former self are particularly painful, because they bring back a whole range of affections and desires which time has deprived of their purpose and which are transformed into a nostalgia for the past.

These inner dramas are the stuff of this book. Apparent causes are of little moment: a society reception or a journey to the seaside. Though for a sensibility so easily moved, the slightest fluctuations are overwhelming. Arriving at the hotel is an event. It is not just a matter of opening up the suitcases but 'of marking things with the soul we are familiar with, instead of theirs which we found alarming'. This spiritual moving-in is at the same time accompanied by the opposite phenomenon which is the defence of the being one is against the being, now rediscovered and reincarnated, that one once was. We must both impose our will on things and defend ourselves against memories. It is a fight that is not without its days of malaise. The odd thing is that this exhausting struggle of the sensibility against itself does not prevent the eye from being very alert, the mind from constructing theories and the hand from drawing portraits. This amazing mixture of touching emotions and ironic observation is not rare in nervous subjects. You think they are carried away by lyricism, indeed they are lost in it, and already they are drawing caricatures. This flexibility makes them both attractive and unbearable. It makes for the richness of M. Proust's book.

NOTE

1 Pléiade II, p. 715.

57. Fernand Vandérem on *SG II*

1922

Notice in *La Revue de France*, 15 June 1922; reprinted in *Le Miroir des lettres*, Paris, Flammarion, 1924, pp. 154–7.

Fernand Vandérem does not overemphasize what might be thought scabrous elements in *Sodome et Gomorrhe*. He recommends the work, as he had done the earlier parts: *Le Côté de Guermantes; Sodome et Gomorrhe I* (see *Revue de Paris*, 15 June 1921) for the objective pictures of society and concludes by proposing a method of reading Proust's work that gets the most out of its richness and complexity.

I find myself here among acquaintances or old friends. . . . I watch them and listen to them. They never bore me. They almost always amuse me. And should my attention wander, M. Marcel Proust is at hand to point out to me their qualities, their absurdities, or even their pitiful misfortunes.

Snobbery is not the least of these and . . . at times, M. Marcel Proust, like a doctor catching his patient's plague, does not seem totally free of contamination from what he observes. But I have also pointed out[1] that snobbery being, in my view, only one of the superior forms of vanity and one of its social manifestations, all the anatomical plates that M. Marcel Proust displays for us have had for me the incomparable value of human documents.

As for the actual episodes of the book, the ones that I would like to impart to you are not the easiest to talk about. Here, for instance, is a newcomer, a small-time musician, by name Morel, who has been discovered by this wretched M. de Charlus who exhibits an affection for him even more frankly described than Vautrin's for young Rubempré.[2] Oh! the sad, comic tale of it! And what a cruel and amusing fellow! I do not say that Balzac is inferior to M. Marcel Proust; but, in the description of similar events, how much less entertaining I find him, and how much less moving. For the grace as well as the ultra-lucidity with which M. Proust analyses these doomed men[3] for us partakes of the miraculous. They are an endless source of laughter for him, and he constantly makes us laugh at them too. And yet he manages in spite of it all to make us pity them. One cannot wait for the third volume, to reach journey's end and get to the bottom of this Sodom and Gomorrah.

As for the general public, I get the impression that the vogue for M. Proust makes further progress every month. There are not many people, who can be said to be anybody at all, who are unacquainted with his characters and who do not speak of them as old friends. They are even cited as types of this or that, almost like financial standards on the stock exchange of fashion. The other evening, at dinner, a lady questioned me about the standing of personages frequenting a certain Paris salon. And as I was, no doubt, a little vague, she said with a smile:

– Well, do Oriane and Basin go there?

What greater joy for a writer, what better reward than to see the characters that he has drawn from the human round come alive again as real beings among real people?

On the other hand, there are readers who are still frightened by M. Marcel Proust's slow episodes, convolutions of style and finicky detail. They declare, not so much with ill-feeling as a certain regret: 'It really is on the long side! It is hard-going!' This is a clear sign that, if they lack a basic cultural development or innate powers of concentration, they need advice if they are to read the author of *A la recherche du temps perdu* with pleasure and profit. So I hasten to present them with a method I have recommended to some of my connections and that I will, if you wish, sum up for you.

To succeed in getting the full flavour of M. Marcel Proust, all you do indeed need to do is adopt the two main principles of physical exercise: progression and follow-through.

You begin, in week one, with about twenty pages each day, twenty-five if you are up to it, thirty at most. Incidentally, a rule not to be broken: never force; at the first sign of lassitude or distraction shut the book and leave it. You continue for a week, at the end of which you increase by five pages a day. In a week this brings you up to the level of about sixty pages a day. You treat this as your limit, but at the same time you do not drop back. And you reach the end after a relatively short lapse of time, not only without any hint of fatigue, but counting from the beginning of the second week, with a pleasure that grows in strength and depth.

However, this is not all. When the volume is finished, you let it rest a little while. Then one morning or evening, you take it up again. Not at the beginning, not so as to engage in uninterrupted reading. A chapter here, a fragment there, to be tasted carefully without haste, soaking yourself in each phrase, in each detail. And that is the moment when at last you will savour completely all the charm, wit and poetry that escaped you, in spite of your efforts, in these delicious books.

The great error of many people, as you see, was to hurl

themselves upon the novels of M. Proust, as if on a run-of-the-mill work and swallow it whole. Let me say, without false modesty, I believe they will abide by my prescriptions and will be able to do nothing else but thank me for them.

NOTES

1 See *La Revue de Paris*, 15 June 1921.
2 In Balzac's *Illusions perdues*.
3 'Hommes damnés', by analogy with the usual euphemism for lesbians, which was 'femmes damnées'.

58. Pierre Billotey: a cartoon in words

1922

From a sketch entitled 'Abondance' in *Les Marges*, 15 June 1922.

Pierre Billotey catches the general mood of amazement that Proust seems to write so much.

'Three volumes of one million, two hundred and thirty five thousand and sixty eight letters.'
(Blurb by M. Marcel Proust's publishers)

I saw M. Marcel Proust, author of so many copious tomes, going into the glass and iron-work chalet in front of the Odéon, on the Luxembourg side. Under his arm he had a moleskin-covered briefcase. As he passed, he nodded to the knitting lady, sitting on her stool on the stone-flagged floor. She smiled back.

M. Marcel Proust pushed open the second door on the left in the corridor and disappeared.

But suddenly a wild demon of a bus, scudding along fast and furiously towards Les Batignolles, comes down the steep hill of the rue de Médicis.

In front of the Odéon, a long vehicle suddenly swerves between the gilded spikes of the railings and the columns of the entrance and blocks the progress of the speeding bus. An accident is inevitable; people will be injured, perhaps killed.

No! With a swing of the steering wheel, the driver of the bus changes direction, avoids the lorry and mounts the pavement. . . . With all the force of its engine, its momentum and its weight, and the weight of its thirty ashen-faced passengers, the bus collided with the glass and iron-work chalet.

At the same instant, the iron supports broke, the glass was shattered and the roof blew off like a lid.

And the crowd that had immediately foregathered saw, on the foundation of the ruined building, this magnificent sight.

M. Marcel Proust was sitting there still, with his trousers round his ankles. On his hairy knees was the moleskin-covered briefcase. Inclining forward, he was writing away, not wasting any time, not having heard a thing, not wishing to hear, and spinning out, with every line he added, the roll of fine paper that miraculously remained attached to a part of the wall that was still standing.

And since that day, I have known that M. Marcel Proust can never, absolutely never, stop writing.

59. An unsigned review of *Swann's Way*
1922

An article titled 'M. Proust; or, Richardson outwritten', *The Spectator*, 11 November 1922, pp. 660–1.

The reviewer closely examines C.K. Scott-Moncrieff's newly published and welcome translation of *Du côté de chez Swann*, and assesses the hardships and rewards of persevering with 'a French where all the words are easy and all the sentences difficult'.

In an article recently contributed to our columns a countrywoman of the now so celebrated M. Proust asked herself and us whether the vast enterprise represented by the words *A la Recherche du Temps Perdu* could in effect be classed as a book? The translator of *Du Côté de Chez Swann* employs perhaps a quaint but nevertheless a happy phrase when he calls his work 'a translation of the first part of M. Proust's continuous novel.' Continuous is the word. It is a work continuous as human life is continuous – far more so than any one actual life – changing a little from one incarnation to the other; *Du Côté de Chez Swann* is not quite the same as *A l'Ombre des Jeunes Filles en Fleurs*. It changes, certainly, as the volumes defile from softness and haze to a sort of limpid certainty, but is liable perhaps to change back to a prophetic mysticism. Yet it is alive through all its length, in all its vicissitudes.

From it, to borrow the words of Doctor Johnson, a hermit might form his notion of the world – not merely of the world of a certain set, or even of the world of one country. Like all great writers M. Proust pierces down to the primary biped. He is neither more nor less interested in Aunt Léonie, the provincial *malade imaginaire*, than in the Duchesses of the Faubourg St. Germain, who appear from time to time in *Swann's Way* and who form the chief *dramatis personae* of *Le Côté de Guermantes*. Swann, the melancholy man of the world, who has refined and refined till elegance and wit – unmasked – have seemed of no more and no less worth than provincialism and buffoonery, has his creator's profound understanding and sympathy. So, too, has the poor little composer and music master of Combray, Vinteuil, whose daughter's disgrace breaks a gentle, ineffectual heart.

Irony, an almost ecstatic sense of the beautiful, a love of the strange and a passion for the commonplace, seem to divide M. Proust's strange and comprehensive mind. But, indeed, when we consider the nature of his task, we can at once see that this must be the case. *A la Recherche du Temps Perdu*, which Mr Scott Moncrieff translates as 'Remembrance of things past', but which could perhaps be more happily rendered by some phrase such as 'The harvest of lost days', is, in fact, an effort to recreate a whole world, and such an effort could obviously only be made by a mind thus passionate and meticulous. And here we must put in a word of warning to our readers. If, in fact, a whole world could be brought back into being, there would necessarily be a great deal in it which ordinarily presents itself only to the eye of the doctor, the lawyer, or the confessor. If for some scientific purpose it were possible to lift (as which of us has not desired to lift) the roofs of all the houses in a town, we know that a great deal would be revealed which we are accustomed to call either common or else unclean. But if the purpose of the research were obviously and comprehensibly a scientific one, we should not for the most part demand that truth should be distorted as omissions inevitably distort. We should willingly admit that the consideration and taking into account of all the elements present were not so much desirable as ordinary and necessary. We should not begin to suspect the good faith of the inquirer unless the proportion of 'horrible revelations' seemed excessive. If it did, then we should be justified in condemning our research worker for a type of distortion far worse and more damaging to the cause of truth than any of the distortions of prudery.

In fine, *A la Recherche du Temps Perdu* is a book for a reader who is fairly far up in the school of life. The 'junior forms' would be not improbably both hurt and bewildered as well as bored by it. But the pathologically, the pruriently minded would dislike it far more. Indeed, this judgment (that it is not a book for 'the young person') is perhaps an unsound one. *Du Côté de Chez Swann* would be a lesson in proportion of the utmost value. For here is a witness who is certainly not on the side of the prudes – a witness, in fact, of a disinterestedness which is almost passionate; and here is all he has to tell us. Are the skeletons in Society's cupboard, when they are all marshalled and grinning, no more seductive or more exciting than this? For the reader of M. Proust will find the simple and happy, the funny and ordinary things of life shown to be as strange and as marvellous as those things for which the esteem of right thinking people (to say the least) must be forfeited. If, then, the novel, as some people hold, is the school of experience without the birch – the voyage in an atlas – then perhaps the reading of M. Proust might be a valuable addition to many a paternal homily.

Du Côté de Chez Swann is concerned with the early life of the narrator, and the complete histories of the people with whom a very quiet existence brought the boy into contact. There are some marvellously subtle descriptions of childish experience in it. Take, for instance, the recurring burden of the earlier chapters, which is the good-night kiss of the boy's mother. Without this kiss the affectionate, imaginative child believes that he cannot go to sleep. The father pooh-poohs this absurd idea, and when there is company to dinner – for instance, that hateful M. Swann – then the kiss must be given and received in the dining-room shorn of any attendant caress or whispered intimacy. This is an agony, and many, but pathetically simple, are the little stratagems to which the child resorts to secure that kiss in its proper setting. How can he carry it intact all the way from the dining-room? One dinner-party night his misery is so overwhelming that he resolves to commit the unheard-of indiscretion of sitting up till his mother comes to bed. And as he waits he tries to imagine what awful form of retribution this conduct will call down upon him. At the least he will to-morrow be packed off to a boarding-school! But when his mother and father come, it is to a sorrow outside his childish power to have prophesied to which he is subjected. For his parents, genuinely distressed, then and there realize that their boy is, indeed, exceptionally highly strung. They tacitly abandon the idea of trying to cure him by a cheerful belittling of his whims. His mother does not scold but tries rather to console him, and promises she will sleep in the room with him for a great treat:

I ought then to have been happy; I was not. It struck me that my mother had just made a first concession which must have been painful to her, that it was a first step down from the ideal she had formed of me, and that, for the first time, she, with all her courage, had to confess herself beaten. It struck me that if I had just scored a victory it was over her; that I had succeeded as sickness or sorrow or age might have succeeded in relaxing her will, in altering her judgment. . . . And if I had dared now, I should have said to mama: 'No, I don't want you to sleep here.'

But we must set before the reader a sample of M. Proust's powers in the well-worn way of the descriptions of natural objects. He is not in the Tchekovian sense a symbolist. If his description is to convey more to us than its ostensible meaning, he will tell us so. He has what many modern writers lack, an appetite for beautiful things for their own sake. The boy is taking one of those many walks with his parents when suddenly they come to a great hedge of hawthorn in full flower. The hedge, irregular and generous, seems to form in its bays a series of little chapels. He is enchanted, carried away by the sight of the sunbathed blossom and by the warm, pulsing waves of scent:

Combien naïves et paysannes en comparaison sembleraient les églantines qui, dans quelques semaines monteraient elles aussi en plein soleil le même chemin rustique, en la soie unie de leur corsage rougissant qu'un souffle défait. Mais j'avais beau rester devant les aubépines à respirer, à porter devant ma pensée qui ne savait ce qu'elle devait en faire, à perdre, à retrouver leur invisible et fixe odeur, à m'unir au rythme qui jetait leurs fleurs, ici et là, avec une allégresse juvénile et à des intervalles inattendus comme certains intervalles musicaux, elles m'offraient indéfiniment le même charme avec une profusion inépuisable, mais sans me le laisser approfondir davantage, comme ces mélodies qu'on rejoue cent fois de suite sans descendre plus avant dans leur secret.'

This passage Mr Scott Moncrieff renders thus:

How simple and rustic, in comparison with these, would seem the dog-roses, which, in a few weeks' time, would be climbing the same hillside path in the heat of the sun, dressed in the smooth silk of their blushing pink bodices, which would be undone and scattered by the first breath of wind.

179

But it was in vain that I lingered before the hawthorns, to breathe in, to marshal before my mind (which knew not what to make of it), to lose in order to rediscover their invisible and unchanging odour, to absorb myself in the rhythm which disposed their flowers here and there with the light-heartedness of youth, and at intervals as unexpected as certain intervals of music; they offered me an indefinite continuation of the same charm, in an inexhaustible profusion, but without letting me delve into it any more deeply, like those melodies which one can play over a hundred times in succession without coming any nearer to their secret.

This translation has a few obvious faults, but the English version as a whole is a piece of work to be proud of. If it is laborious in parts – often a little too literal quite to convey the flavour of the author – how difficult a task it was to translate the work of a writer who is all flavour, whose points are so fine, and whose fine points alone justify whole periods of our reading. The translation, if for nothing else, is of immense value as a 'crib', to be read in conjunction with the French, enabling the slow or uncertain French scholar to read M. Proust at the correct speed. That is a factor which the despisers of translations and of such works as Cowden Clarke's *Riches of Chaucer* often fail to take into account. For every narrative, and, indeed, every piece of literature, prose or poem, is a thing unrolled in time. The speed of this unrolling is always, more or less, consciously borne in mind by the author – poets have many devices with which they delay or increase the reader's speed. Mere pace can deform a work of art. Who does not know the limerick? –

> There was a young lady of Rio,
> Who tried to play Handel's *Grand Trio*.
> But her skill was so scanty
> She played it *Andante*
> Instead of *Allegro con Brio*.

Subjected to such treatment by a slow reading a great deal of M. Proust's flavour is lost. He clearly wrote to be read *Allegro*. This is what Mr Scott Moncrieff's translation will enable many of us to do for the first time, for M. Proust's French is often extremely crabbed in construction, a French to be laboured with, a French where all the words are easy and all the sentences difficult, a French wherein the dictionary will not help us. Let us therefore hope that Mr Scott Moncrieff will continue the good work. There are some passages in the very next section, *A l'Ombre des Jeunes Filles en Fleurs*, upon which this laborious reader at least would be extremely glad to have a second opinion.

What, we wonder, will be the faults which time will reveal in M. Proust's fabric? He is discursive. He has raised the parenthesis to a fine art. He never sticks to his scene. All this is true, and these things would be faults in another. But when he pours out upon us with such unmeasured generous fullness the good qualities which these individualities seem alone to allow to come to flower, it seems surly to challenge them. At any rate, it seems that it is for us of his own generation to praise rather than to appraise. Our censure could obviously not influence the character of M. Proust's output – so our responsibility to our entertainer and instructor is *nil*. And therefore we can – with a good conscience – let 'The harvest of lost days' conduct us as it will, with even less hope of influencing it by act or opinion than we have of modifying that of days yet to come in our own life. We may learn and enjoy with a pleasant passivity, our critical activity left for once on one side.

NOTE

1 Pléiade I, p. 138.

60. An unsigned posthumous appreciation

1922

Part of an article in *The Times* ('From a correspondent'), 20 November 1922, p. 15.

The article harks back to Mary Duclaux's review of *Swann* (see No. 16) by taking up the reference to Henry James, surveys Proust's career to date and pinpoints his arrival on the English as well as the French scene with the Goncourt Prize.

More than any of his contemporaries, Marcel Proust, whose death is reported on another page by our Paris Correspondent, will go down to posterity as the author of one book, a book which there is reason to fear, he may not have completed, but which even as a fragment may confidently be submitted to comparison, as well for the breadth of its observation, the depth of its penetration, the skill with which its material is selected, as for the sheer mass of that (fragmentary though it be) material, with any other work of fiction published in the present century.

It is almost nine years since *The Times Literary Supplement*, in December 1913, welcomed *Du côté de chez Swann* to England, comparing it with the then recent *A Small Boy and Others* of Henry

James, though with the prudent reservation that Mr James's book was 'concise and simple compared to M. Marcel Proust's essay in reconstituting the fresh, vague, shimmering impressions of a child, the wonderment with which it regards places and people which in our eyes possess no vestige of magic or glamour.'

A tantalizing reference in Henry James's *Letters* shows that a little later the English analyst had not yet seen 'the Proust production', which M. Bernstein and Mrs Wharton had successively promised to send him; his opinion of it is not recorded. Possibly this is because it was wholly unfavourable, for even in the first volume of his *Recherche* Proust had begun to seek out those problems and complications of life which James, resolute in obedience to his Puritan instincts, so dexterously and interminably avoided. The briefest comparison of *Swann* with the book of James's that comes nearest to it and may, indeed, have partly inspired it, *What Maisie Knew*, will show the profound difference between the two 'analysts' – Proust, tireless and fearless in the exhaustion of the very last drop from every minutest test-tube; James, using his consummate skill to drain off, or at least deodorize, every remotest hint of 'impropriety'.

[Lists the sequence of publications from *Swann* to *Sodome et Gomorrhe*.]

The year 1919, which followed the publication of the *Jeunes Filles* and conferred on it the Prix Goncourt, established Proust as a novelist of European reputation. *Swann* was reprinted, uniform with its sequel, and another volume, *Pastiches et Mélanges*, in which not only is his literary deftness shown at the summit of achievement, but his literary affinities are clearly indicated. . . .

With these three volumes Proust in 1919 was recognized in England as one of the French authors to be followed. The *Nouvelle Revue Française* was scrutinized monthly lest it should contain, as it sometimes did, an instalment of *Temps Perdu* . . . . In the summer of 1920 appeared *Le Côté de Guermantes* . . . carrying the puerilities of Combray and the Champs-Elysées and the calf-love of Balbec on into the heart of the Faubourg Saint-Germain, which he dissects with a skill so consummate as perhaps to be overlooked by the casual reader, who found the repeated examinations of the Guermantes family, only boring in the fineness of their variety. At the same time, the brain of the writer showed the first signs of that deadly fatigue which is always in store for the creative worker: the volume was accompanied by a list – by no means exhaustive – of over two hundred *errata*, which the reader was requested to correct.

61. Léon Daudet on Proust and Balzac

1922

Extract from 'L'universalité et le roman', *L'Action française*, 23 November 1922.

Léon Daudet's essay, a tribute following close on Proust's death, connects him with Balzac by the grand scale of their approach to the human comedy.

Proust's work like Balzac's has universality. I mean that it has windows opening on all areas of knowledge at the same time as on all circumstances of existence. As for Proust's human comedy, the astounding *Recherche du temps perdu* . . . it too deals with the art of war, agriculture, philosophy, politics, geology, the state of bodies in movement, physiology, sociology etc. and even with microbes and mental illness. But whereas in Balzac, these magnificent, profound digressions are set solidly in the novel's substance – like the jewels of Roman matrons in triumphal arches – in Proust the same digressions are recast and spiritually transformed. It is true that, in other respects, the actual fictional texture, or if you prefer, the dramatic texture is less close-grained than in Balzac, because of the constant presence and intervention of the personality of the author. But, allowing for that, in both the riches are infinite and the mental appetite limitless. Through them one can see the vastness of the field of fiction, which offers to creative genius as many possibilities as the Milky Way on a clear night. Proust's series of novels, like Balzac's, is a life alongside life, a life *over and above* life,[1] differently put together, but as complex, bitter, ironic, sophisticated and guileful as the existence of each one of us.

NOTE

1 In italics in the text.

62. Edmond Jaloux:
an obituary and an appreciation
1922

Part of a front-page article on Proust's death, 'L'oeuvre de Marcel Proust', *Les Nouvelles littéraires*, 25 November 1922.

Edmond Jaloux (1878–1949), after reviewing Proust's literary career, praises his gifts as psychologist (quoting at length from 'Un amour de Swann'), as social observer and satirist and finally as poet.

But we must also admit there is more to him than a psychologist: to start with, he is a satirist, the cruel, sarcastic and pitiless painter of Society, seen first in its aristocratic form (the Guermantes, the Baron de Charlus, the Princesse de Parme) and secondly, in its bourgeois form (the Verdurins, Dr Cottard, Odette as Swann's wife etc.). It is safe to say that no one has described society people and the bourgeoisie with greater irony and truth. The conversation of Proust's characters is extremely accurate; not a nuance of their wit – or lack of it – is left to chance. Had he been endowed with no more than that gift, he would already have been in the first rank! This general picture of a social order could be completed by including his picture of servants of whom he is the only writer to have spoken with intelligence while considering them, to boot, as being full members of the human race.

But isn't there also the poet, a Shakespearian poet, who transforms the perverted girls of his novels into the heroines of a fantastic comedy? The poet of seascapes, of flowering orchards, of communing with the hawthorns (*A l'ombre des jeunes filles en fleurs*)? There is a whole world seething with life in *A la recherche du temps perdu*, a world so complete that Marcel Proust has created in it a town, landscapes, a cathedral, as he has created the unique inspiration of an actress (in La Berma), the ideas of a philosopher (in Bergotte), the art of a painter (in Elstir), a world that would be like ours, were it not that an infinitely poetic spirit hovered over it, a spirit absent from our own – a spirit made up of an infinitely moving and delicate imagination, made up also of love, pity and kindness, made up of a sensibility tender to the point of morbidity, made up of friendship and melancholy – a spirit that was the very soul, the richly mysterious soul, that has just taken its leave of us!

63. Elizabeth Bibesco:
an obituary and a portrait
1922

From *New Statesman*, 25 November 1922, pp. 235–6.

Elizabeth Bibesco succeeds, by anecdote and reminiscence, in transmitting the balance between charm and shrewdness that invested Proust's work as much as his life.

'Marcel Proust is dead.' It seemed like a breach of confidence to read it in a newspaper. It is the price you pay for loving public characters, suddenly to see in cold, hard print a name that you have murmured and cherished and wrapped up in warm folds of intimacy. Out they walk of the firelit room you have known them in, suddenly dispossessed, belonging not to themselves or you but to the world, a foundling, a pauper on the public rates of admiration. When I first met Marcel Proust he had written *Swann* and I had not read it. In fact, I sat next to him without the preparations that are prejudices or the anticipations that are frustrations – I knew that he had written a book – I remembered that it had had a two-column review in the *Times Literary Supplement* which had left vague impressions on my mind, impressions fortunately too vague to be a guide to conversation. Gently, deliberately he drew me into that magic circle of his personality with the ultimate sureness of a look that needs no touch to seal it. How am I to describe the sense that his conversation gave you? Like a sea anemone it kept drawing in and opening out. One's thoughts in his company like those tight paper circles in crackers which, put into water, expanded into flowers. Insensibly you were drawn into that intricate cobweb of irridescent steel, his mind, which interlacing with yours, spread patterns of light and shade over your most intimate thoughts. Marcel was never a monologist. Sometimes he talked at length, but always he made you feel that your thoughts were the accompaniment to his words. You didn't interrupt because you were so much a part of what he was saying that a word would be a separation. When you did say something he would look at you, and the reflection of your idea would play over his face.

When he was talking he listened to your thoughts; when you were talking he gave you his. He never got up till dinner, and rarely then. To see him at all you had to reserve spaces in your life as you put a bag on a seat in a railway carriage. He always asked you to dine at the Ritz. Once he had been in love with someone who lived there; he had acquired the habit. Also, far more permanent than a transitory passion, the head waiter was a dear friend of his. The dinner was always exquisite without being fantastic, unobtrusive but enormously expensive. He would sit in his fur coat in the suffocating restaurant drinking black coffee and eating nothing – 'Comme c'est impossible de lire Swann! Je viens de l'essayer,' and then 'Racontez moi la vérité sur le Lord Mayor de Cork, Céleste (his enchanting *femme nécessaire* of a maid) et sa soeur sont d'un avis différent.'

We walked into the lounge and talked till half-past eleven. The lights began to be turned out. 'Rallumez!' 'Car je veux partir, mais je ne veux pas avoir l'impression qu'on me congédie.'

After ten minutes of a light so bright that we could hardly see we departed. Two hours later my front door bell rang. Marcel walked in. 'Je n'avais pas fini ma conversation,' he explained, and sat talking till four.

His relations with the *monde* were a strange mixture of exaggerated taste and an exaggerated distaste. It provided him with delights and hates, each it seemed to me disproportionately great. In the case of disloyal friends he followed up the proofs of their perfidy with the science of a detective looking for clues or the passion of a lover seeking for tokens. But it was curiosity, not revengefulness. His malice evaporated in certainty.

A very distinguished person wanted to meet him. It was arranged that he should come in after dinner. At 10.30 the conversation had died a natural death. At 10.45 it was suffering an unnatural resurrection. No one had anything that they wanted to say, in consequence of which everyone was laboriously saying something next. At 11.15 Marcel Proust arrived. He went up to the lady (whose claims to fame were not intellectual), apologising for his lateness.

'Monsieur Proust, vous écrivez?'

Smiling down (if he loved you he smiled up), 'Peu, rarement, difficilement, jamais.'

'Comme vous me rassemblez peu,' she exclaimed triumphantly. 'Moi j'écris très facilement.'

Afterwards I asked him about it, 'Heureusement elle m'a parlé de ses livres et pas des miens.'

I remember vividly the last time I saw him. I had been in America, and he had written me those wonderful letters of his – like filet lace they were, written first one way and then the other. He was ill, and I went to visit him after dinner. First there was the hideous cold ante-room, where everything that could be plain was a pattern and everything that could be flat was an excrescence. In the middle stood a portrait of his father on an easel. Hard, varnished and ugly, permitting – like the rest of the room – no compromise with beauty. The cold was so great that one felt like a fish being kept fresh. Finally I was shown into his room. There were the cork walls I knew so well, helping, or supposed to help, his asthma, and there was the resolute assertion that a room is a bed and a waiting room, something you leave with your thoughts and return to with your pains. I was trying to express something very complicated, apologising because my French was lagging behind, though of course I knew that even in English they were thoughts which would not commandeer words. He smiled with half his mouth, as he always smiled when his mind was giving you a benediction. 'Vous colonisez la langue française,' he said. In front of us were some biscuits and some champagne.

And I felt as I always felt with him, as if I walked into a pool – the pool of his personality in which one moved slowly and ecstatically, detached from life. Caught in his gleaming web, spinning ever further through the air on some thread of his fancy, all the time you remained yourself, because he loved you to be yourself, and because out of the abundance of his generosity he created you in his own image.

64. A posthumous appreciation
1922

An article under 'Current literature', partaking of obituary and assessment, signed 'Affable Hawk', *New Statesman*, 25 November 1922, p. 239.

A sympathetic presentation of Proust's background and talents, linking him with Balzac, Petronius, Ruskin, and Henry James as a means of sharpening the focus on his originality.

Marcel Proust died in Paris on November 18th. He was only fifty-one years old. His father was a Professor of Medicine; his mother, Mdlle Weyl, was a Jewess. He inherited a considerable fortune, perhaps some four or five thousand a year, which diminished in recent years. When he was quite young, in his early twenties, he published a little volume of sketches and essays, *Les Plaisirs et les*

Jours (Calmann Levy), now out of print. It contained a remarkable sketch called *La Fin de la Jalousie*, which has strong affinities with Swann's love story. He was recognised at once by 'the passionate few' as a man with rare literary gifts, and Anatole France dedicated one of the stories in *L'Etui de nacre* to him. It would be a mistake therefore to think of Proust as having made no mark at all until the publication of *Du Côté de chez Swann*, the first of his three long consecutive novels, in 1918. But the narrowness of his reputation, however gratifying in quality, is shown by his failure to find a publisher. Even *La Nouvelle Revue Française*, which afterwards became so strong a supporter, turned it down. He published like another triumphantly successful author, Maurice Barrès, at his own expense.

The *Jeunes Filles*, the second, appeared five years later, and its sequel, *Le Côté de Guermantes*, during the next two years in two parts. There were to have been eight volumes in all. After the appearance of the *Jeunes Filles*, Proust was awarded the Prix Goncourt. A volume of parodies and criticisms, *Pastiches et Mélanges*, is the only other book which we have by him, together with some scattered articles, the most remarkable of which is an essay on Flaubert's style which appeared in *La Nouvelle Revue Française*, January, 1920, and two very extraordinary pieces, *Une Agonie* and *Un Baiser (Nouvelle Revue Française*, January and February, 1921). These, no doubt, will be collected, and it is rumoured that there is a long fragment of the continuation of *A la Recherche du Temps Perdu* series in existence.

He also translated beautifully, though he could not speak a word of English, Ruskin's book on Amiens Cathedral, and over the signature *Dominique* he contributed a series of articles on the 'Salons' of Mme Madeleine Lemaire, the Princesse de Polognac and hostesses. I do not know if he publicly acknowledged these. They were elaborate, long and subtle; perhaps they too will be collected. The best literary portrait of him has been drawn by M. Paul Morand, *Ode à M. Marcel Proust*, and Proust afterwards contributed a preface to M. Morand's *Tendres Stocks*. His fame reached England about the year 1919, and it has continued to flourish intensively perhaps rather than extensively. Proustians, like Stendhalians and admirers of Henry James, are conscious of being united by a peculiarly intimate bond.

After the publication of his first early book, Proust became an inconspicuous but esoterically important figure in society, until ill-health, and perhaps satiety, withdrew him into a life of almost complete retirement. How far he disappeared completely from those circles where his company was so highly valued I do not know, but to many who had eagerly sought his company it probably seemed that this young man was one who had had his day. Perhaps they thought about him as the fashionable friends of Swann thought about Swann, after he became entangled with Odette. Meanwhile, Proust was writing in his bed the book which not a few judges of literature consider the most permanent and important work of fiction of the twentieth century, a huge book, 'comparable', as the excellent notice in *The Times* of November 20th said, 'to his master Balzac, if the *Comédie* be regarded as a coherent and fragmentary unit, comparable also to a genius whose reputation is borne upon a far smaller fragment, Petronius Arbiter.'

For my own part, I do not see the affinity between Proust and Balzac. Proust's methods are those of the miniaturist, though they are devoted to a picture on the scale of a fresco, and such an analogy does not hold good of Balzac's work, whose thoroughness is of another description. Proust, too, is profoundly aesthetic in his response to experience, and this implies so fundamental a difference between any writer of whom that can be said and any other of whom it cannot, that it makes superficial resemblances, due to both reflecting in their work a whole environment, uninteresting. On the other hand, I do see an analogy between Proust and Petronius; Proust, too, is an *arbiter elegantiae*, and no one who is not amused by, or who is out of sympathy with, the application of such standards to life, will find much of Proust's writings trivial and unreadable.

> Animus quod perdidit optat,
> Atque in praeterita se totus imagine versat.

'The mind longs for what it has lost, and is wholly occupied in conjuring up the past.' That quotation from the *Satyricon* would have made a perfect motto for Proust's book. It is an odd coincidence.

Readers of Ruskin's *Præterita* may have been astonished at Ruskin's claim to be the possessor of 'the most analytical mind in Europe'. If I remember right, he does not put this forward as his own judgment of himself. (That would be very unlike him); but he quotes it as the saying of another which, however exaggerated in expression, does emphasise the peculiar quality which he himself considered to be his master quality as a writer. Proust was a great admirer of Ruskin.

The qualities which appealed to him in Ruskin were capacity for rapture and this intense analytical faculty dedicated to impressions made upon him by material objects. Proust possessed both himself, otherwise two men could hardly be more different. His analysis of his impressions is more patient and minute than Ruskin's; the impetus, in his case, is never moral fervour, but the resemblance is

189

there; both make an extraordinary intellectual effort to discover what is behind the impressions which have excited them. Proust traces to the last tiny filament root the sources of his impressions of joy, beauty or disgust. He never rests until the confused ideas which have exalted him have been dragged up into daylight. Describing one of his walks as a boy and his literary ambitions he says: 'Alors, bien en dehors de toutes ces préoccupations littéraires et ne s'y rattachant en rien, tout d'un coup un toit, un reflet de soleil sur une pierre, l'odeur d'un chemin me faisaient arrêter par un plaisir particulier qu'ils me donnaient, et aussi parce qu'ils avaient l'air de cacher au delà de ce que je voyais quelque chose qu'ils invitaient à venir prendre et que, malgré mes efforts, je n'arrivais pas à découvrir. Comme je sentais que cela se trouvait en eux, je restais là, immobile, à regarder, à respirer, à tâcher d'aller avec ma pensée au delà de l'image et de l'odeur. Et s'il me fallait rattraper mon grand-père, poursuivre ma route, je cherchais à les retrouver, en fermant les yeux; je m'attachais à me rappeler exactement la ligne du toit, la nuance de la pierre qui, sans que je pusse comprendre pourquoi, m'avaient semblé pleines, prêtes à s'entr'ouvrir, à me livrer ce dont elles n'étaient qu'un couvercle.'[1] 'It was thus, too, that Ruskin looked at a church, a street, a picture, a face; he stared at the object till he believed he had discovered the scent of its exciting power in something else behind it.

Proust has been compared to Henry James. In the preface of that charming book, *A Little Tour in France*, which Messrs Heinemann have recently republished (7s. 6d.), James says: 'From the moment the principle of selection and expression, with a tourist, is not the delight of the eyes and the play of fancy, it should be an energy in every way much larger; there is no happy mean, in other words, I hold, between the sense and the quest of the picture, and the surrender to it, and the sense and the quest of the constitution, the inner springs of the subject – springs and connections social, economic, historic.' There are relations that soon get beyond all obvious appearances of value to us. Their value becomes thus private and profound, and is only to be represented by the process – the quieter, mostly, the better – of absorption and assimilation of what the relation has done for us. Proust's genius was to find the most complete expression of this process.

NOTE

1 Pléiade I, pp. 178–9.

65. An unsigned posthumous appreciation
1922

Article titled, 'Marcel Proust. An attempted imitation', the *Saturday Review*, 9 December 1922, pp. 868–9.

In praise of Proust's insights in *Swann* and *Guermantes*.

November 19th, a Sunday, a typical November Sunday, with a threat of rain in the air that was less a threat than the absent-minded recollection of a threat of bad weather the day before – as I have seen an old gentleman vacantly look round with a suppressed irritation, because he could not remember what he was angry about – was made more like a November Sunday by the announcement in the evening papers that Marcel Proust had passed away full twenty-four hours before. The morning papers had not said a word about it. But the evening papers all adopted, in mentioning the event, a tone or a rhythm, or perhaps the avoidance of a rhythm, that left no doubt even in readers who only vaguely remembered the name of Proust and never suspected that there are Proust societies in England and Holland, that the man who was to be buried on Tuesday – from the same church of Saint-Pierre-de-Chaillot, where so much wealth has sallied forth for Père-Lachaise to be buried in the soft admiration of the poor for the rich – was not a vulgar celebrated author, but one who, writing exclusively for his own pleasure, made thousands of those real friends, the friends who, to speak truly, care nothing about us but care everything for what they, in common with us, love.

Here are the paper volumes, seven or eight of them, distinguished-looking yet paper volumes all the same which henceforth will be what most people will call Marcel Proust. Of how many books can we say, as we say of these, that there is a witchcraft in them? We cannot open 'Du Côté de chez Swann' or 'Guermantes' without knowing at once that we are giving ourselves up to a charm. Wherever we chance to begin, the subtly coloured film is ready to unroll itself and in fact begins to do so to the monotonous incantation of sublimized every-day words. That which blissful states of consciousness or exceptional occurrences – the singing of a Riviera-bound train, a haunting face no sooner seen than it vanished, dreams from which we wake up in tears – only do for us at long intervals, these pages which are nothing else than the chronicle of a humdrum little French town produce in one moment. Blessed be

Marcel Proust, who had read so much, and had enjoyed books as delicate children confined to two rooms alone can enjoy them, for not having, except in his *Pastiches*, imitated anybody, for being dazzled by nobody and for adopting, every time he took up a pen, the simple process of just telling us what he remembered. 'Never invent anything,' was the advice of that astounding liar, the elder Dumas, to young writers. Marcel Proust, the life-long invalid who knew that wisdom in his case was to take his pleasure in his rooms, just sat down and remembered. Memory and Hope are the two great enchanters without whom life would thin itself into nothingness, and even Hope, in time, tires us by always hoping the same things. But Memory is a marvellous teller of stories, which we know, since we lived them, but never seem to have heard often enough. What schoolboy has not felt that he could stagger his master and bewilder the class if he could just make up his mind to tell what he sees and hears in his memory, but knows he will never dare? What old woman, nodding her head under her laced cap, has not been sure, nay, made us sure, that she could give us the last word of human nature if she would only just abridge it from the thousands of selfish acts she witnessed, or performed? Memory shows us scenes more rapid than they happened and faces more distinct than they really were, while we hear the inward commentary explaining both the scenes and the actors, as sometimes adding up figures in our account book, we hear fives and sevens repeated on the other side of our ear-drum by an awfully clear voice. But Marcel Proust never was afraid – perhaps from the moral standpoint was not sufficiently afraid – of pulling the curtain from his soul cinema and showing us what he saw from the time he could see. There it all is, full of the dewy morning poetry and constantly made clear by introspection as deep and clear as that of many Maeterlincks, indeed, as deep and clear as that of a child of six. But the psychologist and the poet, the curious mosaicist who can look at a thing till it looks enormous and finds words to describe it till there is nothing else to say, is also, is eminently a man who can show you life. He may take four pages to describe one smile, or sixty lines to compare the kitchen maid to Giotto's Charity – without letting us feel that he is saying one word too many – but he can let us into the whole secret of Tante Léonie's character by having her drop one casual remark from the window whence she is watching the Combray people on their way to high mass; he can dispense with giving us an elaborate portrait of his grandfather by merely telling us how the old gentleman, irritated by a remark from his saintly but acid sister, turns to his own daughter and asks: 'What is that verse you quote sometimes? . . . Ah! yes: Even you saints can be too provoking.' His books are full of characters floating, all blended with their surroundings yet definite and life-like, down the stream of multitudinous reminiscences. An enchanter, indeed, the man who never aims at any style yet gives us all the time the impression of a superior finish, the psychologist whose butterfly touch leaves the daintiest notations perfectly fresh, the storyteller who never bothers about transitions yet never gives us a jolt. He says himself – in the early part of 'Du Côté de chez Swann': 'We are slow in recognizing in the features of a new writer the cast answering to what is labelled as *exceptional talent* in our museum of ready-made ideas. Precisely because such a physiognomy is new we cannot at first find it at one with what we call talent. We are rather inclined to use, in speaking of it, such words as originality, charm, subtlety or power; and suddenly, one day, we realize that all this exactly means talent.'

66. Middleton Murry on Proust's sensibility

1922

Extracts from *Discoveries: Essays in Literary Criticism*, London Collins, 1924; originally published in the *Quarterly Review*, July 1922.

J. Middleton Murry (1889–1957), essayist and critic, was among the first to give an extended appreciation of Proust in English.

(a) Extract from a chapter on 'The break-up of the Novel', pp. 136–9; expresses his views on the interplay of intellect and sensibility. To be compared with Rivière's similar observations, No. 42.

In the years 1913–1914 three significant books, calling themselves novels, made an unobtrusive and independent appearance. In France, Marcel Proust published *Du Côté de chez Swann*, in America, the Irishman, James Joyce, published *A Portrait of the Artist as a Young Man*, in England, Dorothy Richardson published *Pointed Roofs*. These books had points of outward resemblance. Each was in itself incomplete, a foretaste of sequels to come. Each was autobiographical and, within the necessary limits of individuality, autobiographical in the same new and peculiar fashion. They were attempts to record immediately the growth of a consciousness. Immediately; without any effort at mediation by means of an interposed plot or story. All three authors were trying to present the content of their consciousness as it was before it had been reshaped in obedience to the demands of practical life; they were exploring the strange limbo where experiences once conscious fade into unconsciousness. The method of Marcel Proust was the most subtle in that he established as the starting point of his book the level of consciousness from which the exploration actually began. He presented the process as well as the results of his exploration of the unconscious memory. In the first pages of his book he described how he concentrated upon a vaguely remembered feeling of past malaise, which he experienced in waking at night and trying to establish the identity of his room. It was a particular form of the familiar feeling: 'I have felt this, been here, seen this, somewhere, somehow, before.' We might almost say that Marcel Proust gives us an account of his technique in penetrating such a sensation and gradually dragging up to the surface of full consciousness forgotten but decisive experiences.

This singularity of Marcel Proust's approach – implied in the general title, *A la Recherche du Temps Perdu* – involving as it does a perpetual reference to the present adult consciousness of the author, is important. It gives a peculiarly French sense of control to his whole endeavour, and a valuable logical (or psychological) complete-ness to his work, in which is unfolded the process by which first a distinct and finally a supreme importance came to be attached to these presentiments of past experience. They are the precious moments of existence; they hold the secret of life. The growth of this conviction is the vital principle of Marcel Proust's book. The conviction becomes more immediate, the sense of obligation to devote himself to penetrating these moments more urgent, so that, even though the work is still unfinished, we can already see that the end will come when this necessity becomes fully conscious and ineluctable – an end strictly and necessarily identical with the beginning. *A la Recherche du Temps Perdu* is at once a philosophical justification of its own existence and the history of its own creation.

That internal completeness is peculiar to Marcel Proust, and it gives him the position of conscious philosopher of a literary impulse which arose, quite independently, in two other minds at the same moment. Simply because it is the most conscious, Marcel Proust's effort subsumes those of James Joyce and Dorothy Richardson, though it is not for that reason more important than they. But common to them all is an insistence upon the immediate conscious-ness as reality. In Miss Richardson this insistence is probably instinctive and irrational; it has a distinctively feminine tinge. In

James Joyce it is certainly deliberate, but less deliberate than in Marcel Proust. But the differences in conscious intention are unimportant compared with the similarity of the impulse.

(b) Part of a chapter defining Proust's innovatory features, notably the emergence of a new sensibility. Originally published as an article: 'M. Marcel Proust: a new sensibility' in the *Quarterly Review*, July 1922, pp. 86–100.

The most apparent phases in the evolution of literature are marked by a twofold change, a change in the intelligence and a change in the sensibility that find expression in it. The writers of a new period seem both to know and to feel more than the writers of the period before them; and these separate developments are bound together in the mesh of a continual interaction. They feel more because they know more. . . .

Whatever may have been our final judgment on the strange novel of M. Marcel Proust, *Du Côté de chez Swann*, which appeared in the year before the war – and the book at least had this obviously in common with a great work of literature, that it lent itself to judgment on many different planes – the persistent element in all our changing opinions was that it marked the arrival of a new sensibility. We were being made aware in new ways, induced to perceive existence in new relations. We seemed to be drawn by a strong and novel enchantment to follow the writer down the long and misty avenues of his consciousness to the discovery of a forgotten childhood. And it was not as though his compelling us to enter into and share the process of his self-exploration was accidental; it was most deliberate. . . .

We are conscious that a single sensibility pervades all the parts, even though the power of projecting it so completely as in the episodes of the musical evening and the death of the grandmother is intermittent. And this sensibility is our chief concern. The underlying motive which animates, or law which governs it, is that which appears so plainly in the first volume – the dependence of memory and mental life as a whole upon association. Without the taste of *madeleine*, tbe boy's past at Combray, without the *petite phrase*, Swann's knowledge of the realities of his love for Odette, would have been sunk in the dark backward and abysm of time. This psychological fact at once governs the conduct of the narrative itself in so far as it is presented in terms of a single consciousness, and determines the conduct of the various characters who appear in it. More than this, the act of penetrating through some present circumstances to a fragment of past experience which it seems to hold strangely concealed behind it, is represented as a consummation of personality. To enter into complete possession of the past by means of such present circumstances is to possess oneself wholly; they are, M. Proust says, the door that opens upon *la vraie vie*. . . .

This concealed motive it is which differentiates M. Proust's book from all that have gone before. The metaphysician might call it the history of a solipsist. But such a definition would be as misleading as all other attempts to find a philosophical definition for a particular work of literature. For, though M. Proust is in a sense applying a theory to experience, he is doing so by the strikingly novel method of describing the process by which the theory was gradually and inevitably formed in the consciousness which applies it. If therefore, M. Proust's book ends, as we believe it will end, in its own beginning, it will have a unity – in spite of the apparent discrepancy of certain of the parts – of a kind which has never been achieved in a work of literature before; it will be the first book in the world that has been the psychological history of its own creation, and a philosophical justification of its own necessity.[1] It will belong in this respect to a new order of literature. And that is what we already vaguely feel as we read it. It is something more than a book in an unfamiliar language, more than a fiction of greater psychological subtlety than we are accustomed to. For better or worse, it marks the emergence of a new kind, the arrival of a new sensibility.

That is its uncommon significance. To find an approximate parallel in the history of modern literature we should probably have to go back to Rousseau. There we should discover the paradox of a man not primarily a literary artist whose work revolutionised the literature of the next hundred years. M. Proust likewise is not primarily a literary artist. Nothing could be more significant than the length of the process of his finding his 'invisible vocation'. Like Rousseau, he is ultimately compelled to writing as a satisfaction for his sensibility. The chief point of difference is that where Rousseau was compelled to express his sensibility upon alien themes, M. Proust has been in the privileged position of one who could afford to wait for the truly inevitable occasion. Still, the only work of literature with which *À la Recherche du Temps Perdu* could profitably be compared is the *Confessions of Jean-Jacques*. There is a real likeness between the driving impulses at work in these books, and a careful comparison might enable us to determine the more important differences between the new sensibility of the eighteenth, and the new sensibility of the twentieth century. . . .

But in endeavouring to analyse the singular impression which M. Proust's work makes upon us and to isolate the elements which produce the effect of novelty, in trying to investigate and assess its deeply-rooted originality, we are in danger of neglecting the more obvious qualities of a book which exhibits at least as many beauties as it conceals. It needs no second reading to appreciate the subtlety of psychological observation, the ironic detachment of the writer's vision of high Parisian society. If the dinner-party at the Guermantes is a masterpiece in a not wholly unfamiliar genre, in the description of the musical evening at Mme de Ste Euverte's the same lucid irony is perceptibly lifted to a higher plane and made to subserve a complex emotional effect. And though the biting wit which flashes home again and again through the narrative of *Du Côté de Guermantes* is of the very highest order in its kind, though the semi-satirical portrait of the *bien pensant* ambassador, M. de Norpois, at the beginning of *A l'Ombre des Jeunes Filles* is perfect, they yield in impressiveness to the certainty of the single touch with which in the description of the grandmother's illness, M. Proust sounds the note of the tragedy of death. When the grandmother has had a paralytic stroke in the Champs Elysées, and the boy suddenly sees 'son chapeau, son visage, son manteau dérangés par la main de l'ange invisible avec lequel elle avait lutté', we feel we are in the presence of a great writer indeed. And besides the command of tragic simplicity and wit, M. Proust has also the gift of humour. . . .

But it is not these qualities, rare and valuable as they are, which make *A la Recherche du Temps Perdu* one of the most significant of contemporary works of literature. They are precious qualities, but they are in a sense superficial, and they might be outweighed by the undoubted obscurity, the awkward complication of language, in large portions of the book. It is something much more than a dark narrative with frequent gleams of beauty; it is a book with at least one of the qualities of permanence, an animating soul. It is maintained by a high and subtle purpose, informed by a view of life as a whole, and because this secret fire glows steadily within it, we feel the radiance through the most forbidding pages long before we are able to detect its source. One consequence of this is that though M. Proust's language is sometimes alembicated to a point of grotesqueness, he has style; we might more exactly apply to him a phrase which he himself has aptly used of a great predecessor, Stendhal, and say that his work has *la grande ossature du style*, a thing of infinitely more importance than limpidity or beauty in the detail of expression. M. Proust's style, in this larger meaning, is as new and original as is the sensibility to which it owes its being.

NOTE

1 This essay was written in 1921. There is now, alas no hope either of proving or confuting the prophecy. (J.M.M.)

1923

TRIBUTES AND ASSESSMENTS

67. André Gide on *Les Plaisirs et les jours*

1923

Part of 'En relisant *Les Plaisirs et le jours*', in 'Hommage à Marcel Proust', *La Nouvelle Revue française*, 1 January 1923, pp. 123–6.

Gide became, after the blunder over rejecting *Swann* for *La Nouvelle Revue française*, an ardent admirer. This brief article illustrates how hindsight grants greater value to the text than contemporary critics could allow.

. . . When I re-read *Les Plaisirs et les jours* today, the qualities of this delicate work, that appeared in 1896, strike me as being so brilliant that I am amazed no one was dazzled by it at the outset. Today, of course, our eyes know what to look out for and everything we have been in a position to admire since then in the recent work of Marcel Proust, we recognize here where at first we were unable to find it. Yes, everything we admire in *Swann* or *Guermantes* is already here, subtly or, as it were, insidiously suggested: the child's expectation of the mother's goodnight kiss, the intermittences of memory, time's dulling of regret, the evocative power of names and places, the distress of jealousy, the winsome charm of landscapes – and even the Verdurin dinners, the snobbery of the guests, the gross vanity of the talk. . . .

Yes, everything that will later break into glorious flower in these long novels appears in an emergent state in this book, the tight bud of these huge blooms – everything we will admire later; unless what we admire is just this very detail and abundance, the extraordinary profusion, the exaggeration and the conspicuous multiplying of everything that is here only at the stage of promise, only in germ. . . .

68. Albert Thibaudet on Proust and tradition
1923

Part of 'Marcel Proust et la tradition française' in 'Hommage à Marcel Proust', *La Nouvelle Revue française*, 1 January 1923, pp. 130–9.

Thibaudet draws attention to Proust's affinities with Saint-Simon and Montaigne.

. . . For six years it has become a commonplace in France to mention alongside Proust the two names of Saint-Simon and Montaigne. Indeed, it deserves to be a commonplace and to be integrated into the links in the chain of our literary history. We must give thought to Saint-Simon and Montaigne if we are to understand the fundamental French genius that is concentrated within Proust's work, that sheer mass of lost time restored to us by this time regained.

Saint-Simon does not only mean Saint-Simon. It is well known that his work, so irregular in its construction, is in three parts. The first part is not by him. It is made up of Dangeau's *Journal* . . . .[1] Saint-Simon first of all stuck on to it the *Additions au Journal*, then extended and remoulded the whole lot in his great quest for lost time in the first part of his definitive *Mémoires* . . . . I would call Proust a Dangeau who has evolved into Saint-Simon. For Proust the world, warts and all, is what Louis XIV was in exactly the same way for Dangeau. . . . Proust sees this world with a many-faceted eye and translates it into the style of Saint-Simon. The living force in people and in the pen is with him only the tremulous vibration of one and the same experience. This depiction of a world implies a world within the sentence itself – that many-sided sentence which seems indefinitely extensible and in which is already included, as in a homoeomeric theory by Anaxagoras,[2] the whole complex structure of the book, just as in the book the whole complexity of life is cast before us. . . . Proust like Saint-Simon is one of those writers who, because they do not see or feel things as simple, would reject simple writing as a betrayal. Each sentence has to preserve the complexity, the density, the emotional intensity or joy in description that were there at the origin of the thoughts and images expressed. Having undertaken to force the reader to see and feel a veritable flood-tide of time, life in its progression, they would be loth to divide into separate drops this advancing wall of water carrying with it all that driving energy of theirs that is in turn part and parcel of it. In Saint-Simon we have a tide of history on the move, people in the mass, the whole of France and the living vehement soul of Saint-Simon ever-present and manifest everywhere. In Proust we have a psychological tide, as vast as the former but, so as to yield its full power and make headway, in need only of a soul, either the author's or the soul of a character whom it has failed to exhaust, inexhaustible as all creatures are. The movement of the sentence accords with the movement of this tide. Portraits by Saint-Simon or by Proust, even of Swann in all its hundreds of pages, never give the impression, however rich, vivid or various they may be, that they have exhausted the unexpected sides and the twists and turns of the character they portray. . . .

At first glance the name of Montaigne is less applicable than that of Saint-Simon. The Proust case, like the Saint-Simon case, would seem to be defined almost as a pathological efflorescence of memory. Montaigne takes care to tell us that in no faculty was he more completely lacking than in memory; the *Essays* provide numerous instances of it. It is not upon the world of men and the figures of his time that Montaigne has cast the net of his experience, but upon himself and upon that human condition that marks everyone. In his book there is no other living portrait than his own. On the other hand, in the part of *A la recherche du temps perdu* so far published, the portrait of the author appears scanty and ill-drawn and not to be compared with the portraits of Swann and Charlus.

However, in Proust the portrait painter, the memorialist and novelist, let us not lose sight of the moralist! Surely one day the psychological and moral reflections that he has scattered through the pages of his work will be gathered together and the extent to which he is linked with the pure line of the great French moralists will become evident. For certain good souls, who cannot stand him, this will be both a discovery and an embarrassment. From this point of view, he may be considered as the present representative of the family of subtle analysts that, since Montaigne, has in our literature so rarely been idle.

His invalid's bedroom has been his Montaigne's tower and, if the spirits of solitude have communed with him and made him speak a different language, it is strange to see that this language proceeds by images that are appreciably analogous to Montaigne's. Proust like Montaigne belongs to the race of image makers, and his images, like Montaigne's, are generally images of movement. The visible modelling, the outer skin of things represents for them mere appearances that have to be penetrated to permit access to the inner movement that has been defined or given expression by them. Proust's universe, and Montaigne's, is a projection of dynamic processes, and it is with these dynamic processes that their style, through the agency of images, strives to coincide. Their styles do not, according to the classic definition, give movement to their thoughts but link their thoughts with a pre-existing sense of movement which those thoughts may choose to take up or reject.

These last few lines, it will be recognized, have a Bergsonian ring to them and they bring us to some suggestive views that I introduce with a certain amount of caution.

Could not these analogies between Proust and Montaigne – the strange sense of mobility they share – be linked with another form of kinship? It is certain that Montaigne's mother, a Lopez, was Jewish. Here in Montaigne is the only one of our great writers with Jewish blood in his veins. Proust's similar heredity is well known. Such is also the mixed heredity of the great philosopher whose name I have just used, the founder of that philosophy of movement that he has expressed in mobile, visual-motor images so similar to those used by Montaigne and Proust. . . . A Montaigne, a Proust and a Bergson bring into our complex and rich literary universe what might be called the Franco-Semitic doublet, just as there are Franco-English, Franco-German and Franco-Italian doublets in literature, just as France itself is a North–South doublet. But let us take all that only indirectly, exercising also a flexible mobility on our part. The French tradition to which we must relate Marcel Proust is a living, unpredictable, singular tradition, irregular in its movements, meandering, twisting and turning, a tradition that, like a Proustian sentence or page, always surpasses its particular content by virtue of its inner elasticity and the abundance of its vitality.

NOTES

1 Philippe Dangeau (1638–1720); author of an unpublished *Journal* concerning life at the court of Louis XIV that was used by Saint-Simon as the basis of his own *Mémoires*.
2 View held by Anaxagoras concerning the ultimate homogeneity of all parts of matter.

69. Jacques Boulenger justifies Proust's digressions

1923

Part of 'Sur Marcel Proust' in 'Hommage à Marcel Proust', *La Nouvelle Revue française*, 1 January 1923, pp. 140–5.

Jacques Boulenger relates Proust's originality to his free fantasy method of composition.

. . . [Proust] distrusted any intervention of orderly reason in the search he led within himself for his memories: 'The information that voluntary memory, the memory of the intelligence, gives of the past does not preserve anything of it,' he used to say.

And it is perfectly understandable that a novelist whose intention is of this order should have steered clear of all thought of 'composition', i.e. of proportion and rational design. As far as he is concerned, there are no details or digressions; everything is on the same footing and his book is the exact opposite of a panoramic view. This also explains why, in relation to the whole, he sacrifices nothing that seems to him to have truly intrinsic worth. Only once does he apologise for a digression, viz. in the account of the Princesse de Guermantes' evening reception. And just examine how this account is put together. Once again there is no impression of ensemble, no unity of action, no concern for 'composition' or perspective. He arrives, meets various people one by one and successively exhausts absolutely all the significant facts he recalls about them, then absolutely all the interesting remarks that each of these events inspires in him and then, when there is room, the observations occasioned in turn by these remarks. Proust never considers that a fact, provided it has some sense to it, or a commentary, however slight its subject, should be set aside or curtailed for aesthetic reasons. As long as it is true or right, that is all that matters to him; for him the beautiful is not a selection to be made from the truth, it is the whole truth. And with him the novel takes an astonishing step forward. For, far from limiting himself to giving us merely the 'external world', far from austerely abstaining from any intellectual explanation, Proust does not put forward a fact or a retort (and how superior they are in quality!) without immediately criticizing them, weighing them up, studying them and analysing them with marvellous intelligence; and if need be he comments on his very own commentary, so that his book is like those medieval treatises where the text disappears beneath the embroidery of glosses and of glosses upon glosses; it is a 'summa'. Of course, other examples of 'psychological' novels, 'analytical' novels exist. These are novels in which the author does not restrict himself to showing us his characters speaking and acting, and where at certain moments he enumerates for us their thoughts and feelings. Proust, however, is not content with this enumeration and does not give us merely an analysis – he gives us a systematic analysis. Yes, *A la recherche du temps perdu* is a psychological 'summa'. . . .

70. Edmond Jaloux on Proust's psychological analyses

1923

Part of 'Sur la psychologie de Marcel Proust' in 'Hommage à Marcel Proust', *La Nouvelle Revue française*, 1 January 1923, pp. 151–61.

Jaloux draws attention to Proust's originality in the treatment of the themes of love and time.

(a) The depiction of love.

. . . It seems to me that before Marcel Proust novelists studied it [love] as a function of the feeling that it represents and not as a function of the individuals who experienced it. Hence a certain universalizing, almost anonymous character given to this depiction. The French mentality habitually reduces problems to the state of schematic representations. It is also very rare for us to meet in literature anything other than a partly abstract lover whose features are virtually identical and in whom we do not find any of those personal, curious, unexpected reactions – vouched for by our intelligence, our spiritual life, our health, our sexual inclinations or our character – that we actually experience ourselves. It could be claimed that in these portraits the individual disappears, together with all his dangerous, fortuitous, complex and contradictory elements, and that he is replaced by the Lover. . . .

In the seventeenth century, with the exception of Racine and

Mme de La Fayette . . . love only served to set off characters conceived *a priori*: [Molière's] Misanthrope is more concerned with his misanthropy than with Célimène. . . .

In the nineteenth century, in spite of appearances, the same applies; Balzac uses the same psychological repertory as George Sand. Only the psychological writers of 1880, following the example of Stendhal, attempted a reaction, but the character they created rapidly turned into such a stereotype that the vast majority of novelists have been for forty years depicting a certain type of lover who behaves like a hero by Bourget or Maupassant – very representative of the sensibility of their period – even though the personal reactions of people have been very different for quite a long time.

Bringing the notion of relativity into the conception of love, and liberating it from that myth of the absolute it has depended on till now, will be seen on reflection as one of the essential results arrived at by Proust.

It seems that novelists have always lied on this point, as if they did not dare speak the truth, as if they were pursuing in the novel the quest for those illusions that please women readers and in which they take personal pride in pleasing them. This has led Proust to speak of oblivion and of the causes of oblivion just as much as of the very beginnings of love.

In *A l'ombre des jeunes filles en fleurs* he has devoted, to this particular problem, some of the most subtle and profound pages of his work. The conventional idea that he came up against was the *coup de foudre* of predestined love. Also he first of all shows us in his hero that state of being in a sentimental vacuum, that state of imaginative idleness, that makes over-excited behaviour of this kind possible and even obligatory. . . .

So in this state of complete availability, the narrator experiences agreeable feelings at the sight of a laughing, rumbustious flock of girls; he longs to know them, and dreams of them without at first making a choice. Then one of them, the 'renowned Albertine' attracts him in particular. His imagination works on her image and gradually incorporates in her all the elements of her being that are to converge in the creation of amorous desire. But when he meets her, he experiences a cruel disillusion, so much does the real Albertine differ from the one he had invented. However, he reconsiders the matter and ends up forging a notion of the girl that partly blends together dream and reality. . . . However, in beginning to love her, he loves her so little that he all but falls (out of vanity) for Gisèle, then he all but prefers Andrée, and if his choice finally comes to rest on Albertine it is because she decides to take the first step.

He describes this feeling of multiple loves in these terms:

At the beginning of a love-affair, as at the end, we are not exclusively attached to the object of this affair, but rather the desire to love, out of which the affair will emerge (and later the memory the affair leaves behind), wanders voluptuously about in a zone of interchangeable delights – delights sometimes simply of nature, of nice things to eat or of the place where we live – that are sufficiently harmonically related to each other for the desire to love not to feel out of place with regard to any one of them.[1]

In these incomparable pages, Marcel Proust indicates with rare lucidity how far, since the earliest times, the desire to perpetuate the species . . . has evolved, and also what remains of it in the superimposition of involuntary mental fabrications that love has turned into.

(b) The theme of time.

. . . Here we find an obvious and considerable influence: that of George Eliot. Already in the author of *Middlemarch* there is a profound renewal of psychology similar to his own, though [George] Eliot is especially good at showing us the changes in people under the stress of circumstances. Alongside her I can only see Tolstoy and Turgenev who have had – but to a lesser degree – such an extraordinary gift. It is not only a matter of getting a hero to commit actions at the end of a book that he might not have done at the beginning, and that are consistent with his nature, but of showing under the pressure of what everyday events a character can end up conceiving actions that are the very opposite of those he would have committed at an earlier time. In the opening pages of the novel, old Goriot is already the whole of Goriot, Micawber the whole of Micawber; but the bitter and humbled Lydgate of the last pages of *Middlemarch* is a different individual from the haughty, enthusiastic doctor of his younger years, . . . and Swann who, before his marriage, and without preening himself because of it, was received by the Comte de Paris, is, after marrying a *cocotte*, proud of the fact 'that the wife of a junior minister has paid a call on Mme Swann'. The crowning achievement of a great novelist is to make this work of time visible; and I can see no rarer quality or one deserving greater admiration; the creation of time is essentially the accomplishing of a divine task. The preoccupation with doing so fills the numerous volumes of *A la recherche du temps perdu*.

In writers before Proust, this measurement of time was expressed by short-cuts, by scenes that indicate the work of time already carried out upon an individual and that pointed to the work left to be done. These were views taken obliquely at different periods of a character's existence. With Proust it is quite a different affair, and it is in this respect that his psychology is so new. He demonstrates for us what this work of time involves.

This ceaseless creation and growth of new cells of our spiritual being, weakening, driving out and replacing the old, the at first unconscious modifications, then gradually the consequent revelations, the partly irresponsible reaction of the human being faced with those metamorphoses that take place unbeknown to him and that he can do no more than register and analyse as they present themselves to his consciousness – such is the unique and enormous subject that fills the vast volumes of *A la recherche du temps perdu*.

Never has a literary work come so close to science; it recalls the splendid prophetic remark by Claude Bernard: 'I am persuaded that a day will come when the physiologist, the poet and the philosopher will speak the same language and will all understand each other.'

Marcel Proust has been criticized for concerning himself with tiny details; this is a fair observation if by that one understands that human life is something infinitely tiny. But it misfires if one confers on life a certain grandeur; in fact, what is involved here is nothing less than our whole existence; no man, since Montaigne, has erected as an object of study such a monument as this or assembled a similar sum of human actions. And we must add that Marcel Proust, a son of a doctor and himself an invalid throughout his life, has insisted that illness and death should occupy the place in life that they do in fact have in it and that writers scarcely grant them.

Thus we see following one upon the other, with abrupt or extended transitions – and sometimes no transition at all – the successive 'selves' that make up our personalities. What we particularly see being established, and with rigorous exactness, is the fact that, whatever may be the circumstances we are going through, and even if they remain almost unchanged, we are never absolutely the same for any two moments of our existence and that the fabric that makes up our lives is at every minute being nourished by different elements, like droplets of water in a river. Now, if this is the case, the fault lies with our subconscious mind that receives, with each particle of time, perceptions that it does not immediately communicate to us, that accumulate in it and from which we receive a massive electric shock each time that some current puts us in touch with it. . . .

NOTE

1 Pléiade I, p. 916.

71. Louis Martin-Chauffier on analytical procedures

1923

Part of 'Marcel Proust analyste' in 'Hommage à Marcel Proust', *La Nouvelle Revue française*, 1 January 1923, pp. 172–8.

Louis Martin-Chauffier examines the subjective base of Proust's observation of reality.

. . . Now, as to this admirably defined profundity, it is within himself, in the act of self-examination that he has taken such perfect cognizance of it. And if we wish to discover why his characters are not only constructed with exact, intimate proportions but (unlike Balzac's which are also well-proportioned, though larger than life) given an equally proportioned setting, we must seek the proof that he had the most precise and least limited self-knowledge by examining in his work the two persons who are not only outwardly observed but revealed from the inside: the 'I' and Swann.

One day I made Marcel Proust smile with delight when I shyly presented him with a discovery I had made: Swann and the 'I' are two moments of one and the same man, two aspects, if you like, of a single personality diversified by circumstances, two areas of land of the same type, but, having different plants and different climates, not producing the same flowers. Their original resemblance, besides being obvious from many points of view, can be recognized in the procedure of the painter, who, unlike other practitioners, treats them analytically, because for him they are not an illustration of his discoveries, but the very substance he will dig into to make his discoveries and put his tools to the test.

The danger that lies in wait for analysts who are too subtle is, as they get carried away with excitement, to forget the rules of the game and render their actions more and more barren as these proceed. They think they are being ever more profound and making ever rarer discoveries because they latch on to a previously unsuspected shade of meaning, which they fail to recognize as being less and less interesting the more and more exceptional and individual it is. . . .

Proust's procedure is just the opposite. He himself pointed it out to me. For him the precision instrument is not a microscope, but a telescope. What interests him is not the infinitely tiny, but bringing into focus far off vistas that are lost in mist and outside his field of vision, and clearly distinguishing, and in their corrected perspective, vague distant backgrounds. His sense of proportion, instead of going awry in this search, extends its domain in depth and, precisely because of this clarity of vision, the clouds he describes (or false ideas, or prejudices etc. etc.), far from dissolving away, appear as what they really are, clouds, and are treated from that point onwards, as such, while a mountain-ridge, say, though belonging to a single whole, becomes the glinting spur jutting out of an undefined mountain mass with which, from a distance, it appeared fused. But when you think that these cloudy masses are the very depths of the human soul, and that the look that gives them their form is the actual look of this soul, you are amazed – more than by the new light that clothes them – by the qualities necessary for this brilliance to be able to exist at all. To live and watch oneself living, even in the palpitations of life's extreme fringes, to meditate, to seek and find the explanation for each of these movements and their harmonious accord without distortion (through error, vanity or shame), to avoid breaking this delicate accord in analysing it, to discover in it and verify through it the universal laws of harmony, without being distracted by personal interpretations; then to project this knowledge-laden gaze outwards and apply it, with the same felicity and the same finesse, to everything that lives around one that shares the same, though differently fashioned, life – that is the real miracle. . . .

72. Robert de Traz on Proust and the subconscious
1923

Part of 'Note sur l'inconscient chez Marcel Proust' in 'Hommage à Marcel Proust', *La Nouvelle Revue française*, 1 January 1923, pp. 195–7.

Robert de Traz examines Proust's use of the subconscious in relation to the prestigious place given to memory.

Now that Marcel Proust is dead, what saddens us is not only the death of a great artist of the novel, but also our general inability to define precisely what is essentially innovative in his work. There is none more mysterious; time alone will bring as yet veiled meanings to the surface. . . .

The reason is that this work has been, as much as anything, conceived as a function of duration. Proust's principle is a retrospective one. Between himself and events, he puts not only a historical distance but also a psychological one. His vision is graded in its perspectives. Could the immediate experience, happening before his very eyes, be said to interest him, otherwise than as a future reserve, something to be used only when fully ripe? What constitutes his genius is a long memory.

He used this surprising memory-oriented imagination of his not only to remind himself of the past but to make discoveries. He was the first to see that it provided the only means of communicating with the subconscious. Those obscure zones where our wishes and passions interact have for long been prohibited. It is impossible to know the subconscious directly because to do so would be to make it accessible to reason and cause it to vanish in the light of day, nor is it possible to capture it at the very moment when it functions because to do that would be to render it sterile at the moment of making it lucid. What Proust does is to re-establish links with it after the event, by reminiscence. His point of departure is a forgotten sensation that comes freshly and actively alive and step by step stirs up emotions to the point of laying bare the soul itself. . . .

Hence the complexity of his narratives. His memory restores whole sections to him in detail because it acts like a photographic developer. Pure intelligence would make choices out of a love for fine order but at the expense of variety, and especially of psychological variety. Proust does not invent nor does he exclude: he bears witness to a resurrection. A universe that has been tucked away out of sight reveals itself to him, complete and inextricable. This is the explanation for the homogeneity and the density of his characters. Not one of them is 'reported'; they are all born of a single inner vision, nourished by Proust's own substance. And we have here another of his discoveries: we can observe others only in ourselves. Breaking with the bad example of the naturalists who only saw things from the outside and made picturesque notes, he has set out to look for reality in the place where it is possible to come to grips with it, i.e. within the novelist himself. That is why his commentaries – those amazing solos in which, when the orchestra is silent, a single instrument can sing out – are never out of keeping. Balzac's commentaries interrupt the rhythm of a chapter, Proust's carry that rhythm to its appointed end. He is not a witness who suddenly takes the floor, he is the very theatre of the action – and one of flesh and blood. His novels, taken all in all – characters, episodes, style and commentaries – are made of the 'stuff of his dreams'. . . .

73. Camille Vettard on style and the theme of time
1923

Part of 'Proust et le temps', in 'Hommage à Marcel Proust', *La Nouvelle Revue française*, 1 January 1923, pp. 204–11.

Camille Vettard analyses the relationship of Proust's uses of language to the expression of the detailed concepts of time that he introduces into the novel.

(a) The layout of the novel reflects time in its duration.

. . . From this point of view, the typography of his works – especially that of the first editions of *A l'ombre des jeunes filles en fleurs* – is as revealing as the typography of Mallarmé's *Un coup de dés*. This close, microscopically detailed, dense text, with massive paragraphs broken up by very few indentations, gives, by comparison with the text of other writers, the same impression that a clock-face showing the seconds would give when put alongside a clock-face showing the hours or minutes. Proust divides the ordinary time of other novelists, or, more exactly the intervals of time they are accustomed to using, into an infinity of smaller intervals, and, since this division is carried out not only as regards the inner life but also as regards the external world, he attempts to describe or narrate everything that goes on in each of these infinitesimal intervals. The result is that, as far as the inner life, the psychological life is concerned, Proust has been induced to note, deep within the cycles of the psyche, between the point of departure and the point of arrival, numerous revelations neglected by his predecessors, distinguishing with each passing second the intellectual representations (perceptions, evocations, judgments), the affective repercussions (emotions, feelings) and the external motor displays (reflexes, moods or states of muscle tone, actions) that make up these cycles. We should note that from this point of view his descriptions are truly

Cartesian and not merely Bergsonian and that they do not admit of those 'Rembrandtesque lighting techniques', those 'chiaroscuro effects' that only yield an imperfect analysis and an imperfect inventory. . . .

(b) Detailed analysis and its effect on sentence structure.

. . . In short, Proust has changed the scale of our perception of duration. He has endowed us, so to speak, with an apparatus to register time (or rather to register variations of things and people in time) that is infinitely more true, precise and sensitive than what we had before. This obviously allows us (as does the calculating of a new decimal in science) to formulate more precise, more detailed laws, and in a new form. . . .

The expansion of the individual's inner world, the intermittences and the time-slips in our emotions, the combination of all the different forces of mind and body in the progression of the cycles of the psyche, the infinite nuances of minutes, hours and days – all these things call out for a special means of expression, the sentence itself is transformed by them. I have recently . . . referred to the analogy that to my mind is presented by Proust's sentence and Einstein's intrinsic co-ordinates.[1] Since Einstein had to seek formulas applicable to a universe whose curvature varies at every point, he was led to invent those 'mollusc' or 'octopus type references' that M. Gaston Moch has described as constituting 'axes of co-ordinates which are no longer straight or curved, but filaments continuously moving in all directions, waving about like the tentacles of an octopus'. Similarly, in order to follow exactly the sinuousities and the oscillations of the inner life, as well as the ceaseless variations in its mood, Proust has devised this marvellous and audacious sentence of his (so little appreciated) whose subordinate clauses, parentheses, dashes, innumerable sub-propositions and countless many-sided images alter our vision of things as much as the past definites and imperfects, present participles and certain pronouns and prepositions in Flaubert. . . .

NOTE

1 Cf. Edmund Wilson, No. 140, p. 408 for the notion of relativity.

74. Emma Cabire on subjectivism and love
1923

Part of 'La conception subjectiviste de l'amour chez Marcel Proust', in 'Hommage à Marcel Proust', *La Nouvelle Revue française*, 1 January 1923, pp. 212–21.

Emma Cabire gives an appreciation of Proust's picture of the conflict between personalities where love is concerned. She shows special interest in the obsession with jealousy, where the subjectivist stance is challenged as it clashes with the freedom and demands of the opposite partner.

. . . However, happiness cannot be truly known, for possession substitutes a new state for what was simply a desire for happiness, overlaying it but not identifying itself with it. To look for spiritual possession or just physical possession is still to believe in its reality and its importance where love is involved. As Marcel Proust's hero becomes more and more aware of the pure subjectivity of his feelings, we see his belief in the possibility of this kind of happiness diminish and his belief in the necessity almost of pursuing its realization diminish likewise. This conviction he has about the inwardness of love modifies his attitude towards the women he successively loves and his demands on them. And this is very important. A different emotional hygiene comes into play when we no longer expect of another individual the happiness to be found in our own feelings; we only require the other partner to go along with this idealization and not contradict it too obviously. The pain in love that is not shared lies not so much in not receiving any of the proofs of love for which we have long substituted illusion. It lies in the painful effort – once we have recognized the need to adopt a different attitude – to contain within us a love that otherwise could not be prevented from spilling over in tender words, caresses or loving attentions, and that has to be repressed at all costs since, in anticipation of sexual expression, it could only encounter lassitude and satiety, so strong is our need above all to love and not to be loved.

Among the sufferings of love there is one to which Marcel Proust has given pride of place. For some natures jealousy can indeed be a terrible torment. For them, the precarious happiness of love is clouded at every moment by doubt. Just as the hope of possessing a woman has occasioned the origin of love, the doubt that this possession may somehow escape you becomes the origin of a veritable malady of the imagination, which sends down its poisoned roots into the very feeling intended to bring us happiness, feeding on it, dying with it and occasionally surviving it. Just as that feeling – the shadow of love, a mirror image of it – is made of numerous kinds of love, so jealousy is made of an infinite number of suspicions. Jealousy is the imagination tormented by the unknown elements in someone's life that escape from our control, from our possession.

Until the first suspicion, this life appeared to us to be without any mystery. We imagined that the side we did not know was the same as the side facing us. With the first suspicion actually relating to a moment of this unknown life, a split occurs in the imagination and a construction is put on all the new facts whose significance had escaped us. All that was unknown and enigmatic ferments, increases, becomes frightening and laden with mysteries.

Alongside this incipient suffering a different effect of jealousy – for the very reason that it puts an end to the dullness of habit that diminishes the uniqueness of the individual – is the renewal of love (as always there is an alternating, binary rhythm); but this time the imagination does not follow the same course. If, from now on, we cannot immediately interpret everything that is new about the person we love – a new expression, a new gesture – by reference to what we know, it is attributed by us to the unknown side and becomes a new source of anguish. Where love found reasons for belief, jealousy finds occasions for doubt. It attributes a hidden sense, a secret intention to looks and words. The ground we advance over is mined; its surface is possibly only a thin film. Swann's painful meditations on Odette's comings and goings, on the true reality behind the orangeade he is about to drink one evening at her house in the company of Forcheville make us think of Dostoevsky. Proust has never been more penetrating. . . .

75. Roger Allard on Proust and painting
1923

Part of 'Les arts plastiques dans l'oeuvre de Marcel Proust', in 'Hommage à Marcel Proust', *La Nouvelle Revue française*, 1 January 1923, pp. 222–30.

Roger Allard, having traced Proust's interest in fine art from *Les Plaisirs et les jours* to his translations from Ruskin, concludes by bringing out fruitful parallels between Proust's imagination and painting in *La Recherche*.

. . . In deciding on the features of his characters, Proust most often summons help from the Dutch and Italian painters. There is Bloch who looks like a portrait of Mahomet by Bellini and one of Albertine's friends is like a 'portrait of Jeffries by Hogarth'. Odette makes a timely appearance in Swann's life as someone who enriches his taste in painting. We may recall Swann's delight in the resemblance between Odette and [Botticelli's] Zephora. . . . We may recall also the photographs of figures by Giotto that Swann gives to the hero of the book who only understands the striking strangeness and special beauty they have – deriving from the importance given to their symbolic dimensions – because of a resemblance he finds between these figures and a pregnant kitchen-maid. . . .

All these comparisons, though a lot less frequent in the later volumes, are perfectly precise and felt. Hence the natural air they have in common and that never gives the impression of an author lacking in stamina and looking amongst the bric à brac of art for something to substitute for descriptive genius.

Nothing is more remarkable in this respect than the descriptions of monuments, for example, the unforgettable picture of the church of Saint-André-des-Champs in the second volume of *Swann*. A picture? A narrative rather, for the elements of the scene appear in it in the actual order needed to light up the reader's imagination, or, to put it better, to move the senses, so instantaneously does it seem that the landscapes, objects and faces described by Proust are brought within touching distance. Colour, texture, smell, historic or symbolic dimensions – everything is suggested in one go.

Even if he had never mentioned the name of Claude Monet, who so often recurs in his books, one would have been struck by the deep influence the impressionist masters had on the novelist. He requires a painter not to reproduce what he sees, but to teach others how to see, delighting them with illusion, in a word 'partly to lift the veil of ugliness and triviality that leaves us bereft of curiosity as we contemplate the universe'. Understood in this way, the pleasure provided by drawing comparisons is something complex and refined, and not to be exhausted by a cursory glance.

In this way we can understand Proust's admiration for the painter of cathedrals and water-lilies, whose art he attempted more than once to rival, witness the description of the water-gardens of the Vivonne. It is certain too that he must have shared Ruskin's enthusiasm for Turner and that some of the features of Elstir are rather reminiscent of the latter and also of Whistler. Everyone has read in À l'ombre des jeunes filles en fleurs the description of the sea at Balbec, in which are noted the effects of light as it changes the shape of objects, at times totally absorbing them or breaking them up, bringing distant vistas nearer and modifying perspectives – effects that belong less, to tell the truth, to the impressionists than to those of their successors like MM. Vuillard and Bonnard. Though he does not say much about it, Proust must have thought deeply about Degas, the technical devices used in the lay-out of his pages and his taste for unexpected viewpoints. This is precisely what Elstir's art makes us think about, Elstir who is shown as deriving from a well-known object some singular image, 'an image different from those we are accustomed to see, singular and yet true, and which for that very reason we find doubly striking because it astounds us, shakes us out of our usual habits, and at the same time makes us turn in on ourselves as an impression is brought to mind.' . . .[1]

NOTE

1 Pléiade, p. 838.

76. François Fosca on period colour in Proust
1923

Part of 'La couleur temporelle chez Marcel Proust' in 'Hommage à Marcel Proust', *La Nouvelle Revue française*, 1 January 1923, pp. 240–2.

François Fosca points out the atmosphere and the time perspective Proust creates in his descriptions.

I think that to recognize Proust's novel . . . as partaking as much of memoirs as of fiction is in no way to diminish its merit. It differs from memoirs because it does not give a word for word report of Proust's real life, and does not contain the authentic portraits of the individual people Proust frequented or met. But, even if one might for a moment consider it to be only memoirs, disregarding its fictional element, it seems to me to represent memoirs of a rather special kind. According to the usual practice, the man who writes memoirs, whether he be Saint-Simon, Casanova or Léon Daudet, tells us about past events while allowing them to retain their essential quality as past events. He looks on them with the distance given them by time and their chronological sequence. Proust, on the other hand, tells us about many events belonging to the past, but all his efforts are directed at not restricting them to the past; his efforts are directed at re-establishing them in the present. The memorialist treats facts – and in this term I include characters, places and his own sensations – as a historian; Proust treats them as the spiritualist seeks to treat the dead, in the hope that he will succeed in breathing new life into them.

Among the methods employed to reach this goal, there is one in which he is incomparable, and that I feel no one has pointed out; I mean the manner in which he restores for us the atmosphere of certain times, what I shall call period colour, which is to time what local colour is to space. Consider, in the final pages of *Du côté de chez Swann*, the description of the Bois de Boulogne and of Mme Swann driving in it. The picture dates from 1890–5, and to make the period characteristics stand out, Proust contrasts it with a description of the Bois around 1910 or so. Just as an art historian compares a portrait by Winterhalter to a portrait by Van Dongen, Proust contrasts Odette Swann's victoria with the motor-cars it passes and the little toque hats and fine gowns of his heroine with the 'immense' hats 'covered with fruit, flowers and various birds' and the 'Liberty chiffon dresses dotted with flowers like wall-paper'. All this is specified with extraordinary conciseness, and all he has to do is to describe a 'mauve bonnet' to reconstitute the whole of this period for us. He goes even further in those pages at the beginning of *A l'ombre des jeunes filles en fleurs* where he recounts his visits as a quite young man to the Swanns'. What restores to us the period colour of 1890 is not only the interiors, Odette's dresses, the fashionable behaviour of the day, little touches like the allusions to the Comte de Paris or the meeting with the Princesse Mathilde, but also the tone of the conversations and the language used. Particularly notable is the conversation between Mme Swann, Mme Cottard and Mme Bontemps. . . .

77. Paul Fierens on Proust's modernism

1923

Part of 'Anticipation', in 'Hommage à Marcel Proust', *La Nouvelle Revue française*, 1 January 1923, pp. 243–5.

Paul Fierens, strikingly for such an early date, defends Proust as innovator. His comparison with the art of the cinema shows a daring attempt to 'recuperate' Proust's text from the tendency to misread it because of its novelty. He envisages how future generations will be even more appreciative of Proust's genius. In his article he imagines what would be said in an academic lecture by a figure of the literary establishment.

. . . The time will come when a learned professor will explain his work, just as today we explain *La Comédie humaine* or the *Divine Comedy*.

'Gentlemen,' he will say, 'in the preceding lectures I attempted to show what Proust's discoveries were in the domain of psychology, how he undertook in the area of subliminal consciousness an exploration along paths no French writer could show him; how, as he returned to the regions of lucid consciousness, he describes them with a mastery equal to that of the best historians; how in either case he satisfies better than any author that need for logic, that need to

217

"know why", which in their intensity are characteristic of our nation. I told you, though without forcing the point, that he had no religious sense. It now remains for me to set out before you, from a formal standpoint, questions of technique, certain considerations on his artistic methods and the rhythm and lay-out of his work.

'At the beginning of the twentieth century, aestheticians were greatly given to using the verb "construct" and it was the start of a happy return to purity. But not many cathedrals were built. They constructed – note, Gentlemen, that I speak figuratively – a certain number of beautiful ornaments, paper-weights, a few pieces of furniture, two or three houses. At the same time, poets, with talk of "dynamism", sent up marvellous rockets. There were a lot of damp ones, and they failed.

'Meanwhile a quite young art was awakening the curiosity of all and sundry. By its nature it offered aestheticians movement, "modernism", a vast field of experience and study. It was only later that theoreticians of form discovered its principles of composition, its harmony and counterpoint. I am alluding, as you may well guess, to the cinema. It would be puerile to wish, at all costs, to compare Proust's work, which is so complex and profound, with the earliest realizations of an art form that is very much given to externals. And the comparison, which may be more successfully attempted where lesser talents are involved, would be outrageous if we did not take the precaution of limiting its significance to the area of observation of concrete detail. Also the chroniclers have neglected to tell us if the master attended any cinematographic performances. However, as I hope to show you in the course of this lecture, there exist, between the structural principles of a Proust and the technique of the screen, connections that are analogous to those that can, for instance, be perceived between the conception of Dante and the first Florentine fresco painters, Giotto and especially his successors at the Santa Croce, the Chapelle des Espagnols and the Campo Santo in Pisa.

'What was the technique used by an American film-director in cutting the scenario of a fashionable gathering so as to show the development of the principal characters? It is exactly the same as Proust's when he tells us about an evening reception at the Verdurins or the Guermantes, with rather abrupt changes of angle, close-ups of faces, slow motion passages, a few dissolves, a flash-back to the past, suggesting the mood, breaking off the narrative thread and skilfully picking it up again, without any concern for the inattentive or those whose minds are on other things. Giving the analysis and depicting the scene are simultaneous; there is a rich orchestration underlying the melodic motifs that can, like Vinteuil's little phrase, always be made out.

218

'By pursuing this analogy further, you will bring to light the hidden structure of a work that has long been thought of as dense, – which, after all, was no criticism – and you will affirm with me that *A la recherche du temps perdu* is the finest film in the world.'[1]

NOTE

1 For the cinematic comparisons cf. Nos 95, 103, section (b), and 119.

78. Ernst-Robert Curtius on Proust's originality

1923

An essay on Proust in 'Hommage à Marcel Proust', *La Nouvelle Revue française*, 1 January 1923, pp. 262–6.

Curtius (1886–1956), a leading international critic of French literature at this time, provides a German assessment of Proust's place in the European literary tradition.

What did we experience on our first contact with Proust's books? The sudden surprise of handling something unknown, of touching a new substance whose structure we found elusive. We felt disorientated and forced to apply ourselves to a method of expression for which none of our mental habits was prepared. Disconcerted at first, then intrigued and gripped, we were not slow in allowing ourselves to be overwhelmed by a mysterious power of attraction. Like the companions of Ulysses in the land of the Lotus-eaters, we had tasted of a fruit that made us forget our spiritual past and took away from us the desire to return to our former sources of nourishment. Drunk with our discovery, we could not distinguish whether it was a new form of art or a new level of existence that was being offered us. But taking stock of ourselves, reconsidering analytically the path we had travelled, we recognized the sheer impossibility of making a distinction between aesthetic emotion and the disruption of our whole being as the utterly infallible sign of that quite uncommon thing: the revelation of a great work of art.

I would like to give its full meaning to this term great art that seems to me to be inevitable as a description of Proust. Certainly, there is no lack of finely-wrought, attractive and powerful works among contemporary productions. But do they not seem – almost all of them – to take their point of departure from traditional literary forms, either by continuing them or by challenging them, which is only another way of being dependent on them? But alongside these works that are grafted on to previous literature and whose regular growth would even seem to guarantee their, so to speak, secondary quality, there is a small number of works that come into existence outside the mainstream, as it were, of the literary preoccupations of the day. They seem to be neither called into being by the 'moment' nor motivated by an artistic current; they differ profoundly from ordinary literature without the desire for difference being evident in them. These works, that are less dependent on literature than literature will be on them and that arise from the original energy of a powerful spirit meditating upon life itself, are the ones I was thinking of when I used the term great art.

In the work of Marcel Proust creative power offers a spectacle that is all the more admirable in that it has exercised itself upon the richest literary and intellectual culture, one which, in a mind of lesser calibre, could have presented an obstacle to such a new achievement by paralysing it or leading it astray in a heady, but bookish, alexandrianism. Proust's art, instead of being fettered by the treasures of his literary remembrances, succeeds on the contrary in showing them off to advantage, or, even better, in revealing to us their novelty. He can create spontaneous life out of the whole inheritance of the past. In handling it, he keeps in direct and immediate contact with the elusively fleeting substance that is woven into our lives. Proust offers himself to it with a sensibility that seems totally free of all previous contact – otherwise how would this sensibility succeed in capturing nuances of reality that until now had escaped us? The slightest evidence of experience that might have been transmitted or of habit that might have been interposed between them and the receiving apparatus would have formed a barrier and would have prevented them being registered. This sensibility, however, is reinforced by a mind nourished on the richest and most diverse tradition – as familiar with Ruskin as it is with Saint-Simon. It is from this clash of two seemingly mutually exclusive things – the most freshly spontaneous sensibility and the most culture-conscious intelligence (but which in his case inter-penetrate and mutually support each other) – that Proust's art derives its new and moving beauty.

In a more general way, the profound originality of the great artist who has just passed away is revealed in the fact that attitudes of mind, which we usually consider as being quite distinct, interconnect in him to the extent of forming a homogeneous totality. Intelligence is not superimposed upon emotion but becomes an integral part of it. Feeling and analysis do not appear as two conflicting terms between which it is possible to establish a connection. Art will be the equivalent of life, and vice versa. Briefly, in Proust thought never gives the impression of being an alien and external element. In his work, separate consideration can be given to psychology, poetry, science, observation and emotion. But it would always involve moving towards making an artificial distinction, and one that distorts the truth. All those elements, that analysis attempts to separate, form, in his work, not a mixture or even a fusion, but the burgeoning of an experience that is sui generis, primordial and integrated. In pushing analysis further one would, I think, be led to understand this profound unity that can be perceived beneath the delicious complexity of his work as the externalization of the creative drive from which it originates. His art is born from that single, total vision that constitutes the spiritual life both in its fundamentals and in its full flowering. In Proust I will never be able to dissociate beauty from truth. The grave and purifying emotion suggested by the evocation of the mysteries of life, the intimate contentment brought about by the clarification of the meticulous detail of our existence, the happiness felt at the revelation of its unsuspected riches, the introduction to a deeper inner life – such are the gifts we receive from Proust's art, but all sharing the same atmosphere and combined into one single harmony.

A new era in the history of the great French novel opens with Proust. Solely in the interests of giving a better definition of his originality, and without aiming at a definitive opinion at a time when we are offering our tributes to a great man deceased, one can nevertheless say that he outshines Flaubert in intelligence, just as he outshines Balzac in literary quality and Stendhal in the understanding of life and beauty. So it is that he will have to take his place as the founder of a world he shares with no one else.

He dominates both our intelligence and our admiration like a master among great masters.

He is among the three or four names in contemporary French literature who are already or will be European names. With his roots deep in the most authentically French soil, he goes, nevertheless, well beyond the limits that some seem to wish to impose on the French spirit. He has extended the domain of the human soul and embellished the lives of every one of us. While belonging to the great classical tradition of his country, he has nevertheless broken free of an excessively timorous classicism. He has gone his own way without conforming to a pre-established aesthetic. With the liberty that accompanies masterly skill, he has annexed for the French tradition areas that have until now been left fallow.

Appearing on the horizon at a time when German intellectual life was turning away from manifestations of the French spirit so as to meditate more exclusively on its own heritage, he has made us feel anew – I can say this on behalf of a few while waiting for others to be able to make his acquaintance and bring their own testimony – that today as much as yesterday there are treasures common to the nations of our divided and tormented Europe.

79. José Ortega y Gasset on Proust's innovatory vision

1923

Part of 'Le Temps, la distance et la forme chez Marcel Proust' in 'Hommage à Marcel Proust', *La Nouvelle Revue française*, 1 January 1923, pp. 267–79.

José Ortega y Gasset (1883–1955), in an essay laden with perceptive assessments of Proust's art, and modestly subtitled: 'Simple contribution aux études proustiennes', provides the most rounded, critical, and helpful study in the NRF obituary tribute.

. . . Proust's 'inventions' are of the greatest importance, for they have a bearing on the simplest elements that go to make up a literary object. What is involved is nothing less than a new way of dealing with time and establishing a spatial dimension.

If, in order to give someone who had not read him an idea of what Proust is all about, we were to begin by enumerating his subjects – a holiday in his old village, Swann's love-affair, the emotions of a little boy and girl playing in the gardens on the Champs-Elysées, a summer holiday on the Normandy coast in a luxury hotel facing the fluctuating waves of the sea, against which, gliding like Nereids, the faces of blossoming girls are picked out, etc. – we would immediately understand that such a list leads nowhere and that these subjects, that have been treated thousands of times by novelists, do not suffice to define what Proust brings us. A

222

few years ago, a poor hunchback had got into the habit of going every day to the Saint-Isidore library. He was so small of stature that he could not manage to read comfortably at his desk. He invariably approached the librarian on duty and asked for a dictionary. 'Which one?' kindly enquired the assistant, 'Latin, French or English?' and the little hunchback replied, 'Oh, I don't mind, it's just for me to sit on'.

We would be guilty of the same error as this librarian if we sought to define Claude Monet by saying that he painted Notre-Dame in Paris and Saint Lazare station, or else Degas by pointing out that he made pictures of women ironing, ballet dancers and jockeys. In fact, in the case of these two painters, the subjects of their canvases are only a pretext; they painted these things in the same way that they might have painted other quite different ones. For them the important thing, the driving energy behind their paintings, is the airy perspective, the mass of chromatic vibrations with which these things, whatever they happen to be, surround themselves so as to entertain therein their sumptuous existence.

It also resembles to some extent what happens in Proust. The fictions that surface and resurface in his work have, as far as he is concerned, merely an incidental and secondary interest; they are like buoys floating and drifting on the unfathomable watery depths of things remembered. Until now your writer handled his memories as if they were materials with which he tried to reconstruct the past. However, the information provided by the faculty of memory is not enough and only retains a very arbitrary selection from the reality that once existed. Your traditional novelist, therefore, completes his memories by observing the present; he adds hypotheses and conventional ideas to them and thus blends in with the authentic materials of memory other elements which are fraudulent. There is some sense in this procedure when it is, as usual, a question of the restoration of things past, i.e. pretending to give them a new immediacy and relevance. Proust's plan, however, is the very opposite. He does not use his memories as materials for the reconstruction of former realities; on the contrary, what he seeks to rework on a literary level are his actual reminiscences and to that end he resorts to all manner of methods – comments on the present, analysis of this thoughts and psychological explanations. It is not, therefore, things that one remembers, but the act of remembering those things that is Proust's main theme. Here, for the first time, memories are no longer treated as materials with which to describe some particular thing, they have now actually become the very thing described. This is why the author does not generally add on to the reminiscence those other parts of the reality that memory has not

223

retained; he leaves his reminiscence intact, just as it is, objectively speaking incomplete, perhaps mutilated and waving in its ghostly isolation what miserable stumps it has left. There is a very evocative page where Proust speaks of three trees on a hillock, trees behind which something very important is hidden, but that time has swept away and abolished from the memory. The author struggles in vain to rediscover what eludes him and to reinstate in its entirety this stretch of ravaged landscape, with those three trees, sole survivors of a mental catastrophe, of a raging storm of forgetfulness.

Fictional subjects are, therefore, in Proust mere pretexts, a kind of *spiracula*, basement windows to let in the air, little openings in the hive from which the excited swarms of reminiscences fly forth. Proust did not give his work the general title of *A la recherche du temps perdu* for nothing. Proust is indeed an investigator of lost time. As such, he scrupulously rejects imposing on the past the anatomy of the present; he rigorously abstains from all intervention, guided as he is by the decided wish to avoid any fixed construction. A recollection emerges, springing up from the nocturnal depths of the soul, like a constellation standing out pathetically along the horizon in the dark. Proust represses all thought of restoration and restricts himself to describing what he sees emerging from his memory. Instead of restoring lost time completely he takes delight in erecting the ruins of it. In his case, it is possible to claim that memoirs as a genre attain the dignity of a purely literary method.

So much for what he does with time. But more fundamental still, and more astounding, is his inventiveness where spatial relationships are concerned.

Counts have been made of the number of pages Proust writes to tell us that the grandmother is using the thermometer. Indeed, it is not possible to speak of Proust without immediately bringing out how prolix and meticulous he is with tiny details. But in this case, the prolixity and the meticulousness, far from being defects, become two powerful sources of inspiration, two new muses to be added to the community of the nine. Proust needs to be prolix and meticulous, for the very simple reason that he approaches objects much more closely than people usually do. He is the inventor of a new distance between things and ourselves. This simple reform has had – as I have said – such astonishing results that almost all previous literary creation begins to look like a literature capable only of a bird's eye view, crudely panoramic when compared with this delightfully myopic genius.

The requirements of our existence impose on each object a certain distance, from which this object may seem to us to be best perceived. When we wish to scrutinize a stone we bring it so close to our eyes that we can make out its porosity. But if we wish to look at a cathedral, we will have to forego looking at the porosity of its stones and move far away so as to increase our visual field tremendously. The built-in utilitarianism that governs life has the task of regulating the measurements of these different distances. The poets, however, have perhaps been misled into thinking that this system of distances, while being excellent for daily use, is good also for art. Marcel Proust, weary possibly of always seeing a hand being drawn as if it were a monument, brings it close to his eyes and, hiding the horizon behind it, sees to his great surprise an evocative landscape opening out in the foreground, in which the valleys of the pores yield in turn to the Lilliputian forests of hairs. This is, of course, a manner of speaking; for Proust is not interested in hands, nor generally in physical attributes, but rather in flora and fauna on an intimate scale. He rectifies our distance for human feelings and breaks with the tradition that describes them as monuments. . . .

[Goes on to define the attitude to detail in impressionist art and relates Proust's style to a literary equivalent for the recording of visual effects.]

. . . The monograph on Swann's love affair is a case of psychological pointillism. For the medieval author of *Tristan et Iseut*, love is a sentiment with a clearly marked outline; for him, a primitive in the field of the psychological novel, love is just love and nothing else. Proust, on the other hand, gives us a picture of Swann's love as something that has absolutely nothing like the form of love about it. There is a bit of everything in it: dots of warm sensuality, mauve colours of distrust, brown colours of routine, grey colours of the weariness of life. Only one thing is missing: love. Love is here a resultant function, just as the figure in a tapestry results from the intersection of the threads, not one of which has itself the form of the figure. Were it not for Proust, a literature that seeks to be read in the way Monet's paintings are looked at, viz. obliquely, would remain unknown to the public.

This is why it is best, when we compare him with Stendhal, to qualify our position. In many ways, they are two totally opposed people. Stendhal is above all an imaginative writer; he imagines the complications, the situations and the characters. He never copies; in his case everything is resolved in fantasy, a nervous concentrated fantasy. The souls of his characters are as deliberately 'thought out' as the contour shaping a madonna in a Raphael painting. Stendhal firmly believes in the reality of his characters and he tries consequently to draw their outline without ambiguity. The people in

Proust, on the other hand, have no silhouette; rather they are more like unstable atmospheric condensations, spiritual images that at any moment are subject to the changes of wind and light. Of course, Proust belongs to the tradition of Stendhal 'the investigator of the human heart'. But whereas for Stendhal the human heart is a solid with clear, inflexible lines, for Proust it is a diffuse, gaseous three-dimensional space, varying every minute with the changeability we associate with the weather. Stendhal's line-drawings and Proust's paintings are separated by a distance similar to that which separates Ingres from Renoir. Ingres uses line to create beautiful women such as we could fall in love with. Not Renoir, however; his method does not allow that. The living plasma of luminous dots that constitutes a Renoir woman, gives us perhaps in the highest degree the feeling of flesh in all its texture; but for a woman to be beautiful the lushness of her body must be defined by the exact boundary an outline provides. Similarly Proust's psychological and literary methods do not allow him to create attractive female figures. The Duchesse de Guermantes, in spite of the preferential treatment she receives, seems to us to be ugly and insolent, and that is all there is to it; whereas if we could relive the wild years of our youth, we would surely fall in love with Sanseverina, a woman so outwardly serene in expression but so passionate in her heart.

All in all, Proust imbues literature with what could be called an overall atmospheric design. Landscapes, people, external and internal worlds – everything in his work is vaporized in an airy, widely-dispersed pulse of energy. Proust's universe would seem to be devised to be perceived as pure breath, for it is all atmosphere. In these volumes no one does anything; nothing happens; we have a quite passive series of static situations. And it could not be otherwise, since to accomplish something one must be something fixed and determined. . . .

In his books, the true agents of vital change are, rather than people, the winds and the physical and moral climates that successively surround them. And the life-story of each is dominated by certain spiritual trade-winds that blow this way and that and polarize sensibility. Everything depends on the direction from which the gale blows; and just as there are north-easterlies and south-westerlies, north winds and south winds, so Proust's characters vary according to whether the wind comes from Méséglise way or Guermantes way. And we must not find it surprising that this writer insists on speaking of 'ways', because, the universe being for him a meteorological experience, the essential point is watching the way the wind blows. . . .

The interpretation of life in terms of atmosphere and consequently the meticulousness with which it is described are the inexorable cause of a defect in Proust's books. I refer to a particular fatigue that the reading of these volumes produces even in their greatest admirers. If it was only the common everyday fatigue produced by stupid works, there would be nothing more to say. The fatigue, however, of the Proust reader has specific characteristics and has nothing to do with boredom. One is never bored with Proust. It is very rare that any one of these pages lacks sufficient intensity, or even the intensity needed. Nevertheless, we are ready at any moment to give up reading. Furthermore, throughout the whole work we constantly feel we are being stopped, as if we were not being allowed to move forward at our own pace, as if the author's rhythm were less agile than our own and was applying a perpetual ritardando to our quick tempo.

This is both the disadvantage and the advantage of impressionism in Proust's books; as I have said, nothing happens, there is no drama, no case to tackle. We have a series of views that are extremely rich in content, but that remain static. Now, we mortals are by nature dynamic beings and the only thing that interests us is movement.

When Proust tells us that the bell at the garden gate in Combray tinkles and that, in the dark, we hear the voice of Swann arriving at the house, our attention fixes on this fact and, having absorbed it, gets ready to jump forward to a different fact that will surely happen next and for which this has been a preparation. We do not take up an inert position as regards the first fact; rather, once we have briefly come to know it, we feel ourselves to be propelled towards a new, future fact, because in life, so we believe, each fact is the herald of another and a transition to it, and so on until a trajectory is formed, just as in mathematics each succeeding point forms a line. Proust, however, puts pressure on this dynamic feature of our existence by forcing us, without any let-up, to remain with the first fact, at times for a hundred pages and more. After the arrival of Swann, there is nothing more; to that particular point no other point is added; on the contrary, this simple momentary fact (Swann's arrival in the garden), this moment of reality dilates but does not progress, broadens out but does not change into another, increases in volume and after that there are pages and pages during which we do not move forward, and we simply watch it growing and stretching, filling out like a soap-bubble and graced likewise with spangles and reflections.

Thus we experience a kind of torment in reading Proust. His art acts upon our sense of dynamism, on our appetite for action, for movement, for progression, like a steadily applied brake holding us back; we suffer like a quail jumping about in its cage and hitting against the wire dome that marks the limit of its prison. The fact is that Proust's muse could well be called 'Moroseness' and his style consists of the literary exploitation of that 'delectatio morosa' that was severely punished by the Councils of the church.

We can now see with the greatest clarity how the cycle of Proust's basic 'inventions' is structured. We can now see how his modifying of accepted distance and form is the quite natural consequence of his fundamental attitude to memory. When we use memory as a substance among others to reconstitute reality intellectually, we only take the part of reminiscence that we find useful and, without allowing it to grow according to its own laws, we go on our way regardless. In the process of reasoning and in simple association of ideas our soul proceeds by a trajectory going from one thing to another and the forward movement of our attention is made by the displacements that follow one upon the other. But if, turning our backs on reality, we plunge into the contemplation of memory, we see that memory proceeds by simple dilation without our moving, so to speak, from the initial position. To remember is not, like reasoning, to progress along the highway of mental space; it is the expansion of space itself. ... .

80. Henry Charpentier: a post mortem view
1923

Part of 'Sur Marcel Proust', *Les Marges*, 15 April 1923, pp. 274–9.

Henry Charpentier, journalist and critic, gives an assessment of Proust that takes a more critical stance than the tributes made earlier in the year.

It is a bold thing to seek to give a considered opinion on the work of a man who has just died. For as long as Marcel Proust's friends still keenly grieve his passing, any opinion that is not totally given over to admiration and any effort to establish objectivity, will appear to them to be partial and sacrilegious.

In the meantime, the very review that published Proust's novels is devoting a special number to him described, according to its contents page, as 'Tributes'. More often than not these tributes are so ill-at-ease, so visibly anxious not to get to the heart of the matter, which means, in a writer, the analysis of his work and his method, and at times are so casual in tone considering that the tomb is scarcely sealed (I am thinking especially of the contribution by Maurice Barrès), in a word so contradictory in their praises, that I have no fear of angering Proust's shade when I express, in all good faith, following his friends' – *a well-informed, but hostile critic would be more to the point*[1] – what I admire among the cluttered memoirs he bequeaths us and what I think should be rejected. . . .

[Considers Proust as both exemplar and critic of the snobbery prevalent in the society he satirizes.]

The truth of the matter is that these Guermantes and Charlus are not very good models. Proust has, I believe, been compared with Saint-Simon. This is nonsense. If we avoid taking a superficial view, if we do not linger, for instance, over the length of the period sentences, we notice that the formidable duke's style is free of affectation. If his style often suggests the hand of a master, it does so by nature. He himself claimed that he did not pride himself on fine writing: 'My only thought was for precision and truth.' As for the essential interest engendered by his memoirs, it is above all historical. It resides in the vivid portraits of outstanding figures involved in all the achievements and intrigues of a reign.

Proust, on the other hand, attaches great importance to his style and employs his meticulous observation only in describing very ordinary personalities and facts of no import: one of Swann's love affairs, a fashionable ball, a dinner party or a gathering of empty-headed people who find each other terribly boring.

He has no creative imagination, and he knows it. He replaces the discriminating choice of essential characteristics, which is the only way to bring characters to life, by a faculty of memory that is both patient and scrupulous. This explains his success in writing excellent pastiches and his lack of success in his novels. All great novelists are without exception observers of the reality around them, but their skill is to know how to select what needs to be kept. In a matter of a few pages I know Gobseck[2], and these few pages wonderfully retain their interest for me. This is because they have all the essential features that make Gobseck different from all other men. There is nothing inessential. Anything, indeed, that could be added would be inessential, since it does not, properly speaking, belong to the money-lender so much as to mankind in general.

Whether his subject is avarice or poverty, Proust does not dare leave anything out. He cannot separate what is relevant from what is irrelevant. Out of fear, indeed, of forgetting the former he prefers to include it with the latter, higgledy-piggledy, in the disarray of a narrative that proceeds at headlong speed, acquiring new details, clarifying this, explaining that and repeating itself as the confused thread of memory unravels. This, as may be discerned without difficulty, is the reason for the confusion of his work. There is no getting away from the narrator. He rediscovers lost time rather in the manner of a talkative old maid with nothing to do who has ensconced herself in her provincial parlour and has no intention of letting anyone have a chance to utter a word all afternoon. He never leaves me alone with his characters. I have finished with Swann and still have no precise idea of his physical appearance and mental outlook. All the elements that will make him known to us are, of course, there but we have, so to speak, to gather them all together and re-write the novel for ourselves, otherwise the life of one of the principal heroes remains permanently disjointed, suspect and almost mythical.

Has Proust, by this method of composition, brought his art closer to reality? I do not think so. Day by day, throughout life man unconsciously rearranges the synthesis he makes of the contradictions and the sudden changes in the personalities of those around him. Such a synthesis allows us to recognize each other at first glance; it is not as deceptive as all that. The analysis of an individual restarted from scratch with every new encounter is much more likely to mislead us.

This method is, incidentally, one of the interesting new sides to Proust's exertions. It attempts to pin down psychological variations like a painter painting the same landscape at different hours of the day and giving totally different accounts of it. But Proust has only succeeded by this method in almost completely destroying the unity of his characters and in increasing the confusion created by his attention to detail.

Proust's style is exactly shaped by his manner of thinking. His interminable subsidiary clauses and his continual parentheses perfectly follow the contours of his soul-searching, his misgivings, his anxieties and the endless explanations he has grafted on to the narrative line, and these, irrelevant as they are for a reader of average intelligence, are disheartening for a well-informed one. But Proust is merciless. The sentence subdivides interminably into capillary-like propositions that proceed to extract from the depths of his mind the tiniest drop of juice that he believes is hidden there. Lacking the generosity of mother nature, he only allows us to taste a fruit after involving us in the whole obscure process that has brought it forth from the humus and the alluvial mud.

For fruits and flowers there certainly are. This style, to be deplored as a means of relating an action, tiresome when it comes to explaining the heart, has a sinuous beauty in descriptions, epithets that are precious, ridiculous and charming and a harmonious and supple sway to its sentences.

It is admirably suited to the poems in prose that Proust often inserts in his novels. Clarity is then no longer the essential point and we can take delight in reciting his numerous, richly suggestive periods rather in the way we stop and watch a stretch of semi-transparent water rocking some beautiful sea-weed to and fro, loosely mingling its strands together and unravelling them.

It would be childish to seek to determine today what posterity will retain from Proust's dense oeuvre. Time, 'father of all things', proceeds to assessments none can predict.

I personally think that this work is not a novel and that it is madness to consider it is as a new *Comédie humaine*. His characters do not lead sufficiently real lives to become types. The fault lies with the models, which are wishy-washy and unrepresentative, almost uniquely chosen from an exceptional milieu that has only a very small place in society as a whole. If at times they are individually characterized, it is not by the strength of deep and universal feelings, the only ones that continue to interest people, as in Ulysses, Don Quixote, Dido or Bérénice, no, it is by odd quirks of nature that owe their origin to fashion and that like it age terribly fast.

The fault also lies with Proust who has failed to isolate the tiny element of the eternal that La Bruyère would perhaps have brought out in Swann and the Guermantes and that he would have revealed to us in its uniqueness. Proust's style will interest a few literary people – a dwindling number – but will always be repellent to the real reading public. Proust is bought today on the advice of critics who are also his publishers. Is he widely read? I venture to believe that it would be indiscreet to put questions of any length concerning his work to the fifty writers who sang his praises in the number dedicated to him by the *Nouvelle Revue française*.

Tomorrow, even more than yesterday, we shall be pressed by life. We shall demand that authors give us short works, simple, meaty thoughts, a poem, a maxim easily lodged in the memory and providing it in a slim volume with the most pregnant reflections.

We have had enough of purely bookish analyses and elaborations.

Yet the most engaging character in Proust's work, the one that will still provide interest for future psychologists, is Proust himself. If he was hardly able to vouch for others, he constantly did so for himself. He used everyone and everything as a mirror. It will be through him that future generations will be able to know and study the strange distortions we suffered in the final years of the Age of

231

Literature. From this point of view he was a moving victim. He devoted his life to self-examination and to transcribing this onto the written page; his novels are, in fact, autobiographical memoirs and when his sensibility is directly involved it expresses itself most movingly. All the pages devoted to his grand-mother have a remarkable truth about them.

What we must wish for Proust – and in this I believe I am serving his memory – is that his admirers should provide us with a short anthology drawn from his work and that none of them turns into a disciple.

NOTES

1 In italics in the text.
2 Gobseck is the miser and Jewish money lender who appears in the tale of that name – and elsewhere – in Balzac's *Comédie humaine*.

81. Francis Birrell on Proust as analyst
1923

Part of 'The prophet of despair' in *Marcel Proust: An English Tribute*, pp. 12–30.

Francis Birrell traces Proust's ancestry in the matter of sensibility from Richardson to Rousseau and Stendhal and stresses his pessimistic conclusions in 'this vast epic of jealousy'. For Proust, intellectual analysis is blended with feeling and this process also governs the handling of sexual inversion and the presentation of characters.

. . . Proust is in turn the intellectual child of Stendhal, and has bespattered *A la Recherche du Temps Perdu* with expressions of admiration for his master. In truth, he has taken over not only the methods but the philosophy of his teacher. It will be remembered that Stendhal insists in his analysis of *L'Amour-Passion* that crystallisation can only be effected after doubt has been experienced. So, for Proust, love, the *mal sacré* as he calls it, can only be called into being by jealousy, *le plus affreux des supplices*. We can want nothing till we have been cheated out of getting it; whence it follows that we can get nothing till we have ceased to want it, and in any case, once obtained, it would *ipso facto* cease to be desirable. Hence Man, 'how noble in reason, how infinite in faculty, in form and moving how express and admirable, in action how like an angel, in apprehension how like a god,' is doomed by the nature of his being to unsatisfied desire and restless misery, till Proust becomes, as I have called him above, the prophet of despair. He is a master of the agonising moments spent hanging in vain round the telephone, the weeks passed waiting for letters that never come, and the terrible reactions after one's own fatal letter has been irrevocably posted and not all the jewels of Golconda can extract it from the pillar-box. . . .

Indeed, happiness in love is by nature impossible, as it demands an impossible spiritual relationship. . . .

Proust, having thus reduced all human society to misery, builds upon the ruins his philosophy of salvation: Only by much suffering shall we enter into the Kingdom of Heaven – that is to say, shall we be enabled to see ourselves solely and simply as members of the human race, to perceive what is essential and fundamental in everybody beneath the trappings of manners, birth, or fortune, learn to be really intelligent. Love and jealousy alone can open to us the portals of intelligence. Thus, in the opening pages of *Du Côté de chez Swann*, the poor little boy, who because M. Swann is dining with his parents, cannot receive in bed his mother's kiss, starts on the long spiritual journey which is to run parallel to that of the brilliant, unhappy *mondain* guest. . . . Swann and little Proust, both endowed with sensibility, could shake hands with each other across the generations: all the experiences of one, all the innocence of the other, were as nothing beside that similarity of temperament which calls to us irrevocably, as Christ called to Matthew at the receipt of custom, and bids us share with our friend the miseries of the past and the terrors of the future.

Proust's youth was spent in Paris during that period when France was spiritually and politically severed by the *Affaire Dreyfus*, and for him the *Affaire* becomes the touchstone of sensibility and intelligence. To be a Dreyfusard means to pass beyond the sheltered harbour of one's own *clique* and interest into the uncharted sea of human solidarity. Hard indeed is the way of the rich man, the aristocrat, the snob, or the gentleman, who wishes to find salvation during the *Affaire*. He must leave behind him taste, beauty, comfort, and education, consort, in spirit at least, with intolerable Jews, fifth-rate politicians, and insufferable *arrivistes*, before worthily taking up the burden of human misery and routing the forces of superstition and stupidity. And there is only one school for this lesson, the school of romantic love – that is to say, of carking jealousy, in the throes of which all men are equal. . . .

Such I take to be the fundamental thought underlying *A la Recherche du Temps Perdu* in its present unfinished state, though we cannot tell what surprises the succeeding volumes (happily completed) may have in store for us. I have insisted, at perhaps excessive length, on the general mental background to this vast epic of jealousy, because it is not very easy to determine. The enormous wealth of the author's gifts tends to bury the structure under the superb splendour of the ornament. For Proust combines, to a degree never before realised in literature, the qualities of the aesthete and the scientist. It is the quality which first strikes the reader who does not notice, in the aesthetic rapture communicated by perfect style, that all pleasures are made pegs for disillusion. Human beauty, the beauty of buildings, of the sea, of the sky, the beauty of transmitted qualities in families and in the country-side, the beauty of history, of good breeding, of self-assurance – few people have felt these things as Proust. . . .

It is also worth remark that Proust is the first author to treat sexual inversion as a current and ordinary phenomenon, which he describes neither in the vein of tedious panegyric adopted by certain decadent writers, nor yet with the air of a showman displaying to an agitated tourist abysses of unfathomable horror. Treating this important social phenomenon as neither more nor less important than it is, he has derived from it new material for his study of social relations, and has greatly enriched and complicated the texture of his plot. His extreme honesty meets nowhere with more triumphant rewards. It is by the splendid use of so much unusual knowledge that Proust gains his greatest victories as a pure novelist. Royalty, actresses, bourgeois, servants, peasants, men, women, and children – they all have the genuine third dimension and seem to the reader more real than his own friends. The story is told of an English naval officer that he once knocked down a Frenchman for casting doubt on the chastity of Ophelia. It is to the credit of Shakespeare's supreme genius that our sympathies are with the naval officer, for Shakespeare's characters, too, are as real to us as our parents and friends and more real than our relations and our acquaintances. But to how few artists can this praise be given, save to Shakespeare and to Tolstoy! To read *A la Recherche du Temps Perdu* is to live in the world, at any rate in Proust's world – a world more sensitive, variegated, and interesting than our own.

It is difficult to analyse the ultimate quality of an artist's triumph; yet such is the function of criticism, the sole justification of writing books about books. Proust, it seems to me, had the extremely rare faculty of seeing his characters objectively and subjectively at the same moment. He can project himself so far into the mind of the persons he is describing that he seems to know more about them than they can ever know themselves, and the reader feels, in the process, that he never even dimly knew himself before. At the same time he never takes sides. The warm, palpitating flesh he is creating is also and always a decorative figure on the huge design of his tapestry, just as in *Petroushka* the puppets are human beings and the human beings puppets. For Proust, though the most objective, is also the most personal of writers. As we get accustomed to the long, tortuous sentences, the huge elaboration of conscientious metaphor, the continual refining on what cannot be further refined, we insensibly become listeners to a long and brilliant conversation by the wisest and wittiest of men. . . .

82. Ralph Wright on Proust's insights

1923

Part of 'A sensitive Petronius' in *Marcel Proust: An English Tribute*, pp. 31–51.

Ralph Wright links Proust's originality with the rise of sensibility and the modern obsession with self-analysis.

. . . Some one has said that the difference between a play and a novel is that while watching a play you have the privileges of a most intimate friend, but while reading a novel the privileges of God. However true this may be of the novel as it exists to-day (and, to read some modern novels, one might hardly suspect one's divine position), it is by no means true of the novel throughout its history. It is clear, if we go back far enough, for example, that with Longus, or Plutarch, or Petronius, the reader's position is very nearly as much that of a spectator as when he is watching a play by Shakespeare. And the same thing remains roughly true of all novels up to the middle of the eighteenth century. It is not, indeed, until we come to Richardson and Rousseau that we find anything like the modern insistence on the personal and intimate life of a man or a woman as a thing valuable in itself. No one except Montaigne and

Burton, neither of whom was a novelist, appears to have been introspective before that date. What mattered before was conduct; what was to matter afterwards was feeling. . . .

[Proust] is, perhaps, if we return to that definition of the difference between a novel and a play, more of the essential novelist than any man has ever been. His aim is by a hundred different methods to make you know his chief characters, not as if you were meeting them every day, but as if you yourself had for the moment actually been living in their skins and inhabiting their minds. Everything possible must be done to help you to this end. You must feel the repulsions and attractions they feel; you must even share their ancestors, their upbringing, and the class in which they live, and share them so intimately that with you, as with them, they have become second nature. Nor is even this enough. The man who knows himself is not common, and to know Proust's characters as you know yourself may only be a small advance in knowledge. So every motive of importance, every reaction to whatever stimulus they receive, is analysed and explained until your feeling will probably be, not only how well you know this being, who is in so many respects unlike you, but how far more clearly you have seen into the obscure motives of your own most distressing and ridiculous actions, how far more understandable is an attitude to life or to your neighbours that you yourself have almost unconsciously, and perhaps in mere self-protection, adopted.

But a short example of this is needed, and a short example of anything in Proust is not easy to find. A character just sketched in one volume will be developed in another, and to grasp the significance of the first sketch one has to wait for the fuller illumination of the development. And even then the short sketch is as often as not several pages of the most closely written analysis, quite impossible to quote from, or in full. There is, however, a very small character in the first book, *Du Côté de chez Swann*, who may serve. M. Vinteuil is an obscure musician of genius, living in the country. He holds his head high among his neighbours, and, on account of his daughter, refuses to meet the only other really cultured man in the district, Swann, who has made what M. Vinteuil considers a disreputable marriage. Suddenly M. Vinteuil's daughter forms a disgraceful friendship. There is scandal in the eyes of every man or woman he meets, scandal which he, poor man, knows quite well to be founded on the most deplorable facts. . . .

[Quotes from 'Mais, de ce que M. Vinteüil' to 'une résultante presque mécanique de toutes les déchéances'. Pléiade I, pp. 148–9.]

Here, at least, we have his method compressed. We have M. Vinteuil's unshakable faith in his daughter, as a jumping-off ground, founded on the past and unaltered by the facts of the present. We have also the pitying attitude of the world to himself and its hostile attitude to his daughter. And from this comes M. Vinteuil's other feeling, no less strong than his faith in his daughter, that they too have somehow sunk, become degraded, not only in the eyes of the world, but also, and because of it, in their own eyes as well. Lastly, as a reaction from this, we have the effect of these feelings on M. Vinteuil's manner – his attitude of humility before the world for sins that he has not committed, for the conduct of a person in whom he still completely believes, which, however ridiculous to the logician, can only be recognised by the rest of us as most disquietingly true to our own experience. It is this complexity in our emotions, this capability of feeling many different things at the same time about any one particular incident or person, that the novel alone can give; and it is on these lines that Marcel Proust has adventured farther than any other man.

And here, of course, he has great advantages. Proust, unlike so many of the great creative artists, started late in life the work by which he will be judged. He is mature as few great men have been mature, cultured as still fewer have been cultured. Wide reading is far from common among great artists. The driving force necessary to the accomplishment of any work of art is seldom found in alliance with wide culture; that, more often than not, is to be found among the world's half-failures. Neither Shakespeare, nor Molière, nor Fielding, nor Richardson, nor Balzac, nor Dickens, nor Dostoevsky, nor Ibsen was a widely cultured man. In Shakespeare, the loss is more than compensated by surety of intuition. In Balzac, there is a lack of the critical faculty that makes it possible for him, even towards the end of his life, to give in the same year one thing as beautiful as *Eugénie Grandet* and another as puerile as *Ferragus*, that allows him to compare the novels of 'Monk' Lewis with *La Chartreuse de Parme* and to call Maturin *'un des plus grands génies de l'Europe'*.

But Proust, like Montaigne and like Racine, besides having an extreme sensitiveness to all forms of beauty and ugliness, happiness and misery, that he has met in his social existence, has also read widely in the works of other sensitive men, has compared their impressions with each other and with his own, has learnt from their successes and failures; he is armed with more than his natural equipment, has more eyes to see through than his own. Actually his books are filled from end to end with criticisms of music, of painting, of literature, not in the way that is unfortunately familiar in this country, as unassimilated chunks in the main stream of the narrative, but as expressions of the opinions of different characters. . . .

[Goes on to examine the themes of the novel and especially Proust's picture of the world of snobs and aristocrats as an illustration of 'that theme of sadness that no ideal state is attainable in this world, not so much because we cannot climb, nor even because the ideal becomes illusion on attainment, but because the object to which we attach our ideal is, of necessity, not seen as it really is, but always as we long for it to be. This, with its complement that the mere fact of not being able to possess may lead to desire even when the object in itself does not seem very desirable, is at the very heart of Proust's philosophy.']

. . . Nor, as a fact, is this interest in cliques by any means confined to the aristocracy. Of at least equal importance are the Verdurins, who, in spite of their riches, are at the very opposite pole of civilisation. And yet with all their vulgarity, with all their intellectual snobbery, with all their lack of taste and breeding, with all their affectation of being a *petit clan*, is it not clear, that up to a certain point at any rate, intelligence is on their side of the ledger? Again, there is that glance at life in barracks, through the mediation of Saint-Loup, which, while small, is as good a summary of the military world as one knows. There are some unforgettable pages on the Jews. There is even that little world of the hotel servants that has plainly interested Proust almost as much as any of the larger worlds he has spent so much care in describing. And, especially in the early books, there are those descriptions of the world of the young man's parents and grandparents, so typical of the *honnête bourgeoisie*, so profoundly drawn in their uprightness and their rather limited social ideas, so secure and anxious for security, so loving to their boy and yet so anxious not to 'spoil' him. Never, with the exceptions of Saint-Simon and Tolstoy, has any author succeeded so well in giving the atmosphere of a particular house or a particular party; never has any one analysed so closely the behaviour of people in small homogeneous masses.

In 1896, when Proust was still a young man, he produced a book which, while not of great interest in itself, is naturally of value to students of his work, both for what it contains in the germ, and for what it omits, of the Proust who was to become a master. And to this book Anatole France wrote a charming preface, in which he said various things which must have appeared more friendly than critical to readers of that day. Among other things he wrote the following words:

Il n'est pas du tout innocent. Mais il est sincère et si vrai qu'il en devient naïf et plaît ainsi. Il y a en lui du Bernardin de Saint-Pierre dépravé et du Pétrone ingénu.

The words are a singularly good description of the Proust that we know to-day. He is not innocent and he remains *naïf*. There is a story of how in his last illness he insisted on being muffled up in a carriage and driven out into the country to see the hawthorn, which was then in bloom. The freshness of joy in all beautiful things remained with him, so far as we can see, to the end of his life. It is as obvious in the moving account of the Prince de Guermantes' confession to Swann at the beginning of the last book as it is in the early Combray chapters of the first. He was supremely sensitive and continually surprised by beauty. But, unlike most sensitive people, he neither railed at mankind, nor shut himself up, nor built for himself a palace of escape from reality in his own theorising about the meaning of it all. He set himself to observe and to note his observations.

In many ways Anatole France's description of him as the ingenuous Petronius of our times is extremely intelligent. And our times are in many ways extremely like the days in which Petronius wrote. There is an aristocracy that has lost its *raison d'être*, and a continual flow of new plutocrats without traditions, without taste, without any object in life beyond spending to the best of their power of self-advertisement. The faith in the old social order has gone, and nothing new has arisen to take its place. Where we differ entirely from that age is in self-consciousness. And that, too, is where a modern Petronius must differ from the old one. For better in some ways and for worse in others, we are far more complex than we have ever been; our motives are at once more mixed and more clearly scrutinised. And a writer who can satisfactorily cram this age within the pages of a book must not only be extremely intelligent and extremely observant, but must also have forged for himself a style capable of expressing the finest shades of feeling; he must refuse the easy simplifications both of the moralist and the maker of plots; he must be infinitely sensitive and infinitely truthful. That Marcel Proust personifies this ideal no one would completely claim. But he does, at least to some people, seem to have approached it more nearly than any other writer of our time.

83. Catherine Carswell
on Proust's women characters
1923

Part of 'Proust's women' in *Marcel Proust: An English Tribute*, pp. 66–77.

Catherine Carswell (1879–1946) isolates the ambiguous nature of Proust's attitude to the notion of the feminine and particularly his unwillingness to grant his women characters any autonomy.

The literature of imagination has always been rich in autobiography, confessed and unconfessed. It is in its essence, perhaps one should say in its impulse, largely an affair of passionate reminiscence. Taken, therefore, as merely a recent writer of distinction who has chosen to deal avowedly with *Things Remembered*, Proust must challenge comparison with dozens of eminent men, his forerunners and contemporaries. Tolstoy has given us his own life-history, not only diffusively throughout his novels and pamphlets, but in that wonderful piece of reconstruction, *Childhood and Youth*. Among living men, James Joyce, with an epic gift and an heroic feat of memory, has recorded for us an impression of his past, physical, mental, spiritual, and has shown it interwoven with countless other lives. And these are two taken at random. *A la Recherche du Temps Perdu* – Proust was not the first, nor will he be the last, to choose it as a theme.

Where Proust stands as yet alone is in his manner of approaching his theme. Or, with more exactitude it may be said, his manner, vigilantly passive, eagerly quiescent, of letting his theme encroach upon and claim him. All attempted recapture of the past is for him 'futile', a 'labour in vain'. Not reconstruction, but understanding of things remembered, is his aim. And to this end with deliberation he permits himself what the realist rejects but the plain man all unknowingly cherishes – the glamour in which for every one of us our own past is bathed. Divest the past, Proust seems to say, of the present's gift to it – the light that never was on sea or land – and you take away its essence; treat the present as independent of the past and you destroy its integrity. That this is true we, as human beings – acting, thinking, receiving impressions from moment to moment – must recognise when it is pointed out. Our actual existence is not so much a narrative as a web in which the shuttle of events flies back and forth between the warp and woof of past and present, from neither of which it can escape any more than can we ourselves. The trouble is that it is pointed out so seldom, and least of all perhaps by novelists, who in this matter still lag far behind our common human experience. The grasp with which Proust has laid hold upon the philosophic and aesthetic values of memory – as, for example, in the passage where he describes the eating, after an interval of many years, of a *petite madeleine* soaked in tea – is a new thing in literature. Here is pre-eminently the novelist with a past. None before him has taken *Things Remembered* not merely for theme but for medium as well.

To forget this, or even for one moment to minimise it, in speaking of Proust, is utterly to lose one's bearings. But, accustomed as we are in our own hearts to his treatment of the past, we are so unaccustomed to it in literature that it is really not easy to avoid the artificial standpoint, the more that Proust proclaims his naturalism neither explicitly nor by freakishness of style. So quiet, so classical is his bearing that it hardly strikes one to investigate his premises.

And so, concerning his long book of memory, one hears questions put by intelligent and even admiring readers. There are his 'shadowy' women – 'Did women at any time mean anything to Proust?': there is his disconcerting chronology – 'How old is his hero supposed to be during such or such an incident?': there is his social pose – 'Was Proust not himself as bad a snob as any he describes?' But such questions can be asked only in forgetfulness, answered only in constant remembrance of the author's unique attitude toward his main subject, the past. . . .

But to come to the women.

A man of particular sincerity once said to me that after twenty years of married life he understood his wife no better than on the day he married her. He had of course become familiar with her modes of thought and action which served as knowledge for practical daily purposes. But familiarity had never bred understanding. Her underlying motives, the ultimate significance of her looks and words, remained hidden.

This, I think, is Proust's position, more especially when the woman happens to affect him powerfully. In every case we can *see*[1] his women, and thus far they are the reverse of shadowy. Grandmother, mother, aunts, and servant – the women that surround his childhood; Mlle Vinteuil and the Duchesse de Guermantes – female figures that shock or thrill his boyish imagination; Odette – the mature cocotte that stands throughout his youth for feminine mystery and glamour; Odette's daughter Gilberte, and later

Albertine – the young girls, minxes both, with whom he falls in love; Madame Verdurin and her circle – the social climbers who call forth his most delicate adult irony as well as his most rancid contempt; – these, simply as pictures, leap out at us complete. Nothing could be more objective than their presentation to the eye and ear of the reader. We feel with each one as if we had met her in the flesh – as one has met a casual acquaintance. The mother's submissive wifeliness; the almost masculine incorruptibility of the grandmother; the raciness of the servant; the neurosis of Aunt Léonie; the half-hearted viciousness of the music-master's daughter; the slightly comic social splendour of the Duchesse; the unmeaning melancholy of Odette's eyes; the unredeemed vulgarity of Madame Verdurin; the domineering girlishness of Gilberte, by turns frank and secretive, appealing and repellent; the smile with which Albertine, at once innocent and wanton, receives the youth in her bedroom – in depicting these Proust never trespasses beyond natural as compared with literary experience. We all know with what liveliness in conversation any man with the gifts of observation and wit can create an image for us of some female 'character' met with in his childhood or his travels. But let that same man come to speak out of his emotions of some woman who has moved him deeply, then his heart will cloud his brain, his tongue will falter or run away with him, and he will no longer be capable of outlining a portrait. As listeners our impressions of his subject will be gained, not from what he says, but independently from what we perceive that he feels, which may well be in direct conflict with his words. In life, that is to say, the more important a character is to us the more we are thrown back for our ultimate knowledge on the emotions aroused by that character in ourselves. In fiction it is usually the other way about. It is his central figures whom the novelist pretends to know best. Proust, however, has recognised this discrepancy with scientific clearness. He devotes himself, therefore, where his important women are concerned – aside from the very minimum of detached, objective observations – to a presentment of the effect they have upon the men that love them.

So his women set us wondering and supposing and coming to our own conclusions exactly as we do in life, either when an individual of our own sex is described for us by one of the other sex, or when we are emotionally affected by some one of the other sex.

For this is important. When it comes to his male characters, Proust takes a different tone. Here he finds himself able, quite consistently with his philosophy, for far more positive assertion. In various ways he can allow them to reveal and expound themselves, and even each other, as when Bergotte speaks of the married Swann as a man who 'has to swallow a hundred serpents every day'. The point of view, the intellectual outfit which all males have in common – these give the male novelist a certain tract of solid ground when dealing with characters of his own sex. A man's fellow-felling for other men is very strong. It has but a faint and imperfect parallel as between woman and woman. Proust, accordingly, without any sacrifice of conscience, can, 'by his belief', endow Swann with a soul. But – marvellous and highly characteristic creation as he is – Swann may be put in the same category with other male characters by other male novelists. Odette, Gilberte, Albertine, are in a category by themselves. Outside of Proust's book they are only to be met with in life.

It is in this differential treatment of his women that we perceive how rigorously Proust applies his artistic method. He never seeks to transcend his own personality. In him, the observer, the whole of creation lives and moves and has its being. Men are creatures made in his own image. He can faithfully follow his own emotions, and 'by his belief' can conscientiously endow his men with souls. But women are in a different case. He has no inner guide to assure him that they are anything more than the phantoms they seem. Strictly speaking, this should imply no more than a negative attitude. In fact, however, Proust goes further. Because he has no grounds for belief he passes into unbelief. In his philosophy *esse est percipi*, therefore, the souls of women for him have no existence. Herein it is likely that he has borne out the unavowed experience of most men. Whether or no, he certainly has expressed the truth of his own experience with a purity that few, even among great writers, can rival.

One thing more. There is Proust's mother.

No doubt the avenging eagerness with which I reintroduce her here for my conclusion is due in part to my being myself of the soulless sex. But quite apart from any such feelings, to speak of this novelist's women without reckoning especially with his mother would be inexcusable. That he adored her in childhood he makes manifest. Further, that throughout his life his adoration effectively debarred him from profound emotion where other women were concerned becomes clear enough to the reader. It hardly appears, however, that Proust was himself wholly conscious of this. True, there is a passage in the *Combray* section in which he speaks of 'that untroubled peace which no mistress, in later years, has ever been able to give me, since one has doubts of them at the moment when one believes in them, and never can possess their hearts as I used to receive, in her kiss, the heart of my mother, complete, without scruple or reservation, unburdened by any liability save to myself'. But this is the only place where he seems to allow that the love he bore his mother was even comparable in kind with the love aroused by other women later in his life. Indeed, though he repeatedly speaks of the anguish with which in his childhood he longed for his mother's good-night kiss, the ecstasy with which he received it, as if it were the Host in an act of communion, conveying to him 'her real presence and with it the power to sleep'; though he tells how, for that 'frail and precious kiss', he prepared himself in advance so as to 'consecrate' the whole minute of contact; though he dreaded to prolong or repeat the kiss lest a look of displeasure should cross those beautiful features with the slight, beloved blemish under one of the eyes; yet he describes himself at this time as one 'into whose life Love had not yet entered', as one whose emotion, failing love and as yet awaiting it, happened to be at the disposal of 'filial piety'. No wonder if, when temporary 'love' came, he compared with them as unconsciously as unfavourably this good and gracious mother – so admiringly timid as a wife, so gentle towards strangers, so perfect socially, so full of stern solicitude as a parent ('she never allowed herself to go to any length of tenderness with me') – and found them merely exciting to the senses. He had already, so far as woman was concerned, given his heart away.

Yet, after all, perhaps he knew it well enough and merely takes his own way of saying it. He tells us little enough of his mother, though probably he tells as much as he knows. What her own real thoughts and feelings were we are left to guess. But 'never again', he says, after describing one very special visit of hers to the boy's bedroom – 'never again will such hours be possible for me. But of late I have been increasingly able to catch, if I listen attentively, the sound of the sobs . . . which broke out only when I found myself alone with Mamma. Actually their echo has never ceased.'

NOTE

1 In italics in the text.

84. Ethel Colburn Mayne on the magic of Proust

1923

Part of 'The spell of Proust' in *Marcel Proust: An English Tribute*, pp. 90–5.

Ethel Colburn Mayne provides an example of lyrical criticism that mixes enthusiasm with some perceptive comments.

. . . The miracle had happened. We were spell-bound, for good and all, within the magic ring. We had forgotten what we used to mean when, in the world outside, we had said 'dull'; for here was much that was not merely dull but positively soporific, yet our eyes were glued upon the baleful page, and any interruption seemed a challenge to the occult power that held us. Something was risked, immeasurably worth our while, did we fall short of the required submission.
. . . This was because we now could feel more deeply the extent of what the wizard meant to do with us. We were not passively to stand within the circle. We were, with him, to pace it mystically round, while time ran back to fetch the Age of Gold. *Le temps passé* would be transmuted, imperceptibly, into *le temps retrouvé*; and our aid was necessary to the necromancer's full success. With this flattering divination there began a new excitement, different in action from the old; for soon, instead of rushing at the latest Marcel Proust directly we had bought it, we indeed did buy it, but re-read the earlier volumes first. Here was the very magic ring itself, drawn round our fireside chair! The latest Proust lay ready to our hand, slim or substantial token of the power still unspent; but lest we should have missed a single letter in the charm, we spelt it through devoutly once again; and, in the spelling, found how many an indication subtly skilled at once to warn and to escape us till the moment of reflection or re-reading! And as a consequence, we now perceived so intricate and exquisite a 'pattern in the carpet' as could make the newest volume into something more exciting for anticipation even than we had dreamed.
This is the proof, to me, of Marcel Proust's (as one might think, indisputable; yet by a few disputed) genius. The *Swann* book contains the largest share of interest, no doubt – that merer, franker kind of interest which other books can give us in a hardly less degree. But in the later volumes, as they 'grow on' us, there is far

245

more (if also there is less) than this; and it is through the more that we come finally to clear perception of Proust's purpose and his mastery. For in these less immediately attractive volumes we are conscious of an ever-growing sense of the significance so deeply interfused through the whole work. He had by then become absorbed to such degree in his interpretation of the microcosm which he saw as a sufficing symbol of the irony, absurdity, and the incessant alternation, 'intermittency', and travail of the consciousness of man, that we are sensible, as he proceeds, of powers more transcendent than the highest of the writer's mere accomplishment – stupendous as that is in Proust, who could 'write' anything he chose, and chose to write so many things, from satire that is blighting in its smiling subtlety (so muted as to mock the hasty ear!), to lyric flower-pieces like the paradisal hawthorn-hedge in *Swann*, and the unrivalled comments upon buildings, pictures, fashions in dress and manners (who will forget the monocles at the big evening-party at Mme. de Saint-Euverte's?), books, the drama, even photographs! In the great elegiac glories of the death of Bergotte (not yet published in book-form), and of that *grand'mère* who is the *motif*, as it were, in the symphonic composition of the unnamed central figure's personality, Proust sounded chords which lay till then beyond the compass of his readers' hearing, but were then revealed to sense that shall not lose them while it yet survives.

But over all this virtuosity there rules a mightier gift – the master-gift of insight. Proust, one could say, 'knows everything', in the restricted meaning of the words. No bent, no twist, of modern thought escapes him; yet, as one reader writes to me, 'there is no dead psychology' – no case stretched on a Procrustean bed, with all that does not fit lopped comfortably, and discomfortingly, off. He, unlike Nature, is most careful of the single life. If ever we had questioned that – and we had very little questioned it – the Charlus portrait answered us: that masterpiece of the undaunted, following eye and mind. Proust leads us with him on this journey of the visual and mental powers; we are no more involuntarily drawn on than he has been into the state of an astounded fondness and appreciation for the maudlin, overbearing, ludicrous, yet constantly pathetic or superb old 'invert'. We are offended personally by the insolences of his favourites; the tears in his unholy eyes can well-nigh wet our own . . . and this though, with the master's hand upon our shoulders, we have gone through every phase of the degrading intimacies, seen and heard the tragi-comic outbursts of the princely victim, every now and then remembering his 'rank' and seeking to restore the true relation between him and those whom in his view he honours by his merest word, yet who are his disdainful masters through his helpless depravation.

If there were nothing else than Charlus in the books, Proust must be given pride of place among the masters. But with the plenitude there is – what must we give? More than a master, one would say, a writer cannot be. Yet in the image here suggested of the magic circle, there is possibly the one thing more that causes Proustians to divide their reading lives into the time before and after they have read these books. No spell had yet been worked on us of potency like this; for though we are pent within the ring, we move within it too – the world revolves, for us, as in a crystal held beneath our gaze by one who, moving with us, will reveal the secret hidden not there only but in our own dim sense, when at the last *le temps perdu* shall have become *le temps retrouvé*.

85. A. B. Walkley on Proust's insights
1923

Part of 'A new psychometry' in *Marcel Proust: An English Tribute*, pp. 96–101.

A. B. Walkley (1855–1926) provides an obituary and an assessment; the article originally appeared in *The Times* for 29 November 1922.

To judge from the newspapers, there have been tremendous 'crises' in public affairs during the last few days: the triumph of Fascismo in Italy, the Lausanne Conference, the English elections. But to many of us the great events are merely spectacular; they pass rapidly across the screen, while the band plays irrelevant scraps of syncopated music, and seem no more real than any other of the adventures, avowedly fictitious, that are 'filmed' for our idle hours. They don't, save on reflection and much diligent pondering of leading articles, come home to our business and bosoms. But one announcement in *The Times* of last Monday week shocked many of us with a sudden, absurdly indignant bewilderment, like a foul blow: I mean the death of Marcel Proust. It is not only absurd but impious to be indignant with the decrees of Fate. The wise throughout the ages have prescribed for us our proper behaviour in the face of such an event;

and most of us find the prescription quite useless. But, on the death of an author, there is this peculiar consolation that never fails: his work lives absolutely unaffected by his death.

. . . We can light the lamp, make a clear fire, and sit down to the book with the old thrill. There is only the thought that we must be content with what we have, that we are to get no more from that hand. With Marcel Proust, however, it seems that we are spared even that mortification. He has left behind him the completion of *A la Recherche du Temps Perdu*. This is great news. The announcements from the press of *La Nouvelle Revue Française* will be eagerly awaited. Even a new Anatole France is not so important an event.

It has been said that Proust will go down to posterity as the author of one book. This is only true in a literal sense. For the many volumes of *A la Recherche* that already crowd the shelves are several 'books' in one. It is not a 'story', but a panorama of many stories. Indeed, who reads Proust for the 'story'? His book is really a picture of the modern world and the modern spirit, and that is its peculiar fascination for us. There are 'morbid' elements in it, to be sure – you cannot read a page without seeing that it must have been written by some one who was anything but a normal, healthy human being, and it is not for nothing that *The Times* has compared him to Petronius Arbiter. But one of the advantages of this hyperaesthesia is a heightened sensibility for *everything*,[1] the perception and accurate notation of innumerable details in thought and feeling that escape a normal observer.

Take, for instance, the account of the famous author 'Bergotte'. Proust, little more than a child, but already his ardent reader, meets him at luncheon. And, first, the boy's imagined author, a 'langoureux vieillard', has to give place to the reality, much younger, a little man with a chin-tuft and a nose like a snail-shell. Then comes an elaborate description of his spoken diction, pronunciation, etc., and an attempt to reconcile these with the peculiarities of his written style. . . .

[Quotes from 'Sans doute encore' to 'la règle morale de tous'; Pléiade I, pp. 555–8].

Nor is the portrait finished yet. Bergotte was at bottom a man who really loved only certain images and to compose and paint them in words. Had he had to defend himself before a tribunal, in spite of himself he would have chosen his words, not for their effect on the judge, but in view of images which the judge would certainly never have perceived.

It is this extraordinarily minute 'psychometry' that is the peculiar mark of Proust's work. The sensations Swann derives from a sonata of Vinteuil's, the special quality of Elstir's pictures of the sea-shore, the effect of afternoon light in the church at Combray, glimpses of military life at Doncières, with its contrast of the First Empire aristocracy and the *ancien régime*, – it is the first time that such things as these have been put into words and brought intimately home to you. Then there are the studies of *le grand monde* – the 'gilded saloons', as Disraeli would have called them, of the Guermantes and the rest. Here you have a picture of the Faubourg Saint-Germain that is as true, you are assured, as Balzac's was false.[2]

I confess 'ma mère' and 'ma grand'mère' bore me. And there is just a little too much of 'le petit clan'. But in this vast banquet of modern life and thought and sensation there is plenty of room to pick and choose. Since Henry Bernstein first mentioned Proust's name to me in the year before the war I have returned again and again for a tit-bit to that feast. Proust is dead; but we can still go on enjoying his work. In that sense the cry of the child in Maeterlinck's *Oiseau Bleu* is true enough: 'There is no death.'

NOTE

1 In italics in the text.
2 In his article, published in *The Times* three weeks later, on December 20, 1922, Mr Walkley replied to a criticism of this statement:– 'The old complaint of "misrepresenting" modern France is now beginning to be heard about the great novelist just dead, Marcel Proust. An eminent English novelist tackles me about this. He says Proust is not entitled to the highest rank in literature because his representation of French society is partial only, and therefore unfair; that he writes only of the Faubourg Saint-Germain set, which stands for the "dead" France, and not of the "live" people, soldiers and statesmen and others, who have made and are making France to-day. And he contrasts him with Balzac, who aimed at giving a panorama of the whole social scheme. Well, it strikes me as an unfortunate comparison. Balzac's *Comédie Humaine* was like Zola's *Rougon-Macquart Family*, a mere afterthought, a specious formula designed to suggest continuity and completeness in what was merely casual and temperamental. As a "representation of France" it is not to be taken seriously; what it represents – like any other work of art – is its author's genius. His men of action, his statesmen, his men of affairs, are, frankly, preposterous. Proust never set out to "represent" France; he represented the side of its social-life that happened to interest him. What he did magnificently represent was the hitherto unexplored in human nature and the human mind. As M. Jacques Rivière says of him in the current

Nouvelle Revue Française, "The discoveries he has made in the human mind and heart will one day be considered as capital, and of the same rank as those of Kepler in astronomy, Claude Bernard in physiology, or Auguste Comte in the interpretation of the sciences." That strikes me as better work than producing a portrait-group of "Modern France", with General Lyautey arm-in-arm with Marshal Foch, and M. Clemenceau putting on his celebrated pearl-grey gloves.' – C. K. S. M. (Note by C. K. Scott Moncrieff, editor of *An English Tribute*.)

86. J. Middleton Murry on Proust in search of the Grail
1923

Part of 'Proust and the modern consciousness' in *Marcel Proust: An English Tribute*, pp. 102–10.

J. Middleton Murry assesses the importance of Proust's novel in terms of the desire for self-justification hidden behind its ostensible themes.

For Englishmen Marcel Proust has already become one of the great figures of modern literature. The feeling is common to many of his readers that in some way his work marks an epoch. What kind of epoch it is harder to say. Is he an end, or a beginning? And, again, yet another question insinuates itself continually as we pass slowly through his long volumes. What precisely – if answers to such questions can be made precise – was his own intention as a writer? Not that it necessarily makes the least difference to his own importance whether he succeeded or failed, whether he was consistent or spasmodic in following out his own plan. But we, at least, should be the happier for some indication of the thread to follow. For there comes a time in the reading of a long novel – and *A la Recherche du Temps Perdu* is surely one of the longest – when we feel the need to stand aside, to contemplate it as a whole, to grasp the pattern, to comprehend the general vision of life on which its essential individuality depends. Only thus, it seems, can we really make it our own.

In this respect Marcel Proust's book may be fairly said to bristle with difficulties. Its obvious theme, its surface intention, as we perceive it in the brilliant opening pages of *Du côté de chez Swann*, is the presentation by an adult man of his memories of childhood. We feel, though with peculiar qualifications to which we must return, that we are on the threshold of a spiritual autobiography; we are to be the enchanted witnesses of the unfolding and growth of a strangely sensitive consciousness. . . .

[Explains how the hidden intention is difficult to perceive until we look back and give heed to the reminiscences of the Martinville towers in *Combray* and of the three trees in *Jeunes Filles*.]

At this moment Marcel Proust came nearest, we may believe, to revealing to the reader the hidden soul of his own book. There is room for different interpretations, of course, and it is admitted that in any case he was frequently distracted from whatever plan he had by his delight in a pure description of the human comedy from the angle most familiar to him. Nevertheless, we are persuaded that Proust brought to the exact and intimate analysis of his own sensations something more than the self-consciousness of talent – some element, let us say, of an almost religious fervour. This modern of the moderns, this *raffiné* of *raffinés*, had a mystical strain in his composition. These hidden messages of a moment, these glimpses and intuitions of 'la vraie vie' behind a veil, were of the utmost importance to him; he had some kind of immediate certainty of their validity. He confessed as much, and we are entitled to take a man so reticent at his word.

We may take him at his word also when he acknowledges that the effort to penetrate behind the veil of these momentary perceptions was the chief interest of his life. The first of these illuminations – the vision of Martinville spire – had taken shape in a piece of writing which he gives us. We suspect that the last did also, and that its visible expression is the whole series of volumes which, after all, do bear a significant title – *A la Recherche du Temps Perdu*; we suspect that the last page of the last volume would have brought us to the first page of the first, and that the long and winding narrative would finally have revealed itself as the history of its own conception. Then, we may imagine, all the long accounts of the Guermantes' parties and the extraordinary figure of M. de Charlus would have fallen into their places in the scheme, as part of the surrounding circumstances whose pressure drove the youth and the man into the necessity of discovering a reality within himself. What he was to discover, when the demand that he should surrender himself to his moments of vision became urgent and finally irresistible, was the history of what he was. Proust – and amid the most labyrinthine of his complacent divagations into the *beau monde* a vague sense of this attends us – was much more than a sentimental autobiographer of genius; he was a man trying to maintain his soul alive. And thus, it may be, we have an explanation of the rather surprising fact that he began his work so late. The two volumes which went before *Du Côté de chez Swann*[1] were not indeed negligible, but they were the work of a dilettante. The explanation, we believe, is that in spite of his great gifts Proust was a writer *malgré lui*; he composed against the grain. We mean that had it been only for the sake of the satisfaction of literary creation, he probably would not have written at all. It was only when writing presented itself to him as the only available means for getting down to the bedrock of his own personality, as the only instrument by which his *fin-de-siècle* soul – the epithet is, in his case, a true definition – could probe to something solid to live by, that he seriously took up the pen. It was the lance with which he rode after the Grail – 'la vraie vie'.

Proust at the first glance looks wholly different from a man who rides off on a desperate adventure. There seems to be no room for desperate adventures in the Faubourg Saint-Germain. It is hardly congruous to some senses to ride through the waste land in a sixty horse-power limousine. Nevertheless, it can be done. The outward and visible sign is, not for the first time, different from the inward and spiritual grace.

So by a devious path we return to our first question. Proust marks an epoch. What kind of epoch? Is it an end or a beginning? And the answer we have reached is the answer we might have expected in the case of a figure so obviously considerable. Proust is both an end and a beginning. More an end than a beginning, perhaps, if we have regard to the technique and texture of his work. In the art of literature itself he opens up no new way. And, in the deeper sense, he indicates a need more than he satisfies it. The modern mind, looking into the astonishing mirror which Proust holds up to it, will not see in it the gleam of something to live by; but it will see, if it knows how to look, an acknowledgement of that necessity and a burning desire to satisfy it. By so much Marcel Proust marks a beginning also. It is the flame of this desire which smoulders always through his book, and at times breaks out; it is this which makes it his own, and this which gives it, in the true sense, style.

NOTE

1 I.e., *Les Plaisirs et les Jours*, published in 1896, and *Pastiches et Mélanges*, which, strictly speaking, did not come out as a volume until after *A l'Ombre des Jeunes Filles en Fleurs*, in the spring of 1919. But of the *Pastiches* some at

least had appeared in the *Figaro* in 1908 and 1909, while the *Mélanges* date
even further, and include the introductions to Proust's translations of
Ruskin, *La Bible d'Amiens* (1904) and *Sésame et les Lys* (1906) – C. K. S. M.
(Note by C. K. Scott Moncrieff, editor of *An English Tribute*.)

87 Joseph Conrad on Proust's creativity
1923

A brief contribution, entitled 'Proust as creator', to *Marcel
Proust: An English Tribute*, pp. 126–8.

Conrad (1857–1924) isolates Proust's analytical power as his
essential characteristic.

As to Marcel Proust, *créateur*, I don't think he has been written about
much in English, and what I have seen of it was rather superficial. I
have seen him praised for his 'wonderful' pictures of Paris life and
provincial life. But that has been done admirably before, for us,
either in love, or in hatred, or in mere irony. One critic goes so far as
to say that Proust's great art reaches the universal, and that in
depicting his own past he reproduces for us the general experience of
mankind. But I doubt it. I admire him rather for disclosing a past
like nobody else's, for enlarging, as it were, the general experience of
mankind by bringing to it something that has not been recorded
before. However, all that is not of much importance. The important
thing is that whereas before we had analysis allied to creative art,
great in poetic conception, in observation, or in style, his is a creative
art absolutely based on analysis. It is really more than that. He is a
writer who has pushed analysis to the point when it becomes
creative. All that crowd of personages in their infinite variety
through all the gradations of the social scale are rendered visible to us
by the force of analysis alone. I don't say Proust has no gift of
description or characterisation; but, to take an example from each
end of the scale: Françoise, the devoted servant, and the Baron de
Charlus, a consummate portrait – how many descriptive lines have
they got to themselves in the whole body of that immense work?
Perhaps, counting the lines, half a page each. And yet no intelligent
person can doubt for a moment their plastic and coloured existence.
One would think that this method (and Proust has no other, because

253

his method is the expression of his temperament) may be carried too far, but as a matter of fact it is never wearisome. There may be here and there amongst those thousands of pages a paragraph that one might think over-subtle, a bit of analysis pushed so far as to vanish into nothingness. But those are very few, and all minor instances. The intellectual pleasure never flags, because one has the feeling that the last word is being said upon a subject much studied, much written about, and of human interest – the last word of its time. Those that have found beauty in Proust's work are perfectly right. It is there. What amazes one is its inexplicable character. In that prose so full of life there is no reverie, no emotion, no marked irony, no warmth of conviction, not even a marked rhythm to charm our ear. It appeals to our sense of wonder and gains our homage by its veiled greatness. I don't think there ever has been in the whole of literature such an example of the power of analysis, and I feel pretty safe in saying that there will never be another.

88. George Saintsbury on Proust's originality
1923

A brief contribution, entitled 'A moment to spare', to *Marcel Proust: An English Tribute*, pp. 129–30.

George Saintsbury (1845–1933), in his limited acquaintance with Proust's work (only *Swann*), perceptively isolates Proust's unique blend of dreaminess and analysis.

I have at last found time, or rather, for it expresses our relations better, Time has been gracious enough at last to find *me*[1] – in regard to *Swann*. It was a new and satisfactory experience. His reality is extraordinary – at least in the main part of the book: I hope for the sake of French upper middle-class society of his day that it is not ordinary in such things as the big dinner scene in vol. ii.[2]

Has anybody said that he partakes *both*[3] of De Quincey and of Stendhal? He does to me, and I'm shot if I ever expected to see such a blend! You see, there is in him on the one hand a double measure of the analytical and introspective power that Beyle's admirers make so much of; with what they also admire, a total absence of prettification for prettification's sake. Yet he can be pretty in the very best sense, while Beyle never can, in the best or any other. Then, too, I at least find in him much less of the type-character which, though certainly relieved by individuality in the *Chartreuse de Parme* and other books (especially *Lamiel*), is still always more or less there. But the oddest and to me the most attractive thing is the way in which he entirely relieves the sense of aridity – of museum-preparations – which I find in Stendhal. And here it is that the De Quincey suggestion comes so unexpectedly in. For Proust effects this miracle by a constant relapse upon – and sometimes a long self-restriction to – a sort of dream element. It is not, of course, the vaguer and more mystical kind that one finds in De Quincey, not that of *Our Ladies of Sorrow* or *Savannah-la-Mar*, but that of the best parts of *The English Mail Coach*. In fact, it is sometimes Landorian rather than De Quinceyish in its dreaminess. But, however this may be, the dream quality is there, to me, as it is in few other Frenchmen – themselves almost always poets. Now, the worst of the usual realist is that being blinder than any other heathen in his blindness, he tries to exorcise dream, though sometimes not nightmare, from life. Such a mixture as Proust's I remember nowhere else.

NOTE

1 In italics in the text.
2 I.e., of *Du Côté de chez Swann*; the dinner at the Verdurins' at which Forcheville is present for the first time with the Cottards, Brichot the painter, Swann, and Odette. It is only fair, to both critic and reader, to explain that Mr Saintsbury had read nothing of Proust save *Swann*, and that only in an inadequate translation. On the other hand, it was as impossible for the editor to contemplate a book of this sort without a promise of collaboration from his old friend and master as it was, at the moment, for the doyen of English (if not of European, which is to say the world's) critics to qualify himself for saying more than is printed on this leaf. – C. K. S. M. (Note by C. K. Scott Moncrieff, editor of *An English Tribute*.)
3 In italics in the text.

89. Arthur Symons: some comparisons
1923

Contribution entitled 'A casuist in souls' to *Marcel Proust: An English Tribute*, pp. 138–43.

Arthur Symons (1865–1945) compares various sides of Proust's vision to Petronius, Stendhal, and Balzac among others. Proust is strongest in psychological analysis and closest to Stendhal.

Pater, who desired to find everywhere forces producing pleasurable sensations, 'each of a more or less peculiar and unique kind', says: 'Few artists, not Goethe nor Byron even, work quite clearly, casting off all *débris*, and leaving us only what the heat of their imagination has wholly fused and transformed.' Has the heat of Proust's imagination fused and transformed his material as Balzac and Rodin transformed and fused theirs? Are his characters creations? Has he the strange magical sense of that life in natural things, which is incommunicable? I think not; there is too much *débris* in his prose which he has not cast off.

Proust's books are the autobiography of a sensitive soul, for whom the visible world exists; only, he could never say with Gautier, 'I am a man for whom the visible world exists'; for in this famous phrase he expresses his outlook on life and his view of his own work: Gautier, who literally discovered descriptive prose, a painter's prose by preference; who, in prose and in verse alike, is the poet of physical beauty, of the beauty of the exterior of things. Proust, with his adoration of beauty, gives one an equal sense of the beauty of exterior things and of physical beauty; with infinite carefulness, with infinite precautions, he gives one glimpses of occult secrets unknown to us, of our inevitable instincts, and, at times, of those icy ecstasies which Laforgue reveals in *Moralités légendaires*. Only, not having read books of mediaeval magic, he cannot assure us that the devil's embraces are of a coldness so intense that it may be called, by an allowable figure of speech, fiery.

In his feverish attempt to explain himself to himself, his imaginary hero reminds me of Rousseau, who, having met Grimm and vexed Voltaire, was destined by his febrile and vehement character to learn in suffering what he certainly did not teach in song; who, being avid of misunderstandings was forced by the rankling thorns of jealousy to write his *Confessions*, in which he unburdens himself of the exasperation of all those eyes fixed upon him, driven, in spite of himself to set about explaining himself to other people – a coward before his own conscience. There is no cowardice in the conscience of Proust's hero; his utter shameless sincerity to the naked truth of things allows him 'avec une liberté d'esprit' to compete, near the end of the last volume, in his unveiling of M. de Charlus, with the outspokenness of Restif de la Bretonne in *Monsieur Nicolas.*

Some of the pages of *Sodome* might have been inspired by Petronius. The actual fever and languor in the blood: that counts for so much in Petronius's prose, and lies at the root of some of his fascinations. He is passionately interested in people, but only in those who are not of the same nature as he is: his avid curiosity being impersonal. Some of Proust's curiosity is not so much vivid as impersonal. Petronius – like the writer I refer to – is so specifically Latin that he has no reticence in speaking of what he feels, none of that unconscious reticence in feeling which races drawn farther from civilisation have invented in their relations with nature. This is one of the things which people mean when they say that Petronius's prose is immoral. So is that of Proust. Yet, in the prose of these writers, both touched with the spirit of perversity, the rarest beauty comes from a heightening of nature into something not quite natural, a perversity of beauty, which is poisonous as well as curious.

Proust has some of the corrupt mysticism of Huysmans, but not so perilous as his; nor has he that psychology which can be carried so far into the soul's darkness that the flaming walls of the world themselves fade to a glimmer; he does not chronicle the adventures of this world's Vanity Fair: he is concerned with the revelation of the subconscious self; his hero's confessions are not the exaltation of the soul. He is concerned, not so much with adventures as with an almost cloistral subtlety in regard to the obscure passions which work themselves out, never with any actual logic. With all this curiosity, this curiosity never drives him in the direction of the soul's apprehension of spiritual things. He does, at times, like Mallarmé, deform ingeniously the language he writes in; and, as in most of these modern decadents, perversity of form and perversity of manner bewilder us in his most bewildering pages.

I find to my surprise that a French critic, Carcassonne, compares Proust with Balzac. As an observer of society, yes; as a creator, no. 'Never,' he writes, 'since Stendhal and Balzac has any novelist put so much reality into a novel. Stendhal, Balzac: I write those great names without hesitation beside that of Marcel Proust. It is the finest homage I can render to the power and originality of his talent.' During Balzac's lifetime there was Benjamin Constant, whose *Adolphe* has its place after *Manon Lescaut*, a purely objective study of an incomparable simplicity, which comes into the midst of those analysts of difficult souls – Laclos, who wrote an unsurpassable study of naked human flesh in *Les Liaisons dangereuses*; Voltaire, Diderot; Rousseau, in whose *Nouvelle Héloïse* the novel of passion comes into existence. After these Flaubert, the Goncourts, Huysmans, Zola, Maupassant. I should place Proust with those rare spirits whose *métier* is the analysis of difficult souls. Browning wrote in regard to his *Sordello*: 'My stress lay on the incidents in the development of a soul: little else is worth study; I, at least, always thought so.' This certainly applies to Proust: and, as he seems to me to derive some of his talent from Stendhal and from no other novelist, I can imagine his casuistical and cruel creation of the obscure soul of M. de Charlus in much the same fashion as Stendhal's when he undresses Julien Sorel's soul with a deliberate and fascinating effrontery.

Consider the question of Balzac's style: you will find that it has life, that it has idea, that it has variety; that there are moments when it attains a rare and perfectly individual beauty. To Baudelaire he was a passionate visionary. 'In a word, every one in Balzac, down to the very scullions, has genius.' I have often wondered whether, in the novel, perfect form is a good or even a possible thing if the novel is to be what Balzac made it, history added to poetry. A novelist with style will not look at life with an entirely naked vision.

There is no naked vision in Proust; his vision is like a clouded mirror, in whose depths strange shapes flash and vanish. The only faultless style in French is Flaubert's; that style, which has every merit and hardly a fault, becomes what it is by a process very different from that of most writers careful of form. I cannot deny that Stendhal has a sense of rhythm: it is in his brain rather than in his dry imagination; in a sterile kind of brain, set at a great distance from the heart, whose rhythm is too faint to disturb it. Still, in Proust's style there is something paradoxical, singular, caustic; it is coloured and perfumed and exotic, a style in which sensation becomes complex, cultivated, the flower of an elaborate life; it can become deadly, as passion becomes poisonous. 'The world of the novelist,' I have written, 'what we call the real world, is a solid theft out of space; colour and music may float into it and wander through it, but it has not been made with colour and music, and it is not a part of the consciousness of its inhabitants.' This world was never lived in by d'Annunzio; this world was never entered by Proust. All the same, there is in him something cruel, something abnormal, something subtle. He is a creator of gorgeous fabrics, Babylons, Sodoms. Only, he never startles you, as Balzac startles you.

258

90. Arnold Bennett: some strictures

1923

Final contribution, entitled 'The last word', to *Marcel Proust: An English Tribute*, pp. 144–8.

Arnold Bennett (1867–1931) provides a mixture of praise and blame but firmly concludes by putting Proust in his place.

Two of the contributors to the stout Proust memorial number of *La Nouvelle Revue Française* remind me that I met Marcel Proust many years ago at a Christmas Eve party given by Madame Edwards (now Madame José Sert) in her remarkable flat on the Quai Voltaire, Paris. (Not that I needed reminding.) With some eagerness I turned up the year, 1910, in my journal. What I read there was this: 'Doran came on Sunday night for dinner. We went on to Misia Edwards' "Réveillon", and got home at 4 a.m.' Not a word more! And I cannot now remember a single thing that Proust said.

I have, however, a fairly clear recollection of his appearance and style: a dark, pale man, of somewhat less than forty, with black hair and moustache; peculiar; urbane; one would have said, an aesthete; an ideal figure, physically, for Bunthorne; he continually twisted his body, arms, and legs into strange curves, in the style of Lord Balfour as I have observed Lord Balfour in the restaurants of foreign hotels. I would not describe him as self-conscious; I would say rather that he was well aware of himself. Although he had then published only one book, *Les Plaisirs et les Jours* – and that fourteen years before – and although the book had had no popular success, Proust was undoubtedly in 1910 a considerable lion. He sat at the hostess's own table and dominated it, and everybody at the party showed interest in him. Even I was somehow familiar with his name. As for *Les Plaisirs et les Jours*, I have not read it to this day.

A few weeks before his death, while searching for something else in an overcrowded bookcase, I came across my first edition of *Du Côté de chez Swann*, and decided to read the book again. I cared for it less, and I also cared for it more, than in 1913. The *longueurs* of it seemed to me to be insupportable, the clumsy centipedalian crawling of the interminable sentences inexcusable; the lack of form or construction may disclose artlessness, but it signifies effrontery too. Why should not Proust have given himself the trouble of learning to 'write', in the large sense? Further, the monotony of subject and treatment becomes wearisome. (I admit that it is never so distressing in *Swann*, as in the later volumes of *Guermantes* and of *Sodome et Gomorrhe*.) On the other hand, at the second reading I was absolutely enchanted by some of the detail.

About two-thirds of Proust's work must be devoted to the minutiæ of social manners, the rendering ridiculous of a million varieties of snob. At this game Proust is a master. (Happily he does not conceal that, with the rest of mankind, he loves ancient blood and distinguished connections.) He will write you a hundred pages about a fashionable dinner at which nothing is exhibited except the littleness and the *naïveté* of human nature. His interest in human nature, if intense and clairvoyant, is exceedingly limited. Foreign critics generally agree that the English novelist has an advantage over the French in that he walks all round his characters and displays them to you from every side. I have heard this over and over again in conversation in Paris, and I think it is fairly true, though certainly Balzac was the greatest exponent of complete display. Proust never 'presents' a character; he never presents a situation: he fastens on one or two aspects of a character or a situation, and strictly ignores all the others. And he is scarcely ever heroical, as Balzac was always; he rarely exalts, and he nearly always depreciates – in a tolerant way.

Again, he cannot control his movements: he sees a winding path off the main avenue, and scampers away further and further and still further merely because at the moment it amuses him to do so. You ask yourself: He is lost – will he ever come back? The answer is that often he never comes back, and when he does come back he employs a magic but illicit carpet, to the outrage of principles of composition which cannot be outraged in a work of the first order. This animadversion applies not only to any particular work, but to his work as a whole. The later books are orgies of self-indulgence; the work has ruined the *moral* of the author: phenomenon common enough.

Two achievements in Proust's output I should rank as great. The first is the section of *Swann* entitled *Un amour de Swann*. He had a large theme here – love and jealousy. The love is physical and the object of it contemptible; the jealousy is fantastic. But the affair is handled with tremendous, grave, bitter, impressive power. The one fault of it is that he lets Swann go to a *soirée musicale* and cannot, despite several efforts, get him away from it in time to save the interest of the situation entire. Yet in the *soirée musicale* divagation there are marvellous, inimitable things.

The second achievement, at the opening of *Sodome et Gomorrhe*, is the psychological picture of the type-pederast. An unpromising subject, according to British notions! Proust evolves from it beauty, and a heartrending pathos. Nobody with any perception of tragedy can read these wonderful pages and afterwards regard the pervert as he had regarded the pervert before reading them. I reckon them as the high-water of Proust.

Speaking generally, Proust's work declined steadily from *Swann*. *A l'Ombre des Jeunes Filles en Fleurs* was a fearful fall, and as volume followed volume the pearls were strung more and more sparsely on the serpentine string. That Proust was a genius is not to be doubted; and I agree that he made some original discoveries in the by-ways of psychological fiction. But that he was a supreme genius, as many critics both French and English would have us believe, I cannot admit.

91. Edmond Jaloux on Proust's immediate posthumous reputation

1923

Extract from *L'Esprit des livres*, Paris, Plon-Nourrit, 1923, pp. 151–5.

Edmond Jaloux locates Proust's originality in the truth of his psychological analysis and does not hesitate to make the strongest claims for comparing him with the most important writers of the European tradition.

. . . What characterizes Marcel Proust and makes of him a writer without equal is the fact that he is absolutely *true*.[1] By this I mean that, over the hundred years or so during which the novel has taken on a role of cardinal importance, it has gradually acquired a great number of psychological clichés from which it is difficult to escape. So many spiritual developments strike us as obvious since Balzac and his successors that we all tend to make use of them. . . . Few contemporary writers completely avoid this mistake, and I could name certain novels, including very successful ones, that from one end to the other are nothing but a string of these clichés. Now, Marcel Proust has not been guilty of a single one. It could be claimed that he gives a completely new life to psychology. In spite of the high polish of his writing and the countless facets of a subtle, meticulous style – and one presenting at times an annoying plethora of detail – we have the constant impression in his case of finding ourselves confronting not a book but life itself. The miracle is to make something so direct, so true and so basic out of a stylistic procedure which is so full of allusion, decoration and circumlocution. In one part of his first book, *Du côté de chez Swann*, there are a few pages on love, on its dawning, high noon, and decline that gives the impression that nothing so acute or profound has been written on this subject since Stendhal. When I read Marcel Proust, when I see in his work the elements of life combining, coalescing, splitting up and degenerating like living cells, it seems to me that what I have before me is the work not of a novelist, but a biologist. . . .

What jars on certain readers of Proust is the ambiguity of his style; it is first and foremost the style of a moralist, or of a psychologist, who claims solely to set before us anatomical plates illustrating the human spirit, like a Montaigne or a Stendhal. But onto this traditionally French philosopher nature has grafted an extremely energetic, super-sensitive system obsessed with the world around us. . . .

By way of comparison with such a varied and complex art as this, the name of George Meredith has been mentioned. Marcel Proust also makes us think of the Henry James who used to say of one of his characters: 'Nature took on, where his imagination was concerned, a resemblance to a garden . . . thanks to which introspection seemed to him to be no more than taking exercise in the open air. . . .'

It is also beyond question that Ruskin, two of whose works he translated, inspired him with that – often unnecessary – meticulousness in detail. However, the writer Marcel Proust makes me think of most often is George Eliot. Like her he has the same boldness in his search for the truth, the same refusal to accept the common view of things, the same inspired discoveries that are so profound and new that they make us start with surprise and suddenly exclaim: 'How can it be that no one has ever made that observation? It's so true!'

When we think of what Montaigne, Mme de La Fayette, La Rochefoucauld, La Bruyère, Saint-Simon and Racine have revealed to us about man, at a time when our moralists were creating a new science, we are dumbfounded by what Stendhal, Benjamin Constant, Dostoevsky, George Eliot, Meredith, Henry James and Nietzsche have been able to add in complexity and subtlety to work that was already so complete that it seemed definitive. Make no mistake about it, Marcel Proust, for all his faults, belongs to that same tradition. . . .

NOTE

1 In italics in the text.

92. André Coeuroy on Proust and music
1923

Extract from *Musique et littérature*, Paris, Librairie Bloud & Gay, 1923, pp. 253–62.

André Coeuroy is the first to survey Proust's work for its numerous allusions to, and uses of, music. He quotes several examples of the associative power music has for recalling the past, notably in the role it plays in the Swann–Odette affair where the *leitmotiv* effect is, as elsewhere, reminiscent of Wagner. He concludes by emphasizing the cohesive force music has in Proust's art.

The miraculous thing about Proust is the way sensibility, intelligence and memory reinforce each other constantly. And in his case music has the privilege of stimulating all three extremely, so that . . . it is when he speaks of music that Proust achieves the greatest beauty:

[Quotes 1 From 'Depuis plus d'une année' to 'il assistait à sa genèse'; see *Swann*, Pléiade I, pp. 349–51.
2 From 'D'abord il n'avait goûté' to 'comme un amour inconnu'; see *Swann*, Pléiade I, pp. 208–10.
3 From 'Mais souvent on n'entend rien' to 'la postérité de l'oeuvre'; see *Jeunes Filles*, Pléiade I, pp. 529–31.
All three passages bring out the sensuousness of the Vinteuil sonata and its special associations both for Swann and the Narrator.]

We can now grasp why music is such a marvellous stimulant for Marcel Proust. It is because it relentlessly arouses memory of which it is the prime supplier, because it wells up suddenly from the unconscious at the behest of a vigilant power. For anyone trying, as Proust does, to resurrect a life through memory, music is the most valuable helper. Would Swann be Swann at all, if it were not for musical memories? As for Vinteuil's little phrase, the token of a complex love affair – (what a joy to hear it played on an execrable piano by Odette, who plays badly and with ludicrous taste) – that little phrase is the key to his soul, as in another sense it is the key to Proust's theory of art.

Proust constantly searched in everything for 'the clear flame of purest knowledge'. For 'the misty ideas' that exalt the mind, he never gave up wishing to find 'a slow and difficult clarification'. It is deep into this desire that the very strong predilection he shows for music plunges its roots, because music is the mistiest among those misty ideas that exalt the mind; because the problems it raises (and even its nature) are the most difficult to conceive and because it is at all points similar to those distant objects of which Proust has said that they 'seem to hide way beyond what one can see something they invite us to come and take, something they seem both to contain and conceal at one and the same time'.

To discover what they contain is the whole point of *A la recherche du temps perdu*. If the mind's essential duty is (as Proust also says) to 'get to the very bottom of one's impressions', the mystery of music partakes of those mysteries the mind applies itself to with utter delight. Having the property to satisfy the most intense demands of the spirit, music has inexhaustibly fulfilled this dreamer, rich with the profusion of nature herself, who desired that those misty ideas should eventually, after countless detours, attain 'repose illuminated by knowledge'.

1924–31
POSTHUMOUS WORKS
AND CRITICAL ESSAYS

93. Albert Thibaudet on *La Prisonnière*
1924

Part of a review in *L'Europe nouvelle*, 9 February 1924.

Albert Thibaudet, well known as a sympathetic critic of nineteenth- and twentieth-century writers, shows here how critical opinion has become accustomed to being on Proust's wavelength and ready to accept his language of communication. His review is typical of those that were favourable to *La Prisonnière*. Not only does he bring out its interesting analyses but he also readily uses it as a basis for relating Proust to the tradition of Montaigne.

. . . Now that we have overcome the inevitable surprise of the beginning, now that we are accustomed to a 'Proustian' nature, now that we know the laws, the currents, the growth and the inner life of this nature, it seems to me, as I finish my reading, that there was nothing, in the nine volumes already published, superior to the two volumes of *La Prisonnière*. Analysis is put through its paces, extends itself, twists and turns, enjoys its own powers with a virtuosity and a spirit that puts us in mind not so much of pure analysis, which is a merely technical and cold thing, as the poetry of analysis. And I do not see any other comparison to be made than the old parallel of Proust and Montaigne. One thinks of that intellectual lyricism in the third book of the *Essays*, the most personal book, the most independent, the one that most directly captures things at their source. . . .

The whole of *La Prisonnière* turns on two characters, on whom Proust's countless analyses do not fall (as they do in the case of professional analysts) like drops of rain that could be said to wash them clean, put them back into general circulation and turn them into

265

generalized types, but much more as brush-strokes on a canvas that is never finished, for a portrait that never completes its mission to speak to us, to produce something new, to live unpredictably. What we have is M. de Charlus and Albertine, one representing Sodom and one Gomorrah, both adumbrated in the preceding volumes and developing in them in such a way, and filling the horizon to such an extent, that the author and the reader seem to move about patiently inspecting them like the Lilliputians walking over the body of Gulliver. . . .

It is often said that artistic creations are more true than real people. It could be said of Proust's characters, and for the following reason. The vast majority of men, at a certain age in their lives, almost cease changing and are reduced almost entirely to a state of repetition and automatism. They become closed cycles that you feel could be defined in a formula that would say all there is to say about them. And the novelist and the dramatist who observe them, or recreate them, or who create them, are in fact looking for this formula with the intention of saying all there is to say about them. When they modify them, it appears that their evolution was logically contained in their previous states. There is no one further removed from this ambition than Proust, no one who takes the opposite point of view with greater deliberation. The characters' account in the writer's bank is never frozen; it is, as much as can be a current account, an open account. As long as they have a place in his narrative, something new is always being written down against their assets or liabilities. If *A la recherche du temps perdu* consisted of fifty volumes, we would still see in the fiftieth M. de Charlus, Albertine, the two Guermantes, the Verdurins, Cottard and Françoise taking on new, unexpected facets that were never implied in their former state. This is literally the force of life itself, and we may say that Proust has pushed back the frontiers within which a novelist is permitted to express life. . . .

94. Robert Kemp on *La Prisonnière*
1924

Part of a notice in *La Revue universelle*, March 1924, pp. 636–7.

Robert Kemp (1885–1959), critic and journalist, welcomes *La Prisonnière* in spite of its unevenness and its deviation from normal psychology.

A la recherche du temps perdu reminds me of that domain belonging to Sleeping Beauty . . . that could be penetrated only with difficulty. Proust is our guide; and what a strange traveller he is! He is quick to cover an important stretch of ground when he suddenly stops in front of a clump of flowers; with a magnifying glass in his hand he examines a petal, vein by vein. . . . A mere nothing distracts him from his path and plunges him into meditation. A mere nothing? There is no mere nothing where Proust is concerned. Where we did not suspect there were any wondrous things, he discovers them for us. His curiosity never flags; his sensibility retains prodigious freshness and intensity. One might say he was a 'micropath', if one were not afraid of seeming to ridicule what one admires. He is a sorcerer, a magician, a psychological magus!

The two volumes that have just been published were not revised by their author. If therefore we find, even more than in the preceding volumes, cluttered, interminable sentences and needless repetitions – Proust goodnaturedly points them out himself – we should be quick to excuse them. It behoves us to welcome *La Prisonnière* with gratitude.

The prisoner in question is Albertine . . . who . . . has agreed to come and live in Paris with Marcel; she is accepted more or less as his fiancée; but who could imagine that this hesitant young man, devoted to examining the continuous fluctuations of his own feelings, worrying himself with the questions he asks and finding vague solutions for them, will one day decide to marry her? In fact, Albertine is horribly compromised by living with Marcel; but it scarcely seems to be noticed. Basically what is truly regrettable – though for some readers it is one of the attractions of Proust's work – is that he has attached so much importance to certain aberrations of human sensibility. Whatever one may say, this has impoverished his work. His victories, furthermore, would have been more valuable had they been achieved within a normal psychological framework in areas which Montaigne, La Rochefoucauld or Stendhal had surely not completely exhausted. . . .

95. Unsigned review of *La Prisonnière*
1924

The Times, 12 March 1924, p. 10.

The review ('By Our Dramatic Critic') is titled 'The New Proust. *La Prisonnière*. Two Pathological "Cases"' and betrays a sense of shock at Proust's growing obsession with sexual inversion combined with fascination for his powers of analysis.

They had been discussing Dostoievsky, and Albertine had asked her lover whether the Russian had ever assassinated anyone. Not one of his books but might be called the Story of a Crime; it was an obsession with him, and it didn't seem natural for him always to be writing of that one thing. Her lover answered: 'Je ne suis pas romancier; il est possible que les créateurs soient tentés par certaines formes de vie qu'ils n'ont pas personnellement éprouvées.' And he promised to show her at Versailles two portraits; one of 'l'honnête homme par excellence' and the best of husbands, Choderlos de Laclos, who wrote the most frightfully perverse book, and, just opposite, the portrait of Mme de Genlis, who wrote moral tales and was not content with betraying the Duchess of Orléans but tortured her by alienating her children.

It is possible that Marcel Proust was here glancing at his own case. For certainly sexual abnormality is as much an obsession with him as murder with Dostoievsky, and he may be said to have had a personal interest in pointing out that the lives of authors are often enough the exact opposite of their works. Whether or not this was so with Proust is a delicate question. The appalling Charlus – who reappears in the two new volumes, an even more loathsome monster than before because more sentimental and almost pathetic – it may be said proves nothing save the microscopic minuteness of Proust's observation and his extraordinary talent for portraiture. On the other hand, why choose *that* subject? Why portray *that*, of all types? Further, one remembers in a previous volume a dissertation on the general pathology of the matter which seemed to show something like a first-hand acquaintance with it. One is driven back upon Albertine's word, obsession; and one cannot help wishing he could have been obsessed with something else. I shall be told, of course, that that wish is the one critical sin that shall not be forgiven, being an attempt to interfere with the author's sacred right to choose his own subject. Well, an author is but a man, and his readers are but men, and 'with such a being as man, in such a world as the present one', I submit that authors have no right to choose themes that are bound to disgust the majority of men. I admit that Charlus is wonderfully drawn, a triumph of art, if you like, but *c'est plus fort que moi*, I simply cannot stomach him.

And is there not a tinge of melodrama in the capital scene of the book, wherein Charlus is rescued from his insulters by the Queen of Naples? 'Lean on my arm', says the Queen. 'Be sure that it will always support you. It is strong enough for that. You know that at Gaeta it has already held the riff-raff in respect. It shall be your rampart.' Do Queens really talk like tragedy queens – 'Gaeta' – 'rampart' – and, if they ever do, would they on such an occasion? I can only say I don't believe a word of it.

What makes the romantic falsity of this incident still more glaring is its realistic setting. No other author that I have ever read comes near Proust in the photographic, or rather kinematographic deline-ation of a big social 'crush', with its tittle-tattle and back-biting, the snobbery and insolent condescension of its 'great ladies', its occasional epigrams, its bowing and scraping *super ignes suppositos*, its stifling and noxious atmosphere, its glimpses of queer episodes behind *portières* and in remote corridors. This picture is one of Proust's set pieces; it recurs as persistently as the *motif* of Vinteuil's sonata; and you have it again, with its inevitable (and quite delicious) purple patch about the thrills aroused by a particular piece of music, in this book, in the party given by that remarkable couple the Verdurins to guests invited by Charlus. In such a scene the bit of *bravura* assigned to the Queen of Naples gives you something like the shock you would feel at an extract from Marie Corelli interpolated in a subtle page of Henry James.

After Charlus, Albertine. Indeed, though not so striking a figure, she fills more space in the book. She is the 'prisoner' of the title, and her love for the narrator is the prison from which she at length escapes. Was she ever in love with him? You (and he) are kept perpetually wondering, for Albertine is another 'case' of sexual pathology, and love for her when a man was concerned must have seemed an unfamiliar experiment. The man himself (call him Marcel) in this particular experiment was odd enough. Perhaps the whole set of Proust volumes might be labelled the Oddity of Marcel. He seems to have wanted as much 'mothering' as the other sort of affection from his mistress. And he was as much her 'little boy' as her lover; a fractious and selfish little boy; a sick little boy, too, with nerves worn to a rag; an effeminate and self-torturing little boy. Of all forms of self-torture jealousy, as we know, is one of the cruellest, and Marcel seems to have suffered all its pangs, and then some, as the Americans say. Albertine, of course, being a woman with much to conceal was an easy, natural liar. That again, is a stock situation with Proust; the lying woman *versus* the jealous man. Odette and Swann, Marcel and Gilberte, and now Marcel and Albertine. The third, I think, gives the minutest exploration of the case; so minute and so prolonged that at times it becomes wearisome. For a story of morbid love and morbid jealousy and nothing else soon wearies a third party. Example: Hazlitt's 'Liber Amoris'. We most of us at some time in our lives have our own little troubles of this sort, and are not tremendously excited by other people's. But no troubles were little for Marcel; his jealousy made his affair with Albertine one agony. It is my fault, I dare say, that I find the spectacle of this agony monotonous.

And yet, I remember what Henry James is reported to have said of Proust. 'He bores and fascinates me.' There is always the fascination. Some of us may find it in what Victorian reviewers would have called Proust's profound knowledge of the human heart; let us say, rather, human brain and nervous reactions. Others in his discoveries of unsuspected likenesses – *e.g.* his comparison in this book of Parisian street-cries with the musical services of the Church, and in an earlier one of his own queer sentimental experiences with those celebrated in the august verse of Racine's *Esther*. Others again in the wonderful notation of musical ecstasy, or in the ironical pictures of the Faubourg St Germain, or in the fresh and suggestive literary appreciations. Or shall we not say the fascination is in the *blend* of all these delights? It stimulates in us that sense of the extension and exaltation and richer colouring of life which is what we all seek in imaginative literature.

NOTE

All italics are in the text.

96. Mauriac on *La Prisonnière*
1924

Part of a review of *La Prisonnière* in *La Nouvelle Revue française*,
1 April 1924, pp. 489–93.

Mauriac sees *La Prisonnière* as showing the Narrator, now
called Marcel for the first time, as a character around whom
other characters play only an abstract role. He finds that
Proust's obsessive interest in the analysis of jealousy now
dominates the importance of plausibility in the novel.

The two volumes of *La Prisonnière* force us to revise, to some
extent, our opinion of Proust's work. We had thought that our
friend, though using, I might add, a completely different method,
wanted like Balzac to rival the national registration of births,
marriages and deaths. And no doubt he discovered enough living
people within himself to justify this claim. But those people he had,
as it were, absorbed during his life in fashionable society and then
brought back into the light during his days as a recluse, while using
his illness to dig deeper into his excavations – those people had never
completely detached themselves from him; the most different shared
similarities, because they shared similarities with him. Between
Swann's love for Odette, Saint-Loup's for Rachel and Marcel's for
Gilberte and Albertine, there is no difference of kind. It is the same
sort of love, but to the ravages of which Proust alerts us, in his first
books, as a novelist, while in *La Prisonnière* he studies them almost in
the abstract and as a clinician. These characters, who once greatly
amused him, seem to interest him less and less. Having emerged
from him without the cord being severed, they once more go back
inside him and are lost in his shadow. Pressed by illness and
suffocating under the pressure of everything he still had to say to us
before departing this life, perhaps Marcel Proust felt less indulgent
towards his creations and only saw them as coming between him and
us. Just as in the last year of his life he dismissed his closest friends,
perhaps he did not find it easy to put up with the living world of his
books. For the first time, in *La Prisonnière*, he gives his hero the
name Marcel and resolutely occupies the front of the stage. The
outlines of his most fully drawn characters become less precise. When
Françoise says to him: 'With your pyjamas being all white and the

way you move your neck, you look like a dove . . .' we do not recognize the familiar voice of the old Combray servant. And we certainly meet here a Charlus who is more blatantly drawn than in the preceding volumes, a terrible Charlus; too terrible! We are dealing not so much with a sick man as with sickness itself. The person we used to know was cancerous, now we see only cancer itself. That secret Charlus of the first books, whose sickness is betrayed only by a look, a flower or a handkerchief which is too brightly coloured, here bursts, cracks open and runs like an abcess that goes on endlessly pouring out. In actual fact, nothing matters so much to Proust, in *La Prisonnière*, as giving us the result of his investigations into love. Only in so far as the study of feeling is concerned is he bothered to be truthful and he subordinates his narrative to the demands of this study, adjusting events with no care for plausibility. We are perfectly willing for an experienced girl like Albertine to go and live with a young bachelor; still the author ought to make such extraordinary circumstances credible to us and show us the reasons for them and their consequences. He should – but let us hasten to say that, fully occupied with the terrible discoveries Proust involves us in, we too succumb to his indifference towards anything that is not part of this implacable search. And besides, it is too bad if the other characters are less alive, since he is still with us, more alive than ever, lying motionless in his bed; yet, in spite of the closed windows, all life revolves around his recumbent form. He draws it close to him and tames it, capturing the street-cries, the shafts of sunshine and the sheets of rain. As he does with Albertine, he draws the universe into his sick-room and keeps it prisoner. . . .

Yet, in *La Prisonnière*, psychological analysis, at the same time as it goes further and deeper, gradually becomes restricted and limited, to the point of being no more than the study, albeit an extraordinary one, of a case, an exception. To the extent that the jailer of the beloved, the jealous lover, has fewer pretexts for suffering, he can no longer feel his love, he is no longer in love. Albertine must either torture him or bore him. As soon as he is assured that she has not wanted to join a woman friend at the Trocadéro or at the Verdurins', Marcel, for his part, asks no more than to be alone. He no longer hungers after that body once he believes that no one is stealing it from him and that it in turn is not eluding his desire. . . .

It would only be left to us to admire in silence if Proust did not claim, for the love he has just dismantled before our very eyes, universal characteristics. Proust does not seem to have any doubt that it is here a question, not of a specimen of love, but of love itself. And it is on this point, it seems to us, that there might perhaps be objections to be made to him. Perhaps – but this love, in which the executioner is the very one from whom we expect peace of mind, goes by the name of un-shared love; and if it is true that that is the kind most widely found throughout suffering humanity, shall we refuse Marcel Proust the achievement of having, in *La Prisonnière*, got back to the universal.

97. Fernand Vandérem on *La Prisonnière*

1924

Notice in *La Revue de France*, 1 April 1924; reprinted in *Le Miroir des lettres*, Flammarion, 1929, pp. 81–3.

Vandérem appreciates *La Prisonnière* for its satiric qualities and sees in that a defence against the charge of immorality.

. . . We are here in the hell of Sodom and Gomorrah, among men and women equally doomed.

And yet, in spite of Albertine's morbid fantasizing and diabolical depravity, what humanity is here in the sufferings she inflicts on the hero of the book! What fine analyses of jealousy they suggest to Proust, worthy of those given us by M. Jean Rostand!

What a build-up of epic power the fatal obsession of M. de Charlus acquires! And how by degrees this grotesque case rises to the level of the great comic types in our literature!

On the other hand, I ask you to imagine these three characters executed with panache, but set before us only in a few instances of their mania or their disappointments, in a few accidental encounters, in the clash of a few rapid exchanges, oh! to be sure, they would not fail to entertain us. Only, instead of the long wake of melancholy or the irresistible hilarity left in us, minute by minute, step by step by their strange agony, we might only be said to retain the fleeting, beguiling memory of a few entertaining or weird figures.

But if you want another kind of proof of the general impact of these portraits, then it is in the alarm they are beginning to provoke. At this moment, a certain tendency to denounce them as much for being a calumny on our society as for the dangers of contagion they bring, is beginning to emerge. Our friend, M. Franc-Nohain[1] in particular, has shown himself to be very critical of *La Prisonnière* and, in the technical reservations he formulated against the book, one could sense a secret indignation against its basic theme.

In my view, however, M. Franc-Nohain exaggerates on both counts.

If we take the literary defects he condemns in Proust's work: slow pace, longueurs, repetitiousness, insufficient selectivity, lack of proportion – who is not familiar with them? Did I not point them out myself when *A l'ombre des jeunes filles* was published? Besides, are they not faults inherent in Proust's manner; without them he would, perhaps, not have been able to realize this unique fresco, which has no precedent anywhere? . . .

Moreover, it seems to me that the number of readers who, sincerely disregarding all charges of snobbery, are ready to accept Proust's annoying difficulties is growing steadily. In any case, as far as I am concerned, I have absolved them of blame this many a day. If there are a few repetitions, a few obscurities, a few hobby-horses, I still consider that it is not too much to pay for all the meatiness, all the riches that I encounter in such pages as these; and I would willingly consent to the same trouble if only I could find something of similar quality in many of the books I read every day.

As for the immorality *La Prisonnière* has been charged with, this complaint would hold if these daring chapters constituted nothing more than a series of deliberate obscenities in the style of licentious novels or following the procedures of naturalist fiction. But one must once again intervene here with the memorable difference noted by Baudelaire between the direct and complete transcription of our impressions, of our feelings, and their 'transformation into objects of art'. Any simply subjective or simply objective depiction of vice and debauchery will only yield a wretched and pernicious representation. On the other hand, should irony, or scorn or anger place their mark upon these scabrous descriptions, we have, not an encouragement to do evil, but its denunciation, we have, as in *La Prisonnière*, satire, i.e. one of the most powerful and one of the highest forms of literary art.

Let us recall in this connection the epigraph that Baudelaire, no less, took from d'Aubigné for his *Fleurs du mal*:

> On dit qu'il faut couler les exécrables choses
> Dans le puits de l'oubli et au sépulcre encloses,
> Et que par les escrits le mal ressuscité
> Infectera les moeurs de la postérité;
> Mais le vice n'a point pour mère la science,
> Et la vertu n'est pas fille de l'ignorance.[2]

This would be the ideal epigraph also for *La Prisonnière* and would allow the most rigid moralists to enjoy in peace the profundity, the comedy and the charm that constantly alternate in these two volumes.

NOTES

1 Vandérem is referring to Franc-Nohain's article on *La Prisonnière* in *L'Echo du Nord* (28 February 1924) in which he expresses his disgust for Charlus and Albertine and denounces Proust as 'sick'.
2 Accursèd things, we are told, must be dropped into the well of oblivion and buried in sepulchres, and evil, so they say, if resurrected in words will infect the morals of our descendants; but vice does not have knowledge for a mother and virtue is no daughter of ignorance.

98. Dominique Braga: an assessment of Proust's individuality

1924

Part of 'Admiration pour Marcel Proust', an article on *La Prisonnière, Le Crapouillot*, 1 April 1924.

Dominique Braga, journalist and literary editor, had been critical of Proust's shortcomings, especially over *Sodome et Gomorrhe*. Here he attempts to review positively the general effect of Proust's work to date and then give some close attention to *La Prisonnière*. He tries to come to terms with the intellectual and the emotional sides of Proust and concludes that with *La Prisonnière* emotion saves the day over what would otherwise be a rather dry repetition of *Un amour de Swann*.

You put down your copy of Marcel Proust and yet, if you want to talk about it, you do not know where to begin. From what angle can one come to grips with this monumental work? It is an organism of such complexity and of such moving sensibility that you are never sure you are putting your finger on what are medically called 'nerve centres'. . . .

Marcel Proust's work varies, as do his own characters, according to the place, the hour and the quality of the observer and the reader. . . .

275

Yet this question of atmosphere, of mood favourable to reading does not, in the case of any other work, play the role or assume the importance we give it when confronted by a volume of Proust. Common sense is perfectly right. Would one think of reading *Du côté de chez Swann* or now *La Prisonnière* at just any time of the day, anywhere, in the train, between a story by M. Cocteau and a novel by M. Giraudoux? No, these copious volumes lie around for some time on your table before you decide to open them; you promise yourself to do it when you have some respite in your life, a period of quietness, convalescence and free time that will give you the leisure to reflect and the patience of a genuine experimenter. It seems that before reading Proust, one should put oneself into a propitiatory frame of mind. Then one can plunge headlong into lost time. . . .

[The question of a favourable approach depends also on appreciating the psychological analysis Proust adopts.]

English novelists, and especially Russian, had already, of course, attempted to explain human personality by its 'underside', by its psychological infrastructures. Yet in a Dostoievsky (incidentally very much greater) who proceeds by intuitions and revelations, by sudden brutal illuminations . . . that insistent desire to fill out the progression from unconscious to conscious that we find in Proust does not appear with complete lucidity. The Russian genius impetuously heaves up the waves of hidden existence onto the surface. . . . This French writer, a man clear in his thinking, this Frenchman who is part Jew, proceeds in the exactly opposite way. With him reason goes down into the depths of darkness, with him intelligence claims to be able to launch an attack on instinct, and even reject it as inspiration. Armed with his lamp, the miner strikes the buried rocks and listens with interest to the echoes.[1]

Whatever may be the foreign influences on Marcel Proust, there does not seem to be anything in the history of French fiction that heralds him or opens up a path for him to follow. If we have at all costs to find precursors for him, we must look into the realm of philosophy, to that line of psychological thinkers that, from Maine de Biran to Henri Bergson, carry the transformism and evolutionism of Lamarck into the life of the mind. As for the feeling of continuity, of duration, of becoming, one surely senses to what modern philosophies our novelist is indebted? Is it not significant that at about the same time Freud in Austria should, along medical lines, reach striking analogies, that in England Samuel Butler should extend the field of consciousness well beyond the individual in terms of time and beyond the cells of the brain in terms of the body? In all these researches there is a moving unity. Proust, perhaps, applied them prematurely to aesthetics, perhaps in the neophyte's enthusiasm and exclusive love of his own theories he arrived at a view of the human being that was as limited as the one for which he substituted his own. Nevertheless, this view is in tune with a whole series of spiritual discoveries that it celebrates, and in whole or in part it constitutes a new way of thinking that we can no longer do without. . . .

[Referring specifically to *La Prisonnière*, he regrets the lack of polish and its unrevised state.]

What impression do these two volumes make on us? First, that Marcel Proust gains in authority even if his originality takes us less by surprise than it did. He knows he is a 'master' and is no longer afraid to slip in the 'literary' piece, the anthology piece; the numerous pages devoted, for instance, to the sounds and cries of the street that the invalid hears from his window in the early morning are at first a happy trouvaille, but then end up causing us extreme annoyance, so much does one sense that they correspond to a systematic compilation, the listener being unable to gather together from his own street alone (and in a single morning) expressions that flourished at several periods and *vary according to the district*.[2] Proust's inclination to theorize plays tricks on him. . . . What a pity it is to have to admit that often in his repetitions in the course of his study of jealousy, Proust adds nothing to what he had said twenty times before. . . . That is why this account does not move us as powerfully as the description of Swann's torments in the first volume, at a time when the author had not yet crystallized his psychological theory of jealousy. . . .

[Goes on to examine Proust's lack of adult experience combined with his excessive introversion and critical analysis.]

In Proust there are two men: the intellectual, the man who forced himself to be impassive in the face of feeling and refused to cover it within the deceptive veils of emotional pragmatism; and the poet, always ready to love, admire and celebrate. What is most extraordinary is the fact that the first did not stifle the second and that, while showing himself to be mercilessly cruel, Proust was able to remain naively mystical. . . .

Proust never fled from pain. He almost revels in it: 'I now call love a reciprocal torture. . . . One must choose either to stop suffering or stop loving. . . . If life brings no change in our love

277

affairs, then we will want to bring it ourselves or pretend to, and talk of separation, so much do we feel that all our love affairs and all other things are rapidly moving towards their end.' In spite of this doom, he surrenders to his demon.

Perhaps if Proust had been content, as is often said, to proceed for ever by analysis, he would never have moved us. But this is not the truth of the matter. These sentences quoted here, and many others, turn analytical development on its head; they are dictated directly by suffering. The pitch rises, we catch a sudden glimpse of the man himself.

So we read Proust. Sometimes his commentaries on the nobility, for all the tact and taste of a sophisticate, border on pedantry. Sometimes this apparent absence of selection, this egalitarian system of introspection cause him to linger with equal good faith on profundities or puerilities as he goes in search of a truism.

But suddenly his path takes him to the windy heights of the imagination, without which art would not exist. . . .

I believe I once wrote that Proust had no imagination. I must have been truly stupid three years ago to write such a senseless thing.

NOTES

1 This is especially true of the Proust of the later volumes, to whom it was often pointed out that he was Montaigne and Saint-Simon and that he wanted to be as intelligent as they were. Marcel Proust in *Les Plaisirs et les jours* (1896) still only gave evidence of sensibility. But what charm! What youthful pastiche! (Dominique Braga)
2 In italics in the text.
3 Pléiade III, p. 109.

99. Norbert Guterman on *La Prisonnière*

1924

Part of a review in *Philosophies*, 15 May 1924.

Norbert Guterman (1900–) responds to the emotional content of *La Prisonnière*. He finds it more explicitly 'Proustian' than preceding works and similar to *Un amour de Swann*. However, Proust is seen here less as an objective observer than as creator of a drama in which the Narrator plays a more definite role than hitherto. There is also a clear idea that the book is to be judged for its insights as literature rather than for the absence or presence of moral qualities.

. . . Here we see Albertine living with Marcel (as the narrator, anonymous up to this point, is called). The unstable equilibrium of this very fragile and indispensable routine, the phase of love, in which, after the possession of the object, affection only subsists because of the fear of losing the object and is capable of yielding nothing but suffering, the monotonous and vague development of the jealous lover's thinking: all this creates a painful atmosphere of anguish and at times reaches an almost dramatic intensity. As for Albertine, for all her efforts to appear docile and passive, she still cannot hide certain words and actions that suddenly open up behind her unexpected and frightening horizons, forcing Marcel to search deep into a life that constantly eludes him. And thus the desire for possession, accompanied by ever-changing memories that are distorted by the influence of conflicting passions, pursues its own search for lost time, a search analogous to the one that has inspired the whole work from its beginning and that is pursued to satisfy another desire for possession, perhaps more universal than the possession of a woman. But let us not anticipate what Proust will presently tell us himself in the works whose titles promise so many revelations.

But what we all already know is how much his work has enriched us: if we had not had Proust, would every moment of our lives have been mobilized in the service of beauty and would each one of them have acquired this priceless value? And this is already such an immense contribution that it is really quite unjust to criticize Proust for having done nothing to 'intensify our spiritual lives'. Besides, to demand moral or scientific uses from a work of art is to judge it from the outside and in a very arbitrary fashion . . . it is really astonishing that people have spoken,[1] in connection with Proust, of 'the dissolution of the personality', of 'moral decadence' etc. . . . What is important in Proust's work is the attempt to give a poetic form to the content of a consciousness. Yet Proust has not indulged in psychology; he has not sought to create an objective or scientific work, he has not sought to trace psychical manifestations back to their first causes or principles. In this sense it must be pointed out that he has been more all-embracing than profound, or, if the comparison can be allowed, that his manner is rather that of a painter than a sculptor: his characters, though full and colourful, though always standing out, sometimes even with the sharpness of caricature, lack roundness.

But, on the other hand, there is a character who appears with increasing depth and clarity as we proceed: this is Proust himself – and surely this is the real reason for the whole of this gigantic series. . . .

NOTE

1 Guterman is thinking of an article by Ramon Fernandez: 'La Garantie des sentiments', *La Nouvelle Revue française*, 1 April 1924. The article was reprinted in *Messages*; see No. 119.

100. A. B. Walkley on the death of Albertine
1924

Review in *The Times*, 23 July 1924, p. 12.

The article, titled 'Albertine Dead. A Proust Fragment. The Instalment Plan' and signed A. B. W(alkley), covers a recently published extract, 'The Death of Albertine' in English. Walkley points out the rewards of a close reading of Proust in small doses.

Among the consolations of life as it passes is the knowledge that there is still more Proust to come. It is perhaps with the charitable aim of postponing the moment when we shall be left at least inconsolable that further instalments are being so sparingly – it would seem almost grudgingly – doled out. If we were offered the whole of the remnant in one big lump, we might be tempted to gorge it at a sitting. Fortunately no author lends himself more readily to the instalment plan than Proust. You no more read him than (to take the Johnsonian instance) you read 'Clarissa' for the story. You are never in a fever of excitement about what is going to happen next; one turn of the kaleidoscope is as good as another, where the pattern is always made out of the author's mind. It is about that mind itself that you are in a perpetual fever of excitement, every fresh manifestation of it giving a new inflexion to your curve of temperature.

You get the latest manifestation of it in the July issue of *The Criterion*, in a fragment translated by Mr C. K. Scott-Moncrieff, 'The Death of Albertine'. It is safe to say that the tremendous theme of death has never been so intimately, so truthfully, treated as by Proust. The death of 'ma grand-mère' showed one side of it. The death of Bergotte, another. But these were, strictly, 'death scenes'. 'The Death of Albertine' is nothing of that kind; it is the scene of the lover's mind as affected by the shock of Albertine's death. A brief telegram apprised him that she had been killed by a fall from her horse. This telegram crossed one from himself, begging her unconditionally to return to him.

[Quotes from 'Je demandais l'heure à Françoise' to 'dans l'agate arborisée d'un seul azur!' Pléiade III, pp. 479–80.]

This is emotion in the making, not 'recollected in tranquillity'. You feel that the poet is waiting for it, round the corner. But if it is not yet poetry, only the stuff of poetry, it would be absurd to pretend that it is good prose. I mean Proust's; for Mr Scott-Moncrieff's translations of him are always so conscientious and so close that one can, as it were, hear the original through them. The last thing that Proust troubles about is form; he is too intensely preoccupied with his subject-matter for that. But the absolute veracity of the thing! Where else can you find so accurate a notation of a mood, of the vain striving to throw off the pressure of old memories logically inconsistent with a present grief yet inseparable from it?

Nor does Proust sacrifice a tittle of the truth to the common human solicitude for keeping up appearances. He knows that he will by and by forget his present grief, and must make a clean breast of it at once. A new mental state will, by and by, supersede the old.

[Quotes from 'A vrai dire' to 'comme un coup de couteau'. Pléiade III, p. 482.]

And all this for a woman who, in her life, had kept her lover in one prolonged agony of jealousy. Being dead she would no longer be capable of exciting his jealousy. 'But this was just what was impossible, since it could not find its object, Albertine, save among memories in which she was still alive. Since, merely by thinking of her, I brought her back to life, her betrayals could never be those of a dead woman.' During her life, his jealous fears were for her future; now in retrospect, his jealousy was concerned with her past. Then he drives the point home. 'Her past? That is the wrong word, since for jealousy there can be neither past nor future, and what it imagines is invariably the Present.' (Pléiade III, p. 490)

There are many people who dislike the intrusion of these metaphysical subtleties, as they call them, into the region of the novel. Agreed, that Proust is not their man. The fact is, the novel in Proust's hands has become something of infinitely vaster scope than the old fictitious history. It is still historical in form, a narrative of events and a study of characters – but with how rich and various a content, ranging from a system of psychology with concrete examples to a treatise on the passions with pathological excursions, from disquisitions on heraldry and the philology of place-names to critical discussions of music and painting, from the Book of Snobs to Vanity Fair! *Que de choses dans un menuet!*

101. André Germain on *La Prisonnière*
1924

Part of a review of *La Prisonnière, La Revue européenne*, 1 October 1924, now in *De Proust à Dada*, Paris, Kra, 1924, pp. 31–7.

André Germain (1881–1971), influential journalist and founder of *La Revue européenne*, impressionistically and energetically lambastes Proust for the static nature of his narrative.

What expectations this *Prisonnière* had raised! Extracts published in reviews had already spread the desire to read it and whipped up curiosity about it. Two in particular had been very successful. On the one hand, 'La regarder dormir', a sad and powerful analysis of a love which, as a constant victim of suspicions, gnawed at and diminished by jealousy, does not open up and flower; I was about to say does not come to full realisation, except in the most chimerical of possessions, a possession that links the absence of the other person's soul to the touch of a beloved body, a possession which the adversary, overcome by sleep, can no longer spoil. And on the other, that full, richly flavoured and, as it were, winged piece the 'Vinteuil Sonata', in which, within the portrayal of a society soirée, observations of fashionable life felicitously blended with a kind of escapism, nostalgia and redemption mediated by art.

We rush enthusiastically to meet these dear fragments as we open the volume. But we do not quite recognise them, diminished as they are by the overwhelming ensemble in which they are now incorporated, drained of life in the stagnant waters of their cave, and our pleasure is assaulted, attacked and damaged.

This time what we have is a strange cabbage soup served up by an intemperate cook, in which floating about, tenderised in greasy water, are masses of turnips, carrots and leeks, the occasional consoling potato, indeed even pieces of excellent boiled beef. It is up to us to dig in our spoons and valiantly struggle with the hard work that comes with this murky and uncertain fishing about. At the risk of offending numerous literati, professors and grand ladies, I will maintain that you really need a big appetite and the stomach of a peasant to carry the redoubtable task to its conclusion without nausea and without a fainting fit.

We who have not been chosen for this task are overwhelmed by sleep in the midst of our strivings. And then, as happens when we are digesting our food, a tiresome dream takes hold of us: these monstrous pregnant sentences that, like octopuses have taken us in their embrace, these paragraphs beneath the twaddle of which we lie prostrate, these parentheses that have 'taken us in', are suddenly touched by a fairy wand and transformed into taxis, side-cars and omnibuses that diabolically jumbled up together jig about without making any forward movement in a horrible, vain grinding of wheels. Meanwhile, the author-policeman, turned by a punishment of Biblical proportions into a pillar of salt, permanently forgets to lower the arm whose masterful gesture has created all this immobility and the magic wand – the rigid white stick that refuses to allow these sadly scurrying sentences and paragraphs driven by impotent tramdrivers to move along – remains hanging before our minds like an odious sign and an intolerable obsession.

In all fairness, there is the quarrel between M. de Charlus and the

Verdurins, which though planned with the ingenuity of a well-digger, recited like a rosary and brought to term with all the pains and long hours of childbirth, has nevertheless its sequence of events, interludes and conclusion. The one and only chapter of the three that does not give us constipation and red faces. But as for Albertine's jealousy! Set out in the first volume over nearly two hundred pages taken up again on p. 169 of the second and threatening to spread out over the volumes of the following work, it is something implacable like a food that causes a lingering nausea and will not be evacuated, like a boring guest we will never succeed in throwing out. Eventually, we are begging our author, our torturer for an enema or a bowl. But he pays no attention to our complaints and our sorry faces; he keeps us on the torture-seat where he has placed us, happy as a madman who has at last found his victims and confidants and continues, without making any progress, to unravel the tiresome imbroglio in which his reason will remain imprisoned.

Decidedly, Proust has no sense of movement. That is his cardinal sin. And one can understand why, like an ill-shod street urchin who jumps onto the springs of a carriage, there are times when he latches on without ever letting go, to the rhythm and the witticisms of a conversation which he goes on and on imitating and reproducing for a hundred, a hundred and fifty or two hundred pages. With the help of M. de Charlus, there he is finally dragging himself along and we give our blessing to this progress of his, however snail-like: for the author and for ourselves it was the only way of escaping death by stagnation. . . .

102. Jacques Robertfrance
on Proust and Freud
1924

Part of 'Freud ou l'opportuniste', *Les Nouvelles littéraires*, 11 October 1924.

Jacques Robertfrance stresses the independent paths of the two writers while pointing to the affinities between them.

. . . It is not without significance that Freud and Freudianism were revealed to French writers in the two or three years following the armistice, when Proust gave a fillip to the analytical novel and re-established a tradition that had been so much neglected by the realist and the social novel. We cannot forget that the introductory work, with which the *Temps perdu* cycle was to open, went almost unnoticed and that *Swann* slept peacefully in the obscure files of its young publisher up to 1920. A certain fictional imagination, the fiction of the heart, had not attracted the reader of Bourget, or those, ever increasing in number, of Daudet and Zola. Proust was cautious. Only Stendhal's assurance was held out to him – an assurance Stendhal had had in the future, eighty years on. But the fact that the time of war brought the settlement date nearer meant Proust was about to cash in, with feeble hand and death at his heels, the marvellous toll-fees of well-deserved fame. Everything to do with quiet, disinterestedness, adventure, psychological analysis, man liberated from time, abstracted from contingency, everything that happened outside the stifling circle of social behaviour rallied that public which peace without rest turned away from the world and abandoned without illusions on the edge of the abyss. Pierre Benoit and Marcel Proust did not need the same readership for them to have, nevertheless, a success, the reasons for which are approximately similar. Proust, however, was playing a double game, and at the same time, by taking the prudent path via Charlus and Swann, cut back in one move to the grand classical avenue of passions in conflict and human tragedies.

It is not by chance that Proust's analysis and the psychoanalysis of the Viennese professor should here come face to face, for in his lectures, Jacques Rivière, more than a year earlier, had compared two methods and two names that he failed to separate from each other and about whom he felt that the one could not do without the contributions of the other. . . . Not that Proust's work owed anything to Freud's experiments – Proust had not read Freud – but two parallel lines can only follow the same winding contours and will tend towards the same goal and the same horizon. Proust is not an interpreter. Signs and symbols remain indecipherably enigmatic in his thought. This invalid is subject to all the laws of the heart, to its 'intermittences'. He does not control them; he suffers them and transcribes them, extremely anxious not to cut through their sensitive character and their tonality with some external motive. Freud is a magician. He forces these same 'intermittences', compelling them, mastering them, marshalling them. But in resurrecting them, he takes them for what they are and, in his hands, their worth is never questioned. A psychological litmus test will never betray their personality. Thus the same current carries two works, quite unknown to each other, towards the same shore. . . .

103. Benjamin Crémieux:
a posthumous assessment

1924

Extracts from his essay on Proust in *Vingtième siècle*, Paris, Gallimard, 1924, Première Série, pp. 9–98.

Benjamin Crémieux (1888–1944), journalist and critic, was among the first to analyse Proust's work with sympathy and insight and to clarify its status in the period soon after his death. His comprehensive essay is the best early descriptive account of *La Recherche* and establishes some criteria for the understanding of Proust that have not been bettered for their relevance.

(a) Proust's aesthetic and his 'superimpressionism' (pp. 15–24).

Fundamental to Proust's work is a meditation on reading, an answer to the question: 'how does a book act on the mind and soul of its readers?' Before embarking on his novel, Proust reflects on the effects and possibilities of the art of literature. The result of this analysis and of these reflections is recorded in a study dating from 1904 and Proust devoted all his energies, as we know, to his great work from 1905, basing himself on notes taken as far back as 1891.[1] This study: *Une Journée de lecture* is the preface to a translation of John Ruskin's *Sesame and Lilies*.[a] It provides the key to Proust's aesthetic and will need to be given pride of place at the head of the definitive edition of *A la recherche du temps perdu*. . . .

Proust's ideas on reading, and consequently on the art of literature, derive from an initial and apparently very simple statement. This statement goes as follows: contrary to what Ruskin imagined, reading can in no way play a dominating role in our spiritual life. It is totally illusory to search in books, as do children and ignoramuses, for *real truths*,[2] set opinions on people and things. A book is incapable of providing an answer to anything; it can only give us longings, urges. Reading for reading's sake, only to take what one has read into one's system like a foreign body, is a pointless task. A book has no more reality about it than a church, a town or a woman. It is within ourselves that the real is made, thanks to a personal effort that nothing can replace. . . .

[Quotes at length from *Une Journée de lecture* in support of his general statement.]

The whole of Proust's poetics will be derived from these considerations on reading. For him the role of a work of art will be above all an occasion for dreaming and reflecting, a source of stimulation and an invitation to the reader to see things, people and feelings from an unusual angle. A work of art is a fight against habit. Our normal vision of the real is a passive, automatic one, where habit reigns supreme. The mission of the artist is to break that automatic response, to invite us to perceive the real in an active way and to reveal to us that habit conceals it from us. The artist must therefore be, to a certain extent, an abnormal person.

How will he, as painter or writer, proceed to turn the tables on such habit as this? He will provide such an unexpected image of the feeling or reality in question that it will confront the mind of the reader or spectator with the necessity and the urgency of a re-appraisal.

The great writer, the great artist is a man who does not contemplate anything in the universe with the eyes of habit; he is a man who recreates the universe and rejuvenates it. Art is not an imitation, but an interpretation of nature. To put it in another way, art is impressionist and subjective. . . .

But Proust's impressionism is very special. Admittedly, the gift of the artist is to see things in the 'non habitual' fashion that is characteristic of him. Yet even he must forearm himself against the errors of his imagination, the sluggishness of his intelligence and the fantastic creations of his desires.

Consequently we have a critical impressionism which, in a certain sense, is the opposite of spontaneity as commonly understood. Not only does it aim to rediscover the innocence and the inviolate virginity of the senses, nerves and brain, but it comprises also a merciless critique, a thorough cleansing – conscious or unconscious – of the accepted ways of seeing things. [b] To start with, all art is a critical re-appraisal of current ideas and images; it must make a clean slate of all acquired knowledge before it can reconstruct subjectively a reality that is peculiar to it. An attempt at dissociation must precede the artist's attempt at re-creation.

Nor yet is it enough to take up a personal idea, for all its apparent originality. Behind all appearances, there is an intimate reality to be discovered and that cannot be discovered except at the cost of great effort. Often the most gifted will not have the will-power to reach the suspected reality behind the image. The true artist is the one who goes straight to the heart of things, to the intuition (in the Bergsonian sense) of the real:

The sunlit lines and surfaces [of the towers of Martinville] cracked open, as if they had been the bark of a tree, some part of what they kept hidden from me became evident, I had a thought that crystallized as words in my head and that had no existence at all for me a moment before.[3]

At the root of Proust's art, there will be then a conscious and deliberate search for originality. . . .

The ideal book in Proust's view is the one that, in the most strongly characteristic language possible of a given time, destroys the normal vision of the universe – or of part of the universe – even as it analyses it and reconstructs from it a different one, an entirely original and subjective one, that heightens the spiritual functions of the élite, moves it in a new direction, gradually imposes itself on the masses, is transformed into a stereotype and lasts until the appearance of a new book which destroys that stereotype and gives rise to a new vision.

This was the book Proust attempted to create in these first years of the twentieth century in writing *A la recherche du temps perdu*, keeping to an aesthetic that could conveniently be termed, not impressionist, but superimpressionist, and that has, however one looks at it, led to a thoroughgoing impressionistic classicism.

NOTES

(a) This study has been reprinted in *Pastiches et mélanges*.
(b) 'The effort Elstir made, as he contemplated reality, to strip himself of all notions deriving from his intelligence was all the more admirable in that this man . . . had in fact an intelligence that was cultivated to an exceptional degree.' *A l'ombre des jeunes filles en fleurs*.[4]

1 Crémieux has instinctively perceived what was to be confirmed only in 1952 with the publication of *Jean Santeuil* and in 1954 with *Contre Sainte-Beuve*.
2 In italics in the text.
3 Pléiade I, pp. 180–1.
4 Pléiade I, p. 840.

(b) Proust as social critic (pp. 56–9).

Crémieux compares Proust to Balzac for the way he, like Balzac, 'has challenged the official designation of an individual's status' and has made people think of 'a Charlus', 'a Norpois' or 'a Verdurin'. Similarly, just as Balzac depicted the arrival of the post-revolution bourgeoisie and Dostoevsky illustrated the clash of barbaric old Russia and liberal ideas, so Proust also has a historical perspective though he, unlike them, proceeds to show it entirely from his own subjective angle: 'There is no doubt that Proust realized eventually the objective historical value of his work and, without abandoning his superimpressionist and introspective method, he certainly envisaged it – at least in part – from this point of view.' Crémieux locates a clear beginning for this: 'The moment could perhaps be fixed at the end of *Le côté de Guermantes I*, where the depiction of social and fashionable life comes fully into the foreground.' He goes on to assess the relationship of Proust's social vision to his art as a whole.

Proust's novel, far from being the arbitrary and gratuitous account of an entirely artificial existence in the salons of high society, with no fundamental reference to the essentials of the day, has become the novel of the crisis that characterizes the end of the nineteenth century and the beginning of the twentieth most strongly: the ultimate de-throning of the French aristocratic élite, the first levelling out between old nobility and wealthy bourgeoisie, the prelude to the levelling out between all social classes, brought on by the war, and the shuttling to and fro between social castes that is a feature of the post-war period.

It is not therefore, properly speaking, a picture of society between 1880 and 1914 that we find in Proust (a picture is always static whereas Proust's vision always extends in time), it is rather an essay on the transformation of this society. The drama he writes about is not isolated from the other realities of the same period, it is steeped in the continuity and the development of French life, it is integrated into it. Proust has set the history of this social change within the history of all the other main contemporary changes: the change in the art of writing, represented by Bergotte, in the art of painting by Elstir, in music by Vinteuil; he introduces all the new developments of the period into his work – modern military strategies, the telephone, the car – just as he does survivals of the past – the street-cries of Paris; he emphasises the impressionist renewal in the way of looking at nature – hawthorns in bloom, water-lilies in the Vivonne – so much so that the book as a whole eventually takes on the air of being a *summa*[1] of French life, of the French styles of thinking and feeling between 1870 and 1914 and more particularly between 1890 and 1902.

As his medium for describing this new push forward by the bourgeoisie, Proust has not chosen the epic mode, as this might have contradicted his idea of gradual and barely perceptible modification of people in time. He has discovered an original method to suggest progression and make it evident to his readers while avoiding accelerating it artificially. (Proust has been described as depicting life in *slow motion*[2] and this formula has had a certain success. For all that, it is wrong; it is other novelists who depict life *speeded up.*[3]) Proust has rendered the invisible slipping past of life by putting a whole family, the Guermantes, in which every member is at a different stage of development, plumb in the centre of his work. . . .

But Proust has especially entrusted the detailed translation of this transformation and the transmission of the very colour of his period to his hero speaking in the first person. Marcel's first day-dreams on the name Guermantes and on the duchess, Oriane, his gradual penetration of the Guermantes milieu and habit that gradually robs elegant society life of all the charm his imagination had lent it – these are a condensed expression of the whole history of the aristocracy in the nineteenth century, its gradual loss of prestige and its dying moments.

This character, Marcel, who is both witness and, to some extent, actor in the actual drama of the closing years of the nineteenth century, also helps Proust, if one looks at the work from this point of view, to set his novel within the broad picture of the drama of human destiny which is common to all periods of history and to display the basic feelings of love, jealousy and vanity in continuous activity.

These brief and very summary remarks give a glimpse, perhaps, of the fundamental unity as well as the total complexity of Proust's work. Everything is inter-related. Proust's conception of art and of people has determined the choice of the heroes, the episodes, the central theme and the atmosphere of the book, and the abundance of viewpoints which disconcerts the reader is only a consequence of Proust's prodigious re-creative power.

NOTES

1 In italics in the text.
2 Idem.
3 Idem.

(c) On Proust's style (pp. 79–84).

Endless, exquisitely subtle sentences, crammed with weird meta-phors, with terms borrowed from the vocabulary of philosophy or medicine, a heaviness in expression bringing its share of complication and contortion to quibbles over thoughts and feelings, the need to re-read a periodic sentence two or three times to grasp all its shades of meaning, to be absolutely sure of the connections interlinking the 'who's' and the 'of whom's', a plethora of 'he's' and 'she's' – such is more or less the legend of Proust's style. As with all legends it is based on a series of points which, taken individually, are perfectly accurate. Proust's style does not have readily seductive features: the tinkle of words, the happy or surprising association of noun and adjective and the musical cadence of a phrase are never sought after on their own account.

This style cannot be slotted into any of the well-tried nineteenth-century traditions: it has neither the magniloquent and melodious sweep of Chateaubriand nor the more staccato rhythm and sudden about-turns of Barrès; it is neither related to the style derived from sixteenth and eighteenth century texts and modernized by Anatole France, nor to that of Jules Renard, nor particularly does it recall Flaubert. His complete freedom of manner would possibly make him comparable stylistically to Balzac were it not that the robust temperament, the exuberance, the exaggerations and the vulgarity of the author of the *Comédie Humaine* are poles apart from Proust's morbid temperament, meticulousness, precision and finesse.

The style of *A la recherche du temps perdu* is perhaps not completely realized; it is nevertheless entirely original. The influence of Anatole France could be felt in *Les Plaisirs et les jours* and we are all acquainted with Proust's virtuosity in bringing off pastiches of the most varied authors: Saint-Simon, Renan, Michelet, Sainte-Beuve, Taine and Flaubert. The outstanding characteristic of Proust's style in his novel is precisely the complete absence of virtuosity.

What is virtuosity in a writer? A habit, a piece of pure automatism. Instinctively, his sentences slip into convenient moulds, cluster around a few favourite conjunctions; words take up their places on either side of neatly balanced oppositions; you have the group controlled by 'not only', the group controlled by 'and yet'; nouns assemble in two's or three's or stand alone. The made-to-measure style of your real writer quickly turns into something off-the-peg. Faithful to a few excellent 'patterns', it scarcely varies and depends for its distinction on not being confused with any other. This style can express an artist's profound nature but it could in no way express the variations and the unceasing evolution of his spiritual life.

Proust's whole concern is to avoid 'stereotypes' (even of his own invention). He does not try to create a style that is distinguishable from all others at first glance, but to fix the representation of each of his thoughts, each of his feelings in the most appropriate way. For each sentence he creates a new design on which he refuses to model a second sentence. Hence the extraordinary variety of his style, hence also the flickering and unsteady impression that you first get. Proust demands of his reader a spiritual involvement that is renewed with each sentence; he never allows him to nod off because of a familiar drone in the background. He is always changing key, always playing different scales. You sometimes find it hard to follow him, but it is never a waste of time.

Others before Proust had dreamed of shedding the ready-made style, the chains of sentences that seemed to put their own style in chains. Rimbaud, for instance, felt the hollowness and the burden of the connective articulations of language, so dear to Flaubert. The name illuminations (thereby depriving this designation of the sense given it by Rimbaud) is readily given to these attempts at a liberated language closely modelled on thought and feeling. The futurists, with their free-ranging words, the cubists and the dadaists have sought out this strict stylistic truth. We all know where these attempts generally end up: in impressionistic notations which have the power to fix the fleeting quality of a sensation and the simultaneity of multiple impressions, but are incapable of expressing a reasoned explanation, of providing an abstract and intelligible language.

In Proust we are not concerned with that kind of impressionism at all. Impressionism may well be the basis of his art but it does not seem valid to him unless assimilated, pinned down and deeply analysed by the intelligence. . . .

Proust's impressionism does not consist, therefore, in registering fleeting impressions as they occur but in overcoming the mind's natural laziness and never giving up before uncovering the little scrap of deep, succulent reality contained in that impression. Images decay, having only the meaning our mind clothes them in. Extracting the reality hidden in the impression, such is his aim, that is what constitutes Proust's superimpressionism. . . .

Proust's style, then, is intellectualist above all else. He does not go for the instant expression of the sensation but for the expression of all the profound and essential qualities that the sensation has been able to awaken in him. But far from seeking out the abstract and the schematic in the intellectual result he arrives at, far from expressing it in some generalized aphorism, he requires his thought to remain intimately bound up with the sensation that occasioned it. The thought is the kernel, the sensation sticks to it like the flesh of a fruit.

Proust is not content with handing us the two ends of the chain: the original sensation and the final thought. His intention is to make us follow the full course his sensibility and his intelligence have taken to arrive at the goal. It is a course which Proust's imagination makes particularly rich; it is through precise observations, comparisons, analogies, associations of ideas and unexpected metaphors that, starting out from the impression, we reach the thought at the core of it. This journeying through the ins and outs of Proust's mind gives the sentence its movement and rhythm.

That is why there is no style more dynamic than his and why at the same time there is none less oratorical. Its rhythm is provided not by the movement of the silently uttered word (as in Chateaubriand) but by the movement of the thought itself made perceptible.

Such a style could not have the speed of an oral style. It unfurls itself unhurriedly in continuous duration. It moves through three superimposed and interconnecting levels: the level of impressions, the level of imagination and memory and the level of intelligence. The whole mind – its faculties of reception, preservation and creation – is involved in and conspires with each sentence. Into each one of them Proust puts his whole life-blood. His style may well grow old but it will never become ossified.

104. Cyril Falls on Proust as satirist

1924

Excerpts from *The Critic's Armoury*, London, Richard Cobden-Sanderson, 1924, pp. 201–15.

Cyril Falls (1888–1971) expresses with a certain reserve his views on Proust as social critic, leaving unmentioned all questions of aesthetic theory and memory. This sceptical assessment stems from the reaction to Proust the poet, metaphysician, philosopher, and stylist that had become the accepted portrait just after his death.

There are writers who make their own way to their readers through that jungle which is modern literature, and others who have it hewn for them by the critics. The late Marcel Proust had a good deal of assistance from these woodmen in his own country; but in England he had a great deal more. Seldom, indeed, in our literary history can a path have been cleared so thoroughly, levelled so perfectly, for a foreigner, in so short a time, as has been his case. Most of the English critics of note have set themselves with enthusiasm to the task, and have, in the space of about five years, secured for him an extraordinary notoriety. On the occasion of his death a few months ago they banded themselves together and produced a very readable book filled with their appreciations.[1] As a result this Frenchman is to-day as widely discussed as any of our home-bred novelists. It is possible that he is even more discussed than read. . . .

It is open to doubt whether our critics have not in this case gone too fast. That Proust is a considerable writer is obvious to all who have given him intelligent study, even if short. But is he really all that he has been claimed to be? Is he, for example, our modern – and not decadent – Balzac? I am not prepared to answer No; yet, were there put a stake upon my answer, I should say No rather than Yes. In truth I marvel at the temerity of my fellow-critics. They seem to have no doubts, whilst I find myself full of doubt. Proust appears to me to be very difficult to criticize justly. It is a notable young vintage, doubtless, that suits the present taste; though, even while I say so much, I fancy I detect, like Sancho Panza's kinsmen, some foreign matter in it. That question, however, is not the most urgent. The real difficulty lies in this: how will it 'lay down'? And so, in this short study, I shall attempt to make no definite judgment, because I have reached none. Short of that, the personal impressions of each one of us who has been interested by a writer so extraordinary may have their value in helping to unravel the problem of his position.

Consider first the man's manner of writing, since that is so far away from the common that it is what inevitably first strikes one on picking up any of his books. The critics have exhausted their adjectives in striving to describe its subtlety. Subtlety it has, to be sure, but that is, alas! by no means its sole prominent characteristic. The prose of Marcel Proust is finely expressive, but not in the finest fashion. He does not achieve his object by the happy choice of a word which we feel to be inevitable once we have read it, as is so often the case with M. Anatole France; but rather by the use of many words, by a sustained effort, very conscious and very apparent. It is only rarely that he makes his point at once; more often he approaches it like a hunter stalking game. In his inconsequence, his 'asides', he sometimes reminds us of Sterne, save that with Proust there is never any jerkiness, but a solid and sustained flow of even language, however much caprice there may be in the thoughts to which he is giving expression. That effect of solidity comes in part from the merely mechanical tricks of his style: no chapters or few, long paragraphs, the absence of commas where we should normally expect them. I have found that I experience pleasure at first in reading a passage, renewed each time that I pick up one of his books; but that after an hour or less there comes weariness and an inclination to turn over two pages at a time. Too often he pursues an idea, a joke, a phrase, to the death. When the good Françoise, or even the Duchesse de Guermantes, introduces a provincialism into a sentence, he must needs track it to its historical lair; and not once nor twice, but every time it occurs. He is for ever explaining, and explaining too much.

And yet, the effect of all these deviations and moralizings and descriptions is in its fashion as remarkable as anything in modern literature. The pictures of men and women, the analysis of their emotions, which they achieve, are bewildering in their perfection and comprehension. It were unjust to compare him in this to a Dutch painter, for the detail of that school is lifeless by comparison with the vitality of Proust's portraiture. Harking back to Balzac, it is at least possible to assert that there has been, since his, no such collection of types in French literature. The analysis of their thoughts goes further than the description of their persons. It is not merely personal but universal; so that at his best he seems to give us the analysis of the secret thoughts of all mankind in microcosm. . . .

The matter of Proust springs from his style more directly even than is the case with most great novelists. This is because his descriptions of personages and of *mœurs* – that admirable word which covers both our 'manners' and 'morals' – are what really matter. Of action throughout his series of books there is little. He is never so happy nor so interesting as when he has gathered a party of choice spirits into a room and set them to listen to music and to talk. On such occasions he does continue to keep his reader's full attention for a length of a time so great that few authors would dare to attempt the feat. In *Du Côté de chez Swann* there is a musical party given by Mme de Saint-Euverte of extraordinary length, and one *chez* Mme Verdurin in *La Prisonnière* which, with a conversation that follows it, almost fills a volume. In *Le Côté de Guermantes* the talk in the *salon* of Mme de Villeparisis lasts for ninety close-packed pages, and those pages the finest in the book. It is not, as has been hinted, all talk. There are the inevitable deviations and minute descriptions of persons and their thoughts. There may be more than enough of them, but in this case we must pardon a few *longueurs* for the general brilliancy of the effect. For we have here the world of the modern French *salon* depicted with a delicacy, with an appreciation of its fine qualities of spirit and a gay malice for its foibles, that compel our admiration.

The aristocratic *salon* is, indeed, his own world. He resembles Balzac in this respect at least, one rare among writers of the past democratic hundred years, that he is an aristocrat in spirit and sympathy. But he had this advantage over the elder: Balzac, despite his particle of nobility, was a plebeian. Poor, rough in manners, a recluse and a slave to his work, he had to depend for his pictures of the great world mainly upon his magnificent imagination; and sometimes even that failed him. Proust, on the other hand, lacking the particle, went about in Parisian society and saw its life from the inside. He may laugh at the Faubourg Saint-Germain, but it is quite apparent that it is to him the most interesting thing in this world. The fashion in which he brings out a noble and sonorous name, rolling it, as it were, on his tongue, is evidence of his intense pleasure therein. Hannibal de Bréauté-Consalvi! Robert de Saint-Loup-en-Bray! To the ears of Marcel Proust the words made music as exquisite as the fabulous sonata of Vinteuil.

This passion appears to have disturbed some of our critics, amid all their enthusiasm. Yet there is little doubt that it is his study of the French aristocracy which is the most notable contribution of Proust to literature. The charm of that world, which so greatly appealed to him, is very real. The French aristocracy has, indeed, accomplished an extraordinary feat in self-preservation. . . .

Such is the world that Proust made his own, with another, the arc of which just cuts its circle, that to which he himself belonged: the *haute bourgeoisie* of talent and wealth. A great doctor's wife, herself a patroness of music, like Mme Cottard; a great writer like Bergotte, walk in and out of the drawing-room. A man about town like Charles Swann, with no particular qualification save his wit and a certain simplicity which makes him popular, and also because he *is* a fashionable man about town, goes further. He becomes almost an inhabitant of the circle itself. The whole is tinged with a last shade of that golden aura which enveloped it completely in the eyes of the hero before he himself had entered it and suffered a degree of disillusionment.

It has another side than the bright. Intrigue, jealousy, and snobbery stalk through its decorous ranks. The Duc de Guermantes is a rake and the Baron de Charlus a pervert. The amours of Charles Swann would make him a villain instead of a hero in most English books; for few English novelists would venture to suggest that men of fashion – as well as men who do not belong to fashion – are often like Swann in morals, and at the same time charming and beloved. Yet here, even, the balance is pushed down in favour of the great ones. The aura of the 'Faubourg' never wholly left it for the eyes of Proust, any more than for the hero who is himself in person. Compare the treatment of the Duc de Guermantes and Mme Verdurin. The former is selfish, brutal, a bad husband to one of the most delightful women in modern literature. But he is drawn with a care that has in it certainly more affection and admiration than disgust. We are made to hang upon his words. Manners, wit, physique, air, all combine with his title, his descent and his alliances with royal houses to cover a multitude of sins. Poor Mme Verdurin has no vices but that of being a snob, which she shares with most of the personages, if, not indeed, with all the world, in the books of Proust or outside them. Yet her treatment is almost savage. Her creator has not spared her a tenth of the pains he has given to the man. His portrait is, in fact, not far short of a caricature. He cheapens himself in cheapening her, and in one odious passage, describing the chemical smell of her cleaned white-kid gloves, descends to a piece of snobbery that has been employed by any purveyor of indifferent social fiction any time these twenty years. Proust is always on the side of the social angels, even when they are fallen angels.

And yet, once again, snobbery and injustice counting against him, it is in the picture of the aristocratic life of France and in the realization of its significance that lies the triumph of Marcel Proust. It is because, though he became an ironist instead of a worshipper – just as he ceased to love the Duchesse de Guermantes almost as soon as he knew her – because he never lost altogether that sense of what this world had meant in old times, that his heaviness has its moments of inspiration. It is by reason of this, if at all, that he can be ranked among the great novelists. . . .

There is another side of his work which cannot be neglected, since it fills so large a space in his version of the *Comédie humaine*. Not only is it the main theme of the volumes that make up *Sodome et Gomorrhe*, but it appears again and again in all the others, from the moment when he introduces Mlle Vinteuil in *Du Côté de chez Swann*. That is his preoccupation with sexual perversion. It is exemplified especially by M. de Charlus and the girl Albertine. Now M. de Charlus is one of the greatest figures among all the *dramatis personæ* of Proust. He may be a fallen angel, but he certainly does not lack the stature and magnificence of one. While he holds the stage there may be intervals of heaviness, but they are continually dissipated by bright flashes. Yet it is M. de Charlus and not his theme that holds us. Of it Proust has certainly acute and interesting things to say, but full soon we cry enough. As he goes on, he plunges deeper and deeper into these abysses, till at last it seems to us that in his own mind he really confuses life itself with one of its aberrations. Albertine, for her part, has none of the personality of the baron, and with her our boredom becomes really acute. I confess that I have never read completely through the first volume of *La Prisonnière*. It appears to be not only gloomy but aimlessly so. Analysis of the tortures of jealousy and dissection of women's methods of lying may be admirably done, but do we want to revolve about them for ever and ever? The only remedy for my feelings that I could discover was to skip ten pages when the strain became too great.

We have done little more than glance at the characteristics of *À la Recherche du Temps Perdu*, with its eleven volumes already published and two more, it is understood, to come. It is to be feared that no high hopes need be founded on these latter. The work of Proust was declining long before his death, either through ill-health or because his themes were exhausted and he could do little more than go over them again. From *Du Côté de chez Swann* and *A l'Ombre des Jeunes Filles en Fleurs* to *La Prisonnière* the descent is dismal. The last few volumes will probably have to hang precariously to the reputation of the first half dozen. What is to be the final fate of these?

It seems to me not impossible that they may recede considerably into the shade as time goes on. In many respects they are too up-to-date. That may help to account for their present success, but what is topical to one generation is stale to the next, and sets the third a-yawning. That interminable analysis, carried so far that it often seems pointless, is likely to decline rather than grow in favour as its setting changes and grows dim in the memory. I do not know, nor, having from the first striven to describe merely the writer's effect upon my own mind, will I attempt a comprehensive prophecy. To be quite definite in one's verdict is to be very sure of oneself, or very careless of the weight of one's words, or a *poseur*. I know I am not the first, and I trust I am not the second or third. Yet I cannot think that the charm with which Proust endows the life of the 'Faubourg' will ever wholly disappear. It at least should assure him a certain position if not, as his devotees claim now, one among the highest. The earliest of his books appeared but a few years ago, and he died the other day, yet those pictures seem to take on already the air of an 'old master'; at risk of damnable iteration I add once more, possibly a minor 'old master' only. . . .

NOTE

All italics are in the text.
1 The reference is to *An English Tribute* (ed. C.K. Scott-Moncrieff) 1923. See Nos 81–90 and Introduction pp. 34–5.

105. Philip Guedalla on Proust
1924

Extract from *A Gallery*, London, Constable, 1924.

Philip Guedalla (1889–1944), historian and critic, captures the bemused attitude to Proust in Britain just as his posthumous reputation was beginning to be established. (pp. 272–4)

Believed at first by large numbers of people to be a misprint for M. Marcel Prévost, he approached the critical consciousness of these islands with certain radical advantages. He had a singularly attractive personal mythology; and for the English, who have always preferred their geniuses dead, it counted for something that he was dying. His works, when they reached England, were almost posthumous; and their reception was pitched in a becoming tone of slightly lugubrious appreciation. . . . But since his death, whilst the volume of his published work continues to grow at a rate that most of us find formidable even on a falling exchange, the demeanour of his official admirers begins to do him a singular disservice. Their solemn airs, their hieratic manner, their almost ritual handling of these pleasing works of fiction conspire to render him nearly unreadable. A grave company was recently assembled by an energetic editor, to whom his English readers owe so much. The intention was to lay a wreath of English prose on his grave.[1] But one feels that the gesture was somehow lacking in spontaneity; and it is almost distressing to observe how many of the more distinguished contributors came to bury Caesar, not to praise him. The hysterical commendation of the young (and Mr Walkley is eternally young) is apt to be outweighed by the frank bewilderment of Mr Saintsbury, the desperate endeavour of Mr Conrad to say something polite, and the candid yawns of Mr Arnold Bennett. . . .

But how far all these solemn gentlemen are from that charming, interminable inventory of a young man's sensations. . . It is idle to object . . . that the contents of a man's spiritual trouser-pockets are hardly the most appetising material for the exercise of art. . . . The reader is at liberty to close the book whenever he wants to. But when he does, he will have a haunting memory of long days in French provincial gardens; of shadowy aunts; of church towers and the finer shades of snobbery; of vulgar little ladies and of Duchesses, how vulgar their proud creator never knew; of sunshine, and sickbeds, and concerts, and days in the country, and all the little pieces which fit together into life. He will remember *Swann*; and in that memory he may forget the heavenly host of his admirers.

NOTE

1 The reference is to *An English Tribute* (ed. C. K. Scott-Moncrieff) published the previous year.

106. Guy de Pourtalès on Proust and Ruskin
1924

Extract from 'Note sur Marcel Proust et John Ruskin' in *De Hamlet à Swann*, Paris, Crès, 1924, pp. 227–8.

Guy de Pourtalès (1881–1941) shows in these comments how the theme of affinities between Proust and Ruskin, now that Proust's prose has made its mark, resurfaces.

. . . In fact, the point at which Ruskin and Proust happily converge is in the richness of their miraculous memories, which allows both of them to hear in a seashell not only the Ocean's hymns of praise but the hubbub of an hotel foyer and the lapping waters of consciousness. Yet, if the pleasure of visual sensation satisfies Ruskin, in Proust it is never more than a stage on the path to truth. The pure idea is transmuted by Ruskin into images; he overloads it, splits it up and covers his canvas with so many colours that gradually our eyes, as it were, suffer surfeit.

Proust, on the other hand, is quicker to deploy in its amplitude the immense fresco that covers the walls of his memory. . . . But, by obliterating each detail one by one, gradually reducing the painting to its essential figures, destroying them in their turn so as eventually to leave no more than their blurred silhouettes, he ultimately retains only a sort of spiritual harmony, a shadow (made up of thousands of faded shadows) whose visible, but intangible ghost, bears witness to the real presence of memory.

Philosophical accuracy is really what matters least to Ruskin, who is concerned above all with the artistic value, the brilliance of the colours of his painting. As soon as he is able, he crams his books with sketches and drawings, takes delight in the subterfuges of typography and prints words in letters of gold or vermillion to help his reader meditate with the support of these simple images. His religion of beauty is entirely plastic and, if he could, he would set out its dogmas with the aid of a limner's brush. Proust, conversely, obsessed by the same metaphysical needs, reaches his goal without any external assistance, pressing his scruples to the point of inflicting on himself that manner of composition by large, tightly packed, airless pages, without paragraphs (for which he has often been criticized) that exactly corresponds to the spontaneous creation of his memory and reproduces, both abstractly and concretely, the two-fold film of it. These are surely questions of temperament rather than method that indicate – incidentally rather from the outside – the divergences of two minds of an almost incomparable richness of imagination. . . .

107. Jacques Rivière on Proust's sensibility

1924

Extracts from *Marcel Proust–Conference No. 5*, a lecture for La Société de Conférences, Monaco, Imprimerie de Monaco, 1924, pp. 40–8.

A more considered view than the notice on *A l'ombre des jeunes filles en fleurs* (No. 33) and an attempt to define the character-istics peculiar to Proust's sensibility. To be compared with J. Middleton Murry, No. 66.

(a) On the analytical features of Proust's sensibility.

In Proust, you have poetry; but you also have something more. His intelligence is successful in outlining the minutest contours of this ferment of emotions. The fluctuations between memory and immediate consciousness, the detailed comparisons made in Swann's heart between past and present and the confrontation and intertwin-ing of his states of mind are presented to us with extraordinary refinement and crystallized for us on the page. And in this way they take on a kind of truth that reaches beyond them; they become a moment of the human soul, general expressions of feeling. So much so that . . . at the point where he writes: 'He remembered the gas-lights being extinguished on the Boulevard des Italiens, when he had found her against all odds among the wandering shadows of that night that had seemed almost magical to him . . .', Proust goes on quite naturally, 'and that in fact really did belong to a mysterious world to which we can never return once its gates are shut'.[1] The 'we' without your noticing it replaces the 'he', and the generalizing procedure is so fundamental, so intimate, so bound up with the sentence itself that, in fact, at that moment we are no longer merely thinking of Swann, but applying instinctively to ourselves everything that Proust tells us is happening to him.

When again we are shown Swann looking hard at himself and no longer recognizing himself, it is immediately ourselves that we envisage in this same attitude of profound and intimate reflection to which the resurgence of the past sometimes leads us.[2]

A truth, then, has been extracted, without effort or formality, from a complex of feelings described as belonging to a specific character. I would claim that this is great classic art. And I would claim that Proust, by virtue of his need for the concrete and his longing for something more real than the impressions he expresses, gives us endless examples of it. . . .

(b) On the quality of poetic transcendence in Proust's sensibility.

Something one could call exceptional, or better still, a miracle has occurred in Proust's work, that, in my view, compensates for the complete absence of moral value which is a criticism that can be levelled against it. You will recall that the explicit intention of classical tragedy was to 'purge the emotions' by depicting them as forcefully as possible and with their direst effects. Well, Proust, in a slightly different way, not with that vigorous effort towards a concentrated synthesis that is admired in Racine or Corneille, but rather with a more leisurely patience and equally desirous of clarity, Proust – by mental effort and unflagging curiosity, by a rigorous pursuit of the facts – also 'purges' his sensibility and, in so far as he has interested ours, our sensibility as well. . . .

Now, if in conclusion, we look at his work as a whole, I think that what we will find to admire is something akin to what Swann admired in Vinteuil's sonata, especially the little phrase:

[Quotes 'Quand, après la soirée Verdurin' to 'de moins inglorieux, peut-être de moins probable'.][3]

Of course, what is referred to here is the miracle of music. And a systematic comparison of Proust's work with that of a great composer would lead to distortion rather than clarification. Yet it is surely Proust's particular achievement, as in Swann's eyes it was Vinteuil's, to have struck 'some of the millions of keys of tenderness, passion, courage, and serenity . . . each one as different from the next as one universe from another'[4] which make up the obscure keyboard of our unconscious. It is also Proust's achievement to have struck these keys with an always infallible touch and to have always produced from them a perfectly pure sound. . . .

But on the other hand, in each of his phrases, as in Vinteuil's little phrase . . . one feels 'such a new and original force that those hearing the phrase preserved it in their hearts on an equal basis with the ideas produced by their intelligence'.[5]

This is perhaps the last word – and it is in Proust that we find it – on his genius and on the essential newness and beauty of his work. Whereas all literature since Romanticism has certainly tended to give to our emotions and unconscious perceptions as direct an expression as possible . . . Proust has been working at a permanent fixing, and not any more the mere expression, of the obscure feelings fluttering in the heart of man, so that he has communicated to them 'such a new and original force' that we can preserve them 'in our hearts on an equal basis with the ideas produced by our intelligence'.

His first dream, the one that haunted him in his walks at Roussainville and Montjouvain, is therefore fully realized. His sensibility has taken on an eternal value. It is liberated from time. And so is a whole world that formed part of it. Proust, the great invalid and helpless creature, has eventually, from his bed and by dint of that gentle but unbending stubbornness I have described, won the most difficult of victories: he put all his strength into challenging death and it recoils intimidated before the complete survival of his spiritual essence.

NOTES

1 Pléiade I, pp. 346–7.
2 Pléiade I, p. 347.
3 Pléiade I, pp. 349–50.
4 Pléiade I, p. 349.
5 Pléiade I, p. 350.

108. A. B. Walkley on Proust's modern jealousy

1925

Part of 'Another Proust Fragment', *The Times*, 29 July 1925, p. 12.

A. B. Walkley examines some recently published pages from *Albertine Disparue* and finds in them evidence of an evolution of the imagination that is peculiarly Proustian and peculiarly modern.

The current issue of the *Nouvelle Revue Française* gives another fragment of Proust, to pacify or to whet the appetites of readers who cannot possess their souls in patience: 'C'est un des Pouvoirs de la Jalousie: . . .' It is, of course, concerned with Albertine, so enigmatic in her brief lifetime, and now, after death, almost as puzzling an enigma to her lover. His posthumous jealousy indeed is as intense a torture as though she were there, alive, to excite it. Those pangs never troubled Othello, his death followed too quick on Desdemona's. But even had he survived her, one can scarce conceive him as feeling them. In the first place, he was black or at least of a subfusc hue, with the emotional simplicity of his colour. And then he had not read Proust, was in fact a contemporary of Shakespeare, whose psychology was three centuries behind ours. It is odd – or rather not so odd as startling testimony to the influence of great poetry – how we still take our fundamental notions of love and jealousy and the other passions from those Elizabethans, who were as unlike us moderns as if they had been South Sea Islanders. We have learnt, since their time, strange refinements in the art of self-torture. The commonplace that human nature remains substantially the same throughout the ages seems to me unusually false, even for a commonplace. Oedipus Rex, who slew his father and married his mother and made so much fuss about it, is to me rather a logical (or illogical) construction of the mind than a real man. Today he would say 'Oh well, these odd accidents will happen, and at any rate it wasn't my fault, so let's get on with it', or words to that effect. . . .

Nor can I persuade myself to believe, with Proust, that the constitution of the imagination has remained *rudimentaire, simpliste.* . . . I think that the modern imagination – say, of a Proust – would be scarce recognizable to the ancient imagination –

say, of a Sophocles or even of a Molière – and that the two, side by side, would present as startling a contrast as a modern G.W.R. express engine alongside the queer old ramshackle contraption of George Stephenson's, 'The Rocket'.

It is this thought that makes Proust's elaborate studies of modern jealousy so fascinating. The human race had grown itself during all those centuries an entirely new psychology – blessed Word! – and, as usual didn't know it until an artist arose to express it in literary form. Literary artists are, of course, at this work all the time, it is what they are there for, and they pour out their novels by the hundred a week, but are mostly so inexpressive or so frightened of the truth that we say 'Oh bother your stale psychology! Give us a good detective tale!' Besides, the curious ins-and-outs – the anfrac-tuosities, Johnson would have said – of our own minds and feelings are matters about which we English are taught to keep our mouths shut. Mercifully, no doubt, for there are quite enough bores in the world as it is; but our English reticence has this disadvantage, that it makes us cut a mighty poor figure when we sit down to mirror our new psychology in a novel. Now reticence and Proust – the mere collocation is enough to provoke a laugh. He probes into the most out-of-the-way corners of human nature and sometimes fishes up some very ugly things, but it is all one to him, he communicates his discoveries to the world at large without holding anything back. 'Turn to the left and go straight on till you come to a door marked "Gentlemen"', says Mr George Robey to someone asking his way behind the scenes, 'but let not *that* deter you'; and Proust lets nothing deter him. No ethical prohibitions, no rules of etiquette distress him. His business is to understand the modern mind, and faithfully to express his understanding. And that is why so many of us, despite the enormous difficulties of his laboured, tortuous, parenthetical, 'Byzantine' style, find him a perpetual joy. . . .

NOTE

All italics are in the text.

109. Curtius on Proust's handling of reality

1925

Extract from 'Psychologie und Wirlkichkeit' in his essay on Proust, reprinted in *Französischer Geist im Zwanzigsten Jahrhundert*, Bern and Munich, Francke Verlag, Zweite Auflage, 1960, pp. 312–13.

Curtius provides in the section entitled 'Psychology and reality' one of the earliest and most perceptive, as well as seminal, commentaries on Proust. He makes a basic distinction between two elements in Proust's style: intellectualism and impressionism while stressing that it is the interaction between them that generates the power that characterizes Proust's description of the world around us. Cf. Nos 42; 66; 103 Section c; 107.

Proust's style reveals a peculiar intertwining of intellectualism and impressionism, of extreme subtlety in logical analysis and the most detailed reproduction of nuances in the sensual and spiritual world around us – so much so, indeed, that both are executed in one single movement and constitute a function of the self-same energy. The *mundus sensibilis* and the *mundus intelligibilis* interpenetrate each other to perfection. I consider it to be not totally correct to see Proust purely and simply as a great psychologist. This is the proper designation to ascribe to a Stendhal since he is only interested in the 'moral' side, in the mechanics and the dynamics of the human heart. He could well claim: 'Physical description bores me.' Stendhal remains in this respect in the cartesian tradition of French thinking. But Proust does not recognize the division between the world of thinking and the world at large. He does not chop the world up into the psychical and the physical. The meaning of his work is restricted if it is looked at only from the angle of the 'psychological novel'. The world of sense perceptions occupies the same place in Proust's books as the world of spiritual things. His first endeavours as a writer were to do with the fixing not of a frame of mind, but of an evening landscape with church-towers! That in itself is very typical. But just consider any volume of his work from this point of view. You will find that he devotes pages of detailed description to the smells associated with a house out in the provinces, to the stained-glass windows of a village church, to the plants on the bank of a stream, to the clothes of a lady of fashion, to the furnishings of a room, to the varieties of monocle and such like. It is precisely in the rendering of the material world that his art develops possibilities never suspected by anyone until now. The man who can paint lilacs as Proust does is no psychologist in the traditional sense, as it has been established in France in the works of Montaigne, Racine, the moralists and Benjamin Constant. If one were to call Proust a sensualist one would indeed be capturing an essential feature of his individuality. If Proust is a psychologist, then it is in a completely new sense of the word, in that he immerses all reality, including sense perceptions, in spirituality. But thereby the concept of the psychological has lost its contrastive power – and for this very reason simply cannot work any longer as a description.

110. Edith Wharton on Proust and tradition
1925

Excerpts from *The Writing of Fiction*, London, Scribner, 1925.

Edith Wharton (1862–1937), American novelist and critic, lived in France at the time *Swann* was published and supported its dissemination in her salon and through friends, especially Henry James. By the time of this essay Proust was strongly established; her intention, therefore, is to assess his individuality in relation to tradition for its strengths and weaknesses. Proust's works are examined as part of the art of fiction, following chapters dealing with the short story, the novel, characterization, and situation. Proust is the exemplar of a new vision that renews the art of fiction.

(a) Proust as moralist in the French tradition; pp. 153–6.

Since then [the publication of *Swann*] the conception of the art of fiction, as it had taken shape during the previous half-century, has been unsettled by a series of experiments, each one too promptly heralded as the final and only way of novel-writing. The critics who have handed down these successive ultimata have apparently decided that no interest, even archæological, attaches any longer to the standards and the vocabulary of their predecessors; and this wholesale rejection of past principles has led to a confusion in terms which makes communication difficult and conclusions ambiguous.

An unexpected result of the contradictory clamour has been to transfer Proust, who ten or twelve years ago seemed to many an almost unintelligible innovator, back to his rightful place in the great line of classic tradition. If, therefore, the attempt to form a judgment of his art has become doubly arduous it has also become doubly interesting; for Proust, almost alone of his kind, is apparently still regarded as a great novelist by the innovators, and yet is already far enough off to make it clear that he was himself that far more substantial thing in the world of art, a renovator.

With a general knowledge of letters extending far beyond the usual limits of French culture he combined a vision peculiarly his own; and he was thus exceptionally fitted to take the next step forward in a developing art without disowning its past, or wasting the inherited wealth of experience. It is as much the lack of general culture as of original vision which makes so many of the younger novelists, in Europe as in America, attach undue importance to trifling innovations. Original vision is never much afraid of using accepted forms; and only the cultivated intelligence escapes the danger of regarding as intrinsically new what may be a mere superficial change, or the reversion to a discarded trick of technique.

The more one reads of Proust the more one sees that his strength is the strength of tradition. All his newest and most arresting effects have been arrived at through the old way of selection and design. In the construction of these vast, leisurely, and purposeful compositions nothing is really wasted, or brought in at random. If at first Proust seemed so revolutionary it was partly because of his desultory manner and parenthetical syntax, and chiefly because of the shifting of emphasis resulting from his extremely personal sense of values. The points on which Proust lays the greatest stress are often those inmost tremors, waverings, and contradictions which the conventions of fiction have hitherto subordinated to more generalized truths and more rapid effects. Proust bends over them with unwearied attention. No one else has carried as far the analysis of half-conscious states of mind, obscure associations of thought and gelatinous fluctuations of mood; but long and closely as he dwells on them he never loses himself in the submarine jungle in which his lantern gropes. Though he arrives at his object in so roundabout a way, that object is always to report the conscious, purposive conduct of his characters. In this respect he is distinctly to be classed among those whom the jargon of recent philosophy has labelled 'behaviourists' because they believe that the proper study of mankind is man's conscious and purposive behaviour rather than its dim unfathomable sources. Proust is in truth the aware and eager inheritor of two great formulas: that of Racine in his psychology, that of Saint-Simon in its anecdotic and discursive illustration. In both respects he is deliberately traditional.

(b) Proust and his characters; pp. 160–71.

The sense that, through all his desultoriness, Proust always knows whither his people are tending, and which of their words, gestures and thoughts are worth recording; his ease in threading his way through their crowded ranks, fills the reader, from the first, with the feeling of security which only the great artists inspire. Certain novels, beginning very quietly – carelessly, almost – yet convey on the opening page the same feeling of impending fatality as the first bars of the Fifth Symphony. Destiny is knocking at the gate. . . .

There are many ways of conveying this sense of the footfall of Destiny; and nothing shows the quality of the novelist's imagination more clearly than the incidents he singles out to illuminate the course of events and the inner workings of his people's souls. . . .

Proust had an incredible sureness of touch in shedding this prophetic ray on his characters. Again and again he finds the poignant word, the significant gesture, as when, in that matchless first chapter ('Combray') of *Du Côté de chez Swann* he depicts the suspense of the lonely little boy (the narrator) who, having been hurried off to bed without a goodnight kiss because M. Swann is coming to dine, persuades the reluctant Françoise to carry to his mother a little note in which he implores her to come up and see him 'about something very important'. So far, the episode is like many in which the modern novelist has analyzed – especially since 'Sinister Street' – the inarticulate tragedies of childhood. But for Proust such an episode, in addition to its own significance, has a deeper illuminative use.

'I thought to myself,' he goes on, 'how Swann would have laughed at my anguish if he had read my letter, and guessed its real object' (which was, of course, to get his mother's goodnight kiss); 'but, on the contrary, as I learned later, for years an anguish of the same kind was the torture of Swann's own life. That anguish, which consists in knowing that the being one loves is in some gay scene [*lieu de plaisir*] where one is not, where there is no hope of one's being; that anguish, it was through the passion of love that he experienced it – that passion to which it is in some sort predestined, to which it peculiarly and specifically pertains' – and then, when Françoise has been persuaded to take the child's letter, and his mother (engaged with her guest) does not come, but says curtly: 'There is no answer' – 'Alas!' the narrator continues, 'Swann also had had that experience, had learned that the good intentions of a third person are powerless to move a woman who is irritated at feeling herself pursued in scenes of enjoyment by some one whom she does not love–' and suddenly, by one touch, in the first pages of that quiet opening chapter in which a little boy's drowsy memories reconstitute an old friend's visit to his parents, a light is flashed on the central theme of the book: the hopeless incurable passion of a sensitive man for a stupid uncomprehending woman. The foot-fall of Destiny has echoed through that dull provincial garden, her touch has fallen on the shoulder of the idle man of fashion, and in an instant, and by the most natural of transitions, the quiet picture of family life falls into its place in the great design of the book.

Proust's pages abound in such anticipatory flashes, each one of which would make the fortune of a lesser novelist. A peculiar duality of vision enabled him to lose himself in each episode as it unrolled itself before him – as in this delicious desultory picture of Swann's visit to his old friends – and all the while to keep his hand on the main threads of the design, so that no slightest incident contributing to that design ever escapes him. This degree of saturation in one's subject can be achieved only through something like the slow ripening processes of nature. Tyndall said of the great speculative minds: 'There is in the human intellect a power of expansion – I might almost call it a power of creation – which is brought into play by the simple brooding upon facts'; and he might have added that this brooding is one of the most distinctive attributes of genius, is perhaps as near an approach as can be made to the definition of genius.

Nothing can be farther from the mechanical ingenuities of 'plot'-weaving than this faculty of penetrating into a chosen subject and bringing to light its inherent properties. Neither haste to have done, nor fear lest the reader shall miss his emphasis, ever affects the leisurely movement of Proust's narrative, or causes him to give unnatural relief to the passages intended to serve as signposts. . . .

It was one of the distinctive characters of Proust's genius that he combined with his great sweep of vision an exquisite delicacy of touch, a solicitous passion for detail. Many of his pages recall those mediæval manuscripts where the roving fancy of the scribe has framed some solemn gospel or epistle in episodes drawn from life of towns and fields, or the pagan extravances of the Bestiary. Jane Austen never surpassed in conciseness of irony some of the conversations between Marcel's maiden aunts, or the description of Madame de Cambremer and Madame de Franquetot listening to music; and one must turn to 'Cranford' for such microscopic studies of provincial life as that of the bed-ridden aunt, Madame Octave. . . . But just as the reader is sinking delectably into the feather-bed of the small town, Proust snatches him up in eagle's

310

talons and swings him over the darkest abysses of passion and intrigue – showing him, in the slow tortures of Swann's love for Odette, and of Saint-Loup's for Rachel, the last depths and involutions of moral anguish, or setting the frivolous careers of the two great Guermantes ladies, the Duchess and the Princess, on a stage vaster than any since Balzac's, and packed with a human comedy as multifarious. . . . Every reader enamoured of the art must brood in amazement over the way in which Proust maintains the balance between these two manners – the broad and the minute. His endowment as a novelist – his range of presentation combined with mastery of his instruments – has probably never been surpassed.

Fascinating as it is to the professional to dwell on this amazing virtuosity, yet the lover of Proust soon comes to feel that his rarest quality lies beyond and above it – lies in the power to reveal, by a single allusion, a word, an image, those depths of soul beyond the soul's own guessing. The man who could write of the death of Marcel's grandmother . . . the man who could touch with so sure and compassionate a hand on the central mysteries of love and death, deserves at such moments to be ranked with Tolstoy when he describes the death of Prince Andrew, with Shakespeare when he makes Lear say: 'Pray you, undo this button. . . .'

(c) Reservations on Proust's vision; pp. 171–8.

Hitherto I have only praised.

In writing of a great creative artist, and especially of one whose work is over, it is always better worth while to dwell on the beauties than to hunt down the blemishes. Where the qualities outweigh the defects the latter lose much of their importance, even when, as sometimes in Proust's case, they are defects in the moral sensibility, that tuning-fork of the novelist's art.

It is vain to deny, or to try to explain away, this particular blemish – deficiency, it should be rather called – in Proust's work. Undoubtedly there are blind spots in his books, as there are in Balzac's, in Stendhal's, in Flaubert's; but Proust's blind spots are peculiarly disconcerting because they are intermittent. One cannot dismiss the matter by saying that a whole category of human emotions is invisible to him, since at certain times his vision is acutest at the precise angle where the blindness had previously occurred. . . .

M. Benjamin Crémieux, whose article on Proust is the most thoughtful study of his work yet published, has come upon the obstacle of Proust's lapses of sensibility, and tried, not very successfully, to turn it. According to this critic, Proust's satire is never 'based on a moral ideal', but is always merely 'complementary to his psychological analysis. The only occasion' (M. Crémieux

311

continues) 'where Proust incidentally speaks of a moral ideal is in the
description of the death of Bergotte.' He then cites the beautiful
passage in question: 'Everything happens in our lives as though we
had entered upon them with a burden of obligations contracted in an
anterior existence; there is nothing in our earthly condition to make
us feel that we are under an obligation to be good, to be morally
sensitive [*être délicats*], even to be polite; nor, to the artist, to begin
over again twenty times a passage which will probably be admired
only when his body has been devoured by worms. . . . All these
obligations, which have no sanction in our present life, seem to
belong to a different world, a world founded on goodness, on moral
scruple, on sacrifice, a world entirely different from this one, a world
whence we come when we are born on earth, perhaps to return there
and live once more under the role of the unknown laws which we
have obeyed here because we carried their principles within
ourselves, without knowing who decreed that they should be; those
laws to which every deep intellectual labour draws us nearer, and
which are invisible only – and not always! – to fools.'[1]

It is difficult to see how so deliberate a profession of faith in a
moral ideal can be brushed aside as 'incidental'. The passage quoted
would rather seem to be the key to Proust's whole attitude: to its
weakness as well as to its strength. For it will be noticed that, among
the mysterious 'obligations' brought with us from that other 'entirely
different' world, he omits one; the old stoical quality of courage.
That quality, moral or physical, seems never to have been recognized
by him as one of the mainsprings of human action. He could
conceive of human beings as good, as pitiful, as self-sacrificing, as
guided by the most delicate moral scruples; but never, apparently, as
brave, either by instinct or through conscious effort.

Fear ruled his moral world: fear of death, fear of love, fear of
responsibility, fear of sickness, fear of draughts, fear of fear. It formed
the inexorable horizon of his universe and the hard delimitation of
his artist's temperament. In saying so one touches on the narrow
margin between the man's genius and his physical disabilities, and at
this point criticism must draw back, or linger only in reverent
admiration of the great work achieved, the vast register covered, in
spite of that limitation, in conflict with those disabilities.

Nietzsche's great saying, 'Everything worth while is accomplished notwithstanding' [*trotzdem*], might serve as the epitaph of
Proust.

NOTE

1 Pléiade III, pp. 187–8.

111. Edmond Jaloux on *Albertine disparue*
1926

Part of a review of *Albertine disparue* in *Les Nouvelles littéraires*, 16 January 1926.

Edmond Jaloux reflects the feeling that Albertine has an unreal quality, not so much a person in her own right as an occasion for the Narrator's obsession with jealousy.

Albertine disparue is the first book by Proust on which he did not work in his customary fashion, which was to revise his pages indefinitely, puff them out, nourish them and enrich them in a thousand different ways. This can be felt to some extent. It can be felt by a certain monotony of language; the general tone is more abstract and not so varied. We can see from reading that the perpetual recasting to which Proust subjected his works came directly from life: picturesque details, and constant and immediate connections with the outside world. His formidable memory opened up to his perception thousands of little psychological details. I will not go so far as to say that this feature is missing from *Albertine disparue*, because the story is too enthralling for us to get the impression of this shortcoming; but on proper reflection we do realize its absence.

The book begins with the flight of Albertine. The whole of the Albertine drama is destined to remain rather obscure to us. There is something mysterious in this semi-sequestration of a young woman in the house of a young man who is not sure about loving her but is certain he will suffer if she were to go away from him, and whose jealousy is so violent that she gives him no peace of mind. Until now psychologists had never envisaged that jealousy could develop almost outside love, or rather that it might be in itself the whole of love. The idea that Albertine is able to deceive him is almost all that keeps the narrator near her. He is haunted by all the things she may do when she is not with him and that he seems, furthermore, to have no inclination to do himself when she is. In one of his extraordinary sentences – in which Proust goes further into the human heart than any man has perhaps ever done – he begins to see that this jealousy has its origin in the horror of what is unknown in the life of the person one loves, but at the same time he begins to see that it is this unknown that is coveted in him. . . .

313

Swann's love for Odette had the same theme, though Odette was a kept woman, or nearly so, and Swann's jealousy, because it was precise had something limited about it. . . . The jealousy of the anonymous narrator in *La Prisonnière* and in *Albertine disparue* has something more cruel about it because it is more vague. He suspects Albertine of having affairs with other women and this love, because it is even more elusive, fleeting and capricious, causes him a more irksome pain than Swann's. Perhaps in this feeling there is also at the back of your mind the thought that the woman who deceives you with a man is deceiving you with someone of your own kind who cannot give her anything really different from what you can yourself, whereas where women are involved a seething world inconceivable to a man is opened up for her and carries her far away from you. I mention these things fairly rapidly, but I believe that one day there will be a case for returning to the essential difference between the jealousy of Swann and the jealousy of Proust's hero, because one concerns men and the other women. This Albertine, about whom we know next to nothing, or at least nothing more than a mixture of complaisance, perfidy and evasiveness fills so many pages of *A la recherche du temps perdu* that her vague shadow finally takes on for us a hallucinatory character. . . .

112. Benjamin Crémieux on new developments in Proust

1926

Review of *Albertine disparue* entitled 'Nouveauté d'*Albertine disparue*' in *La Nouvelle Revue française*, 1 February 1926, pp. 216–24.

Benjamin Crémieux sees in *Albertine disparue* evidence of Proust breaking new ground in psychological analysis and in fictional and descriptive inventiveness. It also serves as an exemplar of the essential characteristics of Proust's style.

A posthumous work, *Albertine disparue* is only a draft. No one should be advised to make acquaintance with Proust through these two volumes; it is to be presumed that no one would contemplate it. It is only convinced 'Proustians', in fact, who will get as far as this latest section of *A la recherche du temps perdu*. For them, *Albertine disparue* will provide a pleasure of rare and at times novel quality. It is not, as in *La Prisonnière*, a matter of a single episode followed to the bitter end by a sick man with low vitality and an often failing critical sense. What we have is the earliest state of a text, a first expression that allows us to measure, in Proust, the impetuosity of the inspiration and the violence of the flow. This is a unique document for grasping the mechanism of his art.

The reworking he indulged in, as we may now realize, was on the one hand a process of planing down and touching up set expressions and on the other a task of an architectural nature, intended to balance up the different parts of the work, and fill out some development that had hardly got under way so as to provide a proper counterweight to some other development that had come into full flower at the first go.

The first hundred pages of *Albertine disparue* and, in the following chapters, all the pages that bear on the flight of Albertine, on Marcel's suffering and on the 'irregular progress of oblivion', even on this oblivion itself, are cast in the same mould and their abundance and complexity appear excessive, almost inhuman. Perhaps, also, they are not lacking in monotony and at times give the impression (actually false, when closely investigated) that Proust is repeating himself. All the customary ingredients – already almost too familiar – of Proustian analysis and psychology are present without exception: the subjectivity of love, the intermittences of the heart, the invincible power of habit, the ceaseless renewal of the self, the strength and at the same time the weakness of memory, the different modes of suffering and the multiple aspects of feelings and vices. Proust has used them to the point of satiety in connection with Swann's jealousy over Odette, the death of the grandmother, the forgetting of Gilberte and Marcel's jealousy over Albertine. True, the new situation – the death of a woman that you have loved and been jealous over and who has left you – is amenable to infinite variations on the big Proustian themes.

Exactly so, the main impression here is that we are dealing with variations, with psychological fugues written with a virtuosity, a mastery, you might almost say, with a gratuitousness that are incomparable by a man fully in control of his technique, his methods and his general philosophy, but sometimes too by a man in full possession of the Proustian procedures, the Proustian universe and the Proustian stereotypes rather than by their creator. *Albertine disparue* (or at least the part involving Albertine) could have been written by an admirably gifted disciple of Proust's. . . .

Never until now, indeed, had Proust achieved, in the handling of his 'ideas' and his psychology, such complete ease and sureness. He no longer fumbles. Like an old consultant who, in respect of everything bearing on his specialism, pronounces diagnoses virtually automatically, here Proust almost automatically traces the stages of suffering and oblivion and effortlessly discovers to hand the most exact turns of phrase he has ever devised. Without a shadow of doubt, it is in *Albertine disparue* that you meet the highest number of general maxims that can be separated from the text and that, re-aligned end to end, would give the most complete and best defined idea of Proust's approach.

Even better than a string of spontaneous diagnoses, what we have here is a lecture at the bedside of a hospital patient by a great clinician dealing with a fine example of pathology, and extracting from the typical case submitted to him the series of general maxims most suited to confirming his overall theory of medicine.

The reader's impression (I refer, of course, to someone who has read the preceding volumes) will be that he is being confronted by an analysis which is less true, less faithfully scrupulous, less vivid than in *Du côté de chez Swann* or *Sodome et Gomorrhe*, and that in that analysis he is not watching the movement of each molecule of reality through the magnifying glass of Proust's vision, as he did when he relived Swann's jealousy or the grandmother's death. Proust 'overdoes it' this time, he 'lays it on too thick'; rather than the memorial of Marcel's pain and his progress towards indifference, what he presents us with is the ideal reconstruction – a paleonto-logical reconstruction (like Cuvier and his vertebra) – of what this pain and progress towards oblivion would be in a character ideally endowed for this experience. It is in this sense that the reservation 'almost inhuman' I used earlier should be understood.

There are, nevertheless, in these pages discoveries and revelations as striking and unexpected as in the previous volumes – the idea, for instance, that before reaching oblivion, love retraces in the opposite direction all the phases that it went through from its beginning and finally reaches the same emotional state of availability, and in Marcel's particular case, the same undifferentiated desire for a whole bunch of girls. This idea, which is psychologically speaking so curious and fertile, had not previously been expressed by Proust, and no one had formulated it, I believe, before him. It would not be difficult to quote a hundred other remarks as novel and suggestive.

But we still need to ask if Proust's apparent detachment from the 'I', this slight withdrawal, which is at first a bit disappointing, does not indicate a victory of subjectivism upon itself and a sort of objectivizing of it. If such is the case, *Albertine disparue* brings a new quality to Proust's work, that is not so much unexpected as patiently pursued, realized in fact, and presents us with the ultimate achievement of the Proustian quest, the equivalent in the realm of the psychology of love of the natural history of spirits dreamed of by Sainte-Beuve. Proust has succeeded in systematizing the causes, the progress, the effects and the gradual disappearance of a feeling outside the individual experiencing it and whose personal variation depends on contingencies appropriate to each particular case, but contingencies that are all of the same kind for any given feeling. Thus he arrives at a synthesis, viz. a generalization concerning feelings of the same kind as that provided by classic authors, by Racine and Marivaux. The process of love and oblivion, much more complex than was thought until now, and yet capable of being reduced to a small number of laws, is the same in all people. Behind Proust's subjective psychology, we find a kind of sociological psychology, a kind of mental and emotional universalism. Feelings exist *in themselves*,[1] but with a contradictory and heterogeneous existence quite different from the one described for us by classical psychology.

The fact that feelings exist is the big, essentially new quality brought by *Albertine disparue*, but it is not the only one. Not only do we find in it confirmation of the structured layout and the architectural composition of Proust's novel, denied until now by a number of his admirers, but also we enjoy the unexpected revelation of Proust's gifts as a writer of fiction, inventor of situations and 'sheer story-teller'. Proust as novelist of action – this is another of the great novelties of *Albertine disparue*, a further notion to be added to the idea we have of him.

The surprising series of events that bring Marcel back again to the company of Gilberte, now Mlle de Forcheville, is composed, calculated, arranged and managed with an understanding of the art of preparation and coups de théâtre that professionals in the genre might well envy.

We could claim as much for the episode of the Venice telegram (though a little forced) that leads Marcel to believe for a few days that Albertine, though already quite dead in his heart, has not in fact died. Let us note here, always bearing in mind those who had doubts that *A la recherche du temps perdu* was a properly composed work, that for this episode to have the slightest plausibility, it must have been prepared as far back as *A l'ombre des jeunes filles en fleurs* when choosing the name Albertine, one syllable of which is shared with the name Gilberte, and that Proust is careful to reinforce credibility by insisting, in the chapter entitled: *Mlle de Forcheville*, on the gradual degeneration of Gilberte's hand-writing.

A good illustration of what a concise story-teller Proust could

317

have been is the meeting of Mme Sazerat and Mme de Villeparisis in Venice. . . .

[Explains the preparation of this episode and quotes from 'Je menai Mme Sazerat' to 'C'est elle'. Pléiade III, p. 634.]

We may, indeed, notice that this encounter, as well as the reunion with Gilberte or the telegram incident – people who do not recognize one another or mistake each other for someone else – belong to one and the same order of events: mistaken identities, to be exact, and mistaken identity is the mainspring of light comedy. And it is correct to say that, translated into action, Proust's psychological approach transforms life into a sort of enormously moving light comedy, in the same way as the parallel approach by Pirandello, whose *Henry IV* has been described as tragic light comedy.

In the last thirty pages of *Albertine disparue* Proust has packed in other episodes, other coups de théâtre (Saint-Loup's homosexuality, for instance). And it shows furthermore what an inventor of dramatic subjects Proust could have been had he set himself to it.

Another novelty in *Albertine disparue* and one that allows us to measure Proust's greatness – his pages on Venice. For the first time in his work he tackles a 'bravura aria', already in the repertory of countless predecessors, and in the most natural, simple way, he gives us an original picture of Venice that no one had thought of describing before him and that proves to be one of the most revealing ever given of the city of the Doges.

The form of the Venice chapter, one must admit, is not up to the mark. It is often uncertain, woolly and all the clumsier in that it tackles things that are very difficult to formulate or suggest. To enjoy the pages on Venice to the full you have to keep to the content and not attempt to compare Proust's sentences with those of his more brilliant elders: Gautier, Barrès or d'Annunzio.

[Quotes a number of brief descriptions of Venice.]

Just as it is in *Albertine disparue* that one may well seek out the essential and definitive facts on Proust's psychological approach, so also it is to that work that we need to turn to seek out the essential facts about his style.

The first thing to be noticed is that, as with all original styles, it is built on an oral language, with speech, a particular way of expressing oneself, as its point of departure. Thibaudet observes that the point of departure for Flaubert's style is the speech of the well-off bourgeoisie of Rouen with its provincial background and no doubt purist pretensions. The point of departure for Proust's style is the speech of the Parisian salons of the upper bourgeoisie and the aristocracy. Proust is surely the only French writer since Naturalism whose style is based on the living language of the court. . . .

The striking thing about the manner in which people who frequent salons express themselves is not so much their vocabulary as their syntax, their art of linking sentences together without leaving any space for interruption (exactly the opposite of the jerky conversation and the crackling exchanges of a certain 'fashion-conscious' bourgeoisie). They are the last people to speak in monologues. The extent to which this soliloquizing type of speech suited both Proust's temperament and his purpose is obvious.

The peculiarly Proustian elements in this style are, first of all, the vocabulary he borrows from scientific terminology, from the techniques of other arts and from the lexicon of Symbolism; secondly, the use of tenses and moods, the abuse of the past conditional, most often transcribed in its identical subjunctive form (*il eût pensé, il eût eu* in preference to *il aurait pensé, il aurait eu*) and especially the gliding from one tense to another, from the imperfect to the past definite, the past indefinite, the present and the conditional in one and the same long sentence.

In a hundred years grammarians will also note that Proust's style has marked the return in narrative to the indirect style that has been abandoned in France for a hundred years and even, one might say with some exaggeration, since Voltaire. It is a style suited to interior analysis, to reflections upon the thoughts and conversations of others (which interior monologue tries to evade and that, long before interior monologue, Stendhal tried to side-step by writing: 'Fabrice thought: if I, etc.')

The inherent defects of this style of 'aristocratic' origin will also be noted – the perverse use of '*lequel, duquel*' and of syntactical structures often fraught with danger (also at times high in flavour).

There are surely many other new qualities to be emphasized in *Albertine disparue*. Let us simply point out finally the complete disappearance of that snobbery that seemed inherent in his nature and something he could not objectively study, and let us not attempt to conclude. It will only be possible to come to a conclusion on Proust after the publication of the last line of *Le Temps retrouvé*.

NOTE

1 In italics in the text.

113. Fernand Vandérem on *Albertine disparue*
1926

Notice in *La Revue de France*, 1 February 1926; reprinted in *Le Miroir des lettres*, Paris, Flammarion, 1929, pp. 172–80.

Fernand Vandérem's views on Proust have shifted towards seeing him less as a novelist and more as a man obsessed with confession. While admiring a relentless quality in psychological analysis, he is now less tolerant of scabrous elements and makes no defence of them as satire.

With Marcel Proust's *Albertine disparue* the literary year can, as they say, sleep soundly, since it has from this moment the certainty of being marked by a work of great calibre. . . .

In these two compact volumes, all is not, however, of equal quality. And without any circumlocution, I am going to point out to you, just as if we were chatting together, the chapters among the four it contains – I won't say the least good, for there are hardly any pages in the book that I do not find attractive – but the ones that seem to me to be the least substantial and of slight impact.

First, there is an episode in Venice, where the hero (whom we will call, for want of anything better, *He*[1] spends a few weeks with his mother – an episode rich in subtle and amusing impressions, but which, whether it concerns the psychological portrayal of the character or the development of the story, is of no use whatsoever.

Then a final chapter: *A new side to Robert de Saint-Loup*, over which, if you are at all normally inclined, I do not suggest you linger. In it you will see the niece of the well-known tailor Jupien adopted by M. de Charlus and given in marriage by him to the young Marquis de Cambremer; then again, Gilberte Swann marrying the Marquis de Saint-Loup; then the young Mme de Cambremer dying suddenly and her husband becoming the favourite of M. de Charlus, while Saint-Loup flaunts his taste in women to provide a cover for distractions of quite another nature, and rounding the whole thing off, if I may put it like that, M. Legrandin from Méséglise given over to fantasies of the same stamp. Poor Verlaine, who gave the title *Histoires comme ça* to such innocent little tales! What astonishment would be his to learn the sense that his title has taken on and the kind of talent it now covers! Without being strait-laced or prudish, it seems to me that Marcel Proust would have gained, if not in eliminating these pages, at least in applying to them some severe pruning. In spite of their funny elements, they do not have that comic amplitude to be found in some chapters of *Sodome*, and their seething mass of tiny scabrous details is not so much evocative of grand satire as of the gossip in certain clandestine dens of iniquity.[2]

Proust's adversaries – and there are many – will be quick to shout in triumph: 'Out of four parts, two that are pointless; one of them only made up of travel notes and the other more tiresome than instructive – you can easily see that Proust is no novelist.'

Of course he is no novelist, and the error people have committed and still do lies in considering him to be one and judging him accordingly!

Moreover, as soon as he gives signs of being one, notice how unskilful and awkward he is. And notably in *Albertine disparue* what a lot of examples there are of this clumsiness!

For instance, at Venice, *He* receives a telegram from Albertine who, he thinks, has been dead for several months but who, it seems, is alive and wants to see him again. *He*, who has stopped loving Albertine, puts the telegram in his pocket and does not think any more about it. But, during the return journey in the train taking him back to Paris, he thinks, prompted by a remark from his mother recalling Gilberte Swann, that in the telegraph office Gilberte's handwriting could have caused her name to be taken for Albertine's. So all is explained, and Albertine is well and truly dead. The result of this improbable mistake? Its psychological repercussions? None. Proust has simply recorded the adventure as appearing in his notes or recollections.

But, once the emotion we have felt from this resurrection of Albertine has been dissipated, suddenly a particular feature, at first passing unnoticed, catches our eye. Why, earlier, having received notice of the accidental death of Albertine – an appalling tragedy and one in which *He* is himself nearly brought to death's door – why did he not rush off to Touraine, inform himself of the circumstances of the accident and say his last farewell to his beloved? There could be nothing more human and more natural than such an action. Nothing more obvious and that the least skilled of novelists would not have failed to tell us about in detail. – But Proust is no novelist; what he does is recount the thoughts and deeds of his hero. And *He* not having gone there, why should Proust invent this journey?

Yet another example: on the very day of Albertine's escape, *He* has gone prowling round the precincts of his beloved's house. There he notices a poor young girl who seems nice, takes her home, detains her a few minutes and, after taking a few vague liberties, packs her off with twenty-five louis. That evening, to his utter chagrin, a letter from the courts summons him to appear upon complaint by the parents of abducting a minor; and an indulgent magistrate succeeds only after great difficulty in getting him out of this wretched business. Why, at the height of his grief, did *He* allow himself to be dragged into this dangerous escapade? No explanation is given of this strange behaviour. And the eventual consequences for his thoughts, his feelings and his relations with Albertine? Not the shadow of a suggestion! But Proust is not the kind of novelist to restrict himself to depicting relevant scenes. His sole wish is to give us nothing less than the complete picture of his hero. And, since *He* has yielded to this strange impulse, Proust did not have the heart to let it go unmentioned.

But if *Le Temps perdu* is not properly speaking a novel, could it be a blend of similar genres: memoirs and confessional fiction[3] – something like a concoction made up of the *Confessions* and *Adolphe*? It's not this either, for in these two books, the narrator remains continually in the foreground, considers the other characters only in relation to himself and does not depict them other than as incidental secondary characters involved in the action. Whereas, in *Le Temps perdu*, the hero suddenly disappears for pages, for whole chapters at a time to make way for an observer, a painter, an artist uniquely concerned with the representation, the feelings or the strange behaviour of his models – the book becoming suddenly as objective as a novel by Balzac or Flaubert and setting out before us unforgettable types, with a roundness, a strength of outline and a comic force that those two masters no less could only have bowed to.

Then, immediately after, personal confession will begin its course again, with an abundance, a minuteness and a precision of detail that at times are the equal of Rousseau or Benjamin Constant, but in which neither of them displayed such unbroken attention and incisiveness and such a wealth of unexpected and novel observations. Are not such ill-matched things as these the opposite of art? Assuredly so, if they are appreciated from the point of view of our tradition in fiction and the literary rules in current use. But who is there to say that, by its origin as much as its execution, Proust's work does not break free of all these previous classifications and must not be placed outwith all known genres?

For my part, I would be inclined to see in it not so much a phenomenon of a literary order as a psychological one; the unprecedented case of a particularly sensitive, exceptionally perceptive individual, driven not so much by the desire to make a book as to give complete and utter expression to his feelings, to relieve himself of the myriads of impressions, emotions, joys, sorrows and observations that a tireless memory continually built up in him and who, weighed down by the ever-increasing weight of this oppressive burden, felt a kind of physical need to get shot of it.

Otherwise, how can one explain away what has always been for me the great mystery of Proust's work and that no exegesis seems to me to have attempted to illuminate: this unique intrepidity in the history of letters in piling page upon page, detail upon detail with no concern for being thought over-long, slow-moving or over-complicated, with no other goal than the utter exhaustion of what it is he wants to say, and in spite of all the risks he ran in doing it: boring his readers, repulsing them, disorientating them, tiring them out – or worse still, not having any at all.

Because, as far as literary art goes, Proust was no child. The works of the masters were ultra-familiar to him. In them he had calculated everything a story or poem can gain from selection, concision and synthesis and everything that is to be lost in neglecting these procedures.

Nor was he a coterie writer, living only in his dreams or among his associates and ignoring the reactions of the public at large. He had never given up being in the swim of Parisian life. He knew exactly what would come across in that milieu or remain a dead duck. He knew his readers better than his own family, and the limits of their understanding as much as the limits of their endurance.

In a word, he was no visionary either, one of those lyrical megalomaniacs drunk with words and carried away by their sheer verbosity. There is not a line in Proust that does not show reflection, calculation, maturity of mind, not one that is not rich in substance and original thought.

Arguing *a priori*, none of the losses, none of the obstacles and dangers to which his enterprise exposed him, was therefore to escape his attention. So, for him to have proceeded with such temerity, such tenacity and constancy, we must surely suppose that an instinct different from the literary instinct provided him with support and driving energy: a secret necessity, the imperious and irresistible need to express himself, to drain himself even to the dregs, to the supreme essence, to the last drop.

Rarely however has this private demon of confession and analysis driven Proust to the degree of power and perfection exemplified in the two first parts of *Albertine disparue*.

The subject of the first is one of the simplest and most hackneyed: the old story of the man betrayed and abandoned by the woman he loves, his confusion, his anguish and his desire to capture her again even at the cost of the worst concessions. This is Arnolphe and

Boubouroche. But instead of treating the theme in one or two closely-argued scenes, in one or two closely-packed, fast-moving chapters, Proust will use more than two hundred pages to note the graph of its rise and fall, day by day, hour by hour, studying its slightest variations and hunting out those two great human mysteries: the pain of love followed by its eternal remedy, oblivion, even in their most secret recesses.

There have been long discussions on whether Arnolphe was a comic or a tragic character. Proust shows us he was both, as Guitry had already done. For in the slow unravelling of this astonishing analysis, there is not a page where Proust's irony does not go hand in hand with the emotion that emanates from his extraordinary sensibility, not a painful observation that is not emphasized when necessary by the most knowing, the shrewdest of smiles.

The way we have become used to the beloved, then the habit whereby we initiate ourselves into accepting her loss, how our memories act for the unfaithful lover against us, then how they turn against her, the slow infiltration of oblivion, breaking down our former personality so as to create a new one out of it – one would need endless quotations, one would need to quote almost the whole lot to show with what art Proust has renewed, recreated and enriched in this respect all the comments of his predecessors. . . .

Then, once Albertine has been lost for good, killed in a fall from a horse, another drama begins: no longer the drama of Arnolphe beset by Agnès's sly tricks – but Bovary's challenged by Emma's deception. You may recall the poignant episode at the end of *Madame Bovary* where the widower forces a drawer and discovers a batch of letters that reveal all Emma's excesses. A crushing blow, a man scarcely able to survive, struggling, bewildered, incoherent, stunned and collapsing a few days later in his garden plot like a rotten tree – the whole thing in four or five pages.

But *He*, Proust's hero, is made of sterner stuff and endowed with a stronger curiosity. As soon as Albertine is dead, the suspicions he had of her loose behaviour and perversity, instead of abating, take on a new vigour, and far from crushing him, inject into him a kind of resurgence of energy. A prurient itch to know all torments him and spurs him on. He will not back down from any effort, any enquiry, any manoeuvre to arrange the posthumous trial of Albertine: dispatching his servant at Balbec to Touraine to conduct an investigation on the spot; an affair with Andrée, her friend and accomplice, so as to extract a full confession. And what strange effects these tormenting disclosures have on him! For, if, internally, they slowly eat away his love with their acid, externally they stimulate him and revive him, re-establishing Albertine as his daily companion, bringing the dead girl back to life, re-opening his liaison with her and renewing the scenes, the curses and the interrogations of past times, even at night in his dreams, even in his waking hours where the dreams penetrate with growing intensity – I say it again: no analysis of mine could give you an idea of such analyses as his. Read it you must, the text's the thing. . . .

NOTES

1 In italics in the text.
2 However, he very soon spoke again of satire as being the defence of Proust's immorality. See *Le Figaro*, 20 March 1926:

> Indeed, nothing is more harmful and more odious than those books where the author describes these aberrations obliquely and with an ill-disguised sympathy that almost smacks of an accomplice's indulgence.
> But, on the other hand, these portrayals will only be able to serve morality and art if the author approaches them openly and directly and delineates them with indignation as does d'Aubigné, with pity as does Baudelaire and with humour and satiric bite as does Proust.

3 Proust had mixed feelings with regard to Vandérem's reviews and particularly objected to the misreading of *La Recherche* as memoirs. Such articles 'misjudging the strict composition of my work, give the impression I am composing Memoirs and writing as the whim of my reminiscences takes me.' See *Correspondance générale*, Paris, Plon, 1933, vol. IV, pp. 29–30.

114. Albert Thibaudet on *Albertine disparue*
1926

Review of *Albertine disparue* in *L'Europe nouvelle*, 13 February 1926, pp. 213–14.

Thibaudet stresses the importance of *Albertine disparue* as a study of a character evolving within the memory of the Narrator and as being an example of Proust's affinity with seventeenth-century writers.

With *Albertine disparue* we have the penultimate part of Marcel Proust's great voyage of discovery, *A la recherche du temps perdu*. The last part, *Le Temps retrouvé*, is in the press and in a few months we will have the fifteen or sixteen thick volumes of the Proustian *oeuvre*.

To wait for the end of the work would, of course, be essential if we are to see the whole panorama and become familiar with all its intentions. Indeed, the true nature of Proust's genius lies in revealing ever newer turnings and in making the unexpected one of the elements and one of the continual resources of his psychology. There is not a single important character who does not in the course of the work change his apparent nature several times like a snake sloughing its skin. True, the reader eventually realizes that it was always the same animal under the different skins. It is also true that these characteristics in one and the same character are not only successive states but also simultaneous ones. Depending on the people he is dealing with, a character reveals this or that side. Proust possesses also the marvellous knack of making these successive or simultaneous appearances resemble mobile spotlights illuminating every inch of the view.

There is, perhaps, in *Albertine disparue* even less action than in *La Prisonnière*, and both are also works of psychological analysis that for richness, meticulous detail and the vigorous but amorphous proliferations of our souls have certainly no equal in our literature. Whereas *La Prisonnière* analysed the feeling of jealousy, *Albertine disparue*, apart from a few incidental matters, presents itself as a monograph on memory. It is to do with the person Albertine becomes, after her escape and death, in the heart of the narrator analysing and describing the life she led. In this way, *Albertine disparue* heralds, much more clearly than the preceding parts, the last phase of the work, *Le Temps retrouvé*, in which we will see these

326

forces of memory working towards providing a new, enhanced, enriched and decisive life for an interval of time that had belonged until then only to a kind of duration of indifferent quality.

Reference to this new life that Albertine takes on in the world of time regained, reminds us that this subject had already been dealt with to some extent in a novel by Jules Romains: *Mort de quelqu'un.* In it Romains studied in a quite new way the kind of existence a dead man takes on in the mind and memory of those who survive him. Auguste Comte has studied it from the philosophical point of view in the guise of subjective existence and it was natural for a man like Romains, who was used to giving an artistic form to the thoughts of philosophers, to find it was just what he was looking for. But even though these two writers deal with similar subjects, it is obvious that they have casts of mind that are not only different but completely opposite! Romains is as much a precise, refined artist, with a feeling for caricature and a sense of humour, in line with traditional novelists like, for instance, the Flaubert of *Un Coeur simple* as Proust, for his part, gives free rein to a mass of recollections and images that he refuses to keep in check or sacrifice.

Albertine disparue owes its strength not only to being this incomparable monograph on memory but also to the way many of the characters of *A la recherche du temps perdu* curiously reappear in it. We find a Saint-Loup who has most surprisingly passed over into the amorous camp where we would least expect to find him and where M. de Charlus is colonel and young Morel warrant officer. In particular, we rediscover, in one of the episodic scenes of the work which will one day most certainly be anthologized, the two interesting figures of M. de Norpois and Mme de Villeparisis. They have become a pair of old lovers that the author discovers in a hotel dining-room in Venice and this picture of two nice elderly friends takes on in the Venetian setting an air of admirable sweetness and poetry. The whole story of the stay in Venice is moreover not only one of the fine set pieces but also one of the most important parts of the work. Venice, in a book that, do not forget, was written before the war, marks almost as of right the place in the world where this transformation from real life to the life of memory will come into being. Today it would perhaps not be at all the same thing. . . .

Critical opinion has pointed out that *Albertine disparue* was the first of Proust's books to be published from the author's rough sketches and not to have those long additions and those interminable corrections by means of which Proust went on endlessly adding something new to a book, almost without ever making a cut. The impression has been that the difference has expressed itself in a more summary, more fast-moving and at times less satisfying work. I confess that I have not been very taken with this point of view. Proust would perhaps have added several pages to bring out for us the nature of Saint-Loup which indeed remains somewhat obscure. But it is equally true that this rough sketch of Proust's, this Proust in first draft, reveals indeed the same qualities not only of analysis but of style as the preceding works that had been modified to his heart's content. This is surely how the Duc de Saint-Simon wrote, much admired by Proust and whose direct and exact influence has perhaps, throughout the whole of our literature only been evident in the case of the author of *A la recherche du temps perdu*.

We have, furthermore, in *Albertine disparue* the chance to admire how much more deeply Proust appreciates and continues the tradition of our great seventeenth-century writers than many of those who throw up their hands in horror at him as if confronted by a decadent writer. There are admirable pages here on Racine and on the role of Phèdre. The numerous passages of this kind to be found throughout his work cause us to regret he did not write a book of literary criticism proper. Possibly the publication of his correspondence, from what we know of it, even though it is a long way off, will fill this gap.

115. Armand Pierhal on *Albertine disparue*
1926

Review in *La Revue nouvelle*, 15 February 1926, pp. 44–7.

Armand Pierhal, translator and critic, provides insight not only into *Albertine disparue* but into its place in Proust's work, thematically and stylistically.

A very clear distinction needs to be made between the two volumes entitled *Albertine disparue*. . . . The first, given over entirely to one single chapter, deals with one of the subjects Proust has applied himself to with greatest perseverance: the analysis of the changes which feelings associated with the memory of the beloved undergo to the point of oblivion, an analysis for which the 'Gilberte case' was, as Proust himself said, only a 'preliminary light sketch'. This is the high point of the trajectory described by Proust's work. With the unforced energy of genius it reaches those subtle regions where intellectual tension becomes almost unbearable for the common run of people. . . . These 220 uninterrupted pages do in fact recall certain chorales by Bach in which, having subjected the given theme to the rarest, most ravishing developments, to the extent that you wonder if it is humanly possible to outdo their riches, the composer finds the means in his conclusion to elaborate a mass of blinding inventions that leave you literally devastated. Similarly Proust in this definitive picture of the haphazard progress of oblivion. And the analogy between the composition of *A la recherche du temps perdu* and a musical work can be carried further. What comes to mind is Wagner's writing, Wagner who surely had an imperious fascination for Proust, who was, we should not forget, part of the generation that saw the triumph of Wagnerianism. Like Wagner Proust has this determination to exhaust a subject, to get the last drop out of it, which means that the territories they have each exploited have been ravaged and made sterile for a period of at least fifty years after their deaths, and because of this a fertile literary movement deriving from Proust has been no more possible than a musical movement deriving from Wagner. (Germany is hardly capable of making a recovery from the cataclysm of Wagner.) Yet, one might object, this power to make a wasteland around one is the mark of all the great creators. There are more precise similarities: it would not be impossible for Proust quite consciously to have used the leitmotiv technique to guarantee the unity of his gigantic novel. In this case the leading themes are speeches made up of 'linguistic tics' peculiar to each character and accompanying each of their appearances. This is most evident for M. de Norpois, each of whose appearances is indicated by a 'Norpois-type' set piece. But Françoise, Bloch, Legrandin, old Mme de Cambremer and the director of the Grand Hôtel at Balbec also have their leitmotivs. At first I thought: a surfeit of detail! needless repetitions! No. Deliberate repetitions for a structural purpose. At times the leading theme is of a more subtly psychological order. Thus Swann's love and jealousy regarding Odette is generally recalled along with his name. The evocation of gentleness, that undying, searing, frantic gift from the mother is linked with the grandmother and the mother of Marcel, twin characters scarcely differentiated – and also, and not by mere chance, with the name of Mme de Sévigné, another incarnation of maternal love. If necessary, the themes follow the development of their respective characters. The 'Charlus tone' which is so wildly arrogant at the beginning is not the same in *Sodome et Gomorrhe* where, now fallen and ageing, the supercilious gentleman bows to the insults of Morel, yet this tone preserves, for all that, enough characteristic features for us to recognize vestigial traces of the original voice. This is one of the most marvellously realized expressions of Proust's art. What will astonish future generations, who will be better placed to take in the overall effect of Proust's work, will surely be above all his amazing talent for construction, much more than the intrinsic quality of his style. For, as he was fully aware himself – ('My irremediable lack of talent' are words he so often puts into Marcel's mouth) – he had few of the gifts needed to be an original stylist. Let us be clear about this: few, compared with his powerful originality of thought. With hindsight he will not appear as a creator of forms of language that have a personal flavour to them. The fact that he devoted himself with such loving indulgence to pastiche would be proof, if proof were needed, that he did not have that tyrannical inflexibility in the will to self-expression that makes for original writers. This explains why a single sentence of Barrès is very often enough to recognize his voice while you need a page at least of Proust. This is because Proust is less interested in leaving his mark on the detail than on the general rhythm of the piece, since, once again, his interest is in construction. How can one, after a century of unbroken descriptive prose, speak of Venice with originality? Proust discovers the theme of associations established in his mind between his impressions of Venice and his memories of Combray, and he will draw from them the most unexpected effects. And the fact that he possesses this gift of development – the most admired in music because it is so rare – is yet another similarity between his genius as a writer and the genius of a composer. . . .

The second volume of *Albertine disparue* is, in my view, a lot less good. It marks the point at which the premature death of Proust makes its terrible presence felt. We have an accumulation of sudden changes in the personality of the characters, dramatic reversals and thoroughly unforeseen coups de théâtre without the developments Proust has led us to expect, the absence of which sharply interrupts the general flow of the work. A further disappointment: the stay in Venice announced so early on and long awaited is, in spite of a few delightful details, rather on the short side. Yet there is . . . in this second volume an analysis of the impressions that assail an author reading his first published article, together with reflections on the objective reality of the printed essay, which have the perfection and the profundity of Proust's most successful realizations. But this is not enough to counterbalance the defective composition of the other parts. We have to take it as it stands. In spite of the abnegation and the total sacrifice of the second half of his life, Proust was unable to catch up with 'lost time' completely. A sad reflection on the irremediable imperfection of human effort!

116. Eugène Montfort on *Albertine disparue*
1926

A brief notice in *Les Marges*, 15 March 1926, pp. 219–20.

Eugène Montfort represents a hostile reaction to Proust's reputation and especially to the unfinished impression given by this text.

This is going too far. *Albertine disparue*, the latest work published by Marcel Proust, does his reputation no good. Proust's most fanatical admirers are forced to admit that this book is a 'rough draft'. Why then publish a rough draft? And if it is published, why not preface it with some explanation, some warning? Why indeed, if not to milk the vogue a writer enjoys and exploit a rich seam? The public would not buy the book if it were warned it is a rough draft; not a word is said, people are allowed to believe the work is as important as the earlier books, and the trick is won.

Albertine disparue once again proves Henri de Régnier right when he said that Marcel Proust's work is 'a vast preparation for something'. A preparation, not a realization. This holds for almost all this writer's books, beginning with *Du côté de chez Swann*.

After transports of blind faith and exaggerated expressions of fanaticism an anti-Proust reaction is perfectly possible. A great wave of disrespect is on the way.

117. John Charpentier on *Albertine disparue*
1926

Part of a review in *Le Mercure de France*. 15 April 1926, pp. 409–11.

John Charpentier (1880–1949) was regular reviewer of fiction for *Le Mercure de France*. While not condoning sexual inversion, he defends Proust for his objective approach and his eschewing of pornographic descriptions.

Something that amazes me is that, in the period of libertinage, or rather, vulgar debauchery in which we live, there are writers who, in the name of morality, stand up against the perverse elements in *Les Faux-Monnayeurs* of M. André Gide and in the latest posthumous volumes by Marcel Proust. In spite of my amazement, let no one suspect me of complacency with regard to unnatural behaviour. But no one will make me accede to the view that works like the ones I have mentioned can have some kind of corrupting effect being by their literary character so difficult or so inaccessible to the public that seeks salacious pabulum in books. There is, moreover, no scandalous description in *Les Faux-Monnayeurs*, and, after resorting to almost scientific language to describe M. de Charlus's vice, Proust contemplates the lamentable past of Albertine from behind the veil of death. M. Gide was surely wrong to attempt an apology for sodomites in *Corydon*; but in *Les Faux-Monnayeurs* he restricts himself to a psychological study and I do not think that this study of the dark feelings an uncle has for his nephew has the least seductive effect on a healthy young man. . . . Let us not commit the heresy of speaking of immorality when we are dealing with works that are doubly protected against the actions of swine by the beauty of their art and the nobility of their sincerity. The defenders of virtue have occasion enough to employ their zeal without declaring war on Proust or M. Gide, and we are all acquainted with novels, plays or 'illustrated' journals that have no need to exalt abnormal love in order to corrupt morals. Then again, where is homosexuality more pilloried than on the stages of cafés-concerts that are not, to my knowledge, schools of edification?

If there is something Proust can be reproached for – since these things are said about him – it is not so much that he has studied Sodom and Gomorrah as the society in which the tradition of these accursed cities is perpetuated. Proust, because of the reclusive life he led, had to limit the field of his investigations, and his work loses in extent what it gains in depth. . . .

Albertine disparue, in spite of the beauties it abounds in, seems a little arid in fact when compared with his previous works, because he did not enrich it with the discoveries he added to his trouvailles or that his trouvailles suggested to him. . . . I must return one day, when *Le Temps retrouvé* is published, to the ensemble of Proust's work. . . . For one cannot speak of any of his books, which are by no means novels, in isolation. But in the two new volumes that have just come out, what art again is here in the dissociation of feelings! What a sure touch in untangling them, in clearly examining the way they are superimposed or the way they are inextricably intertwined! What sensibility and intelligence this man has, whose marvellous intuition, so well served by lucid reasoning, links him with the moralists of the seventeenth century! Being, it is true, not so much a philosopher as a psychologist, his generalizations do not have the value of his observations, and in the subtlety of his analysis he is nearer Maine de Biran, whom he does not mention, than Kant, whom he actually quotes and whose synthesizing power he is far from possessing. But it is not the business of an artist to determine laws and this one has admirably filled his role in revealing so many precious truths to us in his exploration of the past – which he chose as his particular domain, and which is perhaps the sole reality for mortal creatures.

118. Raphael Cor on Proust as moralist
1926

Part of an essay on contemporary writing: 'Marcel Proust et la jeune littérature' in *Le Mercure de France*, 15 May 1926, pp. 46–55.

Raphael Cor, journalist and critic, examines the tendency he sees in contemporary writers, notably Giraudoux, to weary the reader with preciosity and treat literature as something coldly decorative or at best a stylistic game. This serves to heighten the unique quality of Proust who is presented as a writer not only with a brilliant style, but concerned also with the very stuff of life, even when drawn into special pleading for deviant behaviour.

. . . If we now pass on to Marcel Proust, how abruptly everything changes! We are confronted by an art which is no longer hot air, but rich in human substance; instead of acrobatics and gymnastics what we have is the human heart, its anxieties and the thrilling analysis of the passions, and instead of today's fad for glass jewellery, the pure gem of self-knowledge.

And surely it is not by his style of writing that Marcel Proust casts his special spell over us, even though that prose of his, with its endless twists and turns so cleverly devised to follow the contour of feeling in its finest inflections, churning up the rarest beauty as it swirls on its course, is marvellously suited to the bent of his researches. But what is really his greatest distinction, what really makes him incomparable is, piercing through his astonishingly penetrating elucubrations, the gaze of the moralist, fixed on our souls and fascinated by only one thing, humanity, his one and only concern. How far-reaching are his analyses of the heart in their profound lucidity, at one and the same time so sharply observed and yet bathed in a half-light that throws over them the mysterious softness of dreams. The amazing revelations of a lucid sleep-walker! The strange magnetism of those sleep-laden eyes that see much more clearly than the eyes of other men!

Is it to be ascribed to his sickly neurotic genius? Yet his profoundest observations, once they have been transformed by his dreaming, appear to us as if surrounded by a halo of strange phosphorescent light. And it is a fascinating sight to see this lone figure meditating on the dark treasure within him, savouring it with a mixture of delight and anguish, making his own auscultations, exhausting himself in the secret examination of his inmost self, listening to the amplified pulse of his arteries and keeping a keen eye on the poisonous growths that blanket his soul. If, from all that, feverish vapours and harmful emanations arise, we should not be surprised. And yet isn't this quivering miasma life itself? His books have the warmth, the stickiness of life at its most fundamental. That is why they exude a perfume with which we remain permanently impregnated. Proust, great poet of nostalgia, marvellous painter of the landscape of our inner life, what does your art, that is so human, that quivers with the throbbing pulse of suffering, have in common with the preciosity of these manufacturers of conceits! . . .

By virtue of his constant self-reflection, together with this inexorable intellectual honesty, Proust is the very opposite of those showy modish authors whose formula would seem to be extravagance and contrivance. Put alongside these improvisers besotted with sheer bad writing, he has no difficulty in standing out. Certainly, it is regrettable that, following the English manner, which is quite unlike ours, he strives to say everything and not sacrifice a single detail, as if he was afraid the essential point – the very one, indeed, that the great artist would keep – might slip from his grasp. Yet this frantic, finicky search for the truth is to be explained by a feverish urge to reach it. The superb perception he displays, the brilliant ideas that spurt forth from the secrets he vouchsafes when, shining his magic lamp, he stealthily takes us down into the innermost corners of his heart – in all that, in fact, he rivals the classic authors themselves.

In this respect, his extremely bold picture of abnormal love affairs shows a rare felicity in its daring. Wasn't it Boileau, in a famous couplet, who granted the great artist the right to contemplate anything and everything?

> Il n'est pas de serpent, ni de monstre odieux
> Qui, par l'art imité, ne puisse plaire aux yeux.[1]

Without a moment's hesitation, Proust arrogates this right to himself as a moralist aware that 'immorality', the precious fabric of his work, constitutes the very basis of mankind and that, in an assorted bouquet of rare blooms, the black iris of sin also has its place.

Certainly he cannot be criticized for underestimating the immense role that secret passions play in life, but rather the opposite, that is, for exaggerating it and, in the course of his wanderings in the forest of sensual desires, lingering at suspect corners – and not without a suspicion of connivance. Coaxing vices with the whispered cajoling of a snake-charmer, he would appear by his incantations to be compelling them to come loping out of their dens. This is how, from among the 'deviants' or would-be 'deviants' of this mysterious tribe, more numerous than the Israelites, he succeeds in creating an absolutely unforgettable gallery. While Morand restricts himself to outlining some scabrous adventure with a few deft strokes in passing . . . Proust tackles the dangerous subject we all know about, and that obviously fascinates him, with untiring, infinite patience. As an expert painter of secret deviations, he reveals them to us with a sure touch.

[Concludes by comparing Proust with Gide on this last point and finds Proust the more honest clinician.]

NOTES

1   No snake, no odious monster can there be
         That art can't paint, and make a joy to see.
                (Boileau: L'Art poétique. Chant III)

119. Ramon Fernandez: some strictures

1926

Part of 'La Garantie des sentiments et les intermittences du coeur', chapter on Proust in *Messages*, Paris, Gallimard, 1926, pp. 147–69.

Ramon Fernandez (1894–1944), one of the most distinguished early critics of Proust, here takes him to task, in a closely argued chapter, on the question of the emotional and intellectual values that may be extracted from a given experience. Fernandez chooses as the subject of his attack the much anthologized recollection of the grandmother in the section called 'Intermittences of the heart' in *Sodome et Gomorrhe*. He makes important comparisons with other analyses of the emotions (by Montaigne, Newman, and Meredith) that, in his opinion, reveal shortcomings on Proust's part.

The objections raised by Proust's work, considered as a total analysis of the heart and as revelatory of the depths of our nature, can, in my view, be reduced to two essential ones: it does not erect a hierarchy of values and, from beginning to end, it gives no evidence of any spiritual progress. This twofold deficiency puts him in an equivocal situation, which allows some to hail in it the foundation-stone of a positive literature, free of false pretence, an architecture of the intelligence, the task of which, it seems, is to bring fantasies and sublimations in line with the actual procedures of the sensibility, and which leaves others, whether more ambitious or more feeble, holding a bitter bouquet of disenchantment. I will restrict my criticism to one single example: in his masterly analysis of the 'intermittences of the heart', Proust raises a problem of extreme gravity, for it is on his solution that our conception of the value of man and the orientation of the future depend. It appears to me to be quite urgent, before echoes resound from all parts to the voice of the master, to examine carefully the problems he has raised without resolving them, or that he has in fact resolved by hasty and often unwarranted generalizations. The Proustian analysis of the intermittences of the heart possesses this particular feature, viz. it reveals all at once, and in one and the same mental act, the mechanism of Proust's thought and its limitations.

[Quotes from 'Bouleversement de toute ma personne' to 'que je venais d'apprendre qu'elle était morte'. Pléiade II, p. 755–6.]

After this come general reflections of high significance, but before quoting the essential part of them I would like to distinguish them from the preceding passage a little more clearly than has been done until now.

Eminent critics who have quoted these reflections seem to see in them the natural result of the emotional turmoil experienced by Proust, as if this experience could only be logically translated in accordance with the law of the intermittences of the heart. Yet, in fact, this abrupt reversal of values, this unexpected vision of reality, this passage, with no intervening phases, from the purely intellectual notion of being to the state of disruption brought on by its miraculous 'presence' in us, in no way imply the dissociation of personality that Proust deduces from it. On the contrary, we have here a normal stage in spiritual progress towards greater consistency and unity, a progress consisting essentially – as Newman has established definitively – of proceeding from intellectual comprehension to *real* comprehension of an object, a feeling or an act. The law of intermittences . . . is only the restricted and to some extent pathological version of a human phenomenon whose sense would be distorted if we did not hasten to place this law in the hierarchy of the laws of the spirit.

[Quotes from 'A n'importe quel moment' to 'où ma grand-mère s'était penchée vers moi' Pléiade II, pp. 756–7.]

What, as a result of his analysis, Proust adds to the phenomenon of *realization* that he has so strongly described, and what he omits from it, is obvious. The real memory – as opposed to the intellectual, fictitious memory – belongs to a framework of sensations, and indeed to imagine strongly we must feel strongly; but as to the hold over the real that the living memory provides, nothing guarantees its effectiveness and its duration, because the new self thus created is part and parcel of the affective and sense framework from which it originates. This self does not react on its own account and does not try to benefit from experience to reinforce the unity of Proust's spiritual side: in other words it does not try to become a true self. Make no mistake about it, whatever the impact of his analysis may be, Proust here creates a confusion by an improper use of the words soul and *self*, or more exactly, he implicitly gives definitions of both that would have to be accepted before we could assert either that he is mistaken or that he has renewed the

338

psychology of the human heart. It appears, in this passage, that by soul he understands the *collection* of our sensitive and emotional experiences scattered through time, and by *self* the passive subject of one of these experiences brought into consciousness by memory thanks to an emotional association. It could well be that these definitions exactly express reality, but in that case there would be frankly nothing for it but to excise these two words from our vocabulary. We would then be composed of independent and transitory waves whose rapid as well as unexpected passage would be registered by our consciousness. They would have exactly the same value as those waves of purely physical pleasure or pain that go through us, compressing or expanding our sensibility, and that we can only prolong by temporary and hasty reveries, or appease only by drugs and the deliberate re-education of our will. In this multitude of relived experiences, the only real link would be assured by memory and the only possible principle of unity would be the intelligence, that would co-ordinate these states by *comprehending* them. The only effective progress would be that of the intelligence, the sole non-illusory improvement would be that of our intellectual consciousness.

If we accept these criticisms and if we direct man towards the practical and put him among his fellows, we are now obliged to revise our ideas of spiritual guarantee and responsibility. . . . If the driving force of our sensibility depends on a phenomenon of reminiscence, if to know a feeling we have to await the emotional spark that will allow us to relive a previous experience to the full, if to understand, to feel, to long for and to desire, we must first undergo a metempsychosis in reverse that can restore to us as imperious and exclusive, the useless forms of our past lives, we are hardly better than those small South American republics which change programmes and promises every month as they change dictators.

The problem is a grave one. Not only, if we are to believe Proust, could man not guarantee his feelings, and consequently his acts, and not only would he be as a result an eternal bankrupt, but he ought also to renounce the consolation of feeling that he is making progress in spite of this discontinuity and intermittent blindness and that he will be able some day to control them and transcend them. Any real progress is growth, and growth of the whole man. There is no progress in a deeper and deeper understanding that one is making no progress; on the contrary, progress consists in deeper and deeper understanding that one's feelings are more and more wholesome, one's desires more and more effective. All spiritual development must be accomplished, not within the intelligence but within the individual person. The problem posed, therefore, by the Proustian analysis of the intermittences of the heart is the problem of spirituality, of the value of the ideal, of the future and of human progress. It can be formulated in the following terms: everything that appears good and fair to us, the inner forces that guarantee our words and our future actions, the aspiration towards that better condition called the ideal, the feeling of transcending oneself called spiritual progress – all that is only a discontinuous illusion of our senses, or at least, we can only guarantee the apparent results of all that thanks to various subterfuges: spiritual gymnastics and making our actions mechanical through habit. If the intermittences of the heart and their corollaries represent basic human nature and the ultimate experience of our *self*, than the life of the spirit must be placed entirely in the category of the imagination, and intelligence is the highest point of human development we can lay claim to. We ought, therefore, to demand of intelligence that feeling of elevation, dignity and beatitude traditionally required of spiritual life. The victory of intelligence would indicate the defeat of the spirit, and man's highest task would become one of denying his age-old striving.

Before concluding with Proust on the renunciation of life and the exclusive cult of the intelligence, we should do for him what he has not done, viz. situate him in a hierarchy. There is, after all, a way other than his of reaching self-understanding without self-transcendence, viz. Montaigne's which consists of taking one's place in an ordered structure while putting oneself in order. . . . The further we advance in our reading of the *Essays*, the more we distance ourselves from the somewhat rhetorical exercises of the beginning and the more we see Montaigne anxious not only to define himself, but also to *classify* himself: his personality does not fill the frame, there is space round him in his noble picture of Epaminondas. The great weakness of Proust's work, though very beautiful in so many respects, is that everything in it is brought down to the lowest common factor of a passive sensibility which gives no indication of maturity and that our field of vision is obscured in it by a *self* larger than life-size which the most lucid analysis cannot succeed in making transparent.

To remedy this defect we have to cross over the barricade, question the men who have found in individual sensibility and imagination the guarantee of our feelings and of the continuity of human effort. It is remarkable, in fact, that the more thought ripens, the more it conceives the necessity, in order to touch reality and dig deep, to rely on the most concrete reactions of the individual which it opposes to the abstract procedures of reason – and rely notably on this real understanding of things that Proust has described in dramatically lucid terms. The most profound analyst of this thinking and of this concrete logic that is so typically modern, Cardinal Newman, has provided an interpretation of it that is very interesting when compared with Proust's analysis.

Newman distinguishes two phases of understanding things: one can understand them *in the abstract* by inferences that bear on notions, and one can understand them *in reality* by an act of assent bearing on concrete representations by our imagination of an experience, a feeling or a particular act. For instance, before the 'shattering of his whole being' Proust understood his grandmother's death and the affection he had for her in the abstract; he had no understanding of it in reality. Newman sees in *real* assent (to be distinguished from abstract assent, the conclusion of an inference) the strongest and most perfect hold that the spirit can have on reality, on true knowledge in the realm of feeling and in the realm of action, and even in the realm of ideas in so far as these are capable of interesting all the forces of our being, and it is in this sense that Proust observes, with great accuracy, that he had just 'learned' of the death of his grandmother a year after the event. Up to this point Newman and Proust are in perfect agreement. Newman even goes as far as to recognize, as does Proust, the haphazard, unexpected, accidental character of the conditions of real assent. We cannot, he says, assure ourselves of real apprehension and assent 'because we have to secure first the images which are their objects, and these are often peculiar and special. They depend on personal experience; and the experience of one man is not the experience of another. Real assent, then, as the experience which it presupposes, is an act of the individual, as such, and *thwarts rather than promotes the intercourse of man with man*'.[1] And later, still in connection with real assent: '. . . it cannot be reckoned on, anticipated, accounted for, *inasmuch as it is the accident of the individual*'.[2] The coinciding of their thinking is significant: there is no doubt that Proust knew and experienced the first phase of this ripening of thought fixed in us by images, which allows us to pin down our feelings and give weight and consistency to our personality.

But it is also clear that the first phase was all he knew: the birth of his spiritual life soon gives all the appearance of an abortion. Newman is as explicit as it is possible to be: for him, the fixation of thought by concrete representations indicates a considerable progress, a deepening of the life of the spirit and human values taking root, so to speak. 'They [real assents] are sometimes called beliefs, convictions, certainties; and, as given to moral objects, they are perhaps as rare as they are powerful. Till we have them, in spite of a full apprehension and assent in the field of notions, we have no intellectual moorings, and are at the mercy of impulses, fancies, and wandering lights, whether as regards personal conduct, social and political action, or religion. These beliefs, *be they true or false in the particular case*, form the mind out of which they grow, and impart to it a seriousness and manliness which inspires in other minds a confidence in its views, and is one secret of persuasiveness and influence in the public stage of the world.'[3] Thus Newman discovers the roots of spiritual life in the very experience that, according to Proust, makes it impossible: he guarantees our feelings and our actions by the operation that for the author of *Swann* brings about the bankruptcy of our personality. And yet Newman's point of view is here clearly pragmatic, his conclusions are independent of any metaphysical postulate. We must conclude, therefore, either that Newman was not properly able to decipher his own experiences, or that there was in Proust's experience an element of corruption that prevented it from developing normally.

Newman's opinion is strangely reinforced by that of Meredith, who, totally opposed to the cardinal's mysticism, in no way anxious to provide rigorous connections with speculative thinking, and preoccupied only with relating to the individual and pursuing him by intuition and analysis, brings back from his investigation of man experiences that confirm Newman's criticism. 'Wilfrid', he says – Wilfrid Pole, the typical 'sentimentalist' according to Meredith – 'was a gallant fellow, with good stuff in him. But he was young. Ponder on that pregnant word, *for you are about to see him grow. . . .* One may also be a gallant fellow, and harsh, exacting, double-dealing,[4] and I know not what besides, in youth. The question asked by nature is *"Has he the heart to take and keep an impression?"* For, if he has, circumstances will force him on and carve the figure of a brave man out of that mass of contradictions.'[5]

Take and keep: Proust takes but does not keep, or rather he keeps in a very peculiar way, and it would perhaps be more correct to say *that he is kept by the object of his impression*. Indeed, his impression, as it filters through his consciousness, is not refined or reduced to essentials so as to form both a nucleus of emotional resistance and a body of tendencies orientated in a certain direction: instead of representing his experience by simplifying it, the impression projects his 'self' outside him and fixes it firmly in this experience. The process described by Newman and Meredith is carried out in reverse order in Proust. For them, to keep an impression is to transpose a particular concrete experience by harmonizing it with the spirit, to cut the mooring ropes of space and time belonging to this experience and confer on it the infinite plasticity of a living personality in constant growth. For Proust, it is to dissolve one's 'self' completely in the experience, set it according to the facts of time and space where it occurred and consequently *to cut it up into pieces, each of which is identified with a particular experience and lodged in a niche in time which thus acquires a fixedness and an exteriority that are the characteristics peculiar to space.* . . .

We cannot compare Proust to the great analysts of concrete thought without perceiving in his work a veritable turning of thought upon its head. Newman and Meredith think in terms of schemata and of procedures favouring the idea of progress; Proust thinks in terms of total reconstruction of past experiences. One can see how the form of Proust's experience inhibits the intelligence from favouring the slightest vital and spiritual progress, since in this case the intelligence, constantly invited to rethink an experience in its totality so as to give Proust that intuition of 'self' without which we cannot live, necessarily functions in the past. One can also see that this particular quirk of his thinking urges him on to exaggerate and show up in sharp relief a sensitive disposition that a different method and a healthier mode of living could perhaps have been capable of modifying. In Newman and Meredith, on the other hand, the permanence of the impression – because it is part of our spiritual being – builds up a strong mental force that allows the intelligence to fulfil its proper function, which is to go beyond the immediate experience and open up the future. And note that I have deliberately chosen two men who are not purely theoretical, who consolidate their feeling by their thought and prove their thought by their life. May we not then conclude that Proust has failed to discover the germ of unity and consistency belonging to the personality and that he has failed to dredge up in the net of his analysis the principle that is fundamental to real feeling? . . .

NOTES

All italics are in the text.

1 J. H. Newman, *An Essay in aid of a Grammar of Assent*, London, Burns, Oates & Co., 1870, p. 80. Italics added by Fernandez.

2 *Ibid.*, p. 81. Italics added by Fernandez.

3 *Ibid.*, pp. 84–5. Italics added by Fernandez.

4 Footnote by Fernandez: Cf. Proust: '. . . my words and thoughts as an ungrateful, egotistical and cruel young man'. It is very remarkable that in the psychological features that Proust attributes to himself, and that he attributes to human nature in general, Meredith sees the temporary characteristics of youth waiting to be modified by experience and the

natural process of human development. Is it possible that Proust suffered a premature fixation on the sensibility, an arrested growth that he would seem to have remedied subsequently by resorting to the intelligence as an expedient? This would perhaps explain the absence, in his work, of any spiritual progress in the proper sense of the word.

5 From Meredith's *Sandra Belloni*, London, Constable, 1897, p. 91. Italics added by Fernandez.

120. Jacques Massoulier on *Albertine disparue*
1926

Part of '*Albertine disparue* et le processus proustien', *Europe*, vol. 10, 1926, pp. 429–34.

Jacques Massoulier provides an appreciation which underscores the feeling that Proust has reached a point in his posthumous publications where he demands to be reassessed afresh.

. . . He gives himself up to us with an abandon and a sweetness for which we are sincerely grateful as we proceed from page to page. He does not think us unworthy of the smallest detail. He confides in us more frankly than in his own mother, as if confiding in himself. Therein resides a part of his charm.

Any other writer chooses a theme and imposes it on us; if he speaks to us about himself, he does so only to give us one or two facets of his personality, only the ones he deems interesting for the 'general public' or only the ones he is capable of distinguishing and treating introspectively. What Proust gives us, on the other hand, is the very substance of his life, transposed onto paper from one minute to the next.

Now that we have almost all the sections of his work, we can try, it seems to me, to define the process that led him to write in such an individual, novel and admirable a manner.

When very young, Proust, who was endowed with an exceptional intuitive sensibility, was struck by unexpected combinations of circumstances. A ray of sunshine, blue sea between apple-trees, three trees on an evening walk, a pebble on a path appeared to him at certain times as riddles he had to solve. . . . Emotions such as these deriving from nature, instinctive and intuitive, form, it seems to me, the basis of Proust's genius. Unfortunately, these sensations, so vivid that they used at times to bring tears to his eyes, were untranslatable. This is why he believed for a long time that he could never put pen to paper. He tried, however, and certain pieces of *Les Plaisirs et les jours* . . . are the sincere and sometimes slightly awkward reflection of this initial stage in his evolution.

A few years later, the music of Wagner left an indelible mark on him and had a decisive influence on the style of *A la recherche du temps perdu*. . . . This could be said to form the second stage. Yet he still could not write. He was certainly in control of the musical translation of his feelings, but not of the literary one. He needed to find a framework based on *intellect*[1] from which, from time to time, visions pure and simple could be made to emerge. He discovered this framework in the salons with which not only was his actual intuitive sensibility involved, but also his intelligence and his critical faculty. The data provided by these last two functions are, by their very nature, easily translated into words.

This development that made it possible for him to compose continued as he went on writing. He even succeeded in neglecting the initial visions so as to devote himself almost entirely to a process of analysis and introspection in which intuition, instead of being in command, became the hand-maiden of critical intelligence.

Though *A l'ombre des jeunes filles en fleurs* is swarming with those visions . . . already in *Le Côté de Guermantes* more space is devoted to analysis. . . .

In *La Prisonnière* evocations of childhood are rarer. Then again, as to the Guermantes, they are linked with that adolescent state of reverie while, in the meantime, being gradually stripped of their fascination. But, whereas his cerebral infatuation for the Duchesse de Guermantes scarcely interferes with these dreams and evocations, indeed even provokes them, his carnal love, with all its anxiety and pain, for Albertine takes over all his faculties, destroys the impassioned indifference of his youth and transforms him through suffering into a marvellous analyst. It is difficult to know which to admire most of these two facets of his work.

Finally, there is a third change that derives from the sudden death of Albertine. *Albertine disparue* reveals Proust as a man of action. Shattered by the passing of his lover, he realizes the pointlessness of his psychological attitude since, to use his own expression he has 'botched it' where both Albertine and Gilberte are concerned. Moreover, throughout his long subjection to the girl's enchantment, events have occurred in the Guermantes world, the origins of which he has not been able to pursue with his accustomed detail, and that confront him, when he ventures forth once more, in the fullness of their crude finality. He is struck down by these *facts*[2] which impose themselves without warning on his new confrontation with society. Stung by this brutal whiplash, he acts. He goes out, sends telegrams and leaves for Venice. . . .

The pages devoted to his sorrow at the death of Albertine are perhaps among the most appealing in the work. Yet Proust has certainly changed. At the time of his grand desire to be received by the Guermantes, that very desire, being quite a cerebral thing, inflamed only his imagination. . . . The sorrow over the death of Albertine, however, reveals someone suffering like any man in the world who is in love and jealous. So we are, perhaps, a little less charmed, now no longer presented with scintillating variety. We are, however, more gripped in human terms by a common grief that could be our own, our neighbour's, though expressed with a frankness unknown till now, with delightful naivety and in a language that is certainly still Proustian, but transformed, made to fit the feelings of the moment: *concentrated*.[3] Here there are now almost no long sentences turning in on themselves and containing a gleaming secret, but, often, short statements, direct and compelling because they spring straight from the heart.

Those subtle connections between social castes, people, things and atmosphere that his disinterested genius revealed to our thick wits have been put to flight by the crescendo of true, simple and painful love. Instead of the fine lace leisurely embroidered by his butterfly-like sensibility, a firm spurt of energy, almost positive, totally human, is born of this crystallization around Albertine. The emotions we feel are healthier. It even seems that the physical departure of Albertine at last gave Proust a place against which to brace himself. It is a fact that hits him with all its bulk in the very core of his being. Everything revolves around this fixed point.

Death and forgetfulness, alas, gradually efface Albertine's solid neck and large face arrested for one moment by grief after all the transformations of the Balbec days when she had been in turn a camellia, a sea-mist, a decorative motif. . . .

What is most striking in the second part of *Albertine disparue*, i.e. after his return to society, are the unusual transformations of people – unusual because of their abrupt revelation: Gilberte becoming Forcheville and marrying Saint-Loup, the friendship of the latter for the man who says 'I' in the book, a friendship that we were accustomed to consider for quite some time as pure and unassailable and that becomes tarnished by a crude revelation. Such reversals in our usual heroes, whose faults, vices and idiosyncrasies we were familiar with, force us to go back over the whole novel of which

Albertine disparue seems thus to be the outcome.

Before the onslaught of such a series of external events, Proust's memories of childhood would seem to disappear for ever. They discreetly resurface, however, in the last pages, softening a little Gilberte's crude revelation. Proust's first, intuitive, manner, the more curious and profound one, resurfaces notably in this image:

'. . . when all we met with in the village was the bluish, irregular and moving triangle of the sheep returning'.[4]

Here we meet again the three adjectives Proust finds necessary for his descriptions. Furthermore, this phrase is not entirely acceptable in purely intellectual terms. The word 'triangle', in fact, appears incorrect. For my part, I have never seen flocks of sheep moving forward in a triangle, only birds. Yet, if we set aside critical attitudes of mind, we feel that the word 'triangle' is well-chosen and that no other could coincide as much as this one with the mysterious and perfect fullness of this impression garnered haphazardly along with so many others.

The last page but one of *Albertine disparue* gives us, I like to think, one of the secrets of Proust's passionate nature.[5] Gilberte, in fact, informs him that, when only a child, she had beckoned to him to come to her one day when she physically wanted him. Proust thought that it was a sign of contempt. It turns out to be lucky for us, and no doubt for him. If he had replied to Gilberte's invitation, he would not have profited later, in Paris, of an anxiety in his love for her that resulted in bringing to life the smell of the dripping trees on the Champs-Elysées, thus colouring the people associated with Gilberte, and in fact all else besides.

If Albertine had been faithful to him, he would not have been able to make head or tail of Charlus.

In both cases, had he succeeded on the physical level, his mind would have remained stagnant. He would not have lived and would not have written.

If he had not been a failure with both Gilberte and Albertine, he would, perhaps, have been a failure himself instead of the composer of genius behind the marvellous symphony of *A la recherche du temps perdu* that was cut short only by death itself. And he even had time to analyse this in the fine pages devoted to the death of Bergotte, pages that we can put as a closing chord, once all his books have seen the light of day, at the end of the magnificent span of his masterpiece.

347

NOTES

1 In italics in the text.
2 *Idem.*
3 *Idem.*
4 Now in *Le Temps retrouvé*, Pléiade III, p. 691.
5 Now in *Le Temps retrouvé*, Pléiade III, pp. 693–4.

121. G. Turquet-Milnes on Proust and the European tradition

1926

Extract from *From Pascal to Proust*, London, Jonathan Cape, 1926, pp. 164–91.

G. Turquet-Milnes (1887–1977) represents the desire shortly after Proust's death to place him in a context of development. Here we have a comprehensive attempt to relate Proust to the European tradition by means of frequent and far-ranging comparisons, to explain his vision in terms of the restrictions surrounding a sick man's view of the world and to justify his obsessions with time and memory by finding a philosophical basis for them in Bergson.

After careful reading of the greater part of contemporary French literature, together with the already considerable bulk (and all has not yet been published) of the work of Marcel Proust, one cannot fail to be struck by the fact that Proust is essentially a sick man who will not react against his malady, and that, as such, he is the representative of a group of writers who, while seeking by means of the hyperæsthesia of their feelings to deify their desires, succeed only in becoming the citizens of a *città dolente* which still awaits its Dante. A sick man: Proust was that all his life, living since 1910 in a room more or less filled with fumigations for relief of his asthma, and finally scarcely going out at all except at night. . . . Proust's genius was Proust's morbid temperament, a malady of the soul. . . .

We have had French writers who were sick men before Proust, and the epithet of madmen has not been sparingly applied to them by the healthy, but these thinkers, like great Pascal or subtle Maine de Biran, following the classic French tradition, sought to turn their sickness to good use, neglecting their self, or at least studying it only in so far as such study should be beneficial to humanity. When suffering threw them upon their own resources, their mind being thus forced to produce from its own meditation or memories, some rule of life, gained in depth, and thus acquired psychological knowledge that no outside teaching could reveal. In a measure this is also true of Proust: he could not escape that law which forces every thinking being to concentrate and reflect upon the problem of its destiny, and it is as well to admit at once that he owes it to his unhealthy – deliberately unhealthy – sensitiveness, that he studied himself, watched himself living with so infinitely careful an attention that he surpasses the great self-analysts, Benjamin Constant or Amiel or Meredith. He uses his malady as a microscope which shows him on an enormously enlarged scale all the molecules which swarm and seethe in his heart. That is how he came to give a new perception of Duration which makes it fitting to set his name beside that of Bergson.

There is then in Proust an unhealthy attraction about illness for illness's sake, just as in his work there is a morbid attraction about vice for vice's sake, a liking for what is base or vile just for the pleasure of forcing us to admit that there are base or vile elements in human nature. Every lover is a seeker of anguish. . . . Marcel Proust in love is very like Marcel Proust in sickness. Both seek deliberately the art of self-torture. . . .

Whilst then the sick men of genius – a Pascal or a Maine de Biran – being chiefly preoccupied with their soul's salvation or the functions of their brain, seek to drive out of their minds all that is false or merely artificial, and above all 'all lusts of the flesh or of the eyes, all pride of life', the better to be penetrated by eternal truths, Marcel Proust, enslaved by his education and his instincts, remains always imprisoned in the dominion of the senses. . . . Far too from any religious feeling, Proust never enters that realm which for want of a better word we call 'Grace'. . . . He is of the earth earthy, and being an artist very sure of his craft, he takes for models a little group of French *mondains*, products of idleness and its kindred vices, men much more artistic and cleverer than the rakes of the Regency.

Somewhere in his *La Prisonnière* Proust evokes the presence of Dostoievsky, he writes very acutely about him, and he is very careful to note the original trait in the Russian which makes him see that 'love and bitter hatred, kindness and treachery, timidity and insolence, are but degrees in one and the same nature'. There is something of that in Proust. His sinners, Baron de Charlus,

349

M. de Châtellerault, M. de Vaugoubert, have a double life – Jekyll and Hyde – though Proust adds the piquant element in that the high rank of these *seigneurs* seems to have no other effect than to make their fall among the *canaille* the greater.

The vision of immortal sin would seem to exhilarate Proust like some horrible concierge primed with low gossip. We should tremble for him were it not that an art about which he has written wonderful passages comes to save him from himself, the art of music. Clearly Proust is of Stendhal's opinion that we enjoy music only in the dreams it brings us – dreams like an eighteenth-century tapestry with cupids on a background of roses, when Albertine plays Rameau, or of Eastern steppes where sound dies in snow-muffled distances, when she plays Borodin. . . .

Proust offers us an original, but not a new, answer to the question asked by countless ages: What is the purpose of music? The answer is more or less of a commentary on the famous myth of the music of the spheres. . . . Proust, by very reason of his being steeped in Bergsonian philosophy, comes very near this conception. For without wishing to depreciate Proust's undeniable talents, it is perhaps not pedantic to point out here that in a sense he is following exactly the same path as Bergson in his effort to understand the audible and inaudible harmony of the world.

This question of music may be seen as the substratum of all modern philosophy as it unquestionably is the factor of its beauty. Music is the lyrical cry of the modern soul tired out with freedom and the effort to rise superior to itself. Its astonishing power lies in its expression of the lyrical soaring of a conscience awakening to Beauty, the impetuous departure of multiple fugitive impressions, ignorant of ideas and words, first essays of the primitive myths. It matters little to us now whether Schopenhauer be right or wrong to see in music the inexpressible thought of the inner principle of the universe, the absolute foundation of things making us leap in the dance as it makes us love.

For the moment one thing matters: music is the work of our self which changes so completely that what we thought even today no longer belongs to us. Just as human personality is divided into countless numbers of beings ceaselessly in pursuit of one another, so music with its fluidity, its harmonies, its discords, and its syncopations, is composed of a ceaselessly changing becoming.

That is why Bergson and Proust attach such great importance to memory, the unconscious and dreams. According to Bergson memory is something other than a function of the brain, and there is not a difference of degree, but of kind, between perception and recollection. . . .

The novelist loses none of his originality – on the contrary – for plunging his roots into the rich soil of a philosophic system whose greatness is undeniable: far from being a destroyer – as has been so often said – Proust becomes a true constructor. This philosophy enables him to revolutionise the novelist's art: since he may devote many pages to a happening which could have lasted only a few instants, while, like the astronomer, he may condense mathematical time into a few lines, one might almost say a few figures.

It may be well to point out that Proust is in this point less of an innovator than may at first appear. Long before Proust, Marivaux and his disciple Sterne had written novels like the cinema moving at infinitely diminished speed. Proust's enemies should study his illustrious predecessors. Sterne is past master (perhaps even more than Marivaux, as is natural, seeing that he followed him) in this art of reacting in the most piquant, unexpected and lingering fashion to the smallest object visible to his perception – a woman or a chance phrase. The capacity for finding food for continuous and gaily-profound meditation in some tiny fact is certainly the stamp of an original mind. Read Sterne again after reading Proust, and you cannot fail to be struck by the resemblance between a certain aspect of their brains: both have a comic gift, the salt of mockery, mimicry which will ever keep their work fresh.

These comparisons would have been eminently pleasing to Proust, convinced as he was of the existence of his many selves, but there is a risk that they may lead us to neglect Proust's really wonderful sensitiveness which led him to quite marvellous discoveries when he meditates about his grandmother or about his mother and his family, or simply about nature and an apple-tree in bloom.

M. Albert Thibaudet in his study of Marcel Proust reminds us of the novelist's Jewish descent on his mother's side and his Catholic heredity on his father's, and naturally evokes the figure of that other son of a Jewess, Montaigne.[1] We must tread carefully on such slippery ground, but we may at least say of both men that they are haunted by two similar feelings: the dismay at fleeting time which hastens the approach of death, and a real need of balancing the account of true realities, of making a delicately graduated scale of certitude in all things. They are obsessed by the Heraclitean paradox of the perpetual imperceptible change in all things: but while the one seeks refuge in antiquity and with the past masters of wisdom, the other turns to art and æsthetic culture. Ruskin is a veritable prophet in his eyes. . . .

If posterity reads Proust it will be for his symbolic rather than for his literary value. There is no need to appeal to medical science nor to search in his ancestors for the explanation of his malady or his work. Never does one realise so well as with him the futility and the impotence of so-called physiological criticism. The world is ruled by the spirit, and what is true of the universe is true of literary history and of novels – no one figures therein except by the justification of a symbol. Proust would have agreed to that.

Proust's real ancestors are certainly the romantic heroes, René, Manfred, Werther, with their spiritual fevers and ideal despair; still more direct ancestors are the neo-romantics with their combination of excited sensitiveness and deep culture, and their effort to see with their eyes rather than with their brains. Not only Adolphe, Obermann or Dominique, but Baudelaire with his countless descendants, Rimbaud as well as Robert de Montesquiou. Most direct ancestors of all are the English school of Swinburne with their master Pater.

The critic who is interested in the 'natural history of minds' cannot but be astonished as he reads his Proust after reading his Pater at the very striking resemblances between the two. Should we see therein a freak of nature, or on the contrary the working of a profound law governing human intelligence which, once started on a certain path, must of necessity arrive at the same goal? Proust is really a second Marius the Epicurean who lives in the real and the concrete, and, to use Pater's phrase, 'by system in reminiscence'. Proust's intellectual activity has never been so well summed up as by Pater some thirty years before his time: 'a strange trick memory sometimes played him; for, with no natural gradation, what was of last month or of yesterday, of to-day even, would seem as far off, as entirely detached from him, as things of ten years ago.'

Proust is a hedonist to whom the grace of God . . . or Plato was mainly lacking, because he never *really* loved nature. Pater has an illuminating little sentence which tells us a very great deal about Marius and explains his spiritual end: 'In those grand hot summers he would have imprisoned the very perfume of the flowers.' Not so Proust, he was never more than the toy of the tropical garden in which he shut himself. The hothouse wherein he breathed the heavy perfumes of most deadly flowers was that little select world in Paris which has no place for a really religious man. In all Pater's work we see the ghost of Pascal overshadowing him, and in the end Pater died, pen in hand, trying to understand the author of the *Pensées*.

But Proust in his eternal pursuit of singular sensations understood that he would never be so completely himself as when relating his own past. Thenceforward humanity is resolved into juvenility. He is always the *Child in the House*. Universal man in his work becomes nothing more than a grown-up child. Sensitiveness becomes the source of all knowledge. Proust's real field is the pursuit of the obscure forces of the human being, the impressionism of the infinitesimal. Whatever may be the final judgement passed on his work, we should be grateful to him for taking us behind the scenes of the unconscious and for having reclaimed a little ground from the seas of mystery encircling us.

NOTE

1 Cf. No. 68, p. 201.

122. Janko Lavrin on Proust and Dostoevsky
1927

Part of a lecture on Proust and Dostoevsky delivered to the Anglo-Russian Literary Society, now in the *Slavonic Review*, vol. 5, 1926–7, pp. 609–27.

Janko Lavrin (1887–1986), the distinguished authority on Russian literature, claims that Proust and Dostoevsky have little in common, yet his study is illuminating for the contrasts he describes. His examination of their psychological approaches establishes the important place of the emotions and the intellect in their analyses of behaviour.

While Dostoyevsky's 'psychology' at its best is, in a way, beyond normality and abnormality, Proust is more at home on that ground which could be perhaps called *before*[1] the normal and the abnormal. In both regions there is an interesting fusion (as well as confusion) of man's conscious and unconscious elements – a flux in which 'good' and 'evil' are often indiscriminately mixed up; in which the greatest contrasts (the ambivalence of impulses, feelings and emotions) 'exist side by side'. This evasive boundary line between the conscious and the unconscious has been crossed by both Dostoyevsky and Proust. But as each of them works in a different direction, the result of their work is bound to be widely different too. Dostoyevsky's psychology

353

is above all a spiritual quest and a struggle with his own 'subconscious' monsters which threaten to destroy his soul. Hence his dangerous divings – a smoking torch in his hand – into those labyrinths of the human spirit which are full of unexplored abysses, and of weird apocalyptic beasts with a cruel lustre in their eyes.

The ground of Proust's art is safer. If Dostoyevsky looks for new spiritual continents, Proust confines himself to average sensations and emotions, as well as to average inversions, which he investigates down to their ultimate 'atomic' elements hidden in our subconscious. So much so that feelings which on the surface seem simple, suddenly prove to be extremely complicated underneath. Take Proust's analysis of Swann's love for Odette, or that of his own love for Albertine. There is no more detailed and finer dissection of these feelings in the whole of modern literature. Constant's *Adolphe* and Stendhal's analytical intuitions look bald in comparison with his sharp and patient eye which catches every change, every *nuance*, and disentangles even the most confused subconscious fringes of our 'simple' psychic states.

It goes of itself that this plane of psychology does not need any 'higher' pretexts, because it is self-sufficient. The only thing required is a calm æsthetic interest coupled with complete objectivity and integrity of statement. And this we do find in Proust. While Dostoyevsky often gives the impression of a spiritual Sysiphus who vainly tries to alleviate his burden by unravelling its mystery, Proust is above all a calm anatomist of psychological 'infinitesimals'. He never raises his voice, never forgets himself, and what he sees he renders in a sure although in a too explicit way. Contrary to Dostoyevsky's fury and frenzy, Proust is the very embodiment of a dispassionate intellectual observer. He seems to be more interested in an analysis of feelings than in the feelings themselves. If Dostoyevsky puts irrational intuition above logical reason, Proust always tries to comprehend intellectually even the irrational chaos of our subconscious *ego*. Yet he is not averse to considering Dostoyevsky's standpoint, as we see from his conversation with Albertine (in *La Prisonnière*).[2]

NOTE

1 In italics in the text.
2 See Pléiade III, pp. 378 ff., for instance p. 379:

Dostoevksy, instead of presenting things in logical order, i.e. beginning with the cause, first of all shows us the effect, the striking illusion. This is the way Dostoevsky presents his characters. Their actions appear to us as deceptive as those effects of Elstir's where the sea gives the impression of being in the sky. We are quite amazed to learn later that some sly gentleman is basically an excellent fellow, or the opposite.

It seems that Proust was beginning to be interested in Dostoevsky in 1897. He wrote to a friend: 'Who wrote the Brothers Karamazoff?' (*Corr. II*, p. 211). Cf. also *Contre Sainte-Beuve*, ed. P. Clarac and Y. Sandre, Paris, Gallimard, 1971, pp. 644–5.

123. Jessie Murray on Proust and Ruskin
1927

Part of 'Marcel Proust as critic and disciple of Ruskin', *Nineteenth Century*, April 1927, pp. 614–19.

Jessie Murray, after introducing Proust as translator of Ruskin and critic of some of his views, goes on to draw important parallels in aesthetic approach that reveal their affinities and divergences. She had previously in *Le Mercure de France* (1 July 1926) made similar points in her comparisons, emphasizing especially Proust's debt to the visual qualities of Ruskin's style: 'It was not as a thinker, but as a painter, that Ruskin was Proust's incomparable guide.' In her second article she perceptively and eloquently reveals how Ruskin acts as guide to a young disciple, who then transcends that influence by his own originality.

. . . The spell that Ruskin was able to exercise over other minds must have been very great indeed when Proust, after condemning most of his arguments and setting aside almost all his doctrines, could still say that he was one of the greatest writers who ever lived. Ruskin, he says, gave him the power of appreciating beauty, of looking on the world with new vision. He reminds us of Charlotte Brontë, saying that *Modern Painters* seemed to give her new eyes, and, in fact, all those who have come under the influence of Ruskin have spoken in exactly the same way of the increased power of vision he gave them.

After reading Ruskin's *Bible of Amiens*, Proust set off on a '*pèlerinage ruskinien*' to see those mediæval stones that Ruskin had loved so much, and this pilgrimage seemed to him a much truer form of hero-worship than a visit to Ruskin's grave or his birthplace. In the stones of Amiens Ruskin had sought chiefly the soul of mediæval sculptors, and Proust, in his turn, seeks the thought of Ruskin. Not Amiens itself, but Amiens as it was re-created in the mind of Ruskin, was the object of his pilgrimage. Moreover, it is this artistic recreation of a thing in the mind of an artist that will be found later on throughout the whole work of Proust to be the one essential thing in his conception of art, nay almost the one essential thing in his conception of life – the sole reality in a world of illusion. To show us the world as he sees it and not as he knows it to be is the work of a true artist. Elstir, the painter who plays such an important part in the work of Proust, is an artist and a creator in this Ruskinian sense. The roses he paints in a water-colour, for example, are, according to Proust, a work of true creation just as much as if, like a skilful gardener, he had grown a new variety of rose.

Marcel, the hero of *A la Recherche du Temps Perdu*, owes much of his education in art to the work of Elstir, and what he constantly admires in him reminds us very much of those qualities which Ruskin so eloquently praised in Turner. With increased powers of vision, Marcel, initiated by Elstir, contemplates a new heaven and a new earth, and for the very reasons which made Ruskin predict that generations yet unborn would see Nature through the eyes of Turner. Not knowledge, but the intuitive vision of reality, is the essence of a true artist's work. This being so, it is the artist's duty to express that part of reality of which he has been granted this interior vision. Proust is in complete agreement with Ruskin in believing that the artist has no choice but to obey the voice that dictates to him. For Ruskin, it is the voice of God; for Proust, the voice of the mysterious prompting of the subconscious mind. Art is the Lamp of Sacrifice and the artist must give his life for it. This doctrine of necessity and obedience is of the utmost importance both in Ruskin's work and in Proust's. Ruskin looked upon himself as a scribe writing down a divine message; Proust considered himself merely as the instrument through which certain thoughts were communicated to humanity. Both Ruskin and Proust accepted this yoke of discipline, but it must be said that in the case of Proust the sacrifice was accomplished without even a gleam of that eternal hope for which Ruskin lived. He knew that instead of discovering at each step of his work the Divine Being he would never find anything but illusion and emptiness.

It is obvious to all readers of Proust that though Ruskin may have taught him to see, yet the world he contemplated was very different from that of Ruskin. Nevertheless, Ruskin, engrossed in nature and in art, and Proust, making psychological investigations into hitherto uncharted regions of the mind, very frequently move along parallel lines. Both aim chiefly at tracking down falsehood, the one in our representation of nature, the other in our interpretation of sensation. This similarity is all the more marked because Proust, in his psychological explorations, very often uses even the language of art, and treats his subject as if it were a design of which he wished to criticise the perspective. Again, as Ruskin is constantly proclaiming the interdependence of things, and that there is no such thing as unconnected colour, but always colour influenced by light, by neighbouring colour, etc., so Proust is always alive to the same 'relativity', and even when he deals with the simplest sensation he realises that it cannot be studied as an isolated thing, but has its place, as it were, in the great canvas of our life, where it stands in proximity to, and under the influence of, many other manifestations of our conscious and unconscious life.

Ruskin as a painter and Proust as a psychologist instinctively dwell on the study of perspective, and Proust, when he examines the workings of the unconscious mind, is content merely to inspect and never proceeds to sum up or to theorise. He aims at viewing things from every possible angle, but he is no more anxious to seek an explanatory theory than Ruskin is to find a formula by which to sum up the different aspects of any beautiful object, be it stone, or moss, or cathedral, after he has carefully examined it from all the points of the compass. Proust feels that to see things in their true perspective is the only end worth aiming at, and if we are bent on achieving that, then the desire to judge or condemn or weigh up in a moral balance will have no meaning for us. It will be something quite irrelevant to the more important business of seeing things in perspective. On this point, of course, there is a gulf fixed between Ruskin and Proust. As a theologian and a puritan, Ruskin puts morals higher than art, whereas the only morality Proust admits is that which compels the artist to sacrifice everything to the one duty of giving to the world the beauty of his art. Nor does Proust find any reason why the artist should thus obey or why he should feel morally bound to strive after the one elusive form which is artistically satisfying although difficult to attain. And yet it is so, and Proust feels as if it was a mysterious moral obligation laid on him in a previous life which compels the poet or the artist to be satisfied with nothing less than a perfect expression of beauty. It is strange that, whereas Ruskin subordinated everything to morality, Proust, in his turn, should regard all moral considerations as being totally irrelevant and that his only conception of a moral bond should be obedience on the part of an artist to the vision of beauty. Surely, if Ruskin made art the handmaiden of morals, Proust has narrowed the scope of morality by considering it to have no existence except as a necessary factor in artistic creation.

This idea of discipline as applied to the artist is at the root of Proust's conception of style. He looks upon the form and even the words of a man's work as being no more chosen by him than his dreams are. Ruskin liked to think of himself as a prophet unfolding a scroll and not knowing what his message was going to be, and Proust tells us that not only in the choice of what he says, but in the selection of his form of expression, he obeys, not his intellect, but an involuntary prompting as sure in its working as the instinct which brings a homing-pigeon home.

Another idea of equal importance in the work of Proust, and which can likewise be traced back to his study of Ruskin, is the conception of memory as being a necessary factor in artistic creation. The part played in the work of Proust by involuntary memory is well known, and Proust in his criticism of Ruskin is very conscious of the fact that Ruskin is constantly resuscitating countless sensations which have been stored away in his mind, and that to write the greater part of his work he simply 'published his memory.' The belief that it is involuntary and not intelligent memory that brings back the past most clearly, although it is one of the most original things in Proust's work, is found in Ruskin, although, of course, the latter does not attach to it the same importance as Proust does, or make it one of the main ideas of his work. Proust, bringing back forgotten days of his childhood by merely tasting a 'madeleine', reminds us of Ruskin resuscitating forgotten scenes of the past because of the form of a branch which he involuntarily recalls. (Locke, whom Ruskin admired and read, and on whose work (*Essay Concerning Human Understanding*) he modelled the plan of *Modern Painters*, had already expressed the same idea when dealing with 'involuntary perceptions.')

It is certain that Ruskin's influence on Proust was only possible because there was a strong affinity between them. They had the same acuteness of perception, the same remarkable receptivity, the same powerful visual memory, and the same capacity for being more attracted by irrational beauty than by intellectual truth. Proust, by far the more intellectual of the two, nevertheless puts aside his intelligence as it were, and seeks chiefly that kind of beauty which mere intelligence can neither produce nor analyse. It is this characteristic in Proust which causes him, though he disagrees with all the doctrines of Ruskin and has nothing in common with him in the world of action which he regards as thoroughly 'inadequate mode of expression,' to feel the irresistible spell of Ruskin's artistic vision and the captivating though irrational beauty of his words.

Finally, this unmistakable influence exercised by Ruskin over Proust seems to bring together in a rather unexpected way two currents of literature which otherwise are very remote from each other in our thoughts – namely, the school of Victorian socialist and moral literature headed by Carlyle and Ruskin and the much more subtle psychological writings of post-war France. It also brings a new tribute to the name of Ruskin by showing that his work, '*l'esthétique d'un homme du nord spiritualiste et protestant*', as Taine called it, has, more than a generation later, been very differently judged and revaluated by a greater mind than Taine's.

124. E. M. Forster on musical and rhythmic patterns in *La Recherche*
1927

Extract from his chapter on 'Pattern and rhythm' in *Aspects of the Novel*, London, Arnold, 1927; reissued 1974, pp. 113–15.

E. M. Forster (1879–1970) in his enthusiasm for Proust's work uses it as a yardstick to measure the achievements of the English and the Russian novel: 'No English novelist is as great as Tolstoy – that is to say, has given so complete a picture of man's life, both on its domestic and heroic side. No English novelist has explored man's soul as deeply as Dostoyevsky. And no novelist anywhere has analysed the modern consciousness as successfully as Marcel Proust' (p. 4). In the following extract he draws out the advantages of the *leitmotiv* effect of musical phrases and associations.

Rhythm in the easy sense is illustrated by the work of Marcel Proust.

Proust's conclusion has not been published yet, and his admirers say that when it comes everything will fall into its place, times past will be recaptured and fixed, we shall have a perfect whole. I do not believe this. The work seems to me a progressive rather than an aesthetic confession, for with the elaboration of Albertine the author is getting tired. Bits of news may await us, but it will be surprising if we have to revise our opinion of the whole book. The book is chaotic, ill-constructed, it has and will have no external shape; and yet it hangs together because it is stitched internally, because it contains rhythms.

There are several examples (the photographing of the grandmother is one of them), but the most important, from the binding point of view, is the 'little phrase' in the music of Vinteuil. The little phrase does more than anything else – more even than the jealousy which successively destroys Swann, the hero and Charlus – to make us feel that we are in a homogeneous world. We first hear Vinteuil's name in hideous circumstances. The musician is dead – an obscure little country organist, unknown to fame – and his daughter is defiling his memory. The horrible scene is to radiate in several directions, but it passes.

Then we are at a Paris salon. A violin sonata is performed, and a little phrase from its andante catches the ear of Swann and steals into his life. It is always a living being, but takes various forms. For a time it attends his love for Odette. The love affair goes wrong, the phrase is forgotten, we forget it. Then it breaks out again when he is ravaged by jealousy, and now it attends his misery and past happiness at once, without losing its own divine character. Who wrote the sonata? On hearing it is by Vinteuil, Swann says: 'I once knew a wretched little organist of that name – it couldn't be by him.' But it is, and Vinteuil's daughter and her friend transcribed and published it.

That seems all. The little phrase crosses the book again and again, but as an echo, a memory; we like to encounter it, but it has no binding power. Then, hundreds and hundreds of pages on, when Vinteuil has become a national possession, and there is talk of raising a statue to him in the town where he has been so wretched and so obscure, another work of his is performed – a posthumous septet. The hero listens – he is in an unknown, rather terrible universe while a sinister dawn reddens the sea. Suddenly for him, and for the reader too, the little phrase of the sonata recurs – half heard, changed, but giving complete orientation, so that he is back in the country of his childhood with the knowledge that it belongs to the unknown.

We are not obliged to agree with Proust's actual musical descriptions (they are too pictorial for my own taste), but what we must admire is his use of rhythm in literature, and his use of something which is akin by nature to the effect it has to produce – namely a musical phrase. Heard by various people – first by Swann, then by the hero – the phrase of Vinteuil is not tethered: it is not a banner such as we find George Meredith using – a double-blossomed cherry tree to accompany Clara Middleton, a yacht in smooth waters for Cecilia Halkett. A banner can only reappear, rhythm can develop, and the little phrase has a life of its own, unconnected with the lives of its auditors, as with the life of the man who composed it. It is almost an actor, but not quite, and that 'not quite' means that its power has gone towards stitching Proust's book together from the inside, and towards the establishment of beauty and the ravishing of the reader's memory. There are times when the little phrase – from its gloomy inception, through the sonata, into the septet – means everything to the readers. There are times when it means nothing and is forgotten, and this seems to me the function of rhythm in fiction: not to be there all the time like a pattern, but by its lovely waxing and waning to fill us with surprise and freshness and hope.

125. Gabriel Marcel on *Le Temps retrouvé*

1927

Review of *Le Temps retrouvé* in *L'Europe nouvelle*, 12 November 1927, pp. 1501–2.

Gabriel Marcel (1889–1973), philosopher, dramatist, and critic, admires *Le Temps retrouvé* for the grandeur of Proust's conception of time as duration in spite of flaws in composition.

. . . As was to be supposed, *Le Temps retrouvé* is the act of inner recuperation that allows the *artist* to grasp, to possess in its actuality that very substance of life which, because of the state of intermittence and atomization to which we are as mortal creatures bound, has throughout his history constantly escaped *man* and deluded him. The pages in which Proust describes those moments of ideal achievement in which his whole life, by an act of concentration and transcendence, receives and simultaneously endows itself with its ultimate meaning, will without any doubt count among the most memorable he has written. This marks the central point of Proust's 'rose-window', or more precisely of the secular mysticism from which the whole work derives – the mysticism of pure memory that, beginning with Combray, the Vinteuil sonata and the towers of Martinville, gradually emerged as the fundamental melody, or even the ground bass of this vast novel. The word mysticism will perhaps be thought surprising; yet it is the only one that suits for here it is literally a question of salvation, of an intuition of, and a technique for, salvation – conditions that are the only ones that allow consciousness to be liberated from the feeling of its own mortality. It is through the resurrection of memory, drained of everything that abstract intelligence brings to it which could adulterate it, and through this resurrection alone that, in spite of the lacunae in our evolving state, the completeness of our inner being can be realized.

[Quotes *Le Temps retrouvé*, Pléiade III, pp. 870–1 where the force of memory is described as releasing the 'essence of things'.]

From this point of view *La Recherche du temps perdu* appears to be totally directed towards a certain way of looking at Spinoza's theorem: 'We sense intuitively and know that we are immortal.'[1] Except that the experience described here, instead of being the permanent base of our spiritual nature and always accessible to the thinker, is in Proust's eyes the result of a kind of miracle, of a sharp break in the mechanism that rules our inner life. We are in fact so constructed that reality is generally perceived by us only at the precise moment when the imagination, which had previously enjoyed it and granted it a value, is reduced to silence, so much so that the thwarting of our expectations is inherent in the nature of things. It will only be at certain privileged moments that the past will be able to find its voice in the present without however losing its wonderful freshness and without the present that it proceeds through neutralizing or extinguishing it. We must not therefore be taken in by the abstract words that Proust sometimes uses to express his thought on this matter, and especially by the rather muddled expression: the *essence of things*. In fact what the Proustian odyssey of the mind in search of itself, as it flees before the eternal flow of time, results in is a sensualism of the timeless.

It is, however, important to observe that there exists a strict correlation between this mysticism of time regained and the picture which is so strangely systematic in its very pessimism that fills the final volumes of *La Recherche du temps perdu*. Even while admitting that Proust's world . . . obeys an internal logic by virtue of which the aristocracy and the upper classes gradually blend into each other, we must, it seems to me, recognize that for the writer it is above all a question of producing in the reader's mind as ample an impression as possible of change, of perpetual recasting, and especially of dissolution and of crumbling away – and the contrast sustained in this way between a human world that is both illusory and actual where everything wears out and is destroyed, a world of alterations and endless substitutions, and the ideal order in which this world is restructured and restored, cannot fail to be compared with the antitheses that form the basis of so many sermons on the fragility of human affections and the eternal quality of things sacred. . . .

[Quotes from 'De ma vie passée' to 'si instructif de l'amour'; see Pléiade III, p. 910; goes on to introduce Proust's obsession with seeing sexual inversion all around him.]

In my view it is scarcely possible to deny that this strange didacticism to some extent spoils the final parts of *La Recherche du temps perdu*. Proust no longer succeeds in interesting us fully in the final transformations of Gilberte and Saint-Loup, even of M. de Charlus or of Mme Verdurin now promoted to the rank of Princesse de Guermantes. It is only too obvious that in his heart Proust has dismissed them, that he is anxious to have done with that kind of refutation they make of each other which will put paid to them once and for all. But what is admirable and surely unique in literature is, in fact, this gradual irresistible process by which he removes one by one all the creatures conjured up by his magical imagination. He stands totally alone on the empty stage, with his work still to be completed, a work through which he will try to perpetuate – by building it into its structure – the fleeting miracle of memory.

[Quotes from 'Je ne savais pas' to 'la porte funéraire'; see Pléiade III, p. 1040.]

I know of nothing in French literature more extraordinary than the great diptych on which the whole work comes to a close – on the one hand, the picture of a society eaten away by old age as if by an acid, already barely recognizable and lit by the cross-lighting of the fires of hell; on the other, a meditation shot through with recollections and premonitions in which all life takes shape and in which the vast poem takes on embryonic form and already comes into being. Now we see all the peaks of the past taking their places according to newly discovered vistas; between so many apparently unconnected episodes a link is revealed that not only allows us to place them but confers also on each a kind of ultimate justification. . . . Each encounter with the past, each experience allows us at last to discern the actual mission given it by a possibly blind destiny, but one gifted for all that with an inexhaustible imaginative power – a mission that is not only uniquely individual but infinitely diversified:

Just as a bucket being pulled up by a windlass keeps swinging to this side and that against the rope, there was no person in my life, not even a single thing almost that did not have at various times different roles to play in it. I had only to find some social acquaintance, even a material object that had been lurking for years in my memory for me to see that life had gone on winding round the remembrance threads of all kinds that finally coated it with the lovely velvet sheen of the passing years such as you might see in an old park encasing a mere water-pipe with a sheath of emerald. (Pléiade III, p. 973)

Imperceptibly, however, the dantesque image and the meditation combine together and both melt into a finale of extraordinary orchestral richness in which the countless themes of the work, reduced to their purest melodic essence, reappear, reinforce each other and interconnect. Ultimately, it seems that all man's individual sensations of duration – the duration of social groups, the duration of individual persons, the duration of feelings – come together to form the august countenance of pure Duration itself. The whole of this final part of the book – chilled by the breath of mortality blowing over it – is like some broad, shallow-banked estuary in which clouds are reflected at twilight, while the sun sinks inevitably into the Ocean where it will soon be swallowed up.

NOTES

All italics are in the text.
1 Spinoza, *Ethics*, Part V; Note to Proposition 23.

126. Benjamin Crémieux on
Le Temps retrouvé
1928

Review of *Le Temps retrouvé* in *La Nouvelle Revue française*, 1 January 1928, pp. 113–18.

A description of *Le Temps retrouvé* that brings out its importance as lynchpin for the whole work and as an explanation of Proust's justification of existence by means of an aesthetic.

If, in many respects, the two volumes of *Le Temps retrouvé* confirm the ideas of an alert reader as to the content and the intention of Proust's work, the way in which they broaden its foundations, its significance and, one might say, its finality is an unpredictable one, though one that would not have been unpredictable to an even more alert reader. This explains why, in spite of repetitions, the lack of 'organization' and the numerous grammatical lapses . . . these drafts of *Le Temps retrouvé* occupy, in the work's overall pattern, a privileged place and perhaps, alongside *Du côté de chez Swann*, the most important one. From the point of departure to the point of arrival, the circle closes so perfectly that the inevitable itinerary through Balbec and Sodom and Gomorrah seems abridged thereby and, so to speak, skimmed over.

No one today questions any longer the unity of *A la recherche du temps perdu*, no one subscribes any more to that assertion made in the *Hommage* of 1923: 'Proust does not compose. . . .' But some recall the announcement made in 1913 of a novel in three volumes, and while admitting the initial desire for composition, basing themselves on the amplitude Proust allowed himself in *A la recherche du temps perdu* and in his 'additions', they deny that that initial desire was entirely respected by him. They quote in their defence the strings of digressions. They willingly agree that Proust may have had a precise plan to start off with, but they consider that, as he went along, he lost all sense of proportion. *Le Temps retrouvé* bears witness to the fact that this is not the case and that the composition of *A la recherche du temps perdu* is even more rigorous than it could have appeared till now, just as *Le Temps retrouvé* shows that the subject Proust deals with, far from being restricted and particular, is vaster still than it appeared even to those who saw in it the fusion of an aristocratic and a bourgeois society, the fusion of the Guermantes and the Verdurin-Swanns. . . .

The sociological subject is in fact the birth, life, death and renaissance of a society, the eternal mixing of social groups by time that destroys and renews them in about half a century, just as the psychological subject of the work is the evolution throughout time's duration of a certain number of representative characters.

As for the composition, the matinée at the Princesse de Guermantes', which takes up two thirds of the second volume of *Le Temps retrouvé*, finally does enlighten us on its subject. What remained to be justified were those enormous sections devoted to society receptions. We realize now that the reception at Mme de Villeparisis', the dinner at the Duchesse de Guermantes', the first evening reception by the Princesse de Guermantes, the Verdurin soirée, the matinée given by the post-war Princesse de Guermantes, who is none other, this time, than Mme Verdurin, represent, according to an expression used recently by Ramon Fernandez, 'spatial sections, cut into the duration of time', into the duration of this society and its constituent elements. There may be no room to say so here, but nothing would be easier than to show how the episodes involving those social ceremonies rigorously correspond to one another, how also those ceremonies are so many altars and look-out points marking the pilgrimage of a society in the act of evolving (as every society always is), what Proust calls 'perpetual re-groupings of forces' destined to 'bring out the most contrastive faces' of men's natures and to vary the reader's points of view. The same goes for those repeats of an identical theme; thus, Swann's jealous love for Odette, Marcel's jealous love for Albertine, his love for Mme de Guermantes and his love for Gilberte balance out to provide a more complete proof of important psychological laws.

Note also, as verification of this rigorous composition, the necessary links between the slightest detail and the whole, the 'interlocking' and the explanation of the slightest allusions; e.g. it was Théodore who had written such a charming letter to Marcel on his article in the *Figaro*; the humiliation of Mme de Saint-Euverte at the Guermantes soirée by the Baron de Charlus was preparation for the final scene where the baron bows to her with such humility on the Champs-Elysées.

If there is any point in insisting on the composition of *A la recherche du temps perdu*, it is because it is of paramount importance to the whole work. This composing – an obsession with Proust – serves to show to advantage and give a structure to that didactic, intellectual part of his work, intended to set off the poetic, extra-temporal reality which is 'in too short supply for the work of art to be composed solely of it', that part of his work that is made up of those 'truths sifted by the intelligence', 'truths that the intelligence extracts directly from reality', 'truths relating to the passions, natures and manners of man' and that in *A la recherche du temps perdu*, refer for the most part to Time, 'to Time in whose stream men, societies and nations bathe and are transformed' and 'to the great moral laws' that 'differ only slightly in relation to the intellectual power of individuals'; so that almost everything in Proust is a reconstitution, a composition in time of imaginary individuals with the help of real fragments of time's duration that have been assembled together and made coherent. The struggle to compose and be coherent, which in the insufficiently revised last volumes leads to a puppet-like oversimplification, is therefore essential in Proust.

However, this composing and these 'studies' of Time and moral laws are not the essence of art; according to Proust, they 'give it a setting', they 'embed it like a precious stone', they complete it. The essence of art is achieved through a miracle, the miracle of involuntary recollection which abolishes time and allows us to reach the essence of things. It is a miracle that has already been performed under our very eyes in *Du côté de chez Swann* when Marcel dipped his madeleine in the tea. It occurs three times in a row on the day of the matinée given by Princesse de Guermantes. . . . Each memory brings back all the circumstances . . . of the past moment to which it refers. . . . But this miraculous re-awakening of an impression is 'fleeting'. It only lasts if we make it permanent by converting it into a 'spiritual equivalent', viz. a work of art. . . . It is only through art that we can 'get outside ourselves'. 'Thanks to art, instead of seeing only one world, our own, we see it multiply and we have at our disposal as many worlds as there are original artists. . . .' The work of art is an 'optical instrument' that grants us an original vision of the world.

We can now come to a conclusion that still escaped us until *Le Temps retrouvé* was published. It seemed that Proust would reach a dispersal of the self and go no further. His mystique of memory seemed to offer no way out. Such was not the case. After casting down the myth of character, of fixed human personality, he shows us the path whereby we can become our own masters, whereby we can reconstruct the world by liberating ourselves from time. To achieve this, he warns us that we must begin by purging ourselves of all passion. In Proust's eyes, what is human is characterized by a detachment from everything. As long as the animal impulse of the senses, of heredity and of imagination are in evidence, the most absolute determinism is in control of us. Our liberty is born with wisdom. Let us not say that reconstructing the world from a few remembered impressions is an impossible or vain exercise. It is very true that only those moments really belong to us that have been so deeply imprinted on our being that they recreate .out of us, once revived by some surprise, all the things we were when they first struck us. Besides, these impressions are not enough; they demand an intense, spiritual effort on our part if we are to succeed in making their reality permanent. Proust's superimpressionism is made up of this poetic sublimation and this spiritualization of the remembered impression.

We would do well to linger long here over Proust's anti-realism, over his notion of art conceived as 'a relationship' between two different objects, a metaphor 'bringing together qualities common to two sensations', liberating 'their essence by reuniting them' and joining them 'by the ineffable bond of words boldly coupled together'.

This revelation within us of a human element that can be translated into a work of art, brings everything tainted with passion and imagination down to the level of the animal. *Le Temps retrouvé* forcefully clarifies this view. Whereas Gide in *Corydon* or *Si le grain ne meurt* was solely concerned to attack the anomaly thesis and consider homosexuality as a special phenomenon, though a natural and not a perverse one, Proust considers all love, even normal love, as a form of perversion and aberration based on fantasy. This fantasy is more often than not dictated by a whim of heredity ('It is possible that, being excessively dark, Morel was as necessary to Saint-Loup as shadow to a ray of sunshine. One can easily imagine in this very old family some blond lord . . . harbouring down in the hold a secret taste for blacks' or again M. de Charlus in chains with his 'dream of virility' and haunted by 'crucifixions and feudal tortures' in his 'medieval imagination' . . .). After this hell of passion, Proust gives us a glimpse of the paradise of humanity and art.

These are the first reflections suggested by the revised and completed 'Proustism' of *Le Temps retrouvé*, but these last two volumes open up so many new perspectives on the work that the whole is modified thereby and its meaning enlarged and heightened. To put it in a nutshell, Proust's negative work is here converted into a positive one. It would be unfair, however, if the new light cast on the whole work by *Le Temps retrouvé* were to cause us to neglect the admirable pages it contains on the war behind the lines, the first pages in which an author has succeeded in dominating this monstrous theme while keeping his distance in describing it.

127. John Charpentier on *Le Temps retrouvé*
1928

Part of a review in *Le Mercure de France*, 15 January 1928, pp. 419–22.

John Charpentier, with Proust's final publication, finds in *Le Temps retrouvé* objections to composition and the portrayal of characters that were among the earliest criticisms of his work.

After a careful reading of the copious volumes of the series entitled *A la recherche du temps perdu* which constitute the essential work of Marcel Proust, one is neither surprised nor disappointed to see, today, that the two volumes that bring this work to a close contribute nothing new, philosophically speaking. Disciple, no doubt of M. Henri Bergson, in that he illustrates his 'metaphysic of the senses' (to use M. Léon Daudet's expression) and because of the importance of the role he attributes to memory, Proust has, however, no gift for construction. Though he has frequent occasion to generalize as a moralist, his intelligence is above all analytical. In any case it was possible to predict that, as long as death did not surprise him too soon, he would strive to extract from his meticulous researches into his past a sort of hedonism that was both artistic and emotional. In the anecdote of the madeleine that some time back had reminded him of Combray, one can find the germ of the incident out of which he seems to wish the illumination in *Le Temps retrouvé* to grow. . . .

'What is, then, to forget, if not to die?'

So said Musset. The whole of Proust's effort is to fill in those gaps between his memories that oblivion excavates like so many graves, and to establish between the various moments of his life a sort of unbroken current. He finds a remedy for the brevity of this life – a brevity that is all the more perceptible the more fragmentary the appearance we give it – by re-allocating events to their dates and by marking out his line of view with these reference points. With him the instinct for mobility develops almost exclusively in time only.

Also, being a memorialist and an essayist, he is only psychologically a novelist by sheer chance. Not only does he not compose, but he does not let his characters have a life independent of his own. . . . But, contrary to what he believed, though one may write admirable books, one does not write novels, properly so called, without imagination. What one gathers from the sufferings and joys of others does not replace the invention of the one Baudelaire calls 'the queen of the faculties', even if the intelligence were to contrive by its alchemy to transmute these dark elements of the sensibility. A significant peculiarity, incidentally, and one that I do not think has been pointed out: the more Proust prizes a character, i.e. the more of himself he puts into it, the less he succeeds in making it expressive, the less we see it standing out in relief against the little world suggested by it. For instance: Albertine, who is certainly both the most caressed or most intimately investigated and the least precise creation I know. As with passion, snobbery makes his pen falter, and causes him to blur the features of the Princesse de Guermantes in the sketch he provides of this noble lady. As for M. de Charlus whom he outlined after the well-known model for the character – the poet of the *Hortensias bleus*[1] – he transforms him, in proportion as he builds up his personality from a range of details borrowed from the whole homosexual community, into a kind of symbol, victim of a pscyho-physiological fate, pursued by the furies to the point of masochistic-ally ending up in chains. On the other hand, Françoise, the cook, the pretentious Mme Verdurin and the foolish Odette are complete successes because he has, where they are concerned, the necessary detachment. The very reverse of Balzac, Proust only discovers or *finds*[2] things in time past; he does not anticipate and takes no possession of the future. His universe was obsolete even as he was describing it and attempting to incorporate present features into it, and he has brought a pre-war state of mind to the picture he has painted, in his last book, of French society during the war. Just as Saint-Simon was historian of the intrigues that surrounded the ageing Louis XIV, so Proust is the historian of the gossip around the Dreyfus Affair. . . . He belongs to a period that is not actually old, but old-fashioned, and the tastes of that period are to be found in his heterogeneous art like the furnishings and decoration of the cluttered salons he used to frequent. But alongside so many unusual, doubtful things, or things characterized by a tormented preciosity, what riches – I will not say in the disorder of his art – but in its complexity. . . .

NOTES

1 Robert de Montesquiou.
2 In italics in the text.

128. Louis Emié on Proust's humour

1928

Part of 'Langage et humour', *Le Rouge et le noir*, 15 April 1928, pp. 82–93.

Louis Emié examines the notions of caricature and humour according to his idiosyncratic definitions. Amidst all the concern to describe Proust as moralist and psychological analyst, very little interest is shown in one of the few 'serious' French writers whose work is invested with humour. Cf. Vandérem No. 97 and Wilson No. 140 who appreciate this side of his outlook.

. . . The exaggeration with which certain characters of Proust's – Mme Verdurin, Bloch, Cottard – reveal themselves could lead one to suppose that Proust sacrificed humour to caricature. This is not at all the case.

Humour is still part of life. It is one of life's most diverting expressions. It can even suffice unto itself, and whole books in which it leaves evidence of itself may thereby acquire a human value of the highest order. Caricature has other concerns; to develop, it needs prepared ground, contrast and characteristic detail around which it can take its time to burgeon. This hypertrophied growth is its goal, its end and its excuse. It makes us laugh – but moves us rarely. . . .

There is no caricature in Proust's works, and when we hear M. de Charlus, Mme Verdurin, Bloch, Cottard and Albertine talking, we must not let ourselves be fooled by the crudity of a range of vocabulary. . . . As for that intense contrast that the characters in question suddenly acquire in our eyes – or to our ears – we must admit it is pure, and if not gratuitous, at least quite disinterested. Here, art abstains from all intervention, and what, in the last century, would have been called 'realism' does not allow similar classification today. Proust's 'verbal realism' borrows all its qualities from the realism of life itself, and life is never exaggerated in the manner of caricature. Life flows, and its rhythm often becomes the rhythm of our thinking and our imagination.

Proust's humour, most of the time, could be said to be involuntary, dictated to him by events and by the individuals whose talk he records, including the talk of Professor Cottard or the director of the hotel at Balbec.

371

It is especially with episodic characters that this humour develops its true proportions. It is, indeed, rather rare to find in the words of Albertine or of the baron the least diverting touch. . . .

[Refers to Cottard's vulgarity, the director of the hotel's malapropisms, and Bloch's grandiloquence.]

From these three examples, we can draw a quite definite conclusion. In Proust, humour is always adapted to the psychological essence of the character, and the mechanism used for one could not, under any circumstances, serve for another. For so much virtuosity to be possible, what deep knowledge Proust must have possessed, and what a sense of values, too. . . .

129. Pierre F. Quesnoy on Proust as moralist
1928

Part of 'Le moralisme de Proust', *Le Rouge et le noir*, 15 April 1928, pp. 94–8.

Pierre F. Quesnoy sees Proust as not so much giving indications on how we should live as how we should analyse ourselves.

. . . The true moralist is not the man who provides *a priori* rules for living and structures that are applicable immediately and in all circumstances, but the one who teaches man to look at himself. The grand principle of all morality, since and before Socrates, remains as always the 'know thyself'. . . . Montaigne and La Rochefoucauld never claimed to provide practical rules of behaviour; they were satisfied to dig deeper into man's knowledge of himself. On this count, Proust is one of the greatest moralists. . . .

'Proust', wrote André Maurois, 'observes his characters with the passionate and distant curiosity of a naturalist observing insects. . . .' Yet people have been mistaken about this attitude – a sort of impassiveness that recalls Montaigne's scepticism. They did not see that it was only a means of introspection, an effort to grasp what, out of cowardice, laziness or thoughtlessness, man hides from himself. . . .

The title of moralist has never been denied, for instance, to Bourget, yet he has fewer rights to it than Proust. Bourget may observe correctly but most of the time he interprets badly for want of investigating deeply the motives of human actions. Proust's penetrating analysis and his acute introspection explore the most obscure nooks and crannies of consciousness and throw light on what, until then, had escaped the moralist. In this respect, he follows the Montaignes and the La Rochefoucaulds in the line of the great French moralists.

Yet if Proust is linked to the French tradition, there is a different aspect of his moralism which is far from negligible. In discussing him, it has often been a question of Bergson and Freud. In fact, the influence of these two philosophers, though indisputable, is less than was generally thought. It is rather a case of . . . ideas 'in the air' at that time. . . . In actual fact, what is common to all these minds and comes out notably in Proust, is this preoccupation with rediscovering the initial reality of man beneath the artificial contribution of civilization, beneath the repressed feelings brought on by our restrictive society. As for that effort towards spontaneity, that quest for *purity*[1] and sincerity, that desire to revise values and particularly the moral values that originate in the thinking of Nietzsche – Proust was one of the architects behind it all. . . .

NOTE

1 In italics in the text.

130. Raphael Cor on Proust and Schopenhauer

1928

Extract from 'Marcel Proust, ou l'indépendant; réflexions sur *Le Temps retrouvé*', *Le Mercure de France*, 15 May 1928, pp. 55–74.

Raphael Cor admires numerous features of Proust's achievement in *Le Temps Retrouvé*, especially his use of memory and his compassionate tragic view of Charlus. Here he draws a parallel between Proust and Schopenhauer to show the balance of a pessimistic outlook and the optimistic saving grace of art.

. . . If [Proust] insists on recreating his impressions through memory, it is in order to transform them into equivalents of the intelligence and confer on them at the same time an eternal value. Certainly, the first requirement is a sensibility that is out of the ordinary, as was indeed that of this great neurotic, from whom emanates some mysterious fluid that you expect to see bursting out in a shower of pale lights. As with those opium smokers whose hearing, sharpened by the drug, manages to perceive indiscernible distant sounds, in him the past sounds its bell and becomes once again present, even down to its finest resonances. But these resurrections, however passionate they may be, have but one goal – to allow him in his evocation of this immense line of forbears, to extract from it the fundamental laws of life. Do not be misled, however; we must see in it not the attitude of the logician, taking up the role of abstract translator of emotion, closing his eyes to the differences constantly produced by nature and trying to encapsulate them in the rigidity of a formula, but the quite opposite attitude of the artist who, meditating on the infinite detail of consciousness, and persuaded that essential reality lies in the discontinuous succession of individual personalities, endeavours to rediscover the exact nuance of each and not to immobilize the dynamic element of consciousnesses but, on the contrary, to rediscover the laws of their mobility. What is there to be said other than that the sensations he exhausts himself in evoking in this way, play in his work a role very close to the role of intuition for Schopenhauer? This is so true that between the scattered developments in *Le Temps retrouvé* and the philosopher's principal views one has all the choice in the world over the correspondences to be noted.

When, for example, we read that the artist is the man who takes a particular existence and depicts it in all its strict individuality, but in so doing presents thereby all human existence, for in seeming to be concerned with the particular, in reality he has in view what belongs to all times and all places (*The World as Will and Idea*),[1] would the reader not think he was listening to a commentary on Proust by Proust himself?

Firstly, that passion for the general, the only passion worthy of animating a work of art according to the novelist, because only the general has the power to liberate the habitually hidden essence of things, with the result that the superior artist has not so much to invent as to translate; secondly, the role assigned to the writer, which, by means of a return to the depths where what has existed lies unknown to us, consists in rediscovering the reality from which we are excluded by formal knowledge,[2] and in summoning from the darkness what we have felt, in order to raise it to the dignity of a spiritual equivalent; thirdly, that conception of the artistic sense, defined by the perfect submission to inner reality, which transforms our spirit into the pure mirror of the universe; finally, that keen sense of the concrete – so close to Schopenhauer's intuition – that authorizes him to relegate realism, that flat summary of lines and surfaces, to its lower status, thus enhancing a fully human art that fathoms its own depths – these are just so many views that, without being any the less felt for it, are akin to the metaphysical speculations of the great German. . . .

NOTES

1 Cor gives the following reference: *Le Monde comme volonté et comme représentation*. Translated by Cantacuzène, vol. II, p. 645.
2 Footnote by Cor: 'The proper goal of all works of art is to show us things and life as they really are; only, in reality, they cannot be understood by everybody, because a mass of fortuitous conditions contrives to veil them. This is the veil that is drawn aside by art.' Schopenhauer, op. cit., p. 612.

131. Ramon Fernandez on aesthetic theory
1928

Article entitled 'Note sur l'esthétique de Proust', *La Nouvelle Revue française*, 1 August 1928, pp. 272–80.

Ramon Fernandez provides a closely argued analysis that counters what he sees as Proust's special pleading in *Le Temps retrouvé* over the role of intuition and intelligence.

This article could not pass over in silence the admirable essay Proust devotes to his art, and more generally to aesthetics, in the second part of *Le Temps retrouvé*. Proust did not like critics. With admirable skill, which must have delighted novelists, he has incorporated into his work the critique of it, announcing it and explaining it at the very moment he was completing it. In about a hundred fervent, urgent pages he has taken up his position on all the problems that perturb contemporary writers, not omitting the inevitable morality of the artist which is intended as justification for his apparent uselessness to society. . . .

These pages of *Le Temps retrouvé* are essentially an essay on style, and another celebrated essay on style, published in 1888 by Walter Pater, allows us to date it. Both essays, despite the forty-odd years separating them, belong to the same spiritual period, i.e. they mark one and the same stage in what might be called the victory of the rights of art. The difference between them, and it is not a small one, arises from the fact that Proust worked from life, while Pater remained in the sublimated regions of culture and ideology. Proust's experience wins in penetration, since it embraces the most fleeting and the most petty details of reality. Pater's wins out in range and in human significance, because the author of *Marius* possessed a suppler and richer spiritual register. As a consequence of this delay, it might well be that Proust's aesthetic views were revised earlier than we think. But they had never been formulated in France with this force and brilliance. And they are necessary if not sufficient for the understanding of the proper nature of aesthetics.

Thomas de Quincey had already established a happy distinction between what he called the literature of power and the literature of knowledge. In the second, the writer communicates facts; in the first he expresses his feeling about the facts. Walter Pater adds that, in so far as 'the aim of the writer, consciously or unconsciously, turns out to be the transcription, not of the world, not of pure facts, but the feeling he has of the world and the facts, that writer becomes an artist'. According to Pater, all beauty is expression and expression is nothing other than 'the finest accommodation of language to inner vision'. These are approximately the terms Proust uses; the agreement between the two aestheticians on this point is complete. Both grant an aesthetic value to expression, to intimate sense experience and to that inner eye which, following Wordsworth, is 'the bliss of solitude'; both leave description and objective sense experience to the literature of knowledge. Reality, in the eyes of the artist, undergoes a singular displacement; it is no longer situated in the object, or in place of the object, as with common sense, but inside the soul, where the impression of the object is associated with other impressions and forms a new object, which escapes from all the measurements of intelligence and ordinary language. The *style* that results from the amalgamating of thought and language that are original and adequate, is a kind of visible mould of the impression. Style is the only means that the artist has at his disposal to render the unique world he carries within him objective and communicable. . . .

Proust's great originality and the great aesthetic interest of his work, come from the fact that he was never satisfied, like the Symbolists, with a world and a language which were the projection of his inner life. Through his work as novelist, psychologist and moralist, he has built a bridge between the literature of expression and the literature of knowledge. He has shown us how, starting from the inner life, it was possible to connect with the objective world, in other words, how the impression led to the general law. I know that some very good minds are embarrassed here by what they call the Proustian ambiguity and I concede that Proust has not emerged victorious from the test without leaving a few feathers behind. There is an incontestable difference of spiritual height and breadth between the pages on Vinteuil's Septet, in which Proust rises to an absolutely pure aesthetic transcendence, and his reflections on feelings, in which he grants more reality to the abstract generality of the law than to the individual and dramatic expression of feelings. What basically was reality for Proust? Was it the poetic impression in its ineffability, in its inability to communicate with reason, or was it the general, abstract, dry, independent idea of concrete circumstances, and such that it can be mechanically deduced without any recourse to observation? There is a great distance between Pater and Taine and many readers, less agile than Proust, fail to cross it with ease. I do not think, however, that the question can legitimately be put. It would be possible to put texts of Proust's in two columns that, compared with each other, would appear contradictory; but it would be on condition that no account would be taken, in this confrontation, of the way in which the general idea in Proust progressively extricates itself from the impression.

There is in Proust a notion of the truth of the impression that he never confuses with the logical notion of truth. But since, to designate either, he uses the same word indifferently, the confusion is difficult to avoid. A lorry goes down the street, I think I can hear a drum-roll and I think of a revolutionary uprising. My impression, in so far as it concerns the objective event, is false, but it is true that such has been my impression. Because I am a poet, I am going to resist the intelligence that functions in me as in everyone and tends towards transforming the drum-roll into the rumbling noise of the lorry. . . . To the classic idea of truth, the aesthetic of expression opposes the idea of poetic truth, which is translated by the close correspondence of style to impression. Poetic truth is nothing other than metaphor, which is something Proust admirably establishes in connection with Elstir. . . .

When Proust speaks of 'life', notably in the second part of *Le Temps retrouvé*, he always means plenitude and intensity of the life of the senses, but a life of the senses taken up and corrected by the mind. 'To realize' one's life is on the one hand to feel forcefully, and on the other to respond to the sensation by the harmonious activity of the spiritual faculties. To live, then, is not only to feel, but also to understand and above all to imagine. In order to imagine life two conditions are required: a sensation and a memory, the sensation leading to the memory which is reconstituted by the imagination. To some extent, there has to be the presence of an absence. This miracle comes about thanks to affective memory which recognizes the sensations common to a present event and a past event. The real presence of the event excludes the imagination and the intelligence, consequently is not really lived, is 'lost', or missing. Proust cannot 'realize' his life at the moment of living it because it drifts down the river of time and because his faculties are exercised upon it *successively*: he first imagines, then he feels, then he understands in such a way that he does not feel what he has imagined and does not understand either how he imagined or how he felt. This revelation of the past that he tells us about in *Le Temps retrouvé* allows him to group all his faculties *simultaneously*, to get them to work together, sustained, enlivened and safeguarded by the sensibility and *so to rediscover the conditions necessary to a spiritual progress, conditions linked by the necessities of experience to a progression in reverse within his own memory*. The parallelism of life and spirit is therefore broken, but it is quite true that Proust escapes time, since his consciousness, from being successive and irreversible, becomes capable of synthesis and independent of duration. Here we touch on a very delicate and important point. Philosophers ordinarily obtain this liberation of mind in relation to empirical becoming by the exercise of a rational activity that puts them in touch with the intelligible essence of things. As for Proust, he never at any time approaches the intellectual intuition of a Plato and a Spinoza; but, in the very world of the senses, he encounters an *equivalent* of this intuition. Does he not, in these pages of *Le Temps retrouvé*, constantly speak of the 'essence' of the real? And indeed, a sensation common to several events, to several periods, is in its way a kind of general sensation, an essence. Proust receives, in the form of an affective impression, that revelation of the timeless that the sages owe to intelligible contemplation. Now, it is very important to note here, for the better understanding of what follows, that this resemblance accentuates precisely the formal contrast between Proust's aesthetic and what, in connection with him, has been called Platonism. Not for a moment does Proust himself see in this miracle a revelation of knowledge: all he sees in it is a revelation of expression. The fact that he rediscovers the three dimensions of life in no way signifies that he is discovering a transcendental reality, which is so to speak detachable from phenomena. And likewise this aesthetic – at least in its philosophical content – is formally opposed to Bergsonism, with which it has incidentally numerous affinities: duration is in no respect creative, the mind creates in spite of it. For Proust the revelation of art is the revelation of possible salvation; but this salvation remains strictly aesthetic and never extends beyond the limits of expression.

Proust never sought to take advantage of his aesthetic discoveries in favour of a non-rationalist philosophy. He was a rationalist down to his boots, in the rather unfashionable manner of Taine. It does not even seem correct to say that his aesthetic is more 'advanced' or more profound than his philosophy. . . . All that one is obliged to recognize is that, for Proust, the moment of expression is more important, more vitally essential, than the moment of knowledge. Above all – as I have said above – as far as he is concerned the knowledge of laws is one of the consequences of the impression subjected to the inevitable influence of time.

Indeed, Proust's spiritual progress is founded on the observation – made for the first time, I believe, about Gilberte – that the maturing of the intelligence consists of filing one's feelings in categories or under general laws, the property of naivety being to believe in the unique, exceptional character of what one feels. Yet we have seen that according to Proust salvation consists in expressing what one feels while respecting this unique and exceptional character by refusing the words and ideas of common consciousness. Is there a contradiction here? None at all, since the impression that the artist snatches from oblivion and permanently fixes for eternity he knows full well to be false where its object is concerned: it expresses but a moment of the inner truth of the person who received it. How do human beings succeed in knowing that their impressions are erroneous? By the repetition of those very impressions and the lesson to be learned from them. If our love for a fellow human being makes us attach an absolute value to this person, the fact that in the course of time we attach the same value to several people is enough to reveal to us to what extent our feelings are deceptive. In a more complex, tragic and longer form it is exactly like the story of the rumbling of the lorry which was taken for a drum-roll. Gradually, the laws of human conduct are released, abstract and dry, from the shimmering envelope of our sensibility. Our personal experiences are confirmed by the history of the people who surround us. Hence the importance of . . . *Un amour de Swann* and Saint-Loup's passion for Rachel. Hence the significance of *Sodome et Gomorrhe*, which teaches us that the sex of the lovers is infinitely less important than the general laws of passion which are the same for all sorts of love. The revelation of the work of art is two-fold: it restores the complete atmosphere of a lived moment, and it allows the emotional and other laws that rule the human world to show through rather like a watermark. The disharmony between life lived and life understood is the source of both the tragic side and the grandeur of art, which is alone capable of making it perceptible to us. In the admirable pages in *Swann* on reading in the garden, Proust writes: '. . . and so during life our heart changes, and it is the most terrible pain; but it is a pain we only know in reading, in imagination: in reality, it changes, just as certain natural phenomena evolve, rather slowly in order that, observe as we may each of its different states in turn, we may nevertheless spared the actual sensation of the changing process.' There we can see to what extent art for Proust is an instrument of knowledge: he makes perceptible to us what we do not perceive in life, for instance, the laws of change. . . .

By his practice, even more than by his theory, Proust has marvellously enhanced a principle that ought to serve as the basis for any future aesthetic. This principle is as follows: the events and the moments of our lives that we most highly prize and that give us the feeling of existing, are not transparent and are accessible to the intelligence only with difficulty, especially in the instant when we live them. However, to feel we are really alive, we need to possess in spirit what we have lived in reality. Art provides us with the means to bring this irrational zone within the control of the spirit by faculties such as memory and by relationships such as metaphors, which constitute sense *equivalents* of thought. Art makes transparent to the spirit what science allows to escape through the overwide mesh of its net; art thus completes the spiritualization of the real. As for the general laws that Proust thought that he was able to deduce from his experience and of which he makes the ultimate essence of the real, it seems obvious that they are not in line with mankind at large. The reason is that they are in fact particular laws, made to Proust's own measurements, to suit his milieu and his time, in short, laws of the human type that he represented. There are more things in heaven and earth than are dreamt of in Proust's philosophy, but that is not a reason to neglect the relationships and the contrasts that he has underlined between the real as felt and the real as thought. A more mature, better armed, better informed aesthetic will no doubt to a large extent reduce these contrasts. But Proust's task will have been to maintain a distinction against which our instincts revolt and yet without which we can no longer see clearly: a strict and sound distinction between what is experienced as real and what is conceived as true.[1]

NOTES

All italics are in the text.

1 Footnote by Fernandez: What is felt is real to this extent, and believed to be true. Proust was not able to discover a truth that was equal in value to his sense impressions. It was his greatness to recognize this difference and to underscore it.

132. Clive Bell on Proust

1928

Extracts from his essay *Proust*, London, Hogarth Press, 1928.

Clive Bell (1881–1964), essayist and critic, associated with the francophile Bloomsbury writers, brings to full circle the pattern of attitudes that Proust's work occasions in his readers: preliminary objections, ardent conversion and cool assessment. His study presents in these three elements the typical critical approaches to Proust's work from 1913 to 1930.

(a) On Proust's faults and qualities (pp. 11–27).

When I began to read *Swann* the first fault on which I pounced was that of which anyone, however, unpouncingly disposed, is sure to complain at first. I complained that Proust was tedious. Tedious he is, but his tediousness becomes excusable once its cause is perceived. Proust tries our patience so long as we expect his story to move forward: that not being the direction in which it is intended to move. Novelists as a rule are concerned, to some extent at any rate, with getting on with their tale; Proust cares hardly more what becomes of his than did Sterne. It is in states, not action, he deals. The movement is as that of an expanding flower or insect. He exhibits a fact: we expect another to succeed it, effect following cause. Not at all: the fact remains suspended while we watch it gradually changing its shape, its colour, its consistency. For fifty pages we watch the process; after which Proust proposes another fact, new and seemingly irrelevant. Because very often there is no progressive relation we have a sense of being thwarted. We are annoyed. Proust does not get forward, we complain. Why should he? Is there no other line of development in the universe?

This sense of weariness, born of continual checking and marking time, is aggravated by the fact that, at first reading, Proust's sentences seem unconscionably and unnecessarily long. For this, too, there is excuse, and good. In short sentences Proust could not have given his meaning. He hesitates, he qualifies, he withdraws a little even; partly because, politest of men, to him a peremptory affirmation seemed sheer bad manners, chiefly because his ruling passion was a passion for truth. Two thousand five hundred years of philosophy notwithstanding, truth is rarely absolute; that is why Proust's sentences are interminable. They are a string of qualifications. For him short sentences would have been mere literature – words corresponding with no reality. His object was to tell the truth about life as he saw it; wherefore he intended originally to write a book without a single paragraph or chapter, so unlifelike – so unreal – did these arbitrary and convenient divisions appear. For the same reason he may have had a horror of full stops. . . . Time overflows punctuation. Also, how is a style to be anything but complicated and prolix when an artist is trying to say four things at once – to give a bird's-eye view and 'a close up' at once in time and space? . . . simultaneously he reacts to the object and his knowledge of the object. Dichotomy for Proust is begging the question. It is a complete experience he pretends to give – his whole experience, as a whole, not in detail: that sort of thing cannot be done in the style of Voltaire. Wherefore, when we complain that Proust's sentences are unarchitectural, illogical and endless, let us add that not otherwise could he have said what he had to say. . . . If Proust was not a stylist after the manner of Flaubert, or of Gautier even, Proust had his reasons. . . .

It is customary to compare Proust, stylist and memorialist of his age, or at least to say that one will not compare him, with St Simon. Certainly his style may be compared profitably with that of the seventeenth-century writers. . . . Proust, like the seventeenth-century masters, is periodic: only, whereas the great prose writers of that age deal generally in general ideas, Proust is plaiting very particular strands of emotion and sensation experienced by a very definite individual, and experienced simultaneously. That is why the interminable dependent clauses, instead of following one another duckwise, go side by side, like horses driven abreast, and sometimes higgledy-piggledy like a flock of feeding starlings. . . . Proust composed in the periodic manner in that his meaning is often not revealed till the close, or near the close, of the sentence. Often a careless or sleepy reader will find himself at the end of the sentence with a principal verb on his hands which he hardly knows what to do with. This shows that the period has been well sustained and that the periodic structure has served its purpose. He who would understand Proust must attend to every word he utters. This means stiff reading. Hence fatigue: hence also the revelation. I see no reason for supposing that Proust acquired his style by the study or imitation of other writers. Like all styles worth the name it was an instrument developed gradually to serve the single purpose of self-expression. . . .

From his heroic effort to translate Ruskin he may have picked up something. But what is there common to Ruskin's verbiage and Proust's press of words – each corresponding to some twist or start of the mind? Rather the style of *La Recherche* seems to me a quite

natural development – but what a development – from the style of
Les Plaisirs et les jours: at its best it is the precise equivalent of the
recaptured and detached experience of the author at his best. How
simple art is!

In my jealous irritation I complained that Proust was not only
tedious but clumsy. He is clumsy: again I was right, and again
wrong in not seeing that as a rule he is clumsy in order to be
something else. Proust's passion was for truth, the whole truth, the
truth about oneself, the untold truth. . . .

Proust wanted to tell the truth as he knew it. He had a passion for
the fact. And this pursuit of truth, of reality I had rather say, is the
only begetter and conditioner of his style. It was the contemplation,
the realisation, of facts which provoked the poet that was in him. He
kept his eye on the object much as the great impressionists had done,
he observed, he analysed, he rendered; but what he saw was not
what the writers of his generation saw, but the object, the fact, in its
emotional significance. And, like the impressionists, he has taught
the more sensitive of a new generation to see with him.

[Quotes 'Mais ma grand'mère' to 'le but vague mais permanent de
ma pensée', Pléiade I, pp. 83–4, and 'Je m'arrêtais à voir sur la table'
to 'changer mon pot de chambre en un vase de parfum', Pléiade I,
p. 121.]

Proust's images were no lucky hits. On imagery he had meditated
much and to the purpose. Metaphors he held the most effective
means of expression; and he has shaken my admiration for
Flaubert – which stands nevertheless – by pointing out with disconcerting perspicacity and temperance how unfine, how commonplace,
are his. In those illuminating notes on Flaubert's use of the imperfect
in *oratio obliqua* and on his suppression of inverted commas, I
discover, by the way, an image which seems worth catching and
exhibiting, so perfect a specimen is it of what an image should be:
'donc, cet imparfait, si nouveau dans la littérature, change entière-
ment l'aspect des choses et des êtres, comme fait une lampe qu'on a
déplacée.' It is difficult to recall an image that throws a sharper or
more helpful light into a dark corner. Proust meditated Flaubert
strictly. They had things in common: for instance, a passion for
verifying references (the passion for truth) and a habit of not always
getting them right. Flaubert travelled to where Carthage was before
writing *Salammbô*, and Proust, fearful of having misused a technical
term in describing a fourteenth-century ornament, pestered Billy
with interrogatory letters. But for the Flaubert-Maupassant doctrine – the doctrine that the artist should stand outside the work,

observe and record – Proust had no use at all. Facts, yes: he adored facts, but he would not leave them alone. Proust, the master commentator, the born showman, had no notion of standing aside. On the contrary, he rarely states a fact without commenting and criticising and reminiscing at enormous length. . . .

Nevertheless, to return to my grumbling, Proust was clumsy. He can be grossly and, what is worse, unwittingly so. He could not leave out. Insignificant facts, platitudinous reflections, the obvious, the well worn, the thrice-told, all, all are set down beside what is stranger, subtler and truer than anything that has been set down in imaginative literature since Stendhal at any rate. Because he will not eliminate he is indiscriminate. He will treat facts as though he were a man of science rather than an artist. Indeed, in his way of piling instance on instance he reminds me sometimes of Darwin; also for piling thus high he has the man of science's excuse – he accumulates that truth may prevail. Proust was too profoundly in earnest not to be repetitious sometimes. Subtlest of analysts, subtlest of observers, he is not a subtle expositor. Far too much of what he says is redundant. Really he seems not to know which of his ideas and observations are surprising and which are trite. Occasionally his lack of finesse makes one positively uncomfortable, and his humour becomes so elephantine sometimes that one hardly knows which way to look.

(b) On Proust's art and ideas (pp. 42–8; 84–9).

In the last volume of his *opus* Proust has published his recipe for catching experience. It is a matter of some seventy pages, a brilliant performance, made ever so little ridiculous by his fancying that he is laying down the laws of artistic creation, whereas in fact he is merely emptying his own bag of tricks. Proust wants to render experience in all its intensity and vividness, at that throbbing moment when emotion has the force and reality of sensation. Now an emotional experience at its most intense and vivid, at the moment of being experienced, is uncapturable . . . . Could we but recapture a past experience, dragging it up from the depths of the sub-conscious, a past experience with all its glamour, its intensity, its reality clinging about it, but with its sting drawn, should we not stand a chance of seeing the monster whole and seeing him steadily? The monster we know can be brought to the surface; he can be brought to the surface by an appropriate shock. Proust's first gift, the gift that conditioned his method, was his capacity for giving himself shocks.

Given this shocking power, one who would create an equivalent for that spate of experience which we call life must acquire and store up below consciousness a hoard of experience . . . . The experience is in the past. It can be remembered, but how is it to be realised? Realised it must be if it is to be seen and described in all its intensity (sterilised and rid of its poison however) – if it is to be seen alive. This is where Proust's genius – and nothing less than genius of the highest order would have served – shows itself unmistakably. Proust brings the past into the present and makes it live there, the present being the only atmosphere in which for us anything can live; and this he does by creating a shape not in space but in time. Time is the stuff of which *A la recherche du temps perdu* is composed: the characters exist in time, and were the sense of time abstracted would cease to exist. In time they develop; their relations, colour and extension all are temporal. Thus they grow: situations unfold themselves not like flowers even but like tunes; and no one, nothing, is for two chapters the same. Nothing ends as it began. There is no absolute. Love, to take the obvious example: a million feelings, ten thousand incidents, and at the end you say 'I have been in love'. M. de Charlus is always going downhill; so, more slowly, is Swann, whose deterioration keeps pace with his humiliation. One hardly notices that Saint-Loup changes completely thrice, so gradually and naturally does he change. Even Méséglise becomes hill 307. So we roll, with this unhappy, ill-heated planet, through time, because the book is a fabric of time. And let me admit, at once, that, to create this temporal fabric, with time the artificer has taken the strangest liberties. He has shaped it to his ends. This bubble of present time which Proust has filled and coloured with a vision of the past is, with infinite precaution, blown out and distended indefinitely almost . . . .

A la Recherche du Temps Perdu is a shape in time; it is not an arabesque on time. It is constructed in three dimensions, and may be described as architectural if we bear in mind that the blocks of which it is built are time-blocks. They are arranged in an order, conceived and determined by the architect with a view to expressing truth, which is not necessarily chronological order. Indeed, Proust cannot well arrange his blocks in sequence, since he is composing in mass. Better to think of the book as a picture – an oil-painting, not a fresco – in time. Because one time-mass stands before another in the composition it does not follow that it precedes it in history; for, like the modern painter dealing with space-masses, Proust moves his hither and thither regardless of their chronological relations . . . .

And is there a moral? To be sure there is; a philosophy of life at all events. It is not very new, but it is true enough. Proust has explored depths hitherto unplumbed, he has stripped the dirt and tarnish from reality till his fingers ache and our eyes, he has seen life from a new angle and described what he saw with a frankness and precision unmatched in prose; and the conclusion to which he has come is the conclusion to which came the Preacher – and Shakespeare:

> All is vanity . . .
> . . . it is a tale
> Told by an idiot, full of sound and fury,
> Signifying nothing.

Not quite nothing: Proust had his illusions. He believed that art and thought did signify something . . . .

He may have wished to believe that by art and thought one can escape. He knew better. He pampered his illusions, but he knew them for what they were. Art and thought, like eating and drinking, have their delights and their narcotic powers; but for human beings, as Proust knew better perhaps than anyone of his age, human relations come first . . . .

Proust's philosophy of life was simple and sound. Honesty, intellectual honesty, is the best policy. Truth is not only stranger, but far more amusing, than fiction. You may call it, if you please, 'a philosophy of despair'; it is nothing but the considered opinion of an intelligent man with a profound knowledge of life and a taste for truth . . . . Also he knew that the only certainty in life is change. About this there is nothing extraordinary; what confounds us is the vision, the imagination, the poetry, the analytical and sheer intellectual force with which he exposes his science. What Proust knew, if he knew anything at all, about the nature of the universe is unimportant; it is what he knew and still more what he could tell about that microcosm which is man, which is the marvel of our age. From the unsurveyed mines of sub-conscious memory he dragged up experience vital yet stingless and made the past live sterilised in the present. Then, on a pin's point, he held his living captive till he had described it, and describing created a world. He was a creator whose philosophy served him to keep ever in the forefront of his mind that critical spirit, that respect for truth, which alone, it seems, can preserve a creator from nauseous egotism or sprawling optimism. From exaggeration he was not saved; but he is never vulgar, never sentimental. And if, some unlucky divagations notwithstanding, he avoided those messy pits into which most modern creators – Dickens, Hugo, Balzac, Dostoievsky – have fallen, that may have been because a philosopher was ever at hand to remind him, that the one wholly good gift the gods have given man is death.

133. Unsigned review of
The Sweet Cheat Gone
1930

The Times, 13 May 1930, p. 10.

The reviewer looks at C. K. Scott-Moncrieff's translation of
Albertine disparue. Though praising the translation he sees the
work as evidence of unevenness in Proust's later writings.

The Sweet Cheat Gone is the English translation of . . . *Albertine
disparue* . . . . It was Scott-Moncrieff's last work, and he had not
even time to add to it, as to previous volumes, an illuminating
translator's note. As a work of art, though the translation is always
excellent, this volume is of unequal merit. It contains a few of the
most beautiful and poignant passages that Proust ever wrote, and
equally some of the most ugly things that, except in his last volume
of all, he ever recorded. The first chapter contains both elements, but
beauty preponderates. Its theme is memory's agony at the loss and
death of a beloved object – an agony inevitably to be merged in the
indifference of oblivion. Proust accomplishes the description of this
tortured recollection with all his inexhaustible resource and music;
yet with it he blends the harsh theme of morbid jealousy and morbid
desire to discover ugly facts about a mistress's past vices. The later
chapters, in which Proust's power and memory were weakening,
describe the narrator's process towards oblivion of Albertine, which
is marked by a reviving interest in earlier characters of the novel.
Gilberte comes to life again, sunning herself in the beams, so long
withheld, of Mme de Guermantes's favour. She finally marries
Saint-Loup; and Saint-Loup, so sympathetic in the earlier volumes,
turns out to be another Charlus. There is a visit to Venice, obviously
fragmentary, but remarkable for some typical passages of Proustian
nostalgia and for the final glimpse of M. de Norpois's diplomatic
virtuosity as he sits beside Mme de Villeparisis. The presence of
Mme de Villeparis is at the hotel in Venice provides one inimitable
touch. Mme Sazerat, the impoverished friend of the narrator's
mother, hears of it. All her life she had longed to see the lovely
woman who ruined her father. She looks round the room, asking
where she is. The erstwhile enchantress is now but a decayed old
lady. Thus, with over-lavish variation, Proust harps upon the

delusions of human memory and the innumerability of the selves
that make up personality in time.

134. Louis de Robert on Proust's 'method'
1930

Part of *De l'amour à la sagesse*, Paris, Eugène Figuière, 1930,
pp. 57–93.

Louis de Robert, close associate of Proust from the time of
Swann, reviews attitudes to Proust's method of composition
and concludes that his genius lies closer to free fantasy than
strict planning.

. . . Most commentators on Proust say of his methods of composition:
'Proust wanted this, he did not want that.' Thus they seem to adhere
to the belief that Proust did as he intended. M. Benjamin Crémieux
has spoken about composition like a rose-window . . . .
   I am not, I believe, mistaken in thinking that what is wrong with
this formula . . . is that it gives us an impression of something
geometric and suggests a rigorous method. Proust's art was more
capricious, more relaxed and more loose in its weave than this. Each
nook and niche could be extended according to the substance he
filled them with. Some of them ended up like protruding hernias and
overlapped onto others, with the result that it is no longer possible to
recognise the rose-window from such distortions.
   However, M. Crémieux's pen adds to the value of what it
describes. So, that particular habit Proust had of going back over
what he had said, forever dreading that he had not given adequate
explanation of the least little thing – a habit that in the traffic of
everyday dealings made him appear a bit pernickety – is prestigiously
honoured by M. Crémieux in these lines:

The composition of Proust's work is not simply static; more than that, it is
also dynamic. It is not unilinear and melodic, but orchestral and symphonic.
It can only be perceived in time, as motifs unfold, as themes are repeated and
progressively enriched.

389

I will certainly not go so far as to say that there is no truth in all that, but I do not think that it was the result of a thoroughly thought-out plan. In his constant repetition of themes, was Proust conforming to a rule, to a law of composition, or was he quite simply following a natural disposition that, as I have said, could be seen in his everyday relationships?

As far as I am concerned, there is not a shadow of doubt. He proceeded in this way because that is the way he was, because he could not change his mental outlook. M. Crémieux thinks that he proceeded in this way because he had so decided. He sees evidence of Proust's will where I only see evidence of his nature.

When of all the Prousts that co-existed in his brain, the greatest – in one of the magnificent digressions he excelled at – had departed a little from its subject, the next day a more sober and moderate Proust would wonder: 'Doesn't that upset the balance of the ensemble?' This Proust used to seek out aesthetic reasons to give himself the authority to preserve what he felt, as far as his work was concerned, was a further enrichment. But the Proust who, the night before, devoured by a sacred frenzy of inspiration, was not inconvenienced either by physical needs or illness or the unbreathable air of the stifling bedroom, that great Proust could not have cared less for all those reasons, and when a little later he would take up his pen again, he began once more to escape from the excessively narrow limits in which a wiser Proust tried vainly to enclose him.

It is possible that in the case of a man of talent everything is premeditated and calculated. Talent is often well-balanced. Genius is almost always characterized by excess. However marvellously intelligent Proust may have been, he obeyed commands that came to him from a higher source than his intelligence, he obeyed something that, for all his incomparable lucidity, he could not have defined himself and that consequently it is pointless to seek to fix in a formula.

That Proust foresaw a thousand or two thousand pages in advance the repercussions of a little fact apparently of no significance to the reader is beyond doubt and reading his work provides many an example of it. To deny it would be to deny him justice. But to take him at his word when he writes to various correspondents to insist on the point that his composition *is rigorous* – sometimes he used to say *rigid* – is to exaggerate in the opposite direction and to bend the knee of admiration too much.

To give you an idea, he loved to repeat that the last page of *Le Temps retrouvé* would close exactly on the first page of *Swann*.

When I read *Swann* in proof stage in the summer of 1913, I knew that the end of the work was written. So what? The winning post was set up before the race; but after that what a lot of stops on the way! What a lot of developments brought in as afterthoughts! What a lot of unexpected events! I will quote only one, because no one will question that he could not foresee it: the war.

When *Swann* was published, the whole work, as Proust conceived it at that time, was to be contained in three thick volumes or in five slimmer ones. This question was debated between us for more than six months. Now, today, his work comprises about fifteen volumes, which goes to show that rigorous composition was, to put it mildly, elastic.

He had his framework, but the matter he filled it with varied by weight and extent, according to the hour or the moment when he wrote, according to his enthusiasm or his lassitude, even according to the whims of his memory. He composed, he constructed, but alongside the builder there was in him, and I say it again, an executant of genius, and the basic building recalls those pavilions that become, by virtue of the addition of wings, turrets and new main structures unexpected, composite châteaux.

If I have somewhat insisted on what I see as the involuntary element in Proust's art, it is because it seems to me that we are committing an error in thinking that he always did what he intended. It even turned out *that he did what he did not think he was doing*. For instance, he believed that his art was not so meticulous. Well, can one honestly deny it?

He used to enjoy saying (he wrote to say so to his childhood friend Robert Dreyfus, and the sentence has made its mark) that he did not use a microscope but a telescope. That's a witty turn of phrase, and that's all.

His genius, well suited to reconcile opposing views, carried the love of detail to a point where it was difficult to follow him and where no one, I think, will be his equal. Like a dragonfly, he seemed to have twenty-two thousand pairs of eyes. But, no doubt, because he was aware of the sheer breadth of his other gifts, the adjective meticulous as applied to his work did not please him. What he saw in that term was not so much what it contains as what it seems to exclude. He was like the runner all set to astonish the world by a performance no one else had achieved before him and who does not like to be told that he is taking small strides, even if that is the truth, *especially if that is the truth*.

There are some who believe that they have found the explanation of Proust's methods in a sentence he wrote on Mme de Sévigné 'who presents things in the order of their perception instead of explaining them by their causes'. If Mme de Sévigné presents us with things in the order of their perception, it is because she is writing letters and is carried away by her nature, her vigour and her verve. Proust behaves in the same way. He writes an enormous letter to posterity to testify to what he has seen and felt; he writes it with all the unevenness associated with fluctuations of temperature, place and altitude, one day in full possession of his means and another day deprived of part of them, now lingering over a passage whose carved detail, finish and state of verbal perfection amaze us, now writing in feverish haste, without a care for repetitions and contradictions, often taking his ease among the ins and outs and the sinuosities of his sentences, surprising us with an unexpected comparison, the notation of an analogy we would never have dreamed of with the most exact detail, an observation of the rarest quality, a sudden image that we watch opening, growing and developing beneath our very eyes with the suppleness and swiftness of a grass-snake uncoiling itself and disappearing and whose shadow, it seems, one can follow across the page, and sometimes setting down a weighty parallel to explain and demonstrate to us what we had understood by the merest hint, one minute original and saying things that no one had said before him and the next insisting otiosely on matters of secondary importance. In all that we must discern the very conditions under which he works. He is a man whose head buzzes with memories, who can see death approaching, who is in a hurry to say all he can, who endlessly repeats a theme, who adds interpolations galore on separate sheets attached to his manuscript, not according to any method but according to a habit of mind resulting from the unstable equilibrium of his health. The familiar letters to his friends often have the same verve as the best pages of his novel and bristle just as much with insights, reflections, suggestions and surprising and unexpected flashes. If he has any rule, it is to surrender to his demon, his genie, and write on everything to the point of exhaustion. He knows where he is going, he has a plan, but he cannot say in advance if the part devoted, for instance, to Albertine will have two thousand or twenty thousand lines. Thus when he describes a mere dinner at the Guermantes' it takes on, as far as the extent and number of pages is concerned, the same importance as that cardinal episode, *Un amour de Swann*.

This observation in no way diminishes his claim to fame. For my part, Proust's main originality lies in this: He is not the master of his subject, he is its servant, its slave. Hence that peculiar enlargement of the original framework, those interpolated episodes, extensions and parentheses. He constantly overflows. Other writers compared to him seem limited and restricted. He, on the other hand, opens up to our view perspectives that stretch to infinity. His richness is inexhaustible, and he succeeds, in a perfectly natural way, in giving

us a vision of the depth, diversity and complexity of things that
makes our minds reel . . . .

NOTE

All italics are in the text.

135. Pierre Abraham: a comparison with Montaigne and Rousseau

1930

Extract from *Proust: recherches sur la création intellectuelle*, Paris,
Rieder, 1930, pp. 70–2.

Pierre Abraham, after quoting parallels between *Les Essais*, *Les
Confessions* and *La Recherche*, concludes by showing how all
three draw their power from their self-analysis, which in turn
can serve as a guide to the reader.

. . . The fact that their first work, following on silence or else the
slightest trifles that count for hardly much more than that, was
published by all three at the same age, the fact that the first pages of
Les Essais, *Le Discours sur l'inégalité* and *Swann* appeared when their
authors were respectively forty-two, forty-one and forty-two years
old, would be of no great significance other than that in this matter
the human body needs a long build-up of experiences, culture,
comparisons and memories. That's looking at the work from the
author's side.

Looking at the work from the other side, I will make the
observation that with *A la recherche du temps perdu* I think that I
recognize something that, as an eternal reader, I first garnered four
hundred years ago with Montaigne and a second time one hundred
and fifty years ago with Rousseau. And it is precisely this that I
would like to define.

In the light of what they have in common – leaving aside what is
particular to each – the three books, viz. *Les Essais*, *Les Confessions*
and *A la recherche du temps perdu*, strike the reader as reference works
for the spiritual problems facing him, or, if you prefer, as

psychological dictionaries. By that I do not mean a cold, purely documentary collection to be skimmed through with some theoretical intent, but a directly proffered aid, an advance made by the author to the reader, a work any hard-working or worried person can turn to. In certain respects, they are three books of *answers*[1].

Answers to what kind of questions? Once again, let us exclude from each work everything we would not find in the others. From Montaigne let us exclude the dazzling brilliance of reason and that preoccupation with the universal which makes him one of the pillars of human civilization. From Rousseau let us exclude the burning passion and the generosity of soul that is the origin of that social neo-Christianism on which more than a century of history has already been modelled. With these exclusions behind us, the fundamental question that we find in them immediately after: What do I do? is What am I? The basic procedure they follow in their replies is to confront themselves with the various appearances of the world around them.

If *A la recherche du temps perdu* is to preserve its value as a reference work, it is precisely because the same fundamental question can be found there, precisely because the same procedure is followed. *A la recherche du temps perdu* is not a work about a hero who, sure of himself and determined on a vocation, exploits himself as if he were a marble quarry for the extraction of statues; it is the testimony of a man who anxiously follows the road leading to his self-discovery, and who, along this road, bumps into all the milestones, falls into all the ruts and gets lost at every crossroads. These milestones, ruts and crossroads are, as in Montaigne and Rousseau, the very ones we bump into on our own road. The shocks experienced by Montaigne, Rousseau and Proust are the ones we feel ourselves. And the more or less exclamatory, more or less qualified reactions these things draw out of them, are the responses that, with a child's matter-of-fact cruelty, we expect from disciple or reader.

These three works, each in its own way, each in its own field, represent a total, a sum, a limit, a maximum. They are, in three different periods, the work-face of those underground galleries where we go drilling into the bedrock of the human spirit. We demand that periodically someone should take stock of the situation up above; in the same way, we need to know that at regular points in history, there are those who are concerned to take stock of the situation within. Once the assessment is made, it is not a matter of complacently coming to a stop. Let those who are – in the juicy, demotic phrase – bone-idle sigh as much as they like with contentment while uttering the observation that 'With sexual inversion and sapphism, Proust annexed a new domain for literature!' In the first place, it is not accurate, and secondly that is not the point. It makes no difference to humanity whether literature either does or does not annex a new domain; but it does matter to humanity to continue its march in the secure knowledge that the geological foundations have been honestly marked out and probed. This is a task that Montaigne, Rousseau and Proust carry out with equal perceptiveness and equal severity on the only material that is constantly at their disposal – on themselves . . . .

NOTE

1 In italics in the text.

136. Samuel Beckett on Proust's style and vision
1931

Extract from *Proust*, London, Evergreen Books, 1931, pp. 66–8.

Samuel Beckettt (1906–   ), in a succinct and incisive essay, gives a writer's insight into the best and the worst of Proust's style.

By his impressionism I mean his non-logical statement of phenomena in the order and exactitude of their perception, before they have been distorted into intelligibility in order to be forced into a chain of cause and effect. The painter Elstir is the type of the impressionist, stating what he sees and not what he knows he ought to see . . . . And we are reminded of Schopenhauer's definition of the artistic procedure as 'the contemplation of the world independently of the principle of reason'. In this connection Proust can be related to Dostoievski, who states his characters without explaining them. It may be objected that Proust does little else but explain his characters. But his explanations are experimental and not demonstrative. He explains them in order that they may appear as they are – inexplicable. He explains them away.

Proust's style was generally resented in French literary circles. But now that he is no longer read, it is generously conceded that he might have written an even worse prose than he did. At the same time, it is difficult to estimate with justice a style of which one can only take cognisance by a process of deduction . . . . For Proust, as for the painter, style is more a question of vision than of technique. Proust does not share the superstition that form is nothing and content everything, nor that the ideal literary masterpiece could only be communicated in a series of absolute and monosyllabic propositions. For Proust the quality of language is more important than any system of ethics or aesthetics. Indeed he makes no attempt to dissociate form from content. The one is a concretion of the other, the revelation of a world. The Proustian world is expressed metaphorically by the artisan because it is apprehended metaphorically by the artist . . . . The rhetorical equivalent of the Proustian real is the chain-figure of the metaphor. It is a tiring style, but it does not tire the mind. The clarity of the phrase is cumulative and explosive. One's fatigue is a fatigue of the heart, a blood fatigue. One is exhausted and angry after an hour, submerged, dominated by the crest and break of metaphor after metaphor: but never stupefied. The complaint that it is an involved style, full of periphrasis, obscure and impossible to follow, has no foundation whatsoever.

137. F. C. Green on a new psychology
1931

Extract from *French Novelists from the Revolution to Proust*, London, Dent, 1931.

F. C. Green (1891–1964), professor of French at Edinburgh, represents the best qualities of sensitive academic criticism, opening up a difficult author to the public at a time when the whole of Proust's novel was at last available. He makes illuminating parallels with philosophy, stressing the importance of the subconscious, intuition, the concept of time and the ideas of Bergson. He concludes, with confident erudition, in placing Proust within the development of realism in the novel since Balzac.

For Proust the true reality of life is subjective and extra-temporal. We must not think of the past as divorced from the present, since each one of us carries the 'past' in his subconscious mind, from which it emerges to the surface of the conscious self, bringing with it, like a water-spider with its crystal bubble of air, a whole milieu rescued from Time and replete with life that was really lived because it was profoundly felt. The true artist, therefore, is he who will find a way of imitating this trick of Nature's and of expressing this rhythmic interweaving of 'past' and 'present'. Thus Proust tells us why he knew the beauty of one thing long afterwards in another; why, for instance, he *realised* for the first time what noonday at Combray was in the sound of an electric bell, the mornings at Doncières in the gurglings of the radiator of his Paris flat, the death of his grandmother in the painful act of stooping to button his shoes. The genius of Proust, in order to express these realities, has created a style which though at first it strikes us as complicated, is actually the only skin that will fit the wrinkles of his thought.

Like Bergson, Proust jettisons the old mathematical conception of Time as something divided objectively into years, days, and hours, substituting for it what Bergson calls *durée mobile*. Mobile duration is Time measured from the subjective point of view of our individual consciousness, for which, as we all know, the term 'an hour' may be hopelessly inadequate to indicate the duration of a state of soul which in reality may be much longer or much shorter. The whole of Proust's long novel, then, is an extraordinary *tour de force*, an unparalleled effort to see the world of men and things situated not in mathematical Time but in Bergsonian Time or Duration . . . .

A la Recherche du Temps perdu is an experiment in a new psychology, and represents therefore an advance in the art of fiction. The novelist, for Proust, is primarily a translator, an interpreter whose function it is 'to seek beneath matter, beneath experience, something different'. And this is the key to Proust's method of notation, since it explains the fascination of his picture of aristocratic Parisian society from the eighties to the present day. His characters acquire a startling vividness, emerging, as it were, in volume. If we look at a photograph with the naked eye and then through a stereoscope we have a very feeble idea of the difference between a character presented by a novelist of the old school and as revealed by Proust. The complexity of the world appears in a new light, and where a Balzac showed the social interdependence of human beings Proust lays bare the myriad filaments, hitherto invisible, that link our souls. The great fallacy exposed by him is that we can observe life objectively or form an inkling of reality from appearances. Habit, passion, intelligence, amour-propre, erect a constant barrier between reality and our comprehension. Take as an illustration the hero's love for Albertine – one of the master-themes of this novel. To express the reality of that love Marcel (if we may for convenience give him

Proust's name) burrows *underneath* the mass of impressions from which the 'Realist' would disengage what he would call the life of these two. Yet, as we see from Proust's novel, he would be entirely wrong. To arrive at the true impressions one must, like Marcel, *decode* what we falsely call life, translate the appearances, since language, gestures and acts are nearly always expressed in a purely conventional form that does not at all correspond to reality. Habit disguises our sentiments, giving them a semblance of truth which we are prone to mistake for the truth itself. Like Marcel, we think that we know what people are and what they think, but that is usually, says Proust, because we are indifferent. Let love, or jealousy, which is the inevitable companion of love, fasten on our life and immediately the scales fall from the eyes of our intelligence. Then, like Marcel, we lift the veil of habit and discover to our grief and amazement that the soul of the woman we love is an uncharted sea of mysteries. Then, like him, we listen to the voice of intuition and, plunging deep within ourselves, look for those profounder impressions which are the only true ones . . . .

Proust is beyond doubt the greatest literary psychologist whom we have yet encountered in fiction, and though his field of observation is limited to the aristocracy and the higher bourgeoisie, his power of penetration is unsurpassed. This picture of the manners of a social era which opens with the presidency of Macmahon and closes with the Great War is not merely a social document: it is an incomparable vision of the eternal passions and foibles of humanity. It was Diderot, was it not? who said that the great literary types should be revised every fifty years. After Molière, after Balzac and Flaubert, Proust has something new to tell us, something which affords us new food for meditation on the queerness of the animal, man. The profound truth that emerges from his characterisation is that in every man there is an arrant fool. Thus a Cottard can be a marvellous clinician but, outside his speciality, a complete *primaire* with the sense of humour of a child of ten; a Brichot – profound well of learning – is as ignorant of humanity as a cart-horse; Norpois, a magnificent diplomat of the old school, passes critical judgments on literature which would shame an undergraduate; Bergotte, an artistic genius of the first rank, tamely submits to the bullying of a Mme Verdurin, the supreme type of charlatan and *bas bleu*. A recent critic of Proust has uttered the amazing statement that his novel has no 'philosophic background'. How is it possible to follow the destinies of a Charlus, a Saint-Loup, a Mme Verdurin or a Morel; to attend a reception at the Guermantes'; to talk for an hour with Charles Swann or to listen to the conversation of the *clan* at La Raspelière, and not realise that we are witnessing a modern version of the eternal human comedy in the company of one of the greatest sceptics of our age. A more childish and, if anything, more inept reproach levelled at Proust is that he is a snob; that he has failed to explore the psychology of the lower classes. The author would reply that the subject of a novel is of little importance. The great artist, to borrow his phrase, 'can make as precious discoveries in an advertisement for soap as in the *Pensées de Pascal*'. And, as Proust turned away from the spectacle of human vanity and selfishness, racked with spiritual and physical suffering, he made what for him was his supreme discovery. It is that happiness is to be found only in Art, in the pursuit of that essential truth and beauty which all of us unconsciously extract from life and secrete in the cells within us. Most men, slaves of habit, seek the reality and the beauty of life in surface impressions, in the outward appearance of things. At times they are naïvely sad when these afford no lasting joy. The true philosopher, in Proust's eyes, is the artist who, like Elstir of the *Recherche du Temps perdu*, looks for the roses in that *jardin intérieur* which is in all of us if, like him, we will only cultivate it.

The world unfolded by Proust staggers us by its complexity as it astounds us by its beauty. Is not that because, half emerged from the age of rationalism, we have grown accustomed to expect simple and material explanations of life's deepest problems and lost to some extent the sense of wonder? As a corrective to this attitude of mind, as a reminder of the profounder and more richly coloured spiritual existence which underlies our rational one, the work of Proust has an enduring value. In *A la Recherche du Temps perdu* the great forces of Idealism and Realism meet and coalesce in a blinding flash through which the dazzled eye of the reader seems to behold the image of a living reality. One thing, however, is certain. It is that Proust's work signalises the complete overthrow of an old dogma; for never again, surely, can the novelist return to the nineteenth-century conception of a purely objective art, of a Realism which confines itself solely to the 'scientific' notation of unidealised life.

NOTE

All italics are in the text.

138. André Maurois on Proust and Ruskin
1931

Extracts from 'Proust et Ruskin', an article written in 1931 and published in *Essays and Studies*, vol. XVII, Oxford, Clarendon Press, 1932, pp. 25–32.

André Maurois (1885–1967) was novelist, biographer and anglophile. In his biography and appreciation of Proust, 1949 and in his discovery of *Jean Santeuil* and *Contre Sainte-Beuve*, he made important contributions to Proust studies. His early essay of 1931 shows his awareness of the comparative problems to be analysed in Proust's creations and heralds, along with No. 140, the interest in Proust and English authors that developed in the 1930s and 1940s.

. . . What did Proust find in Ruskin that was new? In the first instance, a knowledge of the plastic arts and a taste for them . . . . In bringing him a literary image of a work of art, Ruskin became in a way the bridge between Proust's understanding and certain aspects of reality. As soon as you read Proust, you come back to Ruskin. If Proust compares a character to Giotto's *Charity*, it is because Ruskin often talks about this figure. It was with Ruskin's book in his hand that Proust went to see Amiens cathedral, and the ones at Abbeville and Rouen. At first, he went less in search of their unique beauty than in search of the beauty such as the writer he admired had loved . . . .

What is true of works of art is also true of nature. One of Proust's favourite ideas was how impossible it is for us to know nature other than through great artists . . . . For him, Ruskin was one of the spiritual intercessors . . . .

Another point in common: both grant science a very large role in the composition of works of art, with Ruskin claiming that each example of rock, each variety of soil, each type of cloud must be studied and rendered with geological and meteorological exactness and Proust insisting on describing feelings with the precision of a doctor . . . .

But it is especially on the question of style that the influence of Ruskin on Proust seems to me so great . . . .

The use of adjectives is the same in the two men. Both strive, by means of an unbroken series of several adjectives, to narrow down the description of an object to a greater and greater degree. An example from Proust: 'le jet d'eau svelte, immobile, durci'. In Ruskin: 'the thick, creamy, curdling, overlapping, massy foam, which remains for a moment only after the fall of the wave, and is seen in perfection in its running up the beach' . . . . And when, at the beginning of Ruskin's *Praeterita*, I find an admirable description of almond blossom . . . I cannot help thinking of the hawthorn bushes in Marcel Proust.

The theme of the hawthorns has probably come from Ruskin . . . .

All in all, Proust, having learned from Ruskin a new way of seeing both works of art and nature, has developed this vision and finally carried it further than his master . . . .

139. Ernest Seillière on observation versus metaphysics in *La Recherche*

1931

Extract from *Marcel Proust*, Paris, Editions de la Nouvelle Revue Critique, 1931, pp. 287–90.

Ernest Seillière (1866–1955), literary critic and philosopher, sees 1931 as a watershed in Proust criticism when *La Recherche* can be appraised without partisanship and exacerbation ('sine ira et studio') by a contemporary of Proust's own social scene and an analyst of aesthetics. After examining the various sections of the work, Seillière distinguishes the analytical impressionism of the earlier parts from the would-be transcendent metaphysics of *Le Temps retrouvé*. He argues that Proust's art is more deliberately conscious than the mystic aesthetic of involuntary memory would imply and owes, as *Swann* reveals, much more to observation than the ecstatic release of involuntary memory. Cf. Curtius, No. 109.

. . . He did not perhaps at first pursue such an enquiry with the intention of *using* it directly to bolster his literary reputation: as I have said, he must have dreamed for some time of works of a largely philosophical or aesthetic nature in the style of Ruskin. But as soon as he felt that his true path lay in this direction, he rediscovered, more often than not in a perfectly conscious fashion and in his very reliable *voluntary* memory, the 'historical' data that had long been stored in it. Of course, even in the psychological field, he did function at times like the born artist he actually was, i.e. in a partly unconscious fashion. Those moments when he was in true and utterly complete contact with his subliminal affective state were very rare, as his own account makes clear. As soon as he thought it possible to become the theoretician of his art, he preferred to let it be understood that this was his normal attitude as a writer, so as to make himself appear constantly inspired by the God of Beauty . . . .

[Seillière gives instances of Proust drawing his inspiration from the observation of people around him rather than from a notion of the transcendence of reality.]

This kind of interpretation of *Swann* seems to me infinitely more plausible than claiming to explain it entirely by events similar to the cup of tea incident . . . . While it is certain that invention, in the realm of art as in everything else, preserves an element of mystery, it also has a broad, solid, consciously experimental base and it is always unwise to erect too ambitious a mystical structure on the very pinpoint of creative investigation.

All in all, I prefer Proust's first aesthetic stance, viz. Combray and the Opéra Comique to his second, i.e. the reception at the Prince de Guermantes' which I find extremely artificial. The structure of *Swann* is very deliberate, very complicated and ultimately very clever. Throughout, you are aware of the care and precaution taken (alongside certain bold, more or less veiled, strokes like the creation of Charlus). In the drawing of the characters, you are aware of the modifications in their profession, social standing, even sex that required unbroken attention if the flow of memory was not to be halted and the plausibility of the narrative was not to be interrupted either. Constantly, alongside a rich vein of recollection, you meet the forestalling, the control, the ingenious manipulation and the successful evasion of any excessively indiscreet curiosity on the part of the reader. And all that did not just come out of a symbolic cup of tea.

NOTE

All italics are in the text.

140. Edmund Wilson: assessment and placing of Proust in recent literary history
1931

Extracts from *Axel's Castle: a Study in the Imaginative Literature of 1870–1930*, New York, Scribner, 1931.

Edmund Wilson (1895–1972) shows, in this celebrated chapter, how far Proust has travelled in the opinion of critics in the ten years following his death. Here he is confidently and fully examined by means of frequent comparisons with nineteenth- and twentieth-century writers. He is also appreciated for his individual voice and vision.

(a) On Proust's characters and their Dickensian[1] overtones (pp. 136–9).

Having mentioned *Swann* and *Jeunes Filles*, Wilson goes on to examine the social scenes of *Le Côté de Guermantes* and *Sodome et Gomorrhe*:

We are now to be violently thrown forward into the life of the world outside. The contrast between, on the one hand, the dreams, the broodings and the repinings of the neurasthenic hero, as we get them for such long stretches, and, on the other, the rich and lively social scenes, dramatized by so powerful an imagination, is one of the most curious features of the book. These latter scenes, indeed, contain so much broad humor and so much extravagant satire that, appearing in a modern French novel, they amaze us. Proust, however, was much addicted to English literature: 'It is strange,' he writes in a letter, 'that, in the most widely different departments, from George Eliot to Hardy, from Stevenson to Emerson, there should be no other literature which exercises over me so powerful an influence as English and American.' In the descriptive parts of the early volumes, we have recognized the rhythms of Ruskin; and in the social scenes which now engage us, though Proust has been compared to Henry James, who was deficient in precisely those gifts of vividness and humor which Proust, to such an astonishing degree, possessed, we shall look in vain for anything like them outside the novels of Dickens. We have already been struck, in *Du Côté de chez Swann*, with the singular relief into which the characters were thrown as soon as they began to speak or act. And it seems plain that Proust must have read Dickens and that this sometimes grotesque heightening of character had been partly learned from him. Proust, like Dickens, was a remarkable mimic: as Dickens enchanted his audiences by dramatic readings from his novels, so, we are told, Proust was celebrated for impersonations of his friends; and both, in their books carried the practice of caricaturing habits of speech and of inventing things for their personages to say which are outrageous without ever ceasing to be lifelike to a point where it becomes impossible to compare them to anybody but each other. As furthermore, it has been said of Dickens that his villains are so amusing – in their fashion, so enthusiastically alive – that we are reluctant to see the last of them, so we acquire a curious affection for even the most objectionable characters in Proust: Morel, for example, is certainly one of the most odious characters in fiction, yet we are never really made to hate him or to wish that we did not have to hear about him, and we feel a genuine regret when Mme Verdurin, with her false teeth and her monocle, finally vanishes from our sight. This generous sympathy and understanding for even the monstrosities which humanity produces, and Proust's capacity for galvanizing these monstrosities into energetic life, are at the bottom of the extraordinary success of the tragi-comic hero of Proust's Sodom, M. de Charlus. But Charlus surpasses Dickens and, as has been said, is almost comparable to Falstaff. In a letter in which Proust explains that he has borrowed certain traits of Charlus from a real person, he adds that the character in the book is, however, intended to be 'much bigger', to 'contain much more of humanity'; and it is one of the strange paradoxes of Proust's genius that he should have been able to create in a character so special a figure of heroic proportions.

Nor is it only in these respects that Proust reminds us of Dickens. Proust's incidents, as well as his characters, sometimes have a comic violence almost unprecedented in French: Mme Verdurin dislocating her jaw through laughing at one of Cottard's jokes, the furious smashing by the narrator of Charlus's hat and the latter's calm substitution of another hat in its place, are strokes which no one but Dickens would have dared. This heightening in Dickens is theatrical; and we sometimes – though considerably less often – get the same impression in Proust that we are watching a look or a gesture deliberately underlined on the stage – so that Charlus's first encounter with the narrator, when the former looks at his watch and makes 'the gesture of annoyance with which one aims to create the impression that one is tired of waiting, but which one never makes when one is actually waiting,' and Bloch's farewell to Mme de Villeparisis, when she attempts to snub him by closing her eyes, seem to take place in the same world as Lady Dedlock's swift second glance at the legal papers in her lover's handwriting and Mr Merdle's profound stare into his hat 'as if it were some twenty feet deep', when he has come to borrow the penknife with which he is to open his veins. – And there even seems distinguishable in the Verdurin circle an unconscious reminiscence of the Veneerings of *Our Mutual Friend*: note especially the similarity between the rôles played by Twemlow in the latter and in the former by Saniette.

(b) Proust's moral tone in his attitude to his characters (pp. 143–5).

Wilson refers to scenes that exhibit Proust's comic and satiric gifts: In each of these cases, Proust has destroyed, and destroyed with ferocity, the social hierarchy he has just been expounding. Its values, he tells us, are an imposture: pretending to honor and distinction, it accepts all that is vulgar and base; its pride is nothing nobler than the instinct which it shares with the woman who keeps the toilet and the elevator boy's sister, to spit upon the person whom we happen to have at a disadvantage. And whatever the social world may say to the contrary, it either ignores or seeks to kill those few impulses toward justice and beauty which make men admirable. It seems strange that so many critics should have found Proust's novel 'unmoral'; the truth is that he was preoccupied with morality to the extent of tending to deal in melodrama. Proust was himself (on his mother's side) half-Jewish; and for all his Parisian sophistication, there remains in him much of the capacity for apocalyptic moral indignation of the classical Jewish prophet. That tone of lamentation and complaint which resounds through his whole book, which, indeed, he scarcely ever drops save for the animated humor of the social scenes, themselves in their implications so bitter, is really very un-French and rather akin to Jewish literature. The French novelist of the line of Stendhal and Flaubert and Anatole France, with whom otherwise Proust has so much in common, differs fundamentally from Proust in this: the sad or cynical view of mankind with which these former begin, which is implicit in their first page, has been arrived at by Proust only at the cost of much pain and protest, and this ordeal is one of the subjects of his book: Proust has never, like these others, been reconciled to disillusionment. This fact is clearly one of the causes of that method which we find so novel and so fascinating of making his characters undergo a succession of transformations: humanity is only gradually revealed to us in its selfishness, its weakness and its inconsistency. Anatole France would probably, for example, have put before us the whole of Odette de Crécy in a single brief description – a few facts exactly noted and two adjectives which, contradicting each other, would have pricked

405

us with the contradiction of her stupidity and her beauty; Stendhal would have stripped her of romance in the first sentence in which he recorded the simplest of her acts. But with Proust, we are made to see her in a variety of different aspects through the eyes of the men who have adored her; and her mediocrity and moral insensibility, to Proust such a tragic matter, are never fully allowed to appear until the final pages of the novel, when for the first time we hear her express herself on her experience with her various lovers.

(c) Reservations on the content of *La Recherche* (pp. 164–6).

The fascination of Proust's novel is so great that, while we are reading it, we tend to accept it *in toto*. In convincing us of the reality of his creations, Proust infects us with his point of view, even where this point of view has falsified his picture of life. It is only in the latter part of his narrative that we begin seriously to question what he is telling us. Is it really true, we begin to ask ourselves, that one's relations with other people can never provide a lasting satisfaction? Is it true that literature and art are the only forms of creative activity which can enable us to meet and master reality? Would not such an able doctor as Proust represents his Cottard as being enjoy, in supervising his cases, the satisfaction of knowing that he has imposed a little of his own private reality upon the world outside? Would not a diplomat like M. de Norpois in arranging his alliances? – or a hostess like Mme de Guermantes in creating her social circle? Might not a more sympathetic and attentive lover than Proust's hero have even succeeded in recreating Albertine at least partly in his own image? We begin to be willing to agree with Ortega y Gasset that Proust is guilty of the mediæval sin of *accidia*, that combination of slothfulness and gloom which Dante represented as an eternal submergence in mud.

For *A la Recherche du Temps Perdu*, in spite of all its humor and beauty, is one of the gloomiest books ever written. Proust tells us that the idea of death has 'kept him company as incessantly as the idea of his own identity'; and even the water-lilies of the little river at Combray, continually straining to follow the current and continually jerked back by their stems, are likened to the futile attempts of the neurasthenic to break the habits which are eating his life. Proust's lovers are always suffering: we scarcely ever see them in any of those moments of ecstasy or contentment which, after all, not seldom occur even in the case of an unfortunate love affair – and on the rare occasions when they *are* supposed to be enjoying themselves, the whole atmosphere is shadowed by the sadness and corrupted by the odor of the putrescence which are immediately to set in. And Proust's artists are unhappy, too; they have only the consolations of art. Proust's interminable, relentlessly repetitious and finally almost intolerable disquisitions on these themes end by goading us to the same sort of rebellion that we make against those dialogues of Leopardi in which, in a similar insistent way, Leopardi rings the changes on a similar theme: that man is never happy, that there is no such thing as satisfaction in the present. We have finally to accept with dismay that Leopardi is a sick man and that, in spite of the strength of his intellect, in spite of his exact, close, sober classical style, all his thinking is sick. And so with Proust we are forced to recognize that his ideas and imagination are more seriously affected by his physical and psychological ailments than we had at first been willing to suppose. His characters, we begin to observe, are always becoming ill like the hero – an immense number of them turn out homosexual and homosexuality is 'an incurable disease'. Finally, they all suddenly grow old in a thunderclap – more hideously and humiliatingly old than we have ever known any real group of people to be. And we find that we are made more and more uncomfortable by Proust's incessant rubbing in of all these ignominies and disabilities. We begin to feel less the pathos of the characters than the author's appetite for making them miserable. And we realize that the atrocious cruelty which dominates Proust's world, in the behavior of the people in the social scenes no less than in the relations of the lovers, is the hysterical sadistic complement to the hero's hysterical masochistic passivity.

(d) Imagination and decadence in *La Recherche* (pp. 188–90).

And so though we may regret the spoiled child in Proust, the spoiled child of rich parents who has never had to meet the world on equal terms and who has never felt the necessity of relating his art and ideas to the general problems of human society; though the tragedy of the Guermantes' light reception of Swann's announcement of his mortal illness may come to seem to us somewhat less tragic in retrospect – though we may come to feel a little impatient at having our pity so continually solicited for valetudinarian neurotics who are at least always provided with enough money to be neurotic in peace and comfort; though Proust's dramatic progressive revelation of the anomalies and miseries of the world may come to appear to us less profound when we begin to realize the extreme naïveté of some of the assumptions upon which he proceeds – snobbish naïveté in regard to the importance of social differences and naïveté in regard to sex and to human relations in general; none the less, we must recognize in Proust, it seems to me, one of the great minds and imaginations of our day, absolutely comparable in our own time, by reason both of his powers and his influence, to the Nietzsches, the

407

Tolstois, the Wagners and the Ibsens of a previous generation. He has recreated the world of the novel from the point of view of relativity: he has supplied for the first time in literature an equivalent on the full scale for the new theory of modern physics.

Imaginatively and intellectually, Proust is prodigiously strong; and if we feel an element of decadence in his work, it may be primarily due to the decay of the society in which he lived and with which his novel exclusively deals – the society of the dispossessed nobility and the fashionable and cultivated bourgeoisie, with their physicians and their artists, their servants and their parasites. We are always feeling with Proust as if we were reading about the end of something – this seems, in fact, to be what he means us to feel: witness the implications of the bombardment of Paris during the War when Charlus is in the last stages of his disintegration. Not only do his hero and most of his other characters pass into mortal declines, but their world itself seems to be coming to an end. And it may be that Proust's strange poetry and brilliance are the last fires of a setting sun – the last flare of the aesthetic idealism of the educated classes of the nineteenth century. If Proust is more dramatic, more complete and more intense than Thackeray or Chekov or Edith Wharton or Anatole France, it may be because he comes at the close of an era and sums up the whole situation. Surely the lament over the impossibility of ideal romantic love which Proust is always chanting on a note which wavers between the tragic and the maudlin announces by its very falling into absurdity the break-up of a whole emotional idealism and its ultimate analysis and readjustment along lines which Proust's own researches, running curiously close to Freud, have been among the first to suggest. *A la Recherche du Temps Perdu* subsumes, in this respect, *The Great Gatsby*, *The Sun Also Rises*, *The Bridge of San Luis Rey*, the sketches of Dorothy Parker, and how many contemporary European novels! Proust is perhaps the last great historian of the loves, the society, the intelligence, the diplomacy, the literature and the art of the Heartbreak House of capitalist culture; and the little man with the sad appealing voice, the metaphysician's mind, the Saracen's beak, the ill-fitting dress-shirt and the great eyes that seem to see all about him like the many-faceted eyes of a fly, dominates the scene and plays host in the mansion where he is not long to be master.

NOTE

All italics are in the text.
1 Proust seems to have begun reading Dickens in 1897. See *Corr. II*, p. 211.
  'What's the best thing by Dickens (I don't know anything by him).'

Bibliography

BIBLIOGRAPHICAL SOURCES

Eva Ahlstedt, *La Pudeur en crise*, Paris, Touzot, 1985.

D. W. Alden, *Marcel Proust and his French Critics*, New York, Russell & Russell, 1973; first published 1940.

D. W. Alden and R. A. Brooks (eds), *A Critical Bibliography of French Literature* (vol. 6, *Twentieth Century*), New York, Syracuse University Press, 1980.

H. Bonnet, *Marcel Proust de 1907 à 1914*, Paris, Nizet, 1971; first published 1959.

G. de Catalogne, *Marcel Proust: les contemporains*, Paris, Editions de la Revue: *Le Capitole*, 1926, pp. 207–23.

R. Gibson, *Proust et la critique anglo-saxonne* (1913–49), Cahiers Marcel Proust, No. 11, Paris, Gallimard, 1982, pp. 11–49.

V. E. Graham, *Bibliographie des études sur Marcel Proust et son oeuvre*, Genéva, Droz, 1976.

L. Pierre-Quint, *Comment travaillait Marcel Proust*, Paris, Editions des Cahiers Libres, 1928.

L. Pierre-Quint, *Comment parut 'Du côté de chez Swann'*, Paris, Kra, 1930.

J.-Y. Tadié, *Proust* (Les Dossiers Belfond), Paris, Belfond, 1983.

Elizabeth R. Taylor, *Marcel Proust and his Contexts*, New York, Garland Publishing, 1981.

ANTHOLOGIES OF CRITICAL ESSAYS

J. Bersani (ed.), *Les Critiques de notre temps et Proust*, Paris, Garnier, 1971.

Hommage à Marcel Proust, La Nouvelle Revue française, 1 January 1923.

Hommage à Marcel Proust, Le Rouge et le noir (Cahier Spécial), April, 1928.

Gladys D. Lindner (ed.), *Proust – Reviews and Estimates in English*, California, Stanford University Press, 1942.

C. K. Scott-Moncrieff (ed.), *An English Tribute*, London, Chatto & Windus, 1923.

J.-Y. Tadié (ed.), *Lectures de Proust*, Paris, Armand Colin, 1971.

Select Index

References are grouped as follows: I. Characters and places in *A la recherche du temps perdu*; II. Authors with whom Proust is compared; III. General index.

II. AUTHORS WITH WHOM PROUST IS COMPARED

III. GENERAL INDEX

All works are indexed under the name of the author